HUNTING AMERICA'S GAME ANIMALS & BIRDS

HUNTING AMERICA'S GAME ANIMALS & BIRDS

Edited by Robert Elman & George Peper

WINCHESTER PRESS

Library of Congress Cataloging in Publication Data
Main entry under title:

Hunting America's game animals and birds.

   Includes index.
   1. Hunting--North America. I. Elman, Robert.
II. Peper, George.
SK40.H86   799.2'097   75-9252
ISBN 0-87691-172-6

Published by
Winchester Press
205 East 42nd Street, New York 10017

Printed in the United States of America

PHOTO ACKNOWLEDGMENTS

The editors wish to acknowledge supplementary photographs from the following sources, listed alphabetically. The numbers indicate pages on which the photos appear.

Arizona Game & Fish Department: 224 top left
Erwin A. Bauer: 80
Les Bowman: 334 bottom
British Columbia Government: 6 top right
Bill Browning: 252
California Department of Fish & Game: 224 bottom left
Jon Cates: 48
Robert Elman: 179
Illinois Department of Conservation: 307
Maine Fish & Game Department: 177
Michigan Department of Natural Resources: 229, 232
Montana Chamber of Commerce: 5 right center, 21, 22 bottom, 23, 27, 29, 355
National Audubon Society: 162
National Film Board of Canada: 36 top
National Park Service: 5 left center, 9 bottom right
Nebraska Game Commission: 254, 273
North Carolina Wildlife Resources Commission: 174, 276, 308
North Dakota Game & Fish Department: 302
Ontario Department of Tourism & Information: 288 top, 347 left, 353
David Petzal: 190, 191, 193, 194
Quebec Wildlife Service: 6 bottom left, 288 bottom
Leonard Lee Rue III: 18, 22 top right, 66, 95, 126, 132 top & bottom, 136, 138 left, 146 top, 147, 159, 180, 183, 184, 185, 204, 234 bottom, 235, 237, 253, 260, 331, 334 top, 347 right
John P. Russo: 50
Perry Shankle, Jr.: xvi
South Dakota Department of Game, Fish & Parks: 60, 61, 240, 250
Tennessee Game & Fish Commission: 10, 67, 129, 142
Texas Parks & Wildlife Department: 135 left
Russell Tinsley: 63, 138 right, 139, 265, 266, 268
United States Fish & Wildlife Service: 6 right center, 35, 234 top
Utah Travel Council: 22 top left, 31 right
Charles F. Waterman: 230, 242 right, 245 top & bottom, 246 top & bottom, 267, 332 top, 349
Frank Woolner: 231

CONTENTS

CONTRIBUTORS

Erwin A. Bauer

Fred Bear

Bob Bell

Les Bowman

Pete Brown

Jim Carmichel

John O. Cartier

Byron W. Dalrymple

Dave Duffey

Charles Elliott

John R. Falk

Steve Ferber

Grits Gresham

Bob Hagel

Frank T. Hanenkrat

Bob Hinman

B.R. Hughes

John Jobson

Jerome J. Knap

Ed Kozicky

Pete Kuhlhoff

John Madson

Dick Mermon

Jack O'Connor

V. Lee Oertle

Warren Page

David Petzal

Bert Popowski

Jerome B. Robinson

Leonard Lee Rue, III

Andy Russell

Dan M. Russell

Francis E. Sell

Norman M. Strung

Zack Taylor

Russell Tinsley

Lamar Underwood

Charles F. Waterman

John Wootters

Ed Zern

INTRODUCTION

Almost every publisher of outdoor books has dreamed the supposedly impossible dream: that of producing a book covering every kind of American hunting and every major game species, not from the limited viewpoint of a single author but from the collective experience and knowledge of a whole corps of experts. This is not to say that a single author cannot write a very fine book about many kinds of hunting. Some of the writers presented here have done just that. But every one of them will candidly admit that he's more experienced in some areas than others and, being human, is subject to some bias regarding the "best" arms and equipment, the "best" hunting methods, even the "best" or most important, most enjoyable, or most challenging varieties of game.

A book by a corps of renowned experts therefore has great and obvious advantages. Each contributor can deal with a kind of game or a type of hunting that he is particularly well qualified to discuss. And—if enough truly expert contributors can be recruited—nothing needs to be omitted.

That's a big "if." It explains why the dream has been considered impossible by so many editors and publishers. In the preparation of this book, the editors were in a unique position to overcome the difficulty because our company produces the work of more eminent shooting and hunting writers than any other publisher. We had access to just such a corps of experts as other editors have dreamed about.

The men listed alphabetically on the contributors' page preceding this introduction constitute an all-star cast. Readers conversant with sporting literature will recognize their names and can feel confident in using the tips and techniques that are amassed under the by-lines. They're famous because they deserve to be; no one knows more than these writers about the topics they discuss. No one is better equipped to tell you how to find and take game consistently, how to care for your arms and accessories, how to select ammunition for a given purpose, how to conserve game and the environment, how to find the choicest hunting areas, how to train a dog, how to be a better marksman, how to get the most joy out of your hunt.

In some cases, the authors had already written the best possible game-getting advice for recent Winchester Press publications, and we have adapted it for presentation here in an appropriate section. In other cases we assigned an author to write a chapter (or more than one chapter) exclusively for this book, so that we could offer the fullest, most up-to-date information with regard to every kind of hunting. We have included big game, small game, upland birds, waterfowl—and even a chapter on snipe and other shorebirds, which are neglected in most of today's hunting books. We have also included sections on loads, guns, and alternative arms, on how to improve your shooting skill, on hunting dogs, on vehicles, boats, and equipment, and on hunting near at home or far afield. The chapters on where to go and how to arrange trips are of extreme importance in this age of mobility, especially since near-to-home hunting areas have diminished in many parts of the country.

Finally, in a special appendix, we have presented a survey of the best times and places to hunt the major species. The survey was conducted by one of our most eminent contributors, John Madson, in cooperation with many state wildlife agencies. Thus, what this book offers is the complete how, when, and where of American hunting.

Now, because readers often express a desire to know more about the sporting writers they admire, we will complete this introduction with brief descriptions of our contributors and their achievements.

ERWIN A. BAUER is a freelance writer, an avid sportsman and naturalist, and probably the world's most widely traveled wildlife photographer. He is the author of eight books on hunting, fishing, and photography, and his hundreds of articles have appeared in *Sports Illustrated, Outdoor Life* (where he is a staff editor), *Field & Stream,* and a dozen other sporting magazines. Bauer is the recipient of three first-place awards from the Outdoor Writers Association of America.

FRED BEAR is to archery what Arnold Palmer is to golf. Known and respected by everyone who shoots a bow and arrow, Bear is the holder of six world bowhunting records. He is president and founder of the Bear Archery Company and is honorary chairman of the Fred Bear Sports Club. Bear is also a member of the Explorer's Club, the Polar Equator Club, and the Adventurer's Club. His chapter for this book first appeared in the *Winchester Hunter's Handbook, 1971-72.* Bear is also the author of *The Archer's Bible.*

BOB BELL is editor of the *Pennsylvania Game News.* He is a contributing editor to *Gun Digest,* and his articles on hunting and shooting have appeared in all the major outdoor magazines. Bell's first book is currently in press. It deals with his favorite subject—pheasant hunting—which is also the subject of his chapter for this book.

LES BOWMAN is recognized throughout the hunting fraternity as an outfitter without equal. Shooting enthusiasts also know him for his writings in sportsmen's publications such as *Guns, The Rifle, Gunsport, The Handloader,* and even Australia's *Sporting Shooter.* Prior to becoming a professional outfitter and writer, Bowman worked for 30 years in the aircraft industry. He was, in fact, one of the pioneers of

the air age, both as a flyer and as an engineer. During those days both Bowman an his wife, Martie, were barnstormers.

PETE BROWN, Associate Editor and recently retired Shooting Editor of *Sports Afield,* has been hunting and target shooting ever since he was a boy. At the age of 12, after several years of .22-popping at prairie dogs and jack rabbits, he began diversifying with a .38-40 Winchester Model 92 that brought him his first turkeys and coyotes. Once, while hunting upland birds with one of the editors of this volume, Pete described himself as "basically a Western big-game hunter," and apologized for not being a more accomplished wingshot. He then scored a double as a bobwhite covey went up, brought down a pheasant at considerably more than 50 yards, and amiably wiped the editor's eye in a similar manner throughout the day. Brown studied engineering and ballistics at the U. S. Naval Academy and the University of Illinois, later worked for Western Cartridge Co., and served the Naval Bureau of Ordnance as a technical advisor on small-arms and aircraft ammunition.

JIM CARMICHEL is another old friend of this volume's editors, having sold his first outdoor-magazine story to one of them years ago, when Jim was working with the Tennessee Game & Fish Commission. Today he's Shooting Editor of *Outdoor Life.* He still enjoys visits to the old homesite in Tennessee, but he's just as likely to turn up in Africa (where his several safaris have produced excellent trophies) or in Arizona (where he now lives and often hunts). He has won honors in trap, skeet, smallbore and big-bore rifle, and benchrest shooting; he has served as Executive Secretary of the National Reloading Manufacturers Association; he has written magazine articles on all aspects of firearms and the shooting sports; and as this book goes to press he is working on a landmark volume about the modern rifle. Carmichel's chapter on gun care first appeared in the *Winchester Hunter's Handbook, 1973–74*.

JOHN O. CARTIER is the Midwest Field Editor for *Outdoor Life*. During his 25-year career as an outdoor writer he has published articles in all the leading sporting magazines. He is also the author of *Modern Waterfowling*, and is at work on a second book, *The Modern Deer Hunter*. His duck-hunting chapter in these pages is adapted from an article that appeared in the *Winchester Hunter's Handbook, 1972–73*.

BYRON W. DALRYMPLE's articles on hunting, fishing, and camping have been appearing regularly in the major outdoor publications for nearly 30 years, and the dozen books he has written and edited have sold more than a million copies. Few men have a deeper understanding of wildlife or a wider knowledge of the rod and gun sports, and no one, perhaps, is better able to write about these subjects. Dalrymple's chapter on mule deer first appeared in the *Winchester Hunter's Handbook, 1973–74*. His two other chapters—on future game prospects and on javelina—are appearing in print for the first time.

DAVE DUFFEY is a freelance newspaper and magazine writer and is Dog Editor of *Outdoor Life*. He is the author of four books plus scores of articles on dogs and hunting. Duffey has hunted extensively and has judged and reported field trials all across North America. He is especially well qualified to write his chapter on preserve hunting; for the last 15 years he has managed a private hunting club near his home in Wisconsin.

CHARLES ELLIOTT is the Southeast Field Editor of *Outdoor Life*. A former director of the Georgia Game & Fish Commission, he has worked in conservation for nearly half a century. Elliott's writing credits include a dozen books and countless articles on outdoor subjects. His contribution to this book is taken from a chapter on caribou that he wrote for

Byron Dalrymple's *North American Big Game Hunting* (Winchester Press, 1974).

JOHN R. FALK is Manager of Public Relations for Winchester-Western. For 11 years he served as Dog Editor for *Guns & Hunting*. While part-owner of the Shoshone English Setter Kennels in Garrison, New York, Falk bred, trained, and ran field-trial dogs. He has also taken his turn as a qualified and respected field-trial judge. His articles have appeared in *Field & Stream*, *The American Sportsman*, and other leading outdoor magazines. He is also the author of two books. His chapter is excerpted from one of them, *The Practical Hunter's Dog Book* (Winchester Press, 1971).

STEVE FERBER, Shooting Editor of *Argosy*, is listed in *Who's Who of Sports* and the *New York Times Record Book of Sports*. He has established 16 national shooting records in both conventional and International-style competition. While a member and coach of the U.S. Navy Shooting Team, Ferber was awarded the Distinguished Pistol Shooter's Badge by the Secretary of the Navy, the highest award attainable in small-arms marksmanship. To date, he's collected over 1,000 trophies in rifle, pistol, and shotgun competition. (And several years ago, while on a bear hunt in British Columbia with an editor of this volume, he demonstrated nearly comparable skill in collecting steelhead trout.)

GRITS GRESHAM has been called the best duck shot in America. He is also one of the most knowledgeable and lucid of our outdoor writers. Gresham's credits include four books and several hundred articles. In addition, he has produced, consulted, and starred in several of ABC-TV's *American Sportsman* programs. Gresham's chapter is excerpted from his book *The Complete Wildfowler* (Winchester Press, 1973).

BOB HAGEL is a freelance writer/photographer and a firearms consultant. He currently holds posts on four magazines: as Hunting Adviser to *The Handloader*, Hunting Editor of *The Rifle*, Contributing Editor of *Gun Digest*, and

Technical Editor of *Handloader's Digest*. Hagel was a professional guide and outfitter for a dozen years, and has hunted all across North America over a period of nearly 45 years. His articles have appeared in virtually every firearms and hunting publication, and he has contributed to several books.

FRANK T. HANENKRAT is a college English professor who also happens to be one of America's authorities on turkeys and turkey hunting. While in the service, Hanenkrat served as a shooting instructor with the U.S. Army Marksmanship Training Unit, where he gathered the information and expertise to co-author (with Bill Pulling) *Position Rifle Shooting*, a detailed analysis of rifle-shooting psychology and technique. Hanenkrat is also the editor of his father's book, *The Education of a Turkey Hunter*.

BOB HINMAN shot his first duck at the age of eight. Since that day he has hunted virtually every major wildfowling area in the United States, Canada, and Mexico. Hinman is Shotgun Editor of *Shooting Times*, a staff editor of *Hunting*, and the author of two books and a great many articles. He lives in Peoria, Illinois, where he operates a successful outfitting company specializing in hunting, fishing, and camping equipment. Hinman's chapter is taken from his most recent book, *The Duck Hunter's Handbook* (Winchester Press, 1974).

B. R. HUGHES is one of our busiest outdoor writers. Currently Editor of *The Muzzleloader*, Associate Editor of *Gun Week*, and Shotgun Editor of both *Gunsport* and *Gun Collector*, Hughes has been published by most of the other leading magazines on guns and shooting as well. In addition, he has taught journalism on the college level.

JOHN JOBSON, author of *The Complete Book of Practical Camping*, is Camping Editor of *Sports Afield*. He obtained his early training in woodcraft from the Indians in South Dakota, and he has hunted, fished, and camped in every state in the Union and in much of Canada, Europe, Great Britain, and Africa. Before becoming an outdoor writer, Jobson worked in Holly-

wood "doctoring" scripts. The Jobsons live in a house in Layton, Utah, and in a tent just about everywhere else.

JEROME J. KNAP, author of *The Canadian Hunter's Handbook*, is a freelance outdoor writer and photographer. He is the author of seven books on hunting, fishing, and related subjects, and his articles, numbering in the hundreds, have appeared in *Field & Stream*, *Outdoor Life*, *Sports Afield*, and several other sporting magazines. Knap is secretary-treasurer of the Outdoor Writers of Canada.

ED KOZICKY is Director of Conservation for Winchester-Western. A recipient of the Lewis and Clark Trail Commission Award, Dr. Kozicky has also been cited by the U.S. Department of the Interior for meritorious service in the field of conservation. He is the author of over 100 publications on the subject of game birds, and he is the co-author of *Shooting Preserve Management: The Nilo System*. Kozicky's three chapters for this book—all written with John Madson—saw first printings in the *Winchester Hunter's Handbook*—the coyote article in *1971–72*, the grouse-hunting article in *1972–73*, and the woodcock article in *1973–74*.

PETE KUHLHOFF was *Argosy's* Gun Editor for more than three decades before his death in 1972. Until the Winchester Press editors began compiling material for this book, it was believed that Pete's last writing had been published. Then we discovered that several years ago he had left an unpublished article on file in our editorial offices for inclusion in a later work that never saw print. It's the chapter on shotgunning secrets that appears in these pages. Born in Oklahoma, Pete studied art in Chicago and then became a successful magazine illustrator in New York. He was soon writing a monthly gun column and, inevitably, his love of hunting led him into a new career that changed his life and made millions of readers his armchair shooting companions.

JOHN MADSON is Assistant Director of Conservation for Winchester-Western. He is also the author of several books and many scores of articles on wildlife and the outdoors. In 1967 Madson was awarded the coveted Jade of Chiefs, the highest award bestowed by the Outdoor Writers Association of America. Madson's contributions to this book on elk, squirrel, and rabbits are taken from publications he wrote for the Winchester Conservation Department. The chapters on coyotes, grouse, and woodcock—all co-authored with Ed Kozicky—first appeared in the *Winchester Hunter's Handbook; 1971–72, 1972–73,* and *1973–74,* respectively.

DICK MERMON is a freelance writer, a lecturer, and a representative for manufacturers of fishing and archery equipment. His articles on hunting and fishing have appeared in several sporting magazines, and he is currently at work on his second book. Mermon's chapter is adapted from his first book, *Crow Shooting Secrets* (Winchester Press, 1971).

JACK O'CONNOR claimed his first trophy at the age of 12 and has been hunting ever since; today he holds several big-game records. A recipient of the prestigious Wetherby Trophy, he earned the Winchester award as Outdoorsman of the Year in 1972 and was elected to the Hunting Hall of Fame in 1974. A former journalism professor, O'Connor has written over a dozen books, including two novels and an autobiographical work. He is currently Executive Editor of *Hunting,* and his thousands of articles have appeared in *Field & Stream, Outdoor Life* (where he served as Arms and Ammunition Editor for more than 30 years), and all the major sporting magazines. His contribution on sheep hunting is adapted from a chapter of his most recent book, *Sheep and Sheep Hunting* (Winchester Press, 1974). The chapter on sighting-in first appeared in the *Winchester Hunter's Handbook, 1971–72.* "Tips on Hunting Trips" is printed here for the first time.

V. LEE OERTLE is Vehicles Editor of *Sports Afield.* During his 20-year career as an outdoor writer he has sold words and pictures to more than 70 national magazines. Oertle is also the author of three books, and he is currently a regular columnist for seven monthly pub-

lications. The Oertles live in Beaver, Utah, where he has built his own campground and hunting camp. His chapter first appeared in the *Winchester Hunter's Handbook, 1973–74.*

WARREN PAGE, author of *The Accurate Rifle,* is a nine-time winner of the National Bench Rest Championship. Currently president of the National Shooting Sports Foundation, Page served for 24 years as Shooting Editor of *Field & Stream.* Page is a recognized expert on ballistics and was involved directly in the development of a number of popular cartridges, including the .243 Winchester and the 7mm Remington, and he continues to serve as consultant to manufacturers. In 1972 Page was elected to the Hunting Hall of Fame, and in 1974 he won the Winchester award as Outdoorsman of the Year.

DAVID PETZAL is Managing Editor of *Field & Stream.* A hunter and shooter since the age of 10, he is the author of *The .22 Rifle* and has edited *The Expert's Book of the Shooting Sports* and *The Expert's Book of Upland Game and Waterfowl Hunting.* Petzal has long been a connoisseur and collector of hunting knives. He is also a devotee of long-range rifle shooting at targets ranging from paper to chucks to antelope. Not long ago, in fact, while participating in a one-shot pronghorn hunt, he made a perfect kill at 450 yards. Few men can match his qualifications in discussing knives or scopes. His chapter on knives is adapted from the *Winchester Hunter's Handbook, 1972–73,* and his chapter on scopes is from the *1971–72* edition of the *Handbook.*

BERT POPOWSKI has for many years had the prestigious title of Contributing Editor to *The American Rifleman* Magazine, which means he is one of the select group of experts chosen by the National Rifle Association to answer readers' technical questions on hunting and firearms. Perhaps he is best known for his book *Hunting Pronghorn Antelope,* which has come to be regarded as a reference classic since its publication in 1959. He has also written books on crow shooting, game calling, and other hunting subjects, as well as articles for outdoor magazines. In these pages he is represented by a chapter on pronghorns and a chapter on another of his specialties—the prairie grouse he has been harvesting ever since the end of the market-gunning era.

JEROME B. ROBINSON is known to millions of dog-owning fans through his columns and feature articles in *Sports Afield,* whose masthead he graces as Gun Dogs Editor. He writes from practical experience as a breeder and trainer of bird dogs, a field trialer, a dedicated hunter, and an observant reporter of the techniques used by successful trainers everywhere in the country. Although the major outdoor magazines have published his articles on many subjects, ranging from salmon fishing to caribou hunting, he's most thoroughly in his element when shooting over good dogs—or writing about them. Robinson's chapter on the basic commands was first printed in the *Winchester Hunter's Handbook, 1972–73.* His chapter on preseason conditioning is from the *1971–72* edition of the *Handbook.*

LEONARD LEE RUE, III, is author of *World of the Red Fox* and *Pictorial Guide to the Birds of North America,* so it is most appropriate that he has contributed to this book a chapter on fox hunting and another on duck hunting. At last count, in addition to his volumes on foxes and birds, seven more books by Len Rue were in print, with another due to appear soon. All of these works are about game and other types of wildlife. A naturalist and prolific outdoor writer, he's also one of the nation's finest wildlife photographers. His pictures appear regularly in such magazines as *Audubon* and *National Wildlife* as well as in hardcover books by many authors.

ANDY RUSSELL is a well-known naturalist, photographer, lecturer, and writer. Born on the edge of the frontier in Alberta, he grew up and lived in the Rocky Mountains. Russell is the author of four books, *Grizzly Country, Trails of a Wilderness Wanderer, Horns in the High Country,* and *The High West,* and he has written numerous articles for the sporting magazines. He welcomed the assignment to write a chapter for this book because the subject—bears—was one he has been studying for many years. He is one of the country's outstanding authorities on these fascinating animals.

DAN M. RUSSELL is both an upland shooter and a game biologist who has been studying doves for over 25 years. As wildlife biologist for the Kentucky Department of Fish & Wildlife Resources, he has worked with many other birds and mammals as well, and he has published technical and popular articles on hunting, game management, and ecology. Russell's chapter is excerpted from his book, *The Dove Shooter's Handbook* (Winchester Press, 1974).

FRANCIS E. SELL lives in a beautiful wilderness area he owns in southwestern Oregon. There in his log house he writes about the shooting sports for *The American Hunter, The American Rifleman,* and other gunning magazines. His friends know him as "Spud." His fans know him as the author of *Sure-Hit Shotgun Ways, Art of Successful Deer Hunting,* and other books, as well as numerous articles, very often about shotgun performance. Starting with the September bandtail-pigeon season, he hunts all the game birds in his region—quail, grouse, chukars, snipe, ducks, geese. And when he isn't shooting or writing about shooting, he coaches a limited number of shotgunners who want to polish their gunmanship. Sell's chapter on practical ballistics is adapted from his article in the *Winchester Hunter's Handbook, 1971–72.*

NORMAN STRUNG is a licensed Montana hunting and fishing guide who regularly contributes to all the major outdoor publications. His latest book is *Misty Mornings and Moonless Nights: A Waterfowler's Guide.* Strung is a member of the Author's Guild and the Society of Magazine Writers. He is also a director of the Outdoor Writers Association of America. He has hunted ducks and geese in many parts of the country, and he keeps a close watch on the migratory-bird management and population estimates performed by the governments of the United States and Canada, state agencies, and Ducks Unlimited. He was therefore able to write an extremely well-informed wildfowl forecast, the opening chapter of our section on waterfowl and shorebirds.

ZACK TAYLOR is Boating Editor of *Sports Afield*. In the course of his 20-year career as an outdoor writer and photographer, Taylor has written three books and edited another. His articles on boats and boating have received awards for excellence in the field of boating journalism. Since he is also a hunter, he was the perfect man to get the chapter assignment on boats that go hunting.

RUSSELL TINSLEY is outdoor columnist for the Austin, Texas, *American Statesman*. He is the author of seven books on outdoor recreation, and his many articles on hunting, fishing, and related subjects have appeared in all the major sporting magazines. He wrote our chapters on predator calling and on raccoons (which he sometimes trees with hounds and sometimes calls close enough to take them with a bow). Like several of our other contributors, he supplied a number of photos for this book, and his excellent close-up pictures of many species testify to his skill as a caller.

LAMAR UNDERWOOD is Editor of *Sports Afield*, where he has been a writer and editor since 1967. Underwood has also edited two books and has a third one in press. His scores of articles on sporting subjects have appeared in many of the major outdoor magazines. "How to Be a Better Bobwhite Hunter" is adapted from his contribution to the *Winchester Hunter's Handbook, 1973–74*.

CHARLES F. WATERMAN is one of America's most popular outdoor writers. His six books, *The Part I Remember, The Hunter's World, The Fisherman's World, Hunting in America, Hunting Upland Birds*, and *Modern Fresh and Salt Water Fly Fishing*, reflect the measure of his authority and experience as sportsman/author. Waterman is a regular columnist for *Salt Water Sportsman, Fishing World, Florida Wildlife, Florida Sportsman*, and the Jacksonville *Times-Union*. His chapter is adapted from *Hunting Upland Birds* (Winchester Press, 1972).

JOHN WOOTTERS has written of firearms and hunting for *True, Outdoor Life, Field & Stream, Sports Afield, The Handloader, The Rifle*, and *Shooting Times*, among other publications. He has hunted big game extensively on this continent and in Africa. Though he enjoys a reputation as a consistently successful collector of trophy deer, we asked him to contribute chapters about vastly different kinds of game—wild boar and snipe—because few men can match his knowledge of the savagely unpredictable hog or the elusive little shorebird.

ED ZERN is perpetrator of the famous "Exit Laughing" column for *Field & Stream*, and also serves as that magazine's Associate Editor. His half-dozen books include *A Fine Kettle of Fish Stories, To Hell With Hunting*, and *To Hell With Fishing*. His articles have covered far too many outdoor subjects to list here. Zern is a member of the Theodore Gordon Flyfishers and the Anglers Club of New York. There is evidence that, in addition, he was chief founder of the venerable and greatly esteemed Madison Avenue Rod, Gun, Bloody Mary and Labrador Retriever Benevolent Association. On occasion, as he exits laughing, he refers to himself as President or Recording Secretary of the M.A.R.G.B.M.&L.R.B.A. Others refer to him as one of the country's leading wits and outdoor writers.

Part I: Big Game

The Big-Game Outlook— Forecast for the Future

by Bryon W. Dalrymple

1

Nowadays the big-game hunter who is most successful is the one who plans carefully and well ahead. Time was when hunters had little chance to know what game conditions might be, season to season, even sometimes within their own states. Fortunately, however, big-game management has been brought to such a refined science today that game department specialists can predict the abundance of any species, its trend up or down, numbers that safely can be harvested for any given season, and how to distribute hunters via quotas and permits in specified areas so that both desired harvest and hunter success are obtained.

It is even possible to project ahead for some years what the population of any big-game species *probably* will be in any state or province and in general throughout its range. This also is invaluable to the hunter. One who is unable, let's say, to get a booking with a chosen outfitter this year, or in the place he wishes, is well served by knowing what the general expectations are elsewhere or over the next few seasons.

Travel conditions may also cloud the picture a bit for several seasons to come. So it is a good idea to look even somewhat further ahead than usual.

What can you expect, say, over the next five seasons? We have compiled here brief resumés of the probable population trends for each of the big-game animals of this continent.

You'll find that many predictions regarding the best areas conform pretty well to the *present* hot spots listed by John Madson toward the end of this book, in the big-game section of his hunting-region survey for the major game species. In other words, the forecast shows a welcome stability in these particular game populations, except where otherwise noted.

The brightest outlook of all is with the most popular and abundant of North America's big-game animals, the **whitetail deer.** The whitetail has truly learned to live with man's civilization. The only factor that can possibly affect its superb abundance over the next few seasons—aside from localized temporary declines due to severe winters or droughts—is loss of habitat due to urban development and highway construction.

Almost everywhere whitetail population and harvests are moving upward rather than declining. Much of this is because of new and enlightened management techniques. Throughout all of New England, wherever habitat remains stable, deer harvests can be predicted to continue high and stable, or to increase. The Atlantic Coast states and the middle-south states such as Tennessee have, on the whole, been gaining in deer populations steadily, and annually in harvests. This is also true across the Deep South. Everywhere it is predicted that the trend will continue.

The Pennsylvania harvest remains little short of amazing, and there is no sign that it will decline. The Great Lakes states have had a few problems, chiefly problems of growing numbers of hunters and habitat loss. Actually, success percentages may drop slighty everywhere east of the Mississippi, not for lack of deer but because the number allowable must be split among more numerous hunters.

Throughout all the center of the country, from the Dakotas to Oklahoma, whitetail herds are on the increase, and so is the harvest. This appears to be a steady trend. Texas is phenomenal: The present harvest averages an almost incredible 350,000.

The whitetail areas of the mountain states continue to have high populations and show no sign of a downward trend. And in New Mexico and Arizona, where the Coues deer is found, while the kill will not increase, there is no reason to believe it will drop. In Canada, whitetails hold a steady high level within their range in the eastern provinces, and are on the increase in southern Manitoba and Saskatchewan. All told, over the next five years whitetail hunting will be as good as ever—or better— over practically all of their enormous range.

The **mule deer** forecast is not quite as optimistic. This is not to say that mule-deer hunting won't remain good. But recent history has reflected a slow but nonetheless noticeable slide in population. To complicate matters, widely separated states—Colorado, Oregon, Arizona—have experienced mule-deer declines the reasons for which are not easily pinpointed. The general problem, many management people surmise, is that the mule deer has difficulty adjusting to man's ever-deepening intrusions.

The picture stacks up about as follows: In the Plains States, where mule deer are found in modest numbers, predictions for the next few seasons are for stable or even slightly increasing herds. Desert mule deer in western Texas will remain abundant. Up in the Rockies hunters are almost certain to see, spottily, lowered hunt-unit quotas, few multiple-deer licenses such as have been fairly common in the past, and a general increase in restrictions.

Again, this does not mean poor hunting or low success. It will probably mean a gradually reduced number of hunters getting a crack at mule deer. Any decline is certain to be gradual. And studies now underway may bring valuable new management knowledge. At best, herds will remain stable and will continue to have ample trophy deer. But it's doubtful that Rocky Mountain mule-deer populations will rise.

The situation with the Columbia black-tail, the mule-deer subspecies on the western slope of the Coast Ranges in British Columbia and southward throughout coastal slopes of the Pacific states, is much brighter. This hardy variety is superbly abundant, in some places too abundant. It is the most numerous deer in California, makes up at least half the total herd in Washington and almost that in Oregon. Everything points toward continued high blacktail numbers and hunter success. Hunters who've not taken this deer might well relieve some pressure on the larger Rocky Mountain variety by trying it. The heavier coastal cover is a new experience, indeed.

The only problem for **elk** hunters over coming seasons will be the gamble of getting permits as competition increases, or of applying early enough in instances where they are sold first-come, first-served. Happily, elk herds have shown, under expert management these many years, an amazing stability. Elk are now established or re-established on practically all suitable range on the continent. They seem to have few serious problems. The careful cropping of both antlered and antlerless animals keeps the total number with little fluctuation year to year.

The bulk of the elk are within the contiguous United States, a herd averaging year after year a bit less than 400,000, with a harvest just as stable, from 70,000 to 80,000. Six states—Montana, Idaho, Wyoming, Colorado, Oregon, Washington—account for at least 95 percent of the annual harvest.

Predictions are that the figures will change little over the next few years. Disappearing habitat is not likely to be an influence toward decline, simply because most of the elk are in the national forests and in the wilderness and primitive areas. In addition, success figures in general have for so long remained as stable as the herds that they, too, will continue. This means roughly one out of five hunters will bag an elk each season. Those who settle for antlerless permits will have higher success, those who hunt mature bulls only must expect lower success.

A hot tip is to not overlook the low-kill states and provinces. In the past, for example, New Mexico has had, and probably will continue to have, unrestricted licenses during its mature-bulls-only season. This means no rush, no license gamble. There is some prime but little-known elk hunting also on the east slope of the Rockies in Alberta, and if you can wangle a permit for the annual surplus hunts on the Wichita Mountains National Wildlife Refuge in Oklahoma, you can expect close to a 100 percent chance for success.

The **moose** outlook over the next five years, and probably longer, is just as optimistic as for elk—perhaps even more so. The reasons are that moose are almost entirely on wilderness lands, and that game managers are learning more about them, much of it pointing toward the fact that in most of their prime habitat moose are *under*hunted, rather than pressured by too severe hunting.

Success percentages for moose hunters are much higher than for elk hunters. They run a basic low of 20 percent but shoot up in numerous places to anywhere from 40 to 90. And these percentages have not varied much over past seasons, which makes it possible to project the same for numerous seasons to come. Destruction of habitat in moose range is at present not a serious problem.

Byron Dalrymple with fine whitetail—the big-game species with brightest future.

...untain muleys have shown slow, moderate decline.

Good management has kept elk herds very stable.

Wyoming, Alaska, and western Canada will continue to be prime moose regions.

Les Bowman with pronghorn. Herds are stabilized.

Bighorns are best in British Columbia and Alberta.

Below Canada's border, goat permits will decrease.

Despite problems, caribou hunting will remain good.

Washington will continue as top black-bear state.

The projection for the future is that within the contiguous states, Wyoming will continue to be the prime spot, with a kill averaging a thousand annually and very high—up to 90 percent—success. But permits may be increasingly difficult to acquire. Montana will come next, with a harvest half that and success slightly lower, permit chances the same. The sleeper spots will be the Yukon and Northwest Territories, still opening slowly and developing. British Columbia, Alaska, and Alberta will remain hot spots, with 40 to 60 percent success predictable.

Interestingly, Ontario has a tremendous population but gets so many hunters that success is considered high at 35 percent. Yet predictions are that more animals may be taken here in coming seasons. Newfoundland also should remain stable, very good, with a one-out-of-two prediction for success. The startling moose region for everyone to watch is Minnesota. With a season launched only a few years ago, and to date only for residents, the harvest and success here so far have been phenomenal and there is thought that many more animals might safely be harvested. All told, moose hunting is stable or on an upward trend everywhere, and will remain so for some years to come.

The projection for **antelope** is in many ways similar to that for elk. That is, antelope habitat is rather precisely limited, nearly all suitable areas have their quotas, and game managers are able to make annual population surveys rather easily and accurately. Thus each season, knowing what success has averaged over many past seasons, permit quotas can be set and a virtually infallible harvest can be assured.

Careful management everywhere has kept antelope populations quite stable.

Unquestionably this will continue. The only problems likely to arise over coming years concern weather and, in some cases, fencing. Unusually severe weather occasionally decimates antelope bands. Fencing on public lands has on occasion destroyed antelope by cutting them off from drifting to safety in severe weather.

Aside from those "ifs," it can be forecast that antelope hunting will remain excellent, with the usual high success. Wyoming will continue in first place and Montana second, simply because these states have the greatest expanses of quality antelope range, and therefore the largest numbers of animals and annual permits. New Mexico, Arizona, Colorado, and Nebraska all should have fair to good hunting but modest numbers of permits.

Eastern Oregon, once excellent, has had difficulties and probably will offer residents-only hunting and few permits. In the southern portions of the prairie provinces in Canada hunters should not expect much. Antelope populations are low, and are fluctuating due to severe winters. The same is true in the Dakotas, but these two states will bear close attention. If winters are mild or average, look for high populations and a substantial number of permits. Consider these "sleeper" states.

One certain prediction can be made from now on: Trophies will never again be what they once were. Hunters may as well be resigned to this. To be sure, an exceptional head of 16 to 18 inches may be collected here and there, especially on private lands where no hunting has been allowed for a few years. But antelope bands are so closely cropped nowadays, with everyone trying for a "big buck," that horns of 12 to 14 inches are now considered trophies. That situation will remain.

Sheep are of course a great big-game prize, but though they have had much dramatic publicity, the fact is that annual sheep harvests have for many years been only modest. Success is fairly high, in general because almost all hunters must employ guides. There is no reason to believe that either the number of permits or hunter success will decline much over coming seasons.

Alaska will remain the hot spot for white sheep. The population has remained roughly level for many years. So has the harvest of around 1,000 rams. The Yukon sheep bands are in good shape, stable, with both Dall and in some sectors Stone sheep. In the Northwest Territories sheep hunting will be excellent if hunting is further developed. There are ample numbers of white sheep, but so far, few hunters and outfitters and numerous restrictions.

British Columbia, where bighorns, Dall, and Stone are found, is certain to continue as a top location. We might suggest, however, that more hunters get an eye on Alberta for bighorns over coming seasons. Over half of the bighorns in the record book have come out of this province.

Within the contiguous United States it is not a matter now (or in the future) of how good the hunting will be but how lucky one is in drawing a permit. Wyoming, Idaho, and Montana all have quite stable populations, but only two or three hundred permits issued among them. For Washington, Oregon, Utah, Colorado, and New Mexico permits are fewer yet. Sheep in these states are by no means endangered, but small populations keep permits low.

For desert sheep there are fewer still. Nevada, one of the top states for this rare trophy, usually has around 50, and this is predicted to continue. New Mexico may have a half-dozen some years, with possibly one nonresident. Arizona will probably continue to offer the most desert-sheep permits, and success, which has always been high—up to 50 percent—will probably continue about the same. Unquestionably the most desert sheep are in the mountains of Mexico, where there is always much finagling for licenses. It is a sure bet that this will also continue.

The **goat** is one big-game animal not taken in great numbers but certainly not the least bit endangered. It is well known that mountain-goat populations anywhere in their range have never been high. They live in altitudes where specific management, aside from allotment of permits, is not practical. Everywhere that goats are native their numbers, as far as can be ascertained, have remained about the same for many years. The rugged severity of their favored habitat dictates that only so many will survive. But the toughness of this animal so perfectly matched to its sparse domain also makes possible the prediction that goats will be just as plentiful many decades from now as they are presently.

Alaska and British Columbia will continue as the high-harvest spots. The Yukon and Northwest Territories may see more of this activity. So far, few goat hunters have been trying there and the number of outfitters is very limited. In the goat range within the lower 48, the top state will continue to be Washington, where permits will probably continue to be fairly numerous, and success quite high—to 30 or 40 percent. Idaho will offer fewer permits, but success should continue high there also. The same can be predicted for Montana. In Oregon, Utah, South Dakota,

Wyoming, and Colorado there will be a scattering of permits offered, but it is certain that competition will be rough, and that nonresident permits may be few and, in some instances, unavailable.

Many dire predictions have been made over the years about the **caribou.** Supposedly it has been on the brink of serious trouble for a long time. The fact is that caribou are presently in no great danger, and that the herds are well surveyed and managed. Caribou are certainly not nearly as numerous as they were some decades ago. But they are a long way from danger at this time, and it can be forecast safely that over the next decade, even though there may be slight declines here and there, hunting will remain good.

Alaska will continue to be best, the pipeline notwithstanding. The Yukon, for those who are able to get in, should be excellent. In the Northwest Territories, where caribou have been used by natives for meat for many years and sport hunting by nonresidents has been severely restricted, it can be cautiously predicted that things may open up slowly, with more permits allowed and more territory open. If this occurs, the NWT will be one of the best locations on the continent, practically virgin. British Columbia, one of the well-known caribou provinces, should continue about as in the past, with carefully regulated hunting.

Look for some exceptional heads to come out of the Ungava and Whale River regions of the Quebec-Labrador far north. This hunting was launched only about a decade ago. And in Newfoundland, long known as the place for caribou hunters, the decline that the animals were in for some time appears to be over. It can be cautiously predicted that over coming seasons there may be a strong reversal of the downward trend.

All the big **bears** are in one kind of trouble or another. Polar-bear hunting has been stopped almost completely. It is difficult to say what may occur over the next few years—whether or not some hunting may be allowed—but the chances appear slim. Grizzly and brown bears also have caused much worry for game managers lately (and have served in addition as a tub to thump by the instant ecologists who wouldn't recognize a bear if they saw one in a zoo). The fact is nonetheless that grizzlies within the contiguous states are about done in, with only token hunting that probably will and should come to a halt. In Alaska and elsewhere in Canada the big bears are declining. There will probably be some hunting for them for the next few seasons, but it is not at all certain this will continue, even through the present decade.

Black bears are only in difficulty in spots, in the heavily populated states and in regions where development of one kind or another is narrowing their habitat. For the next five years, there is no indication that black-bear hunting will be much different from what it is currently. By far the major number of blacks will continue to be taken as incidentals by deer hunters. This will remain true especially east of the Mississippi.

For anyone in that general region who wants a bear for a trophy, the best bets will continue to be Maine, some of the eastern Canadian provinces, and Ontario. Spring hunts in this region will be the most successful, as usual. The real bulk of the black-bear population, however, will continue to be focused in the West and Northwest. Alaska, Washington (the top spot on

*Hunter levels carbine at wild boar in Tennessee. There and in North Carolina—
traditional hotspots—permits will be limited. Another good bet for boar
is Monterey, Calif. And preserve boar hunting is increasing in many regions.*

the continent), Oregon, Idaho, Montana, and Wyoming will furnish the large share of the total harvest, with lesser numbers in other Rockies states.

Hunting for **wild boar** should remain stable over future seasons, most of it centered in parts of Tennessee and North Carolina. But, as now, hunts will be restricted, and chances of permits will be poor. There will also be about the same amount of boar hunting in Monterey County, California. Big boars are in no danger. They're too wary for that. What will certainly increase will be the opportunity on preserves scattered across the country to hunt feral swine, hogs interbred between "Russians" and ferals. This is growing, and results, needless to say, are pretty surefire.

This, then, is the hunting picture for at least the next five seasons, and probably beyond. It is gratifying that on the whole it can be an optimistic forecast. Let each hunter take personal responsibility for doing his part to help keep it that way indefinitely!

Outwitting Whitetails

by Erwin A. Bauer

2

During over a half century of hunting, my friend Lew Baker bagged more than his share of trophy whitetails. Born on Michigan's lonely Upper Peninsula, his natural habitat consisted of the birch thickets and balsam swamps along the Manistique River which once was prime deer country. There he bagged both his first buck, at age 11, as well as his last, at 77. In between were more than he can possibly recall. But Lew always felt that he was never really a match for *Odocoileus virginianus*—and in fact that no human hunter really was. The last time we were together, the old-timer repeated what he had often stated before . . . that "our own whitetail buck is the greatest game animal on earth, bar none." I have to agree with him.

Look at it this way. Given unlimited time, money, and the determination to hunt seriously and hard, you could probably collect a bragging-size trophy of any big-game species for which hunting is permitted. Go ahead and name your choice: lion, kudu, any of the sheep, moose, elephant, leopard, mule deer . . . all except

one, the whitetail, would be easy. I know of no open season in the United States where, no matter what is spent for guides and guns and whatever, the hunter could be *guaranteed a really good head*. That is true even though whitetails are very abundant animals and the annual kill runs well into six figures.

Let me clarify the above. Just bagging a whitetail, any whitetail, isn't always easy. Nationwide each fall, fewer than one in every four hunters is successful. But for a really heavy buck with a heavy rack, the ratio is more like one in twenty.

To be consistently successful, hunting deer as anything else is largely a matter of knowing the target and what makes it tick. So let's take a close look at the whitetail to see why Lew Baker and a million other American sportsmen rate it so highly.

Standing nervously in a dark spruce forest, even a mature male whitetail may seem to be a frail and gentle animal. Bambi—you know. But nothing could be much farther from the reality. The species is a product of 15 million years of evolution, during the past four centuries of which it has been intensively hunted, first for the market and most recently for sport. Whitetails have survived the same glaciers and droughts, the same severe climactic changes that wiped out mastodons and saber-toothed tigers. No wonder such a tough and durable critter evolved.

A deer's toughening process begins the moment the animal is conceived. All winter long the fetus is carried by a doe living on starvation rations, compounded by biting cold and, in the North, deep snows. Other animals hibernate or migrate; whitetails can do neither. So any female which survives the winter ordeal bears a fawn just as tough as she. By fall of his first year, "Bambi" will be able to sprint 30 mph over a tough woodland course and clear a six- or seven-foot barrier from a standing position. If he happens to survive his first and most dangerous hunting season, the reward is only to face the same starvation test and wintry cold his mother survived.

Even very good shots have trouble connecting on deer. The reason is that few animals in Nature have been supplied with so many and such effective escape mechanisms. Not many animals can be out of sight so quickly as a whitetail, thanks to the ability to clear 25 to 30 feet in a bound, therefore being out of sight or in deep cover before a gun can be pointed. When really under pressure and traveling at top speed, a deer becomes only a blur of buckskin in the forest. You are fortunate if you have time to flip off the safety. But no matter how fast it is going, a deer can brake abruptly to a stop and be away in a different direction. Such a maneuver would break another animal's legs, but a curious ball-bearing anatomy makes this possible. A whitetail's front legs do not

connect directly to the skeleton, but instead are separated by a tough rubbery tissue which is actually a shock absorber.

To its remarkable physical ability, add any deer's good hearing, a phenomenal sense of smell and uncanny eyesight. Some hunters understandably believe a deer's vision is about eight times as keen as any man's. Vision is a difficult thing to compare, but one fact is absolutely certain: Rarely does a hunter spot a whitetail before he himself is already seen and identified.

Waiting at strategic location is often your best bet for taking a whitetail buck. Tree stands are popular because they give hunter good view and reduce chance that deer will see him or catch his scent.

It would be easily possible to fill this entire book with biological and physiological facts about whitetails, but let's explore now about how to outwit them.

A few big bucks are bagged each year by luck alone, but it is an infinitesimal number. Normally the best, the most skilful, cautious, and experienced woodsmen have the best chance of scoring.

Woodsmanship comes from both practice and confidence, as well as from experience. Not many of us today live in the same area long enough, or spend enough time in the same deer woods, to be considered experienced. But almost all of us *can* get out often enough to feel at home in the mixed hardwood-evergreen forests that whitetails prefer. Long before any season opens, it's good advice to get out and hike, all the time trying to stay in the shadows and to make no noise while moving along.

Develop powers of observation by actually looking for deer or other wildlife—and even by bird-watching. The latter may seem silly to some, but any man who can walk quickly and quietly through a woods and accurately identify the woodland birds he sees will also be able to spot the telltale movements of deer before it is too late. Squirrel hunting is another excellent way to tune up for whitetails.

Being out in the woods frequently develops confidence in not getting lost—in always being able to find the way back to a starting point. A factor too often overlooked is that a sportsman not confident of his bearing cannot possibly concentrate on his hunting.

Learn to know deer sign—and how fresh it is. Fortunately, deer leave behind all kinds of evidence of their presence. The most conspicuous are the trails and crossings. In many areas (because they have been used so long by so many animals) these are as clearly marked as bridle trails across a country club pasture. Look for them, see where they lead, and where they cross, and in time deer will come along. Pellets are signs that deer are present and so are the matted-down places which serve as beds. Just before the fall rut, males strip the bark from saplings by rubbing their antlers against them. These stripped places are easy to see, often for a long distance. Browse lines—where all the trees in a grove have been evenly clipped to a certain height—are another, more subtle sign that deer (perhaps too many) are or were somewhere nearby.

One of the best woodsmen and whitetail hunters I have ever known was Frank Sayers who, by coincidence, also served his hunting apprenticeship in upper Michigan. A good bit of his great success could be credited to "jumping the gun" every year.

This isn't to intimate that Frank poached or broke the law in any way. On the other hand, he simply planned to arrive in hunting territory, wherever it was, at least a few days before the season opened. He then spent his time setting up a very cozy, comfortable camp and reconnoitering the area. With camp chores completed and all firewood cut, there was never any last-minute rush to get it done and maybe delay hunting. And the reconnaissance gave him a jump on all other hunters. By opening morning he knew exactly where the most deer were concentrated and which trails they were using. As a result, I can remember more than one occasion when on opening morning, a fine field-dressed buck was hanging beside camp before other hunters had their bearings.

Even big bucks like this one can make themselves almost invisible in heavy cover. When trying to spot whitetails, it's important to watch for movements and for telltale "bits" of deer behind screening brush.

Let's recap the above because it is important. Assume you have allotted ten days for this fall's deer hunt. You plan to drive to the hunting area the day before opening. But why not split it up another way? Drive to the spot four or five days early and leisurely get acquainted with the topography, the deer, the whole picture. It just might prove to be the smartest strategy of all.

There generally are three ways (or combinations of these) to outwit whitetails. Call these still-hunting, driving, and standing—the waiting game. The last of these—playing the waiting game—is usually the best by far for an inexperienced hunter.

Several years ago the following story was widely circulated by one of the wire services. An obviously green hunter in brand new clothes appeared in the bar of a small northern Michigan town on opening day of the deer season. "I'm up from Detroit," the man said, "and have to be back there tomorrow. Where can I bag a big buck fast?"

"Just go outside town anywhere and sit down near the edge of the woods," the bartender replied. When the man was gone, everyone in the place had a good loud horse laugh.

But the last laugh was on the barflys. An hour or so later the neophyte returned with a huge buck lashed onto cartop carriers. "Thanks a lot," he said, "for the tip."

Of course the news story was meant to be comical, but it also contains a strong message. Any hunter who can station himself in a good spot in good deer country has a far better chance than a hunter who wanders aimlessly, noisily, across a landscape in search of a target. But playing the waiting game calls for great patience and the ability to sit perfectly still for long periods of time, despite cold, winds, and maybe even monotony. Smoking is out and so is standing up to stretch. You have to dress warmly. Success also depends on being in a good spot, perhaps a place where deer will seek to escape from other hunters circulating about. Perhaps the most of the largest bucks everywhere are taken by playing the waiting game.

Despite their wariness and keen senses, whitetails (like many other big-game animals) do have an Achilles' heel; although alert for danger from all around, they seldom look up. The explanation probably is that no natural enemies exist above them. But wherever it is legal (as it is in most states) hunters can take advantage of this weakness by playing the waiting game from a tree or other overhead blind.

Driving pays off well when executed properly by small rather than large parties and when the terrain is broken up, rather than consisting of vast stands of unbroken woods. Parties of four, five, never more than six for safety, are divided up among standers and drivers. A chunk of woodland, hopefully bounded by a river, lakes, or meadows is selected for a given hunt and the standers placed strategically on one end. The drivers then begin at the opposite side and hunt slowly toward the standers in order to sandwich deer in between—

so that somebody gets a good shot.

Success obviously depends on planning—on how well the standers are placed. A common mistake is to drive an area that is too large, from which deer can elude all hunters by dodging between them unseen. Another error is not to consider the direction of the wind. Few drives directly into the wind are ever successful because deer will easily scent the standers and avoid them. A crosswind is the best bet for pulling off a drive.

One person who best knows the region must be in charge of any drive, and all participants must know the role and location of all others. Outline each drive on a map. Standers should not move or shift positions until the operation is finished. In regions such as the Southeast, where deer hunting with hounds is legal, dogs can serve as drivers in what is usually very dense or lush cover.

No technique of deer hunting is more challenging nor more fascinating than still-hunting, either alone or with one other hunter. And there is no more fulfilling way to bag a trophy whitetail buck. You really earn and deserve your venison this way.

Still-hunting means going out on foot in direct pursuit of the target. You pit your own skill, lore, and experience against a shy, suspicious, and elusive animal. You make plenty of footprints and cover a lot of beautiful country. You probably see many criss-crossing tracks and, too often, just the white flag of a deer vanishing into underbrush too far away. It's a game of disappointments and frustrations, but it's far from dull. Persistence pays off, too.

For veterans the following is very basic advice, but it should be emphasized again here that any still-hunter must blend into his environment and travel as quietly as his

Author kneels behind massive rack of once-in-a-lifetime trophy whitetail.
Bucks don't grow this big without learning to avoid humans, but
Bauer outsmarted his quarry by picking his stand well and playing waiting game.

own shadow. Always go upwind—or at least against a crosswind—and hunt with one eye on the ground, the other ahead. Stop often and listen. Change directions slightly, follow a course by zigzagging, and watch both sides as well as ahead.

Still-hunting (as almost any whitetail hunting) is always better when a fresh fall of snow covers the ground. Deer sign is more easily seen then and the animals themselves are better spotted against white than against the dull dark colors of a winter woodlands. Of course the hunter is more easily spotted, too.

But no matter how it's done, outwitting a whitetail is not easy. After all, the target is among the world's greatest game animals. Luckily, it is also among the most available to the American outdoorsman.

Author snapped this photo when he jumped bedded buck. Sometimes you can collect your venison that way, but if you aren't very careful you may glimpse nothing more than raised white flag disappearing into cover.

How to Collect Your Muley

by Byron W. Dalrymple

3

The most encouraging statistic a beginning mule deer hunter can have at hand is that the success percentage among mule deer hunters is at least twice as high as among whitetail hunters, and in some states four to five times as high. Nonetheless, of our 8-million-plus U.S. deer hunters, the great majority have had experience only with whitetails. Mule deer are abundant in just eleven states, and there is a modest amount of hunting for them in only six others. Thus, though the tyro may be encouraged by learning of his overall chances of success, this may not do him much good unless he knows what sort of animal the mule deer is, and has firmly in mind the basics of how to collect one.

Mule deer and whitetails are really quite different personalities. The whitetail is exceedingly nervous and jumpy. The mule deer is a far more placid animal. That doesn't mean it is dumb. It is simply more of a wilderness creature, and deliberate rather than impulsive. Further, although mule deer are found in western forests, they are fundamentally animals of rather open country, and it is interesting and valuable also to know that mule deer do not range to any extent in flat country. They are deer of the slopes, the canyons, and the mountains.

Each season thousands of whitetail hunters comb woodlots practically on the edge of towns and cities, and bag some big bucks, too. Whitetails have learned to cope with man's civilization. Except in winter situations in high mountains where mule deer are forced by deep snow to consort near populous valley places, they are withdrawn. If you're willing to settle for a small mule deer buck, you may find one along a back road in one of the western states. But if you are after a trophy buck you had better be resigned to getting way, way off the beaten track.

Mule deer are extremely gregarious. This is of immense advantage to a hunter, for it can happen that most of the good racks on a mountain that you are hunting will be gathering in only three or four groups. Diligent searching may be required to locate one of them.

You won't hear alarmed or suspicious mule deer snort and blow, as whitetails do.

*This is no record-breaker, but he's a good five-point buck. It's easiest
to judge mule deer's rack when you get full front or rear view. If antlers look
massive and extend fully six inches beyond his ears, he's a real trophy.*

And you won't catch glimpses of an erect, waving flag as they flee. The mule deer runs with its stringy little tail down. It also has gaits quite different from the whitetail, and hunters who know the meaning of these gaits can read what the deer intends to do. For example, scores of times I've watched a good muley buck, caught unaware in the open, simply stare for a few seconds and start to walk away, almost as if embarrassed. No whitetail buck does that! It runs first and wonders later what frightened it.

The mule deer buck will suddenly begin to hop. It bounces into the air and comes stiff-legged down on all four feet, a kind of "pogo-stick" gait. This tells you it is alarmed but puzzled. This is not a fast getaway. In fact, a mule deer hopping like this is easy to hit. But hold up! Chances are it will cover a few yards thus, then stop, and like as not turn broadside and look back. I don't have to tell any deer hunter that a frightened whitetail never stops to look back!

When a muley really takes off, it moves with astonishing power and speed. The back feet strike *behind* the front feet and push it in great bounds. The whitetail in a dead run places the hind feet *past* the front ones at each bound. Running tracks, in areas where both deer are present, can be separated this way.

If the fleeing buck goes over the top on the run, he's still not necessarily gone for good. Whitetail hunters know well that a spooked buck will run over the next several ridges before slowing down. Mule deer commonly follow a kind of out-of-sight-out-of-mind plan. If the wind is right, a prowl up and over the ridge where the deer disappeared may find it within easy shooting distance, browsing along again.

Many excellent mule deer are overlooked by beginning hunters who don't understand that what these deer consider a perfect bedding spot would terrify a whitetail. The large whitetail buck invariably selects a dense thicket in which to hide. He doesn't necessarily want to see out and he wants to be sure no enemy sees in. Mule deer follow an exactly opposite routine. In open country I have seen trophy bucks lie down beneath the shade of a single small bush on an otherwise open slope. Usually such a bed spot is not too far below the crown of the ridge. The deer can see the entire valley, but it is surprisingly well hidden. Many an average hunter would not remotely believe a deer would be there. He may even sweep a glass across the slope and miss it. Further, during the day, thermals in mountain country move upslope as the air is warmed. The deer drinks in scent from everywhere below.

If there are high rock buttes, or, in forested country, high ledges or points overlooking a valley, glassing these during the day will often discover bedded bucks. Perhaps only an antler shows. Approaching such a rocky point on the deer's level is tricky. Old bucks bedded thus will invariably have two escape routes. But many a muley has been done in by a pair of hunters, one moving in from one direction, the other waiting to waylay the old gentleman as he bounds along the far side of the point.

Because of their rather sedentary, placid nature, mule deer are invariably much fatter than whitetails. They dislike heat, and, living in high altitudes, what may seem cool to a hunter may seem too warm to a fat muley buck. Thus, especially in sparsely forested areas, rimrocks, those great jumbles of broken strata coursing ridge or mountain tops, form prime resting spots for big bucks. From far below these may seem incapable of hiding deer. But once you climb up, you find slabs big as houses, with endless shady crannies.

On days of pleasant fall weather the deer will start up to the rims either at dawn or shortly after. They will go to water on the way. A knowledge of this trait can collect you a good buck early in the morning, near a watering place that abounds with tracks, or along a much-used mountainside trail. During the day, however, a hunter who prowls the rims—always, mind you, on the shady side—will jump bucks from their beds. This in fact is a dramatic, even though physically difficult, sport. Shots commonly are at only a few yards.

There are several curious mule deer hiding traits which newcomers should know. On numerous occasions I have watched a big buck that suspected it was being pursued simply ease into a small thicket and lie down. It would stay right there and let a hunter pass within a few yards. In desert mountains I've seen one run up a slope, slow to a walk, head down, put a Spanish bayonet between it and the hunter, flop onto the ground and lay its head flat out, apparently thinking it was hidden. In fact, a buck *can* disappear that way, unless a hunter is onto its tricks. A third trait concerns a running mule deer, even one shot at and missed. I killed a big 10-point a couple of years ago that I jumped from its bed beneath a single piñon. I missed on the first shot at close range. Instead of running over the ridge, the deer wheeled behind a small, dense thicket, turned back and plunged into it, and stood immobile. This is a rather common trick. An excited

hunter might believe his quarry had gone over the top. In this instance, I walked to within 50 yards, finally made out the outline of its neck in the deep shade, and concluded my hunt.

When jumped, mule deer invariably go up, whereas whitetails may pour off a ridge down into a valley. Furthermore, a wounded mule deer doesn't necessarily go downhill. It's often said any wounded deer goes down because that's the easy way. To a mule deer, safety means up, and a badly wounded muley may go up the steepest mountain. When hard hunted, whitetails simply learn to hide better and better on their home range. Trophy mule deer bucks will not tolerate much disturbance. They are used to big country. They simply move back into more secure wilderness reaches.

Because mule deer country contains such vast expanses, time spent glassing every rock and shrub on a mountain or across a valley, or numerous mountain meadows in view from a single vantage point, is worth far more than incessant movement. If you are riding a horse, get up where you can see distantly, tie your mount, and spend an hour studying the terrain. Don't let anybody tell you mule deer aren't afraid of the sound of a rider. I've watched them run at half a mile when horse hoofs clinked shale. Although it is hard work, prowling on foot just inside mountain meadow edges or along canyon rims, slowly and quietly, will show you the most deer at shootable range.

As many readers may know, mule deer in many mountain areas—but not all—make vertical migrations in fall, moving down from their summering grounds near timberline to lower valleys when deep snows push them out and obliterate forage. If you time your hunt to coincide with

Hunter and guide in Montana examine buck taken with .264 Magnum. This hunt took place late in season, when deep snow near timberline had prompted mule-deer migration to lower wintering grounds where buck was intercepted.

such a downward movement, and bone up locally on the ancestral migration routes, bagging a good buck can be rather sure-fire. Or, after the deer are concentrated on their wintering grounds, they are often so concentrated that a hunter can just about take his pick.

However, there are two pitfalls. First, you must be certain that the deer, in the state and area where you hunt, actually do move down in winter. For example, in West Texas, parts of New Mexico, Arizona, and Nevada, and in several Rockies states where the "high country" isn't really so very high, there are no migrations to winter range. The deer stay on the same ranges all year. Second, each season many first-timers unacquainted with mule deer

habits and terrain hunt early, discover a lot of shed antlers, droppings, and browsed shrubs, and think they have found a great place to hunt—when what they are seeing are signs left from the previous winter. Even droppings when moist from rain or dew will appear fresh. Such a winter range may indeed be swarming later on, but unless severe snows hit the high country as the season opens, the deer won't move down to winter range for some weeks.

Take time to make a small study of what the chief forage of the deer is in the region where you're booked. It's certain to be drastically different from that of whitetails where you hunt. A visit with a local game warden or a query to a game department about a specific locale will fill you in. Once

Above left is fine muley buck standing in meadow edging Utah timber. Deer above right is excellent specimen of blacktail subspecies on West Coast. Note that blacktail's rack tends to be narrower.

Hunter at left is in steady prone position for long shot at mule deer. Scene is in open meadow but locale is in Rockies; even here in mountainous country, "plains-style" accuracy is frequently essential.

*Sometimes you'll find several good bucks browsing, resting, or
traveling together and you have to make fast choice of the best trophy—in this
case bringing up the rear. These muleys slowed down after topping ridge.*

you know the plant species, make a point of learning to recognize them. At times, this alone can point you to success.

Be sure to carry a good binocular, not a cheapie. Glassing for a mule deer is mandatory. These spaces are wide, indeed. Further, be sure you are properly gunned. The old .30-30 lever without scope might be all right in the Maine or Pennsylvania woods. But most shots at mule deer are likely to be long simply because in the mountainous West you can see a long way. You need a flat-shooting caliber, one you can sight in for 250 or 300 yards on the money and still not be much over four inches high at midrange. Additionally, shoot a cartridge with plenty of steam. Anchor your buck right where it stands. You might wound a whitetail in farm country, trail it down, and have no problems. But let a big buck mule deer lead you into the mountains and you just may have to sit beside it until you eat it up! There are many opinions about scopes. I will just say that in my view the variable with top rating of 7X, 8X, or 9X beats the fixed power.

There are two items one needs to be able to judge. The first is range. In stand-on-end country, forested or open, range is deceptive. You'll be looking at terrain not at all like average whitetail range. So, when you arrive on the hunt grounds, make it a point to guess at a few distances and then pace them. This is how you learn. The second concerns what is and is not a trophy. The antlers of very modest-sized mule deer look big by comparison to what whitetail hunters are used to. An 18- or 20-inch whitetail spread is a pretty good trophy. It's just a so-so mule deer.

A good way to judge is to know ear length. Mule deer ears are long, about 11 to 12 inches. Cocked up at a "looking" angle they won't spread as wide as their sum plus skull width, of course. But if antlers extend several inches on each side past the ears, you are looking at a pretty fair specimen. If they are out a full six inches on either side, or if with the deer going straight away they spread well past the rump outline, you'd better try to collect.

These basics of mule deer hunting should at least give you a good start. As with all hunting, of course, there's many a fine point to be put in your book as you go along. Experience in this, as in any other endeavor, is still the best teacher!

A Guide to Elk

by John Madson

4

There are deer hunters and sheep hunters who scorn elk. They claim that the wapiti isn't particularly hard to find, stalk, or shoot.

Maybe, in some places. But the game value of an elk is proportional to wariness, which is proportional to hunting pressure, which comes back to game value. Elk in remote areas aren't likely to hit the stampede button at the sight of a distant horseman. But when a bull elk's faculties are honed by danger, he becomes sly and cunning and adopts catlike traits that might seem ludicrous for an animal of his size if he didn't carry them off so well.

Smell is his most important gift, and he relies upon it absolutely. He may never hear or see danger, but he'll take his nostrils' word for it and often verifies the sight or sound of danger by smelling it. Elk can locate a hunter by scent with amazing accuracy, and may panic if wind eddies carry a scent that can't be located.

Their hearing is extremely sharp, and elk are curious about strange noises. Elk don't have binocular vision, nor is there any evidence that they can see color. But they have splendid long-range vision that's a working combination of sharp eyes and stature that puts those eyes high above the ground.

The elk also has a definite sense of awareness—a sort of taut interest in the immediate environment that keeps him attuned to goings-on. A man might sneak to within a hundred yards without much difficulty, masking his movements and sounds in the ceaseless wind of the moors. Suddenly, however, the approach grows more difficult. Within fifty yards of the elk herd, the sound of wind in the heather may virtually cease, and the slightest movement of an intruder seems to cause a great deal of sound. The elk seem to rest in places where they can easily hear trespassers.

Like smart old eastern whitetails, hard-hunted elk adapt as the situation demands. Old bulls, in particular, often hang out in dense thickets that are nearly impossible for a man to penetrate without making noise. Early in the season, when elk are in alpine meadows or high-country parks, they aren't usually too touchy. But once they've been hunted, an alarm may cause them to run for five miles and not stop until they're in the densest thicket on the mountainside.

For this reason, it's important that your first shot be in the money. An elk is a tough critter that can pack a lot of lead and still run many mountain miles. You must hit your elk in the right place, and very, very hard.

There are expert elk hunters who shoot light rifles. In fact, it hasn't been many years since the little .30-30 carbine led the elk-hunting pack in many western states. We've even known of a .243 being used in bison control with deadly results. But day in and out, in the hands of average hunters under average conditions, such calibers are too anemic for elk.

Yellowstone Park rangers working on elk control have used many rifles, and have developed some strong personal convictions. They have come to rely on magnum calibers of .300, .338, and even a few .375's.

But the average elk hunter may compromise. He can usually be more deliberate about his shooting and pick his shots with some care. He doesn't doubt that the .300 and the .338 are better elk cartridges. However, they kick. For an experienced rifleman who understands recoil and how to handle it, such loads are ideal. But the sometime rifleman likes to go a bit lighter.

Gil Hunter, Colorado's chief of game management, says the most popular calibers for elk in Colorado are the .30-'06 and the .270. Gil has several favorite elk rifles and loads—the .30-'06 with a 220-grain bullet, the 8mm with a 175-grain bullet, the .270 with a 150-grain bullet, and the .300 with a 180-grain bullet. In open country the hunter needs a flat-shooting cartridge with well-sustained energy—a mod-

ern, long-bulleted outfit somewhere between .27 and .35 caliber.

Scope sights? You'll probably want 4X. A 2½X is very good, but 6X is probably more than you need. Whatever scope you buy, get a good one—coated lenses, constantly centered reticule, windage and elevation screws protected by screw caps, and nitrogen-filled scope tube. You may be doing some hunting in rain and in sharp .temperature changes, and a sealed scope with no internal fogging is a good investment.

Elk country is cool in autumn. The mountain wind can bite a man to the bone, and it can blow in a sharp weather change in a matter of minutes.

Windproof clothing is a must, especially a down-insulated jacket. For much of the rest, wool is the best choice: shirts, underwear, and thick, fleecy socks. Wool pants are also popular as are heavy duck "tin pants," levis, and denims. And don't forget the underwear—a light woolen full union suit, made of cotton laminated to lamb's wool. It's warmer than a bedful of fat beagles, and light, free, and easy to move in.

Boots? Your flatland favorites may be best. Some packers and wranglers probably like their "cowboy boots" because they learned to walk in them and don't know any better. Such boots are built for riding, not mountain-walking. Rubber-bottomed shoepacs are good for mountain elk hunting, especially when you may encounter a few inches of wet snow. Get them one size bigger than your street shoes. Take plenty of the finest wool socks you can buy, and spare sheepskin innersoles.

Heavy, unlined buckskin gloves can come in handy for general riding and shooting, and you won't go wrong to take

Many hunters scoff at bugling, but if not overdone it can sometimes locate rutting bulls early in season. This elk revealed his position near stream crossing by answering well-blown whistle. Hunter then stalked up close.

along some light wool mittens. Woolen "chopper mitts" with leather shells are excellent.

Good rain gear is essential for a high-country elk hunt. For all-round mountain hunting, it's hard to beat a good two-piece rainsuit. The pants are fine to ride in, keep you dry to your ankles, and the top is a handy jacket. Never hunt in a slicker. Get a rainsuit.

If you hunt in an all-day mountain rain, you'll bless your Stetson. We often wear a cap in the high country and pull the rain-shirt's hood over it, and the cap's bill keeps some rain out of the face. But hunting in a parka hood is never much of a bargain. By all means, take a serviceable cap (with earlaps) on your elk hunt.

On a remote elk hunt your sleeping bag is almost as important as your rifle. It's basic equipment. Buy a goose-down bag with at least two pounds of down. By the way, you'll probably like the new poly-foam sleeping pads. Conventional air mattresses can be cold, but the new foam sleeping pads are excellent insulation, very warm, and easy to lie on. No inflating chores or punctures, either.

The average outfitter provides you with tents, horses, saddles, pack animals, cooking gear, and food. The rest is up to you: rifle, raingear, clothing, toilet articles, sleeping gear, camera, and binoculars. And by all means, *bring your own saddle scabbard for your rifle.* Your guide will likely have his own binoculars and spotting scope, but you'll certainly want good, compact binoculars of your own. For all-round use, the 7x35 is excellent. The heck with a rifle scope for long-range scanning. There's no substitute for binoculars.

If you should want a guide, write the state game department in the capitol of the state in which you'd like to hunt. Ask for a list of licensed guides and outfitters. Then write to the guides, ask for their price lists and literature, find out what they do and do not provide on the hunt, and ask for references from banks and former clients. For a full discussion of guide hunts see "An Outfitter's Plea," page 341.

Elk hunting has come a long way since the Indian method of trapping them in pits. But it still comes down to a man, a mountain, and an elk—and the problems of getting in, getting the elk, and getting out.

A horse is usually a must. And it's best when there's someone along who understands horse-packing. A mounted man can also see farther than a man afoot, and elk aren't particularly frightened by horses. Then, too, there's the fact that elk don't stay put. Tomorrow they may have drifted miles from where they are today, and hunting them is no job for the walking hunter. As one old cowboy said: "If the good Lord had meant man to walk, He'd have give him four laigs!"

Some western horses are pretty good hunters in their own right and may sense elk or deer long before their riders do, nickering or pricking up their ears. Don't use buckskin or palamino horses while elk hunting. Use darker horses with plenty of red on their bridles and on your clothing. In Montana several years ago an eager hunter shot two horses out of a packstring travelling in timber before he knew what he was doing.

Some westerners who hunt elk from horseback dismount only for the actual shooting. Others cover the elk range on horseback but dismount when fresh tracks or sign are found, and proceed afoot. This is much quieter, and the hunter is ready to shoot at any instant. But be sure to leave your horse where he'll be easy to find again, such as at the edge of an open park.

In heavy wind, elk may be found on the protected sides of ridges. So when you top out on a ridge, don't skyline yourself. If you are riding, dismount below the crest, leave your horse, and ease up to the top and have a look. Try to get above the elk. Like bighorns, elk are usually more alert for danger coming from down-mountain.

During the peak of the rutting season when the bulls are bugling, you may see a number of elk in the sparsely wooded basins, ridges, and meadows below timberline. Open grassy areas and aspen "parks" are excellent places to hunt. In the middle of the day, try still-hunting in heavy timber around areas of feeding activity. Pick a good lookout at the edge of a park and wait for the elk to feed out into the open—a technique that seems to work particularly well in northern mountains. In the southern mountain ranges of New Mexico and Arizona—such as in the Gila National Wilderness—elk are hunted about like deer.

Montana outfitter Howard Copenhaver (left) congratulates client who stalked
magnificent wapiti located by bugling. Hunter wisely left whistling to
the pro, counting on his skill and experience as well as knowledge of the area.

In heavily hunted country, elk may be easily found in timberline parks and pastures only early in the season. Later on, hunting becomes hard work and you must take advantage of all openings in which elk might appear—fire lanes, avalanche paths, small burns, natural clearings between bodies of timber, and open benches above streams.

Elk can be maddening devils in the deep woods, and it's not uncommon for a hunter to actually smell the rank, musky-wallow stench of a bull elk and never see him. Like wise old buck whitetails, bull elk in heavy timber may freeze while a hunter walks within a few yards. Or, an elk may sneak silently ahead, staying just out of sight. In other cases, bull elk hole up in incredibly dense stands of pine or spruce in which a hunter can be heard for a quarter-mile.

Big as he is, a bull elk can melt into heavy timber like a wraith. However, the elk's best defense of stealth and infinite alertness can be the best weapons of the hunter. To the alert hunter who is painfully attuned to the forest, a skulking bull elk may materialize as if outlined by neon tubing.

A light tracking snow is an immense help in timber. Groups of tracks often indicate cows, calves, and spike bulls, while solo sets of large tracks are probably those of grown bulls. It works best when two trackers hunt together—one man tracking while the other parallels him and watches well ahead.

Like deer, an elk often travels in wide loops and beds down at a point where his back trail can be watched. More often than not, lone elk seem to expect to be followed. They may stop occasionally and examine their back trail, and when they bed down or watch for pursuers, they often do so from the edge of dense cover where one jump will put them out of sight. When you're tracking elk through timber and come to a clearing, stay in the woods and carefully examine the opposite edge of the forest before crossing open ground—just in case the elk is standing there watching for *you.*

In extremely heavy cover, some hunters may rush headlong toward an elk when the animal is jumped. They believe that a rapid change in position can sometimes offer a quick shot, and there's a chance the elk will look back at all the commotion and make one last, fatal pause. It's tough shooting. You must set your feet, decide if it's a worthwhile elk, pick your target, mount your rifle, and snap off a shot—all in about one second. Good luck.

Elk drives work best in canyons or abrupt valleys. Like deer drives, they should be well planned. Certain hunters are assigned points of vantage overlooking the elk routes. These gunners must *never* move from their positions until the drive is over, and the drivers must always be alert for elk sneaking back through the line.

Horses are used on some elk drives. If a band of elk is found in a patch of timber, one group of riders can move downwind, dismount, conceal men and horses, and watch any open meadows through which elk might move. The other riders enter the timber from upwind, giving the elk plenty of chance to smell and hear them. The elk are supposed to leave the timber and run downwind toward the riflemen, and sometimes they do. But in country where stalking, driving, and several parties of hunters are likely to get all tangled up with each other, the best bet is still to watch known game trails and crossings.

Outfitter will have plenty of work packing out this great bull. Hunter who insists on going it alone—employing no outfitter—may fail to bring out trophy and meat.

This Utah elk came out of timber into sparsely wooded basin. Such spots, as well as ridges and meadows below timberline, are good places to take your stand during peak of rut.

Early in the fall, when a gentleman elk is stoked with passion, he takes a dim view of any other bulls hollering on his mountain. A hunter can exploit this situation with a proper "elk whistle" and some knowledge of what a gentleman elk ought to sound like, and it's not hard to acquire either.

There are commercial elk whistles, but many westerners prefer to make their own. Harry Woodward, the director of the Colorado Game Fish and Parks Department, makes his calls from stiff plastic tubing. Norman Hancock, the chief of game management of the Utah Department of Fish and Game, makes elk whistles of thin-walled electrical conduit tubing. Norm has finally settled on these dimensions: 12″ of ½″-diameter pipe, ⅝″-hardwood doweling for plugs at each end, and a notch cut about 1¼″ from the tip of the whistle. In the blowing end, about ⅛″ is shaved from the top of the dowel plug.

A man-made elk whistle is designed to imitate only the higher registers of an elk's bugling, and must not be blown too often. It should be used only to locate the elk and then only enough to fire his curiosity and outrage his sense of property. Novices usually overdo it.

Choose a calling place where you can watch a large area, and where the sound will carry. It's most effective early in the season, and in areas that haven't been heavily hunted. There are mixed opinions about the value of elk calling—and some men feel that it's only good for calling up other hunters. But there are times and places that it works well. And, like any type of calling, it adds to the sport.

O.K. You have a fine, long-range rifle and you're a fine, long-range rifleman. And now that we've established that, let's shoot the elk as closely as possible. Elk are big and are always farther away than they look. In fact, they are the biggest long-range game in North America. So shoot your elk when you think he's at a hundred yards, because chances are that he's really at two hundred.

Use good judgment; *if you can't pack an elk out, don't shoot him!* We recently heard of a Washington hunter who dropped a near-record Olympic bull at the end of a blind canyon in a jungle of vine maple and salal. It was impossible to get any part of that elk out of there, and nearly a half-ton of meat was left to the ravens.

Where do you hit an elk? The same places that you hit a deer—but much harder. One favorite is the neck shot, for this is supposed to either give a clean kill or a superficial wound. Maybe. But a neck shot can be tricky on a swollen-necked old bull. Some hunters like the head shot, but it is to be avoided on trophy bulls because a broken skull may be barred from trophy competition. The shoulder shot is good. No elk can travel far if he's broken down in the foreparts.

The all-odds favorite, however, is probably the chest shot, for there's a three-way chance of getting the job done. If the bullet is too high, the spine may be broken. Anywhere in the center of the chest area will hit the lungs. A bit lower and a heart shot may result. The heart offers a good shot if you're sure of yourself. It lies in the bottom of an elk's chest just behind the front leg in the normal standing position. The lung shot is highly effective—especially in the upper lung area—but don't expect spectacular results. A big bull elk can be mortally stricken in the lungs and not even leave a blood trail for the first fifty yards. So if you are sure that you've solidly hit an elk but see no blood sign in the immediate area, don't give up.

On quartering shots where the lung area is your best target, proper bullets become very important. Such a shot at a large bull elk may require punching through an arm-length of living leather, thick packs of muscle, and even heavy bone. It's no job for a flit gun.

You Never Know About Caribou

5

by Charles Elliott

We were hunting the far northern part of the Yukon Territory, up where the Bonnett Plume River flows toward the mouth of the Mackenzie on the Arctic Ocean. When we'd first ridden into that country, we had seen caribou singly and in small groups every day. But when we had collected fine specimens of sheep, moose, and grizzly, and turned our attention to locating a caribou rack as creditable as the other trophies we'd taken, every one of the tundra deer seemed to have disappeared. We covered miles in every direction and even set out two spike camps. We found tracks and droppings that were not too old, but sighted not a single caribou for five days.

We made ever-widening circles from camp, but not until the sixth afternoon did we come on fresh sign of several animals travelling in a southerly direction through a long valley between massive ridges. I managed to find, stalk, and shoot a good bull that day. And then, as if the sound of the rifle had been a signal to the herds, the whole wilderness around us suddenly erupted with caribou. For the next week

we were in sight of bulls and cows most of the time.

What we had witnessed has for uncounted generations been a problem with Indians of the North Country, who depend on the herds for their winter meat. For a few weeks each year for many years the herds may stream by in migration, and then suddenly for no apparent reason, the migration course is changed and the caribou do not come. The tribes who have counted on them may then face a starvation winter. This behavior continues to remain a mystery.

Depending on the subspecies and where it ranges, the caribou stands from 3½ to about five feet at the shoulder, and weights run from 300 to 400 pounds for the smaller varieties, up to 600 for the mountain caribou, and even occasionally 700 for the Osborn caribou, which is close kin to the mountain race.

Throughout the range, each subspecies has its own color characteristics, most marked by summer coats that shade from mouse gray to chocolate brown, with lighter-colored neck and cape. The winter coat is much more striking. Over the main body it is lighter in color, with the neck, cape, and long throat ruff or mane extending from the chin to the chest, turning from a light gray in some subspecies to pure white in many barren ground bulls. Each kind of caribou has its own color peculiarities which help to identify it; the mountain variety, for example, is often called the black-faced caribou.

The hooves are uniquely adapted for a habitat encompassing vast regions of swamp, marsh, mud, and tundra, all boggy through the warm months and frozen in the winter. The caribou has the biggest foot in proportion to its size of any hooved animal. The hoof is cleft almost to the hock and he can spread it until his track is often wider than long. Before winter, the rim of the hoof hardens to tough, sharp horn that gives the animal a better footing on ice.

One of the most peculiar things about the foot is that the ankle bones are so constructed and arranged that when the caribou walks, it makes a clicking sound loud enough to be heard for some distance. A number of times I have heard this sound before I saw the animals.

Who could ever aptly describe the configuration, much less the majesty, of the rack that a bull caribou carries high and at such a regal tilt? Technically the antlers have been described as "bifurcated, palmate, wide and branching with many points, and with brow tine compressed laterally." As apt as that may be, it hardly expresses the eloquent beauty of a trophy head. Both sexes wear antlers, but those of the female are much smaller.

Unlike the antlers of most other deer, caribou racks tend to be extremely variable. The brow tine, which parallels the top of the face and often extends beyond the nose, is called the "shovel" and gives a rack distinction. An especially attractive trophy may have a double shovel. No one seems to know what utility the shovel has. One theory is that it's used to clear away snow above the ground plants, but this is generally discarded by the experts, who point out that the shovel is not much longer than the nose—if that long—and most of the low-growing vegetation for feed is uncovered by pawing.

Over many years I have talked with guides about caribou and never cease to marvel at the difference of opinions regarding its status as a game animal. A few guides look upon it as a rather dull-witted species and not too difficult to add to a trophy list. When the herds are on the move, they say, the only question is finding a rack that suits your fancy and shooting it in the right spot. I have never found this opinion quite accurate. With one exception I've had to work for those heads I've taken. The exception was a nice bull in Alaska's Talkeetna Mountains. We rode through the willows of a wide creek bottom and to within 30 yards of a bull that stood in the open on the far edge, watching us. The animal continued to stand while I slid out of the saddle, pulled my rifle from its scabbard, threw a shell into the chamber, and broke its neck.

They come easy and they come hard, depending on hunting pressure and on the individual animal. Consensus among the guides is that the caribou is often very excitable, especially if alarmed by some unaccustomed sight or sound. Biologists have told me of seeing a group, suddenly frightened, run in circles or bound back and forth without leaving the immediate vicinity, and they say that now and then an animal will get so wrought up that it dies of a heart attack.

A caribou is said to have as much curiosity as an antelope and will come to a red or white flag waved by a hidden hunter. I've never decided whether my experiment with this was a failure or success. In the Northwest Territories I crawled to within 200 yards of two small bulls and, completely hidden, I slowly waved a handkerchief. They stared for a long minute, then whirled and made tracks as if they had only a short time to reach the next province.

I sat there ruminating on this for a while, then put my glasses on the bulls; they had stopped on the brow of the next ridge to stare in my direction. I heard movement behind me and froze for an instant, hoping it wasn't an old grizzly that had sneaked up on me and scared off the two caribou, then turned slowly, my rifle ready. A bull caribou stood there, not 50 feet away, looking me over. Those critters are entirely unpredictable.

So far no one has been able to explain the mechanism of caribou migration, which seems to be as notional as the animals themselves. They may follow a route for years and suddenly abandon it, or they may appear in entirely unexpected places. Some observers say that in summer the herds seek open spaces where the wind blows, to help keep off the flies and other

These caribou were released on Adak, in Aleutian Islands National Wildlife Refuge, to build up herd there. Earlier, less successful experiments involved Asiatic reindeer, but game managers have learned much from past errors.

insects, especially while the female is bearing young and the male is growing his new set of antlers in a soft velvet-like cover. The barren ground caribou goes to the treeless tundra and the mountain caribou climbs above timberline.

Both food and shelter are also thought to motivate migration. Winter is a lean season and with the open tundra locked in ice and bitter cold, the herds trail south to the tree line for protection and for food, which consists of moss, lichens, grass, and willow and birch twigs where they are available.

Authorities differ on the number of subspecies on the North American continent. For the purpose of keeping adequate trophy records, the Boone & Crockett Club recognizes four kinds of caribou. These are the barren ground (across far north and northwest Canada and Alaska); the mountain (which includes the Osborn—largest of all caribou—with ranges of the two forms in British Columbia and extending up into the Yukon Territory); the woodland (across southern Canada); and the Quebec-Labrador form (from the upper portions of these two provinces, and thought to be a woodland-barren ground hybrid).

To be on the safe side and possibly to keep down any confusion which might result in wrong identification of a trophy head by an outfitter or hunter, Boone & Crockett not only lists the form, but the region from which it may be considered. The exception to this is the barren ground, though all but a few heads in this listing (which includes the subspecies Grant) have come out of Alaska. The others are listed as: mountain caribou from British Columbia; Quebec-Labrador from Quebec-Labrador; and the woodland from eastern Nova Scotia, New Brunswick, and Newfoundland.

Outside of covering a country by saddle or afoot, looking over the herds in migration or an occasional bunch of bulls, picking out the best possible head, then making your stalk, there is no set procedure for taking a trophy caribou. Most of my caribou kills have been made when I was on a hunt for several big-game species, such as bear, sheep, and moose, as well as the big northern deer itself. No matter what trophy we were after, we stopped to study heads whenever we saw a group of caribou bulls. The best rack I ever took was above Chickaloon in southeast Alaska while the guide and I were concentrating on sheep. We were afoot in high sheep country when we spotted two bulls a thousand feet below us on a barren ridge.

With our glasses we studied the best approach to get within range without disturbing the animals should they happen to be spooky. When we moved, the caribou saw us and stood with heads up, watching us walk away from them to the crest of the ridge. We ducked out of sight and they went back to grazing.

We made a wide circle of perhaps two miles to come in on the downwind side of the caribou, and crawled within a hundred yards. The largest bull was even more magnificent then he had appeared from above. He was close enough to down with a neck shot and I was lucky enough to place my bullet in just the right spot.

On their migration routes, caribou have favorite crossing places over rivers and narrow necks of lakes. Scouting migratory crossings can be worthwhile, of course, and if the herds haven't changed routes unexpectedly you might on occasion be able to watch for a good head as animals funnel across. A rifle of any caliber above a .30-30 can bring down a bull, but most hunters prefer the more high-powered

*Though caribou may unaccountably switch migration routes, they'll
follow one general course repeatedly, so it pays to watch favored passes like
this one. As with elk and sheep, it also pays to do plenty of glassing.*

*On Canadian hunt, sportsman Jack Keller (left) and guide inspect double-shovel
bull. Trophy judgment is complicated by variability in shape and
number of points, but Keller sized this one up carefully with his spotting scope.*

*Whitish lichen called reindeer moss (also known as caribou moss) is
vital food for barren ground caribou. However, herds also feed on other lichens
and mosses, as well as willow and birch twigs and grass where available.*

*Close-up photo of Manitoba bull
shows outsized hooves, which
are perfectly adapted for walking on
muskeg or ice. As animal walks,
unique ankle-bone structure clicks so
loudly it often alerts hunters.*

guns with long range and flat trajectory,
since one never knows when he must make
a long shot for an exceptional head.

Alaska possibly has the best caribou
hunting on the continent. This northern
deer is the state's most abundant big-game
animal, with the total herd estimated at
more than half a million animals and with
an annual kill of 20,000 to 30,000. The barren ground caribou is the main type; the

lesser-known Grant (in the southeast corner) is included in Boone & Crockett records together with the barren ground. Of the 11 recognized herds in this state, one of the most accessible is the Melchina, which ranges chiefly in the Talkeetna Mountains north of Palmer and Anchorage. The Arctic herd, far off the beaten trail, has little hunting pressure, and that's also true of some of the smaller isolated bands scattered through the state. Game officials feel that the caribou is much underharvested in Alaska, for meat as well as for trophies, and they worry that some of

Successful hunter poses with impressive rack that will dominate his trophy room. During hunting season, antlers are apt to be still in velvet, but are fully developed and hardened.

the faster-growing herds may cause a depletion of their natural food supply.

The Yukon Territory is also a top caribou spot that gets too little hunting. The record books show a number of barren ground heads out of the Yukon, as well as two mountain caribou, one from the Cassiar Mountains and the other from Snake River. Range maps show the barren ground caribou across the western half of the territory and the mountain (the Osborn subspecies) through the east and southeast portion.

Not until the past few years has the Quebec-Labrador herd been "discovered." Only 15 records of this big animal appear in the books, and all but one were taken after 1964. The best heads are said to come out of the Ungava and Whale River regions.

Newfoundland has long been a mecca for caribou hunters. The earliest record shown in the B&C book is 1881, and several others go back half a century or more. The caribou population deteriorated there for a while, but is said to have been making a strong comeback over the past few seasons and now numbers more than 15 herds. Hunting is by permit and the season lasts about six weeks. The two top regions are reported to be Area 1 (LaPoile, in the southwest) and Area 2 (Buchans, just to the north, between Grand and Red Indian lakes).

Caribou were once common in both Nova Scotia and Maine, but disappeared from both places decades ago. In 1963, 23 woodland caribou were stocked around Mount Katahdin, in Maine, and recent stockings have been made on Cape Breton Island in Nova Scotia. There is hope that, in the future, caribou hunting may be possible again in both the state and province.

Moose East and West

by Bob Hagel

6

Moose seem to thrive on cold weather. Starting at the southern end of their range, both body and antler growth gradually increase as you go north until you run out of timber where the rivers all flow toward the polar icepack. Not that the very largest moose come from the North Slope, but the largest do come from Alaska, Yukon Territory, and perhaps some of the Northwest Territories. Compared to their cousins living in the moose country of the lower 48, the Alaska-Yukon moose are true giants.

How many subspecies of moose there are is hard to say, but only three are generally recognized. Starting at the southern end of the range in Montana, Idaho, and Wyoming, the smallest moose, the Shiras or Wyoming moose, is found in limited areas where all hunting is done on a permit basis. As soon as you cross the Canadian border all moose are considered Canadian moose no matter where they are found—from the Pacific to the Atlantic—except those from the Yukon Territory. Canadian moose are usually larger than the Shiras, smaller than the Alaska-Yukon,

but vary in size of body and antlers, depending a lot on where you find them. One thing for sure: The very biggest moose killed anywhere in the contiguous 48 will be very small compared to a big Alaskan bull (but any of them are big).

As an example, few mature Shiras bulls stand much over six feet at the shoulder, while the largest-bodied Alaskan bull I ever shot measured an even seven feet from humped shoulder to the heel of his front foot. A big bull I shot near the head of the Tanzilla River in the Cassiar country of northern British Columbia measured 78 inches at the shoulder.

No matter where you find moose, they all have one thing in common—they like water. Perhaps this is what limits their range in the mountain states; as the high mountain ranges wind southward they get drier and the moose population peters out. In fact, moose hunting is often thought of in connection with lakes, portages, canoes, and birchbark horns, and a great many moose are taken every year by this method of hunting. Almost all of this kind of hunting is done in eastern Canada, where some kind of boat is about the only way to pack out a moose from where it is killed to where it can be picked up by some other form of transportation. Here they call moose in much the same manner as elk hunters bugle elk in the West. I've never hunted moose where calling was done to any extent. I know Alaskans who have tried it without great success. If it works in one area it should work in another, but for some reason it has never caught on anywhere I have hunted in the Northwest.

Water transportation is used very little for hunting moose anywhere in the Northwest, either, although it can be highly successful in some areas. The reason for this is that in much of the moose country other means such as horses and aircraft are used to get there, and boats are not available to hunt with. Also, while there are moose along the rivers in Northwestern moose country, they do not spend a great deal of time feeding in or at the water's edge because most of these rivers are swift and do not afford aquatic feed. Rather, they forage around small lakes and ponds and browse the willow-fringed meadows.

A few years ago, a hunting buddy and I made a moose-caribou hunt on the Alaska Peninsula. We took a commercial plane to King Salmon, then chartered a Grumman Widgeon to fly us to the Ugashik Bay area and set down on the King Salmon river. We had with us a large Folboat and out-

Toughest part of moose hunting often occurs after the kill. Most moose are brought out by pack horse, boat, or backpack. Here, Bob Hagel plods across Alaskan tundra, nearly staggering under load of meat and huge antlers.

board motor. With this outfit we hunted the river for many miles, but this hunting was far different from cruising the canoe country of eastern Canada. There is no timber other than a few stunted cottonwoods on the Peninsula, along with great areas covered with willows. There was little moose feed on the river banks, and the only moose we saw there were crossing from one side to the other. The country is very low and flat, with the higher ground being only 100 feet or so above sea level. The boat proved to be good only for moving up and down river, as the moose ranged back from the river for the most part, feeding in basins of swamps, and small ponds, or on the willow-covered slopes. You stopped at any high point of land near the river, climbed to the top, and glassed the surrounding country. And you had second thoughts about most moose you saw because you would have to backpack them a mile or so to the river.

It was delightful hunting and there were lots of moose, but I turned down some good bulls because they were not in the class I cared to pack on for three or four days through knee-deep muskeg. When I finally did decide to take one, we had to pack it three-quarters of a mile through hair-thick willows and hip-deep muskeg to a feeder creek where we managed to line the boat up a mile from the river. Like most moose, that bull was unforgettable.

Northwestern moose hunting usually requires pack train, and outfitter, guide, or wrangler will take care to balance each horse's load evenly, as in this photo. Horse carries trophy taken in British Columbia's Cassiar Mountains.

Where lilies or other aquatic plants are important in moose diet, bulls are often found in or near water. Hunter held his fire until this Idaho Shiras bull reached shore, thus avoiding tough dressing and butchering problems.

This brings up one of the main points of moose hunting: There are few easy moose. I know that meat hunters kill a lot of moose along the roads in Canada and Alaska, and most of them probably don't come too hard, but for the trophy hunter it seldom works out that way. In fact, even a moose shot very near the road can cause you all kinds of trouble.

Several years ago I killed an Idaho Shiras bull (the only one I'll ever kill there because Idaho allows only one moose to any hunter) that was little more than 200 yards from the road, and only 100 yards from where a pickup could be driven. In fact, I saw him late in the evening while driving to the head of a big meadow, and I stalked to about 175 yards for the shot. He was feeding in a big beaver pond in the willows. If he got back into the willows I wouldn't be able to see him. Waiting until he stepped up on the edge of the beaver dam, I clobbered him with a .375 H&H. It killed him all right, but it took about three minutes for him to realize it. In the meantime he backed out into the belly-deep mud and drink, breaking an inch of ice as he splashed around. Twice he came to the bank, and then backed out into the pond again. On the last try he got his big nose over the dam and died with his posterior in three feet of iced mud soup.

After dropping the water level a bit by chopping a hole in the dam, I finally got him dressed long after dark, and spent most of the next day skinning and packing him a scant 100 yards to the pickup. So even a moose near a road is not always easy. You'd better take a hard look at where a moose is standing before you shoot him, and if he's in the water give it some serious thought.

Some moose in Montana, Idaho, and

Trophy begins float down creek on Alaska Peninsula. Water can be troublesome if moose is shot in it, but waterways help hunters find moose in some regions and then transport meat and rack out of wilds.

Wyoming are killed as they feed in or around rivers or lakes, but, for the most part, they are found in the high, swampy mountain meadows with small, meandering streams. Like other hoofed game, they feed mostly in early morning or late evening, and if you don't see them then you'll have to go into the heavy timber or brush and try to get a shot where they bed for the day. Some are killed in that kind of thick stuff.

In hunting this kind of moose country it is best to locate where they have been feeding recently, then find a vantage point where you can see a great deal of the feeding area, then watch it at dawn and dusk. This way you'll be able to size up the head and see if the moose under it is an eatin' moose or if the head is fit to hang on the wall. If you can find high ground to do your looking from, so much the better.

Sometimes shooting moose far from water is more troublesome than shooting one in water. After butchering, this big Alaskan bull had to be backpacked almost full mile through willows and muskeg to be boated out.

Being above the moose not only gives a better view but your scent is less likely to reach him.

I can't say that a moose has a better sense of smell than other game animals, but that big nose is not just for show. His ears are also among the best. It is often said that his eyesight is quite poor. Compared to sheep, goat, and antelope, whose lives revolve around their ability to see their enemies, a moose's eyesight may be pretty shabby, but don't try to walk up to one that has been hunted and think he won't see you or know what you are. It's better not to let him see you so you won't regret that he did.

While moose are usually found in meadow-swamp country whenever they are away from lakes and big, quiet rivers, not all of these areas in moose country are good habitat. Like other game ranges,

good moose country must produce good moose feed. Many mountain meadows and swamp lands run mostly to grass, and grass is not good moose fare. Except for sucking up water plants they find just below the surface, moose are mostly browsers. Good moose meadows have a lot of willow, birch, aspen, and other browse species, and young second growth, as after a fire, is much better than mature stands. That is why recently burned-over country makes the finest moose habitat. If you want to find an area of many moose, big moose, and big antlers, look for moose country that has been burned off a few years before. This applies to most of the Rocky Mountain moose country in the U.S. and western Canada, and on up through most of Alaska. Of course, most of the country on the Alaska Peninsula and some of the Arctic Slope where there are few if any conifers, produces mostly browse species anyway, so fire is not as important to moose here as in country timbered with larger trees.

Another impression that is often given, and we may have added to it here, is that most moose are found strictly in the river bottoms or lake basins. This is by no means always true. Many times they are found high on steep mountainsides where there is water enough to produce the right kind of browse. I once killed a huge bull far up on the slope of Mount Fairplay at the head of the Fortymile River in interior Alaska, and that was several miles from the nearest river or lake. The big Canadian bull killed on the Tanzilla was also high on the mountain above the river valley. This is especially true of the old trophy bulls before the rut in early September. Moose killed in this rough country always pose a problem in getting them to where they can be picked up by wheels or wings. Here the packhorse is the normal means, and even then it is not easy. A really big bull is too large to just quarter and pack on each side of a pony. It requires cutting into smaller pieces. The big Mount Fairplay bull made four heavy packhorse loads of boned meat with antlers and cape.

So far we haven't touched on the rifles or, more specifically, cartridges that are best suited for moose hunting. Sure, you can get by with most rifles and cartridges used for deer hunting, but that doesn't make them the best moose medicine. A moose is a big animal, and while he is not overly difficult to kill if you get a bullet into the right place, which is the heart-lung area, it will take some doing to get it there if he is not in the right position. You need a long, heavy bullet designed for deep penetration, and preferably of fairly large caliber. Even then the bull will probably stand there for a couple of minutes before he becomes aware that life has run out. I've never seen one drop in his tracks from a shoulder-lung hit, and I've seen them whacked with several calibers ranging from the .308 Winchester to the .378 Weatherby.

Normally we don't consider moose shooting as likely to be long-range work,

but it may well be. Of the moose I've killed, the closest was about 150 yards, the longest range 300 yards. The reason for this is that very often the shot is across a pond or lake, from one side of a meadow or swamp to the other, or even from one side of a canyon to the other, with little or no chance to get closer. So it is a good idea if that heavy bullet steams along at fairly high velocity so that it stays reasonably accurate and packs some authority out to at least 300 yards.

The kind of rifle is not so very important as long as it suits you, is reasonably accurate and functions well. As with any other big-game hunting, a scope of up to 4X is desirable.

There's another way of looking at moose-hunting cartridges: If you live in good moose country and have a lot of time to hunt, and especially if you hunt for meat so it doesn't matter too much what you kill, you can afford to wait for a near-perfect shot. Which means you can use a cartridge that may be something less than a desirable moose cartridge. But if you spend dollars in four figures to look for a trophy bull, it is only good sense to pack a rifle that will do the job under adverse conditions. You may not get a second chance!

The Art of Sheep Hunting

by Jack O'Connor

7

The outfitter and the guide were making camp by the last stunted trees at timberline that chill September day high in the Wyoming Rockies. While they were taking off the pack and riding saddles, hobbling the three saddle horses and three pack mules, and pitching our two tents, I volunteered to climb up above the timber to a little lake and bring back a bucket of water.

A game trail covered with the tracks of bull elk snaked up through the last stunted trees and came out on the flat top of a lofty plateau. I was in fairly good condition but the climb made me puff. Timberline there was between 10,500 and 11,000 feet. Beyond the far side of the plateau, dead white against the blue sky and the brown earth and rock, the sharp peaks of the snowy Teton Mountains thrust up stark and cold. Far below I could see an enormous canyon purple with timber, misty with distance, and at the bottom lay the wandering silver thread of a creek. A little breeze was blowing. The air was icy with altitude, fragrant with the breath of the stunted Alpine firs and whitebark pines.

Ahead on that barren plateau I could see the sheen of the water in a shallow little "lake" that was hardly even a pond. As I drew close I could see that the edge was all tracked up by mountain sheep— and that every track had been made by a ram. Some looked as if they were not over a couple of hours old. My outfitter, the late Ernie Miller, had told me that this lofty plateau was a favorite summering ground for rams—and it looked as if he knew what he was talking about.

It was the day before the Wyoming sheep season was to open, and I decided it wouldn't hurt to take a look at some of the rams that had made the tracks if in the process I did not spook them. I carried the bucket of water back to the camp.

"While you guys make things shipshape, I am going to take my glasses and look around from on top," I said. Ernie grunted. I picked up my binoculars, puffed up the trail again, and worked up toward the end of the long, narrow "peninsula." There were sheep tracks and droppings everywhere.

The first game I saw, however, was a bull elk. He was a quarter of a mile away

In this band of Rocky Mountain bighorn rams, two animals at extreme left are excellent full-curl trophies. Author would prefer to take ram second from left because he favors broomed, close-curl heads typical of bighorns.

and far below me. I picked him up with my 8×30 binoculars as a movement behind a whitebark pine. From the color I knew it was an elk. When he walked out he stood in the open, a big six-pointer. As I watched he battered a tree with his antlers, and a moment later I heard his bugle ring through that lonely canyon.

I went on. Every time I came to a new prospect I stopped to glass to make sure I didn't blunder into anything. In the second canyon after the one in which I had seen the bull elk, I sat down to look things over carefully. I was right on a well-used sheep trail, and in every direction there were sheep beds where the rams had scratched out little hollows in the soil and had got rid of the large stones. I could smell the characteristic odor of sheep urine. I picked up a couple of pellets in a bed beside me and squeezed them. They were still soft.

Below me the side canyon fell away thousands of feet into a great darkling valley below. There were scrubby trees, little slanting meadows filled with grass and the little tender plants that wild sheep love. Resting my elbows on my knees to hold the glasses steady, I went over the canyon foot by foot. Sheep trails across rock and shale told me it had long been used, but right away I saw nothing. Then I made out something concealed by the branches of a whitebark pine. It didn't quite belong. I watched it carefully. Presently I became convinced it was part of the horn of a bighorn ram. Then it moved—and I knew it was. I kept watching and presently I could make out other parts of a bedded ram. Then I became conscious that not far away another ram had got up and had started to graze. The sun was slanting down in the west and it was now sheep dinnertime.

Sometimes trophy rams are alone rather than in bands. When you spot one near edge of high, sheer cliff, as in this case, you have to consider that if you shoot, trophy may fall and be ruined or impossible to retrieve.

In a few minutes seven rams had materialized out of their beds behind the scrubby timberline trees and had started to graze. All were shootable. Watching them carefully so I could freeze if one looked my way, I worked my way slowly back up to the top of the plateau out of sight and hiked back to camp. The next morning the guide and I were back there early. The rams were feeding almost exactly where I had left them. When I got through the scrubby trees into the clear, I dropped into a sitting position and shot the ram I had picked. He was across the canyon between 150 and 200 yards away.

This short and simple tale illustrates most of the principles of sheep hunting. Most elementary is that it is exceedingly helpful to know where ram country is. On that occasion Miller told me that during the summer and early fall the rams over a wide area concentrated on that one long flat-topped "point," bedding down at the heads of the side canyons, feeding along the sides and on top. Many other areas looked just as sheepy and a hunter might find ewes and lambs in them, but for some reason the rams always came back to that one lofty plateau. Miller's dudes had taken a ram or two out of there each season for many years. He said that if we had hunted the entire plateau carefully we probably would have located about 30 rams.

Another principle this tale illustrates is the importance of seeing the ram first and then staying out of sight. None of those rams saw me until I had pushed my way through the stunted timberline trees on top of the ridge across the side canyon and was ready to shoot. Another lesson we might draw from the experience is the wisdom of stalking as close as possible for a

Two outstanding desert bighorns, both taken in Arizona. Their headgear is of argali type, with definite overhanging ridges on outer edge, like horns of Stones and Dalls that are hunted far to the north.

sure shot. When I first saw the rams I was somewhere around 400 yards away. I could have started shooting them up right then. I might even have killed one. However, at best it would have been a sloppy performance and chances are that I would have missed or wounded. It is a commonly held notion by people who don't know much about sheep hunting that shooting rams is a long-range proposition. I have been hunting sheep with a fair degree of regularity since the early 1930s. I can remember very few sheep I have taken with long shots but a good many that I have taken at less than 100 yards, two or three at less than 50 yards. The good sheep hunter never bangs away in hopes that he will hit something—he waits until he is sure!

Wherever they are found, wild sheep have about the same habits. The rams prefer their own company to that of the ewes and the bleating pestiferous lambs. They join the ewes, however, at the time of the annual rut. For the desert bighorns with which I am familiar this is in late August and September, so that young can be born at the time of the winter rains in February. The northern sheep, whether Rocky Mountain bighorn, Stone, or Dall, mate in late November and into December, so that the lambs are dropped in the spring. From the time of the rut on the rams are apt to be with or near the ewes, but as the lambing season approaches they drift apart. The rams go off in bunches. Sometimes there will be only three or four rams together. At other times there will be a dozen or more. For whatever the reason it seems to me that I have seen seven rams together quite commonly. I can remember seeing bunches of 15 to 20 rams and once in Sonora I saw somewhere around 30 desert rams together. But for desert sheep this a very rare happening.

I am convinced that rams like to associate with other rams about their own age, and that if there are plenty of sheep in the country the rams tend to sort themselves out in age groups. I also feel that if I see a bunch of rams with one old-timer 12 or 13 years old, a couple of four-year-olds, a seven-year-old, and one about eight or nine, it is generally a sign that there are not many rams in the area. (This is my observation. Frank Cooke, Jr., my guide on my 1971 Stone-sheep hunt, does not agree with me.)

Sheep get out of their beds and start feeding as soon as it is light. Sometimes they begin to feed near their beds. They choose their bedding grounds for safety, and often it is a considerable distance from where they feed. Desert bighorns, for example, often bed high on a mountain and then come down to feed in the valleys. After they have filled up they work slowly back to their bedding grounds and take it easy until late afternoon, when they get up and begin their serious feeding once more. Sheep are dry-country animals and under ordinary circumstances do not water very often. In some areas they get along indefinitely without water. I have not seen many sheep watering, but those I have seen at water have gone there after their morning feed or before the evening feed. In desert mountains where sheep must have water because there is little dew and not many water-bearing cacti, lying in wait for sheep in rock blinds at water holes was a favorite method of meat-hunting.

Sheep, and indeed most herbivorous animals, get hungry along in the middle of the day, get up and browse or graze for a few minutes or a half-hour or so, and then lie down again. Often I have glassed all likely spots hoping to find bedded rams without seeing a hair. Then between noon and one o'clock I would see a ram feeding where I

had seen nothing before. Instead of snoozing away the midday hours the sheep hunter should be plying his binoculars!

I first started hunting sheep in Sonora long before sheep hunting became fashionable. At first I did not realize that a good binocular and the ability to use it is more important in sheep hunting than the rifle. I also spoiled some sheep hunts with some wild shooting at long range. I spoiled others by starting my stalk too early and then finding the sheep gone when I had got to the place where I had marked them.

I think it is wisest when feeding sheep have been located to wait until they have bedded down unless the stalk can be completed quickly. When that happens they will generally stay in the same spot for several hours except for a brief period in the middle of the day when they get up for a snack. Sometimes sheep will move after they have bedded down, but they seldom move far. The sun may get too hot, the wind too strong, or the sheep may decide that the shale around the point is a little softer. For whatever the reason they sometimes move, and during the last stages of the stalk, the hunter should exercise the greatest caution every time he sticks his head over a ridge or comes around a point.

Deer are born suspicious. Sheep have to learn to be afraid of things which have not previously threatened them. If they are in their chosen escape territory, they know they can outrun and outclimb bears or wolves. They have to learn that men with rifles can kill at a distance. Once I shot a ram at about 150 yards. The other rams did not panic but stood around their fallen companion wondering what had happened.

Sheep have wonderful eyes but only for moving objects. Often I have found sheep with 8X and 9X glasses only to find they had discovered me first. But a stationary object doesn't mean much to a sheep. I have had sheep stare at me a few yards away and not know what I was.

Some sheep hunters insist that sheep have poor noses and pay no attention to what they smell. I think they believe this because sheep live in areas of shifting unstable winds and often they appear to be getting your wind when they are not. To see how sheep smell I deliberately have given them my wind. When they get it they always react. Because sheep usually dwell in an area of unstable rock where stones are always rolling, they don't pay much attention to what they hear. Their eyes are their principal warning system, their wonderful legs their defense, but they should always be stalked upwind or crosswind.

Sheep usually bed where they can see a long way—on a point, on a ridge, in a shale slide at the foot of a cliff, at the head of a basin. They watch for danger from below and seldom look up. They should be approached out of sight and if it is possible they should be approached from above. Some believe they always post sentinels. I do not think so as I have seen bunches too many times with no outposts whatsoever. Often the "sentinel" is simply a sheep that has got hungry and wandered a little way off. Or maybe it is a nervous sheep that has once had the hell scared out of it by a wolf. However, often when rams bed down one of them will come back to take a look over a ridge to see if anything is on their backtrack.

Fortunately sheep can't count and on several occasions I have taken advantage of this to collect some mutton and a trophy. The last time was in 1963. My wife and I were hunting Dall sheep in the Yukon when on a shale slide about 500 yards away and below us we saw three magnificent rams. They had seen us first and there was no chance to stalk them where they were. Eleanor's guide took her down the draw while the other guide and I walked up and down to keep the rams interested. Those rams kept staring at us while my wife and her guide scrambled down the draw to within 50 yards of the rams. It was an exciting thing to watch with binoculars. I could see the hunters and the rams at the same time. I saw the hunters pause to catch their wind. Then the guide handed Eleanor her 7×57. I saw her bend over, sneak up the point. I saw her lift her rifle and the rams start to run. Then one of them went down. A moment later I heard the distant crack of the rifle.

One stunt that smart rams sometimes learn after they have been shot at is to bed down on big open hillsides or in big basins so that nothing can approach unseen within 500 yards or so. If the hunter tries to come at them from above, he will be seen as many of these smart sheep have learned to look up for danger now and then as well as to look below. If the hunter tries to approach from below he is whipped from the start. Rimming around on the same level with the sheep won't work unless there is cover of rocks or trees. When rams choose beds like that a patient man may get one by making a stake-out, watching until they can be taken at a disadvantage—going to water, for example. Or the only solution may be for one hunter to stay out of sight above the sheep near a notch or saddle where the sheep might pass. Then another hunter can show himself below. The instinct of mountain animals is to run up when danger threatens, and if the concealed hunter has guessed right he may get a shot. This, however, is nowhere near as sporting as stalking.

The sheep hunter should use his glass in the steadiest possible positions. If the glass wobbles around he will get a headache. I sit down and rest my elbows on my knees, or lie down with the glass in my hands and the weight on my elbows. Look, look, *look!* Come back to all suspicious objects. Be patient. Spend an hour with the glass for every hour walking, maybe for every half-hour.

A spotting scope saves a lot of wear and tear on the legs. It can distinguish a sheep from a stone at great distance, a ram from a ewe, a shootable ram from an unshoot-able one. Before I got a spotting scope I made many unnecessary stalks on rams I didn't want when I got up to them. A 20X or 25X spotting scope will enable the hunter to evaluate heads at ranges impossible with excellent binoculars. Incidentally, the spotting scope should always be used from a tripod.

Once the hunter has decided he wants a ram and has decided the ram will stay put for a sufficient length of time for him to make the stalk, he should pick a route that will keep him out of sight. He should also pick out a conspicuous object near the sheep so he will know where the sheep is when he gets there—a peculiar tree, a certain stone, a well-marked rock stratum.

The hunter should neither bang away at long range nor try to get within a few yards. He should take his ram at the first good spot where he is *absolutely* certain he can make a one-shot kill. Then he should take the steadiest possible position and squeeze that trigger. I have shot a good many sheep from prone with the fore-end of my rifle resting over a hat on a stone or moss hummock, a rolled-up jacket—even once with it resting across my guide's fanny.

The successful stalk, the pause to get the wind back, the steady position, the squeezed trigger. This all adds up to the clean kill and the happy hunt. There is nothing so good to cure buck fever and flinching as the crosshairs resting rock-steady on the ram's shoulder. When you know you can't miss, you don't.

Jack O'Connor rests behind fine Stone ram he took in 1971, using .270 Winchester Model 70. Center photo facing this book's title page also shows him with best American sheep he has yet taken—Dall ram shot in Yukon in 1950.

Getting Your Goat

by Bob Hagel

8

The original range of the Rocky Mountain goat started in the mountains of southern Montana and central Idaho and ran north through western Canada into Alaska. Goats were unknown east of the eastern slope of the Rockies, but they were plentiful along the coastal ranges adjacent to the Pacific from Washington to Alaska's Kenai Peninsula. In fact, there are probably more goats concentrated in the extremely rough country along the southeast Alaskan coast than anywhere else.

In recent years there have been many transplants of goats, and the small herds in Wyoming, Colorado, and South Dakota are examples of the success of these efforts to spread the range of *Oreamnos americanus.*

There is one thing that goats have in common no matter where they are found: The country all stands on end. Sheep like rough habitat but also do well in terrain that is not so rough; goats, on the other hand, will not stay in an area that is not mostly bare rock, and so rugged that even sheep shun it. In fact, a goat's very existence depends on being in or very near such rough land that its enemies cannot negotiate it. Man is about the only predator

who can give a goat a bad time, once it reaches the protection of the most rugged part of its home—the part it invariably seeks when danger threatens. And even man has his problems in reducing a goat to a trophy under most hunting conditions.

It is the extreme ruggedness, the isolation, and the usually inclement weather of goat country that has allowed the animal to exist down through the years, and it is the only natural protection it has from the hunter. Due to natural hazards, goat populations increase very slowly, and the hunter take must be strictly regulated in most areas.

In goat hunting, it is safe to say that 90 percent are spotted from below. Not that this is the best place to do your goat spotting, but it takes great effort to reach an area where you are above or even level with the goat. If you really want to see the great majority of the goats in an area, the best method of spotting them is to climb to near the same level you want to glass on the opposite side of the canyon or adjacent mountain. No matter how you cut it, little goat hunting is done without a lot of climbing.

To start with, goat hunting requires as much looking as any hunting I know of, and while goats are not hard to locate with the unaided eye due to their color, no animal requires better optical equipment for successful hunting. They are at times harder to locate than the uninitiated would think because there are usually white rocks and patches of snow from which the goats have to be sorted out. But the main reason for using top-quality optical aid is to tell the boys from the girls and more important, a poor set of horns from mediocre spikes, and the mediocre ones from the good ones. This requires not only good binoculars of about 7X, but a spotting scope that is ice-clear and razor-sharp, and as light and compact as you can find in a quality glass.

All mature goats look alike, and I've known a lot of goat hunters and even guides who couldn't consistently tell a nanny from a billy. They both have long beards and chaps on their front legs, and they all look a lot bigger than they are, especially if alone. The only sure way of telling them apart is by the shape and girth of the horn. Some of the longest horns are found on females, so you can't go by length, and spread means nothing, either. But a nanny's horns are much smaller at the base, and they usually have a rather sudden bend rearward near the tips. The billy has heavier bases and his horns normally run in a more even curve from base to tip. Sometimes, especially near or during the rut, the scent glands behind the base of the horns will show plainly on a billy.

As for judging the length of the horns on a trophy or record-class goat, this takes some doing, and it requires the best in optics. A good trophy is anything over nine inches, and anything over 10 will probably make the record book. Don't use a spotting scope with too much magnification because mirage, haze, rain, snow, and lack of a rock-steady position can make a scope with too much power completely worthless. a 20X–30X glass is ideal.

It has often been said that a goat hunter should always attempt to get above his quarry because goats always look for danger from below and they invariably head up when disturbed. It is claimed that they seldom see you if you are above them, and that if you do spook them they are quite likely to run right by you. All of this is partially true, but should be modified to fit the circumstances. The very steepness of the goat's home mountain usually makes seeing him from above difficult if you complete your stalk on the same slope or cliff with him. Also, if in completing that stalk you dislodge a rock that tumbles down by him, he is likely to spook, and as he knows it came from above he is almost certain to leave in some other direction, often down.

Goats don't pay a lot of attention to rolling rocks because they hear them all the time, but if the rocks come bounding down on them it is another story. It is best not to make any more noise than necessary. While goats spend more time looking down than up, they will also spot you if you skyline yourself or make a noise, and if they do, they are not going to come up just to be climbing.

If possible, it is best to plan a stalk to get in a position where the goat is across a chute or canyon. This usually puts the goat in full view while you stay hidden as you look him over, and it will afford a better chance for keeping track of the goat after you shoot. Another advantage of approaching with a canyon between you and the

Goat hunting consists chiefly of climbing and looking. For high-country scouting of this kind you need quality optical equipment to scan one mountain from another. Here author rests 20X spotting scope over fallen tree.

goat is that if you must show yourself the animal is less likely to spook. Goats seem to feel safe when there is a chasm separating them from another animal. I have approached and photographed many goats with the whole stalk right out in plain sight under these circumstances.

This brings up a common error. Someone once said a goat's vision is not especially good, and most hunters and writers have been repeating it ever since. There is nothing wrong with a goat's eyes; they are perhaps as good as those of a sheep, but most goats don't get excited about what they see as long as it is a long way off. A sheep may spook as soon as it sees you, but few goats do unless they've been hunted hard. It follows that if you go after goats that have known hunting pressure, the less you show yourself the better.

Another misconception is that they either don't have a good sense of smell or don't pay much attention to human scent. Don't believe it! They don't like your odor any better than an elk or deer does, and they'll leave in a hurry when it reaches them. The reason they seem not to mind is

that a wind which appears to be blowing directly to them is often turned aside by air currents found in all rough country. That same fickle breeze may also undo the best-planned stalk.

But there is a great deal of room for failure between getting within range of a goat and hanging his head on the den wall. It's not that goats are hard to hit or kill. It's where he is when hit, and what happens thereafter that can leave you with little more than a sour memory. A goat's horns are very brittle and a fall of only a few feet often breaks them. The best advice is to be sure that the goat is in a spot where it is not likely to fall off when hit. In the worst cases it may fall into some hole where it is impossible to retrieve under any circumstance. Also try to avoid wounding it because it is almost certain to pull itself to a place where it will go over a cliff when finished off, or else you'll find it almost impossible to get to and skin. At times, goats will deliberately pull themselves over the edge when they are pursued. No matter how many other goofs you may make in getting a shot at a goat, give a lot of

Best way to hunt goats is to do plenty of climbing over high, rough terrain. To find a really good billy, take your backpack and spend time exploring up there where big old males feed and bed.

Most goats are smaller than they appear but some old billies are twice as large as average mature males. This one, sporting 10-inch horns, is obviously big since hunter, if he stood up, would be over six feet tall.

serious thought as to whether it will stay where it is after being shot, and how you are going to retrieve it if it does. Your trophy will depend on it!

Goats are usually considered very tough and hard to kill. True, they are very tenacious of life, and they often show little sign of being hit, but this doesn't mean it takes an extremely powerful rifle to kill one. In fact, any good deer cartridge will do that. Generally speaking, goats are not large animals (although some old billies are nearly twice as heavy as average mature male goats) so penetration is not a great problem. A fairly small caliber will do, and I've killed a couple with no trouble whatever with a 6mm Remington. What is needed is a high-velocity cartridge firing bullets with good ballistic coefficient at high velocity for accuracy at long range.

It is true that the broken nature of the land in goat country often allows the hunter to get within petting distance, but that same ruggedness often makes it impossible to get close and still see the goat. It is also often possible to get a shot at a goat from long range in a place where it will not roll or fall a great distance—and this would be impossible if you tried to get closer. If you find you don't need the long-range cartridge it will work just as well as close range, and if you do need it you have it. Bringing home a trophy is the purpose of most goat hunts.

Pronghorn—Boss Buck of the Plains

by Bert Popowski

9

Once, according to several estimates, the burly North American bison numbered somewhere on the plus or minus side of 60,000,000 head! The buffalo was the meat-and-hide commissary of both Indians and whites travelling our Great Plains. And right with those herds, like fleeting quicksilver shadows, were equally immense herds of pronghorned antelope. Some observers of that era claimed that one species exceeded the other in numbers, but there could be no accurate census. The point is that, when the buffalo were shot down to fragmentary numbers by the 1870s, the antelope population dwindled correspondingly. Whatever the reason, the fact is that both species crashed in population at about the same time in American wildlife history.

Following that double debacle, a Bureau of Biological Survey of 1922–24 came up with a total of slightly over 30,000 pronghorns on the plains areas of North America. Of that fading total the United States' total was counted at 26,604, with Mexico having 2,395 in four provinces and Canada numbering 1,327 in Alberta and Saskatchewan. These antelope were in

widely scattered little bands of a dozen here and a score there, virtually lost in an immense sagebrush sea. But nowhere on this continent could they be legally hunted as recently as 50 years ago.

Due to a method of live-trapping mixed-age herds of pronghorns, originated in 1937 by Paul Russell of New Mexico and implemented by Pittman-Robertson excise tax monies, antelope herds were rapidly re-established over much of their original range. Hunters have since taken many times the number censused for all of North America in the mid-1920s. Wyoming, our leading pronghorn producer then and now, has had several seasons when hunters harvested more antelope annually than existed in all North America at that low ebb. And the herds are now in such healthy shape that sporting hunting is permitted in most of the states where pronghorns once challenged the American bison in abundance.

Since 1942, which marked the resumption of pronghorn hunting in many states, I've personally taken 90 antelope (when licensed) in several states. Some residents who guide visitors to such game may have done as well, or better. But it is significant that a plainsland species which might otherwise have been doomed to extinction has been saved as a huntably plentiful game animal.

My many instructive days in antelopeland were always delightful. I had the satisfaction of being almost alone in that sea of sagebrush and greasewood, along with my rifle, binoculars, and a fascinating form of game to use them on. For pronghorn range is spacious, from one horizon to the other, with only infrequent meetings with other hunters. I know of only one other type of hunting that resembles it: the top-of-the-world pursuit of mountain goats and wild sheep.

Because of fabulous antelope eyesight, the hunter has to be armed with good glassware, both for observing his game and for accurate aim. Pronghorns, like sheep, have been described as having eyes with the resolving power of human eyes assisted by 8X binoculars. I'll subscribe to that. Many times I have thought myself unobserved when crossing a piece of range, only to be halted in my tracks by the blowing or coughing bark of pronghorns that had seen me.

But I have also learned that when closely and stealthily approached, the animals seem confused, as if they're so farsighted they can't recognize danger when it suddenly comes upon them at short range. This is a hunter's opinion, not that of an optometrist, but observed frequently enough to have caused me hours of wonderment. If the hunter stays motionless upon such short-range discovery, pronghorns will hesitate, milling around for some minutes—ample time for a careful shot—before they finally shift into escape gear.

The three most exciting and satisfying ways of hunting antelope are by stalking, by placing yourself in their travel route, or by laying an ambush in areas which have a regular attraction for them. All of them place a premium on the hunter's patience and often require that he leave his hunting friends and transportation for hours on end. Guided hunters will seldom stand for such slow but sure means. They want immediate action, no matter how sloppily executed, which produces quick results. But it is such intimate association with game and its habitat which gives the painstaking hunter his greatest appreciation of both.

Most pronghorns are shot at fairly long distance, but skilled hunter can sometimes stalk to close range. Jerry Popowski, author's son, took this fine buck at just 49 paces with his scoped .308 Winchester Model 70.

As part of long-term management program, pronghorn antelope have been successfully trapped and then transplanted to re-occupy large parts of their original range. These mixed-age bucks and does are in South Dakota.

I have found that pronghorns are best stalked from below; that is, by approaching them from a lower level than their position. This is the opposite from the method by which all other big game is best approached. But the hunter who skylines himself during a pronghorn stalk will often find his game leaving the vicinity while he's still far out of rifle range. And, like most game, antelope are adept at watching their backtrails for any hunter foolish enough to follow directly behind them. The only way, then, is to circle widely to get ahead, no easy chore even when the animals are merely cruising along.

Perhaps the most interesting buck of the 90 I've harvested was the boss of a harem of does and kids taken during a blistering Wyoming afternoon. As usual, I'd parked my vehicle on a small eminence so it would be visible from any similar elevation within a half-dozen miles. Then, regardless of where my wandering stalks might take me, when I was ready to call it a day or got my buck, whichever came first, I could readily find the easiest route back to water, food, and transportation.

My binoculars picked up an earthen dam, used to trap runoff water for livestock. Wildlife also uses such watering spots and it's a good place from which to sight pronghorns. So I dropped into the channel below the dam and cautiously worked up behind a sagebrush clump atop it. Sure enough, a half-dozen head were loafing some 300 yards up the slope. I immediately started to evaluate the buck. But he was a youngster, probably 2½ years old, judging by his smallish horns.

However, I saw interesting action almost immediately. Over the far ridge came a sizable herd—evidently parched, for they were hurrying. At its rear, closing up the stragglers, was the boss buck of that harem. He had poise, authority, and determination, a combination that assured me I'd found what I was looking for. When he saw the little buck and his miniscule herd he didn't miss a step in turning off to investigate. The wee buck, diffident and hesitating, came forward to meet him.

When they were about 10 feet apart the boss exploded in a lightning charge, hit the small buck broadside as he turned to get out of the way, and knocked him flat. Seconds later the little fellow was raising a plume of dust as he streaked away. The big fellow watched him go, then went to water among his increased harem members. I never did see any other buck in that harem larger than spring kids. Evidently that boss wouldn't tolerate even minor competition.

The mass of animals at that waterhole kept me from getting a clean shot at the boss buck at about 175 yards. Then he was so busy rounding up his charges that I couldn't risk a crippling shot. But the herd strung out to pass behind a hillock to my left, which I hurriedly circled. Then I flattened out in a position to overlook their route. With luck they'd string out so the buck would be fully exposed for my shot.

There were only two scrawny sagebrush bushes to cover me in front and nothing to hide my prone length on a broadside view. Visually, it was a critical situation. Moreover, the wind was blowing solidly, directly from me to intersect the herd's route. The situation seemed made to order to spook that harem. But they only raised their heads as they got my scent, then went on, drifting and browsing.

One doe, at the rear of the herd, turned off toward the top of the hillock. The buck instantly cut over to see what had attracted her and to bring her back into the harem. She saw me, fully exposed but motionless, and stared. The buck threatened her with a swing of his horns, then himself went to the top of the hillock to examine the country beyond. Maybe he was looking for more harem.

There he was, fully broadside and standing like a statue at 75 yards. With my Model 70 rifle good and steady, I squeezed off a shot. It was a .270, a caliber that I still think is about as perfect for prong-

horns and other plains game as any in existence. The 130-grain hollow-point drummed into his ribs, he wheeled and sprinted out of sight, but I got up leisurely and watched that bossless harem of 33 head leave the country. My confidence in my shot was so complete that the empty brass of my cartridge was still chambered in my .270.

At the very top of the hillock I paused for a final look at the bereft harem. As they raced up a long slope here came a smaller dust cloud to intercept them. It was the little buck that had been whipped out only minutes earlier! I was smiling broadly as I watched the two dust clouds meet and saw the little guy take on a harem master's multiple chores. I wished him well.

South Dakota conservation worker releases young pronghorn he has trucked to prairie land where feed is adequate, fencing is absent, and there's no intensive human activity or competition with domestic livestock.

The Czar of Swine

by John Wootters

10

The European wild boar (often miscalled "Russian") in America is a little like the itinerant Russian noblemen knocking around this country after the Bolshevik Revolution—proud, aristocratic, touched with an aura of Old World glamour, and endlessly adaptable to whatever environment. He is not exclusively European, or Russian, although found throughout both areas; he is also native to most of mainland Asia and northern Africa. Since 1893, when the first imported stock of boars from Germany was released on private property in New Hampshire, he has been a naturalized American.

During the 80 years since that experiment, other herds have been established in the States, one in New York's Adirondacks, another in Tennessee's Great Smoky Mountains, still another in North Carolina. There have been other releases, most recently being on Santa Cruz Island off the California coast. Mysterious rumors of "pure" Old World boars ranging free in such out-of-the-way places as northeastern Texas, Arkansas' Ozarks, and spots in Louisiana and Mississippi keep turning up, unsubstantiated.

Since the European boar has the same genus and species names (Sus scrofa) as all domestic swine, interbreeding is not only possible but inevitable wherever the two breeds meet. This means that the bloodlines of all "Russians" running free on public land have almost certainly been degraded by crossing with feral hogs, and the only purebloods remaining today are those held under fence or private land. Some of those outside the preserves, however, still have most of the physical and temperamental characteristics of their European ancestors.

Those characteristics add up to a formidable animal. He is long-legged, lean, burly-shouldered, fast as a deer and quick on his feet as a fighting bull, 400 pounds of muscle wielding saber-sharp tusks up to nine inches long. Scientists who study such things tell us he is among the most intelligent of hoofed animals, and he is certainly one of the wildest, wariest, and most evil-tempered. Throughout his native ranges he has the reputation of man-killer, and there is at least one instance on record, in northern France, of a boar which became a confirmed man-*eater* and terror-

After long chase through thick, tangled cover and over broken ground, dogs have boar at bay. Hunter wants to get there before any hounds are injured or hog gets away; his next problem will be to maneuver for clear shot.

ized a village until hunted down.

The boar has always been prized game for the sportsman, mostly the royalty of Europe, and has been considered a challenge for the most courageous and skillful hunters, using lances and knives.

Only one such hunt is known to have taken place in the U.S., in 1920 in Tennessee. Records of this American experiment in pig-sticking are sketchy, but in the melee, many of the boars escaped through a preserve fence. Their descendants populate the area today. How many hunters escaped is not recorded.

The usual method of hunting the wild hogs in the remote and rugged areas they inhabit today is with specially-trained packs of hounds, and it's still a game for the hunter who is stout of leg and long of wind, who's excited by a dash of danger in his sport. The chase is apt to be long, fast, and through tangled, steep mountain thickets which demand stamina from hogs, dogs, and hunters.

The idea is that the hounds will bring the boar to bay and hold him until the hunters come up and shoot him. In practice, it's not usually quite that simple. In the first place, a fighting boar is both brave and deadly with his weapons, and more than a match for an ordinary pack of hounds. Mortality is high among hog dogs; those who fail to temper their courage with caution rarely reach retirement age!

The pig usually bays in the densest rhododendron tangle he can find, and the action is furious. A clear shot is very difficult without endangering the hounds as the enraged boar rushes this way and that at his tormentors. And if the hunters maneuver too close in their excitement, it's quite common for the brute to charge, wading through the dogs as though they were dolls. A wounded but not disabled boar can be counted on to come for the hunters if he recognizes them through the din and fury of the hound pack around him. When he comes, he means business as surely as a Cape buffalo; it's time to shoot and shoot straight.

For such nip-and-tuck action, a rifle or handgun heaving a heavy slug of large diameter is a comfort, although any cartridge capable of taking a whitetail cleanly will do the job on a boar with selected shots. A 12-gauge shotgun firing rifled slugs is also a popular and effective boar gun.

The hunter who hangs a boar trophy taken by this method on his den wall will have a memento of a gruelling, action-packed experience.

There are other ways to hunt the czar of swine, however, even though less frequently used. The animal can be still-hunted and stalked like a whitetail, or a stand can be taken over a feeding ground freshly plowed up by the boars' rooting. The animals live in herds of as many as 20 or 25 individuals, most of them young-of-the-year. Old boars may be solitary year-round, and the boars tend to form bachelor bands during the mid-winter breeding season.

The hunter who tries for a boar by one of these methods will find himself up against an animal whose senses are every bit as sharp as those of a whitetail. The "little piggish eyes" are keen, though the boar's head position places his plane of vision lower than that of a deer. Even so, I've had a boar see me and recognize danger in my form at more than 200 yards.

The meat from an old male is something less than a gourmet delight, to understate the case, but meat from a sow or young pig is delicious, vaguely pork-like, never fat, really more like venison in flavor. Having tried to eat a real old trophy boar, however, I heartily recommend that you be satisfied with the trophy and the hide, which tans into the toughest of glove-leather.

At the moment, guided hunts for "wild boar" are offered by several outfitters in Tennessee, Pennsylvania, and North Carolina. Florida is, I believe, the only state which grants "European boar" the status of game and the protection of a closed season. The purest-blooded hog populations left in the U.S. are all on private hunting preserves, and I do not know whether any

Tennessee's Great Smokies still shelter boar that retain temperamental and physical characteristics of big, ferocious European ancestry. Note impressive tusk protruding from this one's snout, directly in front of hunter's hand.

of these are open to trophy hunters for a fee (if so, it's likely a pretty fancy fee), nor do I know the status of the Santa Cruz herd.

Most of the other reports of "Rooshian" boar you'll nose out will prove to arise from a little glamorizing of ordinary razorbacks, or feral domestic swine; the local folk find a touch of the European aristocracy more interesting and profitable in their wild hogs. Not that a wild razorback isn't a very challenging game animal in his own right!

But the real, Old World article is in a class by himself. He is the czar, the king of all *wildschwein* in the world, a prestige trophy on any wall and a quarry any hunter will remember with respect. No people anywhere in the world who knew the wild boar ever treated him lightly, and it's no different here in America, where we really are more impressed with royalty than we like to admit!

The Truth About Bears

11

by Andy Russell

When I hear some nimrod recounting a horrendous story of peril concerned with the pursuit of a bear, I'm inclined to suspect his veracity, wonder at his luck, or question his ability as a rifle shot. If the bear is a grizzly and has been pursued in the southern Canadian Rockies or anywhere south of the 49th parallel, my reaction is one of sadness and disgust with management that allows any hunting at all in this fast-shrinking portion of the big bear's range, where it has been reduced to numbers far below that affording any justification whatever. If the story involves any kind of baiting to set up the hunter's chances for a shot, my inclination is to report him to the authorities for violation of the law and deride him for his lack of ethics.

To be sure, the grizzly can be an extremely dangerous animal on occasion, as when some territorial claim stake is in question. More than one man, upon going back to a kill to pack out meat, has found himself faced with big trouble, and more than one has been attacked and mauled by the big animal claiming it for food. There have also been some unfortunate incidents when a wounded bear was followed into thick cover.

By and large, in proportion to its bulk, no bear has the pound-for-pound ability to soak up the terrific shocking power and bullet penetration of the modern rifle that is often demonstrated by the mountain goat, pronghorn antelope, or whitetail deer. A bear is one of the easiest varieties of big game to knock down, but if the bullet has hit somewhere around the outside edge of its target, the animal can recover with amazing speed and can then be astonishingly hard to kill. A bruin can be extremely dangerous under such circumstances.

In 50 years of wilderness wandering as a trapper, professional guide, and nature observer in bear country, the closest shave I ever had was when I walked up close to a big cattle-killing black bear that was supposed to be dead. I stalked and shot this big male at close range on the edge of some thick brush along a creek. My bullet smashed his shoulder and ripped into his chest cavity, causing havoc. It should have anchored him for good, but the bear had got a snoot full of my scent a second before

*Silvertip grizzlies like this are scarce in most of their remaining
U.S. range. To discourage hunting where species is threatened, Boone & Crockett
Club now accepts no trophy records of grizzlies taken below Canadian border.*

and adrenalin had already produced its powerful influence. The bear went down, rolled over, and got up to bound into cover as thick as the hair on his back. I quickly circled to head him off, tangled with him at a range of 50 feet, and slammed another shot into his neck. He fell in a heap, lying on his back with all four feet up on a log. Then I did a most stupid thing. I walked up within 10 feet of him for a closer look. At first glance he looked about as dead as anything can get, but something warned me that all was not well. I was just starting to lift my rifle for another shot when that bear uncoiled and lunged at me with his mouth wide open. I had a good look at a mouthful of yellow, worn, broken snaggle teeth as I stepped back, hooked my heel in a forked stick under a foot of snow and fell.

As I went down, I had the strange impression of everything happening in slow motion. By sheer reflex, I poked my rifle muzzle under his jaw and closed my hand on the trigger. This last shot from my .257 Roberts—too light for a close-range bear gun—smashed his neck near where it had been lightly grazed by the preceding bullet. As I sat in the slush, his head lay within a foot of my boot toes.

The incident was more a result of sheer carelessness than using too light a rifle. The rifle was the only one I owned; it was my overconfident direct approach that almost cost me my life. A moose, elk, or buck deer in like circumstances can be deadly, too, as more than one man knows for sure.

When it comes to comparing a black

Most black bears are encountered unexpectedly and taken as bonuses by deer hunters but in some regions bears are actively sought, with or without dogs. In hound hunting, traditional timber lever-actions like Model 94 are popular.

bear to a grizzly for power and sheer courage, it's like observing the differences between a sack of goose feathers and a case of dynamite. The grizzly is generally bigger, stronger, and much more inclined to be warlike when hurt or crowded. Indeed, on the rare occasions when the two animals have been known to tangle, the grizzly has always won.

My son John once found a place where a grizzly had stalked a black bear of almost equal size after a fresh fall of light snow in April. As the track story attested, the battle was short, fierce, and fatal to the black. Its nose was broken off just ahead of the eyes, both ears were torn out and there were numerous other severe injuries. The grizzly had buried the black under a heap of dirt and forest debris and was sleeping on top of it when John jumped him. The grizzly, showing no inclination to fight the man, ran away into thick timber. But when we revisited the place a week later, it was to find the dead bear completely

consumed except for some ragged bits of hair, hide, and bone.

Given any kind of chance to mind its own business in wilderness country, the grizzly will do just that, and even on the occasion when its trail meets head-on with that of man, the big animal will try hard to avoid trouble on all but the rarest occasions. It is when man persists in making trouble for the bear, or is careless about how he leaves enticing food lying around, that serious trouble can sometimes boil over with this extremely intelligent and powerful animal.

To survive, the grizzly bear must have plenty of wilderness country—all the room necessary to live without human intrusion and conflict. Men just won't tolerate the proximity of grizzlies to settlements, even when a bear is inclined to be peaceful. Most people are afraid of the grizzly, and what they fear they are inclined to destroy, even if it means losing something of inestimable value in this living world. Unlike his cousin, the black bear, the grizzly cannot adjust to civilization, and as a result this big animal has disappeared completely from what was once prime range. Where the black bear has successfully learned to cope with human pressure, the grizzly has gone under.

Taking a broad view of the grizzly species, it cannot be assumed to be endangered. However, in certain portions of present habitat it is severely threatened. Poor management and ignorance is largely to blame. In southwest Alberta and southeast British Columbia, and in Montana and Wyoming (the largest portion of good grizzly population and habitat south of the International Border) habitat destruction, low priorities in wildlife budgets, and indifference have largely contributed to decimation of grizzly numbers. However, very recently there has been a dramatic change in policy in British Columbia. Alberta no longer allows hunting of females with cubs and is enforcing a complete closure of season south of the Bow River, where grizzlies have nearly disappeared outside the national parks. Wyoming has closed the season for any kind of grizzly hunting, but Montana still blithely continues to sell permits for grizzlies. And those are about the last of free-roaming grizzlies outside the parks in the U.S.A.

Even in nearly all the western national parks, too many grizzlies have been destroyed by bad management—chiefly through failure to take care of tourist garbage properly. Careful research of the more recent maulings of people in the parks has inevitably revealed that attacks can be directly attributed to poor garbage disposal in most cases.

So grizzly hunting has largely become a matter of the hunter's conscience. The law has proven to be inadequate over large areas of habitat. Sadly enough, human ethics have in no way kept up with population numbers or development of arms. In these times, when the grizzly is backed to the wall in a struggle to survive against industrial intrusion and human pressures of other kinds, no man with any decent sense of responsibility to the sport he claims to love will take more than one grizzly in a lifetime, regardless of opportunity or where he hunts. To be sure, even where hunting is still allowed there are some areas in which no man has the moral right to kill a grizzly.

The black bear is something else, for this species has learned to cope. Given anything like half-decent management, black bears will survive. I have seen fresh black-bear tracks on the slopes of the Catskill Mountains within sight of Manhattan's smoke.

Alaska is the state with the largest population of black bears—something like 75,000 of them—and Washington is next with about 30,000 to 40,000. There are timberlands where the bears kill so many trees by girdling them to get at the edible cambium that hunters get a big welcome, and sometimes professional hunters are hired to trim the numbers of bears.

There is no doubt that black bears are most often harvested by hunters who are out seeking deer or other game. A bear's eyesight isn't very sharp, but his hearing and sense of smell are very keen, and he's a smart, wary animal. Tracking or still-hunting may occasionally produce a shot, but for the average sportsman that kind of bear hunting isn't very productive. Some states permit baiting—meaning that the hunter waits patiently in a hidden position or blind before just about any kind of enticement from a mess of entrails to a ripening calf's head—and I've already expressed my personal opinion of that technique. Some states also allow springtime hunting, but if you're dreaming of a bear rug remember that when the weather grows warm enough the bruins begin to rub and shed. In looking for sign, you may find well-tufted rubbing trees that show bears are in the area and also show that the pelts are no longer prime.

The use of dogs is permitted in some areas, and hunting with a hound pack is an effective as well as popular way to get within shooting range of a black bear. Generally speaking, a guide or hunter in a northern state might have half a dozen good bear dogs such as Plott hounds. There are parts of the South where traditional hunts involve 30 or more dogs and just about as many men. In some states (notably Washington) an often-employed technique is to drive a pickup slowly along logging roads, with "strike dogs" perched behind the cab. The hounds will sound off where hot scent tells them a bear has emerged recently, and the hunt begins there. With a treed or cornered bear, the range is so short that anything from a .357 Magnum handgun to a deer rifle or a rifled shotgun slug or even buckshot will serve. In other situations, too, a rifle in the .30-caliber class will as easily kill a black bear as a deer.

A hunt specifically for a big grizzly is another matter. You'd probably want to be armed with nothing less than a .30-06. And in the far Northwest the hunt would probably consist of scouting and glass, or else haunting the streams during a salmon run. But that brings us back to the discussion of conserving the species by caring more about the grizzly's future than about the expense of the next hunting trip. At least for the present, we ought to refrain from hunting grizzlies where they've been depleted, even if that's closer to home, and we ought to support the stricter Canadian regulations now in force.

Having been privileged to hunt the grizzly when the big animal was virtually lord of the mountains, and having known the spine-tingling thrill of stalking close with only a camera in my hands on many occasions, I have come to know something of the bear. As a professional guide, I also know something about hunters, and if the grizzly is to be saved it has to be the hunters' concern that swings the favorable balance. Hunters have proved many times that they can influence management in the proper direction. They are also the first to reach into their pockets for the money for required research and management—something that can't be said for a greater part of the anti-hunting, preservationist cultists who are so loud in their condemnation of the recreation.

Part II: Loads, Guns, and Alternative Arms

Practical Shotgun Ballistics

by Francis E. Sell

12

Over the past 20 years, shotgun ammunition has improved tremendously. However, the most important ingredient in hunting or target-shooting success has not changed at all—and that ingredient is you, the man behind the gun. The successful scattergunner must equip himself with a smoke pole that fits, must practice with it, and must have a basic knowledge of what happens after he pulls the trigger. That's where this little treatise comes in.

When a gunner touches off a shot, the resulting ballistics are either working for him or against him. A successful application of proper ballistics to a gunning situation is a matter of knowing your requirements beyond the shadow of a doubt.

Effective pattern density at the target is one element of ballistics that every serious gunner should understand. For most effective coverage at *all* maximum ranges, the *improved-cylinder pattern* is best as it delivers about 45–55 percent density in a 30-inch circle. Long range or short, upland or swampland, a 45–55 percent pattern is the end of the line.

Where the larger-size shot is used, such as 5's, 4's, or 2's, and a pattern average of

85 percent is achieved at 40 yards, the average pattern dissipation is around 9 percent for each 5 yards of range beyond this distance. At 45 yards, the pattern average is around 76 percent, at 50 yards, about 65–67 percent. At 55 yards this 85-percent-patterning gun delivers about 58–60 percent, and at 60 yards the pattern average is 45–50 percent.

Pattern density of a load averaging 85 percent extra-full choke at 40 yards also *increases* at about 9 percent for each 5-yards *reduction* in range. At 35 yards that 85 percent is a whopping 94 percent, and at 30 yards or less, *all* the shot charge is contained in a 30-inch circle or less.

Pattern dissipation for a full choke, delivering a 40-yard 70-percent pattern, is greater for each 5 yards of range beyond this distance, about 10 percent, instead of 9 for each 5 yards of additional range when the gun delivers 85-percent 40-yard patterns.

A modified choke, producing 60-percent 40-yard patterns, loses pattern density at about 12 percent for each 5 yards of range beyond this distance. The modified choke can be expected to deliver about 72 percent patterns at 35 yards, 84 percent at 30 yards. Obviously, the best pattern coverage for the modified choke is between 45 and 48 yards.

These figures for pattern dissipation are average. At some range brackets, the rate of dissipation is greater than the figures suggest. For example, a 12-gauge, delivering 70-percent 40-yard patterns, using 1¼ ounces of 6's, will lose more pattern density between 40 and 45 yards than it will between 45 and 50 yards, especially if unplated shot is employed. Quite a large number of deformed shot make a contribution to the 40-yard pattern, but rapidly loose their effectiveness between 40 and 45 yards, with very few making any contribution to pattern density at 50 yards. This is true, though to a lesser extent, even when shot sleeves are used to keep the pellets out of bore contact.

Where copper-plated shot of the best grade, such as the Winchester-Western Lubaloy, is used in long-range handloads, the pattern dissipation for each 5 yards of range is considerably less than it is with "black" shot. This is also true when nickel-plated shot is employed, though to a lesser extent than with copper-plated pellets.

Turning to the extra-full patterns of 88 to 94 percent, obtainable with some of the better factory loads and with the best of the long-range handloads, pattern dissipation beyond 40 yards is about 7 to 8 percent for each 5 yards of range beyond this distance. Before reaching the range where these spreads have become improved/modified patterns, the distances spanned by these loadings are considerably greater than those achieved by shells delivering lesser pattern percentages.

These tight patterns may be exploited

Long-range pattern density is best with copper-plated shot such as Lubaloy (far left). Three other types are (from left) hardened lead, nickel-plated, and steel. Regardless of pellet size, steel is unreliable beyond 40 yards.

by going to lesser shot-charge weights and consequently, lighter, more dynamic guns. For even with a 1⅛-ounce charge of 4's, delivering 90-percent 40-yard patterns, the maximum range where the gun delivers an improved/modified pattern is about 60 yards, ducks the quarry. With the use of 12-gauge Magnum factory loads, 1⅞ ounces of 4's or 2's, the maximum range on ducks and geese, respectively, is about 70 yards, with an improved-cylinder pattern or slightly less delivered at this distance.

In upland gunning, with the gun choked to throw improved-cylinder patterns at 40 yards, the increase in pattern density short of 40 yards is a very pertinent consideration. With a gun delivering 45 percent pattern at 40 yards, a gunner can expect 57 percent patterns at 35 yards, and about 69 percent or full-choke patterns at 30 yards.

The upland gunner, as well as the man shooting shorebirds, has two solutions to his problem of extra-dense, short-range patterns. Spreader, or brush loads, will bring that all-important improved cylinder in to around 25 yards. If handloads are used, these spreader loads are easily made, or flattened shot may be used in a regular handload for wide-spreading, uniform, short-range patterns.

Pattern densities have been increased about one choke designation in all constrictions with the inception of plastic shot sleeves. At present many shotguns are actually overchoked for best results. When this occurs, a full choke delivers very *low* pattern densities, and the uniformity from shot to shot leaves much to be desired. The solution, of course, is to have a gunsmith take out about .004-inch constriction. This, however, should be done on a test-

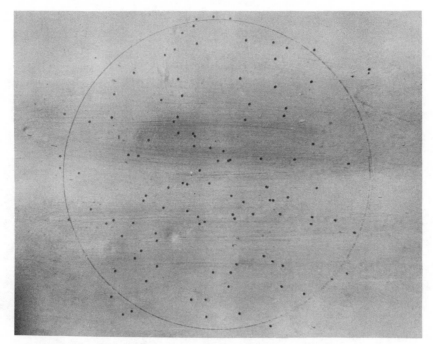

Using 1¼ ounces of Winchester Lubaloy 4's, author put together long-range 20-gauge load that produced excellent duck-shooting pattern— 101 pellets (adding up to 59 percent density) in 30-inch circle at 60 yards.

and-try basis. Usually the job requires not more than .005 relief to bring the choke to a 70–80 percent designation. This is also true when the modified choke's patterns must be reduced in density. Even when the improved-cylinder choke is used, it is quite often feasible to reduce the constriction by .002 or so for better short-range performance.

Considerable confusion exists among gunners as to the increase in range from the *same* pattern coverage when heavier shot charges are used. A good rule of thumb is to consider a 20 percent shot-charge weight increase as giving a 10 percent increase in range for the same pattern coverage. This presupposes the same pattern percentages for the lighter and heavier load at 40 yards. For example, if you are using 1¼ ounces of 4's in a 20-gauge Magnum, then turn to a 2-ounce, 10-gauge Magnum charge of this size shot, the increase in range for the *same* pattern density in a 30-inch circle is a modest 22 percent. If you are getting proper pattern coverage at 55 yards with the lighter load in the 20-gauge Magnum, changing to the 2-ounce 10-gauge Magnum load would extend this range to about 67 yards for the same coverage.

Shot size, performance, and velocities at extended ranges deserve much more consideration than is commonly given them by most gunners. That improved-cylinder pattern at maximum range must be complemented by proper shot sizes to deliver a killing hit on the usual targets of the long-range gunner. It is usually conceded that a 5-pellet hit, with an individual pellet energy of 2 foot-pounds *at the target,* is about right for ducks. When geese are the target, the same 5-pellet hit requires at least an individual pellet energy of 3 pounds for a clean kill.

Proper individual pellet energy, obviously, is an essential requirement for a long-range kill. But it must be tied in with pattern density. If a gunner is using 1⅞ ounces of 2's, he has a load with sufficient individual pellet energy for clean kills on geese to 80 yards or more—even farther on ducks. As a matter of plain ballistic fact, this loading of 1⅞ ounces of 2's couldn't carry pattern density to any greater yardage than 1 ounce of 5's assuming the same pattern percentages for the two loadings at 40 yards. Consider the following:

Shot Size	Shot Charge Weight	Pellets
5	1 ounce	172
4	1¼ ounce	168
2	1⅞ ounce	167

From the standpoint of pattern density, where one expects a 4- to 5-pellet hit on ducks, the range limitations of these three loadings are essentially the same. Of course the energy of 2's is much greater than of the smaller sizes, and this would be of some help if only a 2- or 3-pellet scratch hit is made.

There is a "yes, but" ballistic question to be answered at this point. While an improved-cylinder pattern of 45 to 55 percent might be considered the end of the line from the standpoint of effective coverage with 1, 1⅛, and 1¼ ounces, would this hold true of the 12- and 10-gauge Magnum loads of 1½, 1⅝, 17/8, and 2 ounces? The answer is a qualified no.

The only justification for these heavy Magnum loads is to increase pattern density at maximum range with shot sizes having sufficient individual pellet energy for a clean kill—4's and 2's. Pattern saturation at maximum range is reached with the smaller shot sizes and with much smaller

Goal is to get clean kills like this by matching shot size and pattern density to range. When gunning potholes with 20-gauge double (left) author uses ounce of 6's and gets improved and modified patterns at 40 yards.

shot-charge weights. There is no point in using 1⅞ ounces of 6's in a 12-gauge Magnum when the individual pellet energy of this size cancels out its effectiveness at 45–50 yards. Actually, good pattern coverage with this size is obtained with 1⅛ ounces.

In evaluating the Magnum loads of 4's, 1½, 1⅝, 1⅞, and 2 ounces, pattern density at maximum range can well be considered as 40 percent for the smaller of these charges, and 32 percent for the larger. With the smaller shot-charge weights, the patterns at maximum range can be calculated at 55 percent for the 1⅛-ounce loading of 4's, and 50 percent for the 1¼-ounce loading. Using 2's, the percentage figures may be slightly reduced—though they will be still retained in the improved-cylinder-choke bracket at maximum range.

Muzzle velocity of a shot charge weight may vary widely without its long-range effectiveness being greatly changed. Consider the factory loading of 1⅞ ounces in a 12-gauge Magnum. This is pushed at a muzzle velocity of 1220 feet a second, using either 2's or 4's. Start a #2 shot out at 1330 feet a second and it arrives at the 60-yard mark with a remaining velocity of 730 feet a second. Start the same shot out at 1220 feet a second and it arrives at 60 yards with a remaining velocity of 695 feet a second. The muzzle-velocity difference of these two loadings, 110 feet a second, is reduced to a scant 35 feet at 60 yards, scarcely a significant difference. Usually, though, the lower-velocity loading pro-

duces the denser, more uniform patterns.

Another ballistic dividend of the lower velocity loading is lessened recoil. Take, for example, a 1¼-ounce shot charge at 1330 feet a second. In a 7½-pound gun the recoil of this loading is 32 foot-pounds. Using the same shot weight of 1¼ ounces in a 20-gauge Magnum loading with a muzzle velocity of 1220 feet per second, a gun of the same gun weight would recoil at about 26 foot-pounds—a substantial reduction.

Quite a number of gunners believe that any reduction in muzzle velocity is reflected in increased lead requirements, but that is not necessarily the case.

Assume that a target, whatever its nature, is passing at a 90-degree angle at 40 yards. The speed of the target is 50 miles an hour, about 73 feet a second. With a muzzle velocity of 1330 feet a second, using #4 shot, the flight time of the shot charge is about .1187 seconds. During the flight time of the shot charge, the target will move about 8.66 feet—the lead requirement, disregarding gunner reaction time.

At a muzzle velocity of 1220 feet a second, the time of the shot charge of 4's over the 40-yard range is .1268 seconds. The difference in lead requirements for these two shot charges is less than a foot—eight inches or a fraction more.

Practical shotgun ballistics has a direct application that pays off in more successful gunning. The most important factor is the matching of patterning and shot sizes to the ability of the gunner. There is no profit in going prepared for 70-yard wildfowling if there isn't a matching skill, along with a matching shot size and choke performance.

WINCHESTER-WESTERN SHOTSHELL BALLISTICS*

Muzzle Velocity	Shot Size	VELOCITY IN FPS AT			ENERGY IN ft.-lbs. PER PELLET AT				TIME IN FLIGHT IN SECONDS TO			DROP IN INCHES AT		
		20 yds.	40 yds.	60 yds.	Muzzle	20 yds.	40 yds.	60 yds.	20 yds.	40 yds.	60 yds.	20 yds.	40 yds.	60 yds.
1330 f.p.s.	BB	1085	915	790	34.37	22.87	16.27	12.13	.0502	.1107	.1815	0.5	2.4	6.4
	2	1045	860	730	19.07	11.77	7.98	5.76	.0513	.1148	.1908	0.5	2.6	7.0
	4	1010	815	685	12.70	7.34	4.77	3.35	.0522	.1187	.1993	0.5	2.7	7.7
	5	990	790	655	10.08	5.60	3.56	2.36	.0528	.1210	.2047	0.5	2.8	8.1
	6	970	765	630	7.61	4.04	2.50	1.70	.0535	.1238	.2108	0.6	3.0	8.6
	7½	930	715	580	4.88	2.38	1.41	0.93	.0548	.1291	.2228	0.6	3.2	9.6
1315 f.p.s.	2	1035	855	725	18.64	11.56	7.86	5.69	.0518	.1159	.1923	0.5	2.6	7.1
	4	1005	810	680	12.42	7.22	4.71	3.32	.0527	.1197	.2009	0.5	2.8	7.8
	5	985	785	655	9.86	5.51	3.51	2.43	.0533	.1221	.2062	0.6	2.9	8.2
	6	960	760	625	7.44	3.98	2.47	1.68	.0540	.1248	.2124	0.6	3.0	8.7
1295 f.p.s.	2	1025	845	720	18.01	11.28	7.71	5.60	.0525	.1173	.1944	0.5	2.6	7.3
	4	990	800	675	12.04	7.05	4.62	3.26	.0534	.1211	.2030	0.6	2.8	8.0
	5	970	780	650	9.56	5.38	3.45	2.40	.0540	.1235	.2083	0.6	2.9	8.4
	6	950	750	620	7.21	3.89	2.43	1.66	.0547	.1262	.2145	0.6	3.1	8.9
	7½	910	705	575	4.63	2.30	1.37	0.91	.0560	.1316	.2265	0.6	3.3	9.9
1255 f.p.s.	4	965	785	665	11.31	6.72	4.45	3.16	.0549	.1240	.2074	0.6	3.0	8.3
	5	950	765	640	8.98	5.13	3.32	2.32	.0555	.1264	.2128	0.6	3.1	8.7
	6	930	740	610	6.77	3.71	2.34	1.61	.0562	.1292	.2189	0.6	3.2	9.2
	8	880	675	550	3.69	1.80	1.07	0.70	.0581	.1367	.2358	0.6	3.6	10.7
1240 f.p.s.	2	990	820	705	16.58	10.53	7.28	5.33	.0545	.1214	.2006	0.6	2.8	7.8
	4	960	780	660	11.04	6.59	4.38	3.12	.0555	.1252	.2092	0.6	3.0	8.4
	5	940	760	635	8.76	5.04	3.27	2.29	.0561	.1276	.2145	0.6	3.1	8.9
	6	920	730	610	6.61	3.65	2.30	1.58	.0568	.1303	.2206	0.6	3.3	9.4
	7½	885	690	560	4.24	2.16	1.30	0.87	.0581	.1357	.2332	0.6	3.6	10.5
1235 f.p.s.	4	955	780	660	10.95	6.55	4.36	3.10	.0557	.1256	.2097	0.6	3.0	8.5
	5	940	755	635	8.69	5.01	3.25	2.28	.0563	.1280	.2151	0.6	3.2	8.9
	6	920	730	605	6.56	3.62	2.29	1.58	.0570	.1307	.2212	0.6	3.3	9.4
	8	870	670	545	3.57	1.76	1.05	0.69	.0588	.1382	.2384	0.7	3.7	11.0
1220 f.p.s.	2	975	815	695	16.04	10.26	7.13	5.23	.0553	.1230	.2029	0.6	2.9	8.0
	4	945	775	655	10.69	6.43	4.29	3.06	.0563	.1268	.2115	0.6	3.1	8.6
	5	930	750	630	8.48	4.92	3.21	2.25	.0569	.1292	.2169	0.6	3.2	9.1
	6	910	725	605	6.40	3.56	2.26	1.59	.0576	.1319	.2230	0.6	3.6	9.6
	7½	875	680	560	4.11	2.11	1.28	0.86	.0589	.1372	.2350	0.7	3.6	10.2
	8	860	665	540	3.48	1.73	1.03	0.69	.0594	.1394	.2399	0.7	3.8	11.1

*First determine muzzle velocity for specific loads, and match with muzzle velocity in first column.

WINCHESTER-WESTERN SHOTSHELL BALLISTICS*

Muzzle Velocity	Shot Size	VELOCITY IN FPS AT			ENERGY IN ft.-lbs. PER PELLET AT				TIME IN FLIGHT IN SECONDS TO			DROP IN INCHES AT		
		20 yds.	40 yds.	60 yds.	Muzzle	20 yds.	40 yds.	60 yds.	20 yds.	40 yds.	60 yds.	20 yds.	40 yds.	60 yds.
1200 f.p.s.	4	935	765	650	10.34	6.27	4.20	3.01	.0571	.1284	.2140	0.6	3.2	8.8
	5	915	740	625	8.21	4.80	3.14	2.22	.0577	.1308	.2193	0.6	3.3	9.3
	6	900	720	600	6.19	3.47	2.22	1.54	.0584	.1336	.2255	0.7	3.4	9.8
	7½	865	675	555	3.97	2.06	1.26	0.85	.0597	.1389	.2375	0.7	3.7	10.9
	8	850	660	540	3.37	1.69	1.02	0.68	.0603	.1410	.2423	0.7	3.8	10.3
	9	820	625	505	2.38	1.11	0.64	0.42	.0615	.1462	.2538	0.7	4.1	12.4
1185 f.p.s.	4	925	760	645	10.08	6.15	4.13	2.97	.0577	.1297	.2159	0.6	3.2	9.0
	6	890	715	595	6.04	3.41	2.18	1.52	.0590	.1348	.2274	0.7	3.5	10.0
	8	845	655	535	3.29	1.66	1.00	0.67	.0609	.1423	.2442	0.7	3.9	11.5
1165 f.p.s.	4	915	750	635	9.74	5.98	4.04	2.91	.0586	.1314	.2185	0.7	3.3	9.2
	5	895	730	615	7.74	4.58	3.03	2.15	.0592	.1338	.2238	0.7	3.5	9.7
	6	880	705	590	5.84	3.32	2.14	1.49	.0599	.1366	.2300	0.7	3.6	10.2
	8	835	650	530	3.18	1.62	0.98	0.66	.0618	.1440	.2469	0.7	4.0	11.8
	9	805	615	495	2.24	1.07	0.62	0.41	.0630	.1492	.2584	0.8	4.3	12.9
1155 f.p.s.	4	905	745	635	9.58	5.90	4.00	2.89	.0591	.1323	.2198	0.7	3.4	9.3
	5	890	725	615	7.60	4.52	3.00	2.17	.0596	.1347	.2252	0.7	3.1	9.8
	6	875	700	585	5.74	3.28	2.12	1.48	.0603	.1374	.2313	0.7	3.6	10.3
	8	830	645	530	3.18	1.60	0.97	0.65	.0622	.1449	.2482	0.8	4.0	11.9
	9	800	610	495	2.20	1.06	0.62	0.40	.0635	.1500	.2597	0.8	4.3	13.0
1150 f.p.s.	9	800	610	495	2.18	1.05	0.61	0.40	.0637	.1505	.2604	0.8	4.4	10.1
1145 f.p.s.	7½	835	655	540	3.62	1.93	1.19	0.81	.0621	.1437	.2447	0.7	4.0	11.6
	8	825	640	525	3.07	1.58	0.96	0.65	.0627	.1458	.2496	0.8	4.1	12.0
1135 f.p.s.	4	895	740	630	9.25	5.74	3.91	2.83	.0600	.1342	.2226	0.7	3.5	9.6
	5	880	715	605	7.34	4.40	2.93	2.09	.0606	.1365	.2279	0.7	3.6	10.0
	6	860	695	580	5.54	3.19	2.07	1.45	.0612	.1393	.2341	0.7	3.7	10.6
	7½	830	655	540	3.56	1.90	1.18	0.80	.0626	.1446	.2461	0.8	4.0	11.7

*First determine muzzle velocity for specific loads, and match with muzzle velocity in first column.

WINCHESTER-WESTERN SHOTSHELL BALLISTIC DATA

Gauge	Shell Length	Dram Equiv.	Shot Weight	Shot Sizes	Muzzle Velocity Feet/Second
Super Speed & Super X—Long Range—Short Shot String					
10	2⅞	4¾	1⅝	4	1330
12	2¾	3¾	1¼	BB, 2, 4, 5, 6, 7½, 9	1330
16	2¾	3¼	1⅛	4, 5, 6, 7½, 9	1295
20	2¾	2¾	1	4, 5, 6, 7½, 9	1220
28	2¾	2¼	¾	6, 7½, 9	1295
410	2½	Max.	½	4, 6, 7½, 9	1135
410	3	Max.	¾	4, 5, 6, 7½, 9	1135
Super Speed & Super X—Long Range—Short Shot String—Magnum Load					
10	3½ Mag.	Max.	2	2	1255
12	2¾ Mag.	4	1½	2, 4, 5, 6	1260
12	3 Mag.	4	1⅜	2, 4, 6	1295
12	3 Mag.	4¼	1⅝	2, 4, 6	1280
12	3 Mag.	Max.	1⅞	BB, 2, 4	1210
16	2¾ Mag.	3½	1¼	2, 4, 6	1260
20	2¾ Mag.	3	1⅛	4, 6, 7½	1295
20	3 Mag.	Max.	1¼	4, 6, 7½	1295
Super Speed & Super X Double X Magnum					
12	2¾ Mag.	4	1½	2, 4	1260
12	3 Mag.	Max.	1⅞	2, 4	1210
Super X with Lubaloy (Copperized) Shot					
12	2¾	Max.	1¼	2, 4, 5, 6, 7½	1330
20	2¾	Max.	1	4, 5, 6, 7½	1220
Super X with Lubaloy (Copperized) Shot—Magnum Loads					
12	2¾	Max.	1½	2, 4	1260
12	3 Mag.	Max.	1⅜	2, 4, 6	1295
12	3 Mag.	Max.	1⅝	2, 4, 6	1280
20	3 Mag.	Max.	1⅛	6	1295
20	3 Mag.	Max.	1³⁄₁₆	4	1295
Super Speed & Super X Mark 5 Super Buckshot Loads			Pellets		
12	2¾		9	00 Buck	1325
12	2¾		12	0 Buck	1300
12	2¾		16	1 Buck	1250
12	2¾		27	4 Buck	1325
16	2¾		12	1 Buck	1225
20	2¾		20	3 Buck	1200
Super Speed & Super X Magnum Mark 5 Super Buckshot Loads					
12	2¾ Mag.		12	00 Buck	1325
12	3 Mag.		15	00 Buck	1250
12	2¾ Mag.		20	1 Buck	1050
12	3 Mag.		41	4 Buck	1220

Gauge	Shell Length	Dram Equiv.	Shot Weight	Shot Sizes	Muzzle Velocity Feet/Second
Ranger & Xpert Field Loads					
12	2¾	3	1	4, 5, 6, 8	1290
12	2¾	3	1⅛	6, 8	1200
12	2¾	3¼	1⅛	4, 5, 6, 7½, 8, 9	1255
12	2¾	3¼	1¼	7½, 8	1220
16	2¾	2½	1	6, 8	1165
16	2¾	2¾	1⅛	4, 5, 6, 7½, 8, 9	1185
20	2¾	2¼	⅞	6, 8	1210
20	2¾	2½	1	4, 5, 6, 7½, 8, 9	1165
Ranger & Xpert Brush Loads					
12	2¾	3	1⅛	8	1200
Winchester-Western Double A Trap Loads					
12	2¾	2¾	1⅛	7½, 8	1145
12	2¾	3	1⅛	7½, 8	1200
Winchester-Western Double A International Trap Loads					
12	2¾	3¼	1¼	7½, 8*	1220
12	2¾	3¼	1¼	7½, 8	1220
*Nickel Plated Shot					
Winchester-Western Double A Skeet Loads					
12	2¾	2¾	1¼	9	1145
12	2¾	3	1⅛	9	1200
20	2¾	2¼	⅞	9	1200
28	2¾	Max.	¾	9	1200
410	2½	Max.	½	9	1200
Western Field Trial Popper Load					
12	2¾	—	—	—	—

Whereas jump-shooting ducks at potholes is usually short-range work, open-water gunning (even with decoys) often demands long shots. One handload can't be equally effective for both types of sport.

Handloading Basics

by Pete Brown

13

The first American shooters—Dan'l Boone included—loaded their own ammunition, by necessity if not for pleasure. When the invention of the self-contained cartridge finally revolutionized traditional firearms, gunners happily let the factories do the loading. Handloading steadily declined until only the most unreconstructed of mountain men and moonshiners still practiced the dying art. Then—just as it seemed the industrial revolution would stamp out even the ancient practitioners of an honorable craft—handloading's ranks were gently swelled by a new breed, the devoted amateur ballistician-shooter. A scattering of eager rifle enthusiasts kept handloading alive through the first decades of this century.

The majority of dealers then knew nothing and cared less about reloading components and equipment. Most of the equipment business was handled on a mail-order basis, and you could count the number of retail dealers who carried any components on the fingers a hand or two.

All this has changed in the last generation. Literally millions of reloaders—be they laymen technicians striving for a new rifle load or economy-minded shotshell as-semblers—now contribute to the health and welfare of hundreds of manufacturers and thousands of dealers. Handloading has added a new dimension to both the sporting game and the business behind it.

In spite of today's widespread knowledge of handloading, I still receive a lot of questions on the subject. Naturally, the predominant queries are from newcomers to the game. The most popular questions I receive and the best brief answers I have been able to provide break down about as follows:

"Why bother?"

I've been handloading for so long that when anyone asks me, "Why handload?" it is as if they asked, "Why eat?" Assembling my own cartridges has become second nature. If the questioner is a casual hunter who may—or may not—use about five cartridges a year for zeroing his rifle before tossing off a shot or two during big-game season, there really isn't much of an argument in favor of his loading his own.

However, if the neophyte handloader follows the usual pattern, he'll become fascinated and the first thing he knows, he'll be doing a lot more shooting during the process of experimenting with various

Though some shooters think of handloading only in terms of target rifles, you can also tailor shotgun loads (above) and high-performance loads for hunting rifles. One result is shown in photo of author and pronghorn on page 70.

combinations of loads, guns, conditions, etc. Considering the fact that for most cartridges there are four or five powders which can be used in combination with several makes of bullets in various weights plus different makes of primers, the possibilities seem limitless and the search for better accuracy is endless. Groups will indicate that it can be narrowed down, but never pinpointed.

Loading is a truly fascinating hobby which can make anyone—particularly those with a suppressed desire to venture into the world of science—an addict. This is a warning to all budding handloaders.

Once you find that probing for better accuracy pays off in personal satisfaction and better hunting—plus year-round shooting sport—you'll also become aware that handloading, as you engage in more shooting, saves a considerable amount of money.

"How can I handload and save money?"

If you figure your time at what you hope it's worth, it is highly unlikely it will pay

to handload. However, all the handloaders I know charge their time off to recreation. Not counting your labor, in your cost accounting, provides a good start toward arriving at an impressive money-saving figure.

There is another big money-saving factor. When you salvage a fired cartridge case, you can use it again and again for perhaps 20 times, depending on the type of cartridge and the nature of your loads. Since the cartridge case is the most expensive ammunition component, it is most fortunate that it is the one re-usable item.

After commercial factories have manufactured all the components, including cases, bullets, primers, and powder, they still have assembly costs based on turning these components into a complete round of ammunition. That's why they can sell the necessary components for considerably less than loaded and boxed ammunition. A handloader amortizes the cost of a shell over several loadings *plus* saving the factory loading costs, resulting in an ammunition cost cut of at least half.

"What's a good load?"

This is one of the popular questions. For example: "I have a certain make of gun in such and such caliber. What load will give me the best results on antelope in Wyoming?" I simply can't give my correspondent a well-seasoned answer to this and I don't think anyone else can. Since the question deals with antelope in big open country, the problem concerns accuracy as well as performance of the bullet after it hits the antelope. I can recommend a choice of two or three bullet weights and that's about all. If I go much beyond I won't know what I'm talking about. True, certain loads are generally better than others and there is such a thing as selecting an appropriate powder for the cartridge. But this information is readily available in the handbooks and data sheets.

Every rifle, within certain limitations, has individual characteristics all its own; this is one of the challenges that add interest to handloading. There is only one way to determine which load will give the ultimate accuracy in a particular rifle. A man has to shoot and shoot and shoot on the range with different loads. Then evaluate the results and go back and shoot some more. This is the most reliable as well as the most interesting way of arriving at superior performance.

"Is handloading safe?"

Handloading can certainly be considered safe but, as with anything from crossing the street to climbing out of a bathtub, if done with reckless abandon the consequences can be disastrous.

Concentrate on what you're doing. You can't listen to another shooter's hair-raising hunting yarn and do a good job of as-

Reloaded cartridges cost less than factory ammunition, and you soon begin to turn out tailored loads you can be proud of. You then have hobby that's relaxing, enjoyable, and likely to improve your shooting.

sembling ammunition components at the same time. With a little practice, you can let a visitor talk without listening to a word he says. You can nod, smile, look concerned, or repeat the same old appropriate comments by conditioned reflex. He'll give you the signals if you learn to watch for them. He'll be perfectly happy while he can talk and you can devote your active mind and energies to your loading.

Loading to achieve the ultimate in rifle accuracy and hunting bullet performance is one thing; flirting with the margins of safety by building super-velocity loads is needless danger because there is little, if any, possibility of significantly stepping up power. What little might be gained is not worth the risk. Say that the loader succeeds in boosting the velocity 100 feet per second. Now contemplate the short distance the bullet travels before losing that 100 feet and you'll see the gain is actually insignificant.

Play it cool with your powder and avoid those hot loads. Start loading at least a couple of grains below the maximum recommended in the loading tables, and don't go above maximum. A load that produces normal pressure in one rifle may give high pressure in another rifle. Even after carefully feeling your way, don't use *more* powder than the maximum load recommended.

Most safety practices are commonsense things, but special caution is necessary when loading powder. Check and double-check to see that you have the proper powder and the proper charge. Be sure to double-check the setting on your powder scale. While charging powder, have only one container on the job. If another can is within easy reach, there is always the possibility of using the wrong container. After putting powder in your measure, put the lid back on the can and set it to one side by itself. Make these safety procedures a matter of habit through constant and deliberate practice.

A loading block for holding the cartridges during the loading process makes for orderly and safe loading. A loading block can be made by drilling holes—large enough in diameter to take the head of the

cartridge—in a block of wood. Plastic and wooden loading blocks are commercially available at reasonable cost. Every handloader should have at least one loading block that holds 50 or more cartridge cases.

"My son is 12 years old. He has his own rifle and hunted with me last year. Now he wants to load his own ammunition. Do you think a youngster should be allowed to do this?

Handloading is good experience for a young fellow. It is educational, it saves money, and it can be done safely. I do think that any boy who handloads should have either parental supervision or help from adult friends in whom you have confidence. You could easily provide the essential adult judgment in determining loads and seeing that safety procedures are established and carefully adhered to.

The age at which a boy should start loading depends on the boy. I don't believe in any hard and fast rules in this regard. Certainly a boy with a parent who joins in the boy's interest is in a position to start a lot sooner than a boy whose parents are not able to work with him.

*Secret of effective handloading is
simply to take care with each
step from decapping and sizing to
seating bullets or crimping shotshells.
You can improve your pistol loads
as well as shotgun and rifle cartridges.*

The Case for the Magnums

by Warren Page

14

On the next shoulder of the Absarokas, across a deep ravine and with cows and spikehorns scattered below him, stood a strapping granddaddy of a bull elk. When he straightened his neck to bugle, the top tines of his rack scraped clear back to his rump. The spotting scope had already proved that if he wasn't a candidate for the Boone & Crockett trophy list, only careful taping could prove him otherwise. But across thin Rocky Mountain air, guessing the range precisely was a real problem; his scattered harem would surely tip off a closer stalk; and failure to anchor the bull with the first shot might mean losing him in the canyon tangle of mountain mahogany and oak brush.

Earlier in the hunt perhaps we'd have checked the bet, hoped for an easier chance. There may have been still other solutions, but the best answer to the problem rested in the hunter's hands, a scope-sighted sporter in a Magnum .30 caliber. With the range guesstimated as somewhere between 400 and 425 yards, the rifle zeroed to strike three inches high at 100 yards, on at close to 300, settling the horizontal crosswire of the scope steadily along the elk's withers should mean that

the bullet would drop in 12 or 14 inches below that line, tear into the heart and lung area halfway up from the brisket. And it did just that, so that a half-hour later we had the cameras out for pictures of that trophy bull. He had been dropped in his tracks by skilled use of a Magnum-calibered rifle.

Now had this particular hunter been toting an ordinary .30 caliber, say a .30-06, the problem might, perhaps, have been solved, but it would have been considerably tougher. Even with the rifle set the same way for a like 180-grain bullet—and remember that the plus-3-at-100 system is good for most modern cartridges when you head for mountain country—at that range the scope would have had to be steadied on an imaginary spot at least another full foot over the bull's withers.

The bullet, if and when it hit, would have whammed home with only somewhat more than half the killing force of the Magnum slug. Because of the more curved trajectory of the slower standard load, the elk might well have been missed. Because of the lesser wallop and tissue destruction of the slower standard load, the elk, if hit at all, might not have been properly clob-

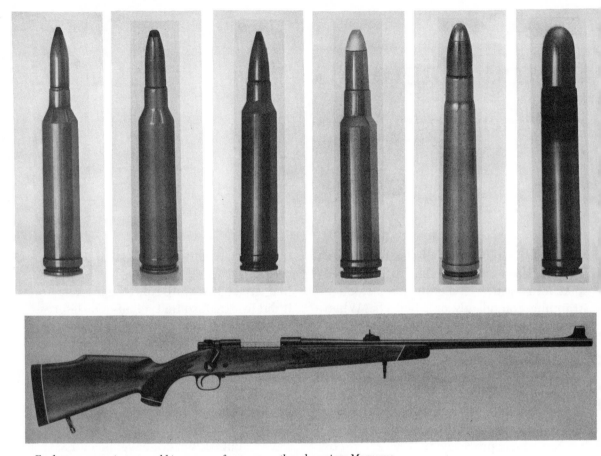

For long-range trajectory and big-game performance, author champions Magnums.
Above is Winchester Magnum 70, chambered for (from left) .264 Win.,
7mm Rem., .300 Win., .338 Win., .375 H&H, and .458 Win. Magnum cartridges.

bered. And therein, essentially, lie the arguments for the Magnum type of cartridge—more speed for easier hitting, more belt at any range.

The Magnum idea is not new. In recent years, however, particularly since the Hoffman and Holland & Holland .30 Magnums, first loaded for U.S. consumption by the Western Cartridge Company, stirred matters up during the 1920s, demand has steadily swelled for Magnums in every conceivable diameter. Not surprising.

The history of cartridge development is largely one of continuing quest for bullet velocity, just as the search for speed has motivated our airplane and automobile designers.

In this country the true father of the Magnum idea was undoubtedly Charles Newton, a fair lawyer, poor businessman, but a superb ballistic thinker. Newton was first known five decades back for small high-speed items like the .22 Hi-Power and the .250–3000; but he must also be credited with the .256 Newton (a 6.5mm cartridge "Magnumized" by using a case of the same size as the .30-06) and the .30 and .35 Newton rounds, true Magnums in the sense that their cartridge cases are markedly oversized as compared to brass ordinarily available for the same diameter of bullet.

Though Newton did not use the outside-belted head of the later H&H types so generally, though not inevitably, associated with Magnums, he stuffed his economy-sized brass bottles with the best slow-burning powders of his day, items like Dupont 10, 13, 15, and 15½, to claim velocities incredible at that time: 123 grains at 3,103 foot-seconds, 172 grains at 3,000, even 250 grains at 3,000. With the propellants available during the first quarter of this century, such figures were probably opium dreams, but with contemporary powders they can handily be reached and exceeded.

Had Charles Newton been able to use fuels like Dupont 4350 or 4831, or better yet the even slower ball powder types developed in recent years by Winchester-Western, and had the shooting public then been ready for the extreme-velocity idea, it is probable that a sort of Magnum millennium would have been reached by Newton alone, even before Finland had paid off its World War I debt!

Newton was not alone, but save for a few speed fanatics among riflemen, the general shooting public was not ready for Magnums, though Western Cartridge for a time loaded Newton calibers. It took a generation of wildcat experiments, some of which developed into commercial cartridges, to prepare the public. It took steps like the .280 Ross and the .280 Halger, even the .270. It took the work of such as Dubiel, Gibson, Davis, Ackley, the OKH trio, Baden Powell, and Miller with their PMVF and CCC chamberings, and others to accustom shooters in general to the glamorous Magnum idea.

The major ammunition-loading and armsmaking companies, keenly aware of the problems of pressure and propellant development, came along more slowly.

Having briefly tried the Newton types, they adopted the Holland & Holland belted Magnums of .275, .300, and .375 caliber, but did not until after the Second World War open up for a crop of Magnums in nearly every size.

That crop includes such as the .222 Remington Magnum, perhaps admissible in that its case is 1/10-inch longer than the original .222, the belted-head .264 Winchester, 7mm Remington, .300 Winchester, .338 Winchester, .350 Remington, and .458 Winchester Magnum types. These will handle every game species from prairie dog to elephant. It might be argued that even the rimless-cased .280 Remington and .284 Winchester are Magnums in that for 7mm bullets they use cases one full step larger than that for the original 7mm Mauser. And the end is not yet in sight, though the area for wildcat experimentation has been sharply narrowed. Smart money says there will be commercial U.S.-made rounds of Magnum character in some of the intervening bullet sizes.

Nearly all these modern Magnums, even including the Magnum-styled handgun cartridges such as the .357, .41, and .44 Magnums, and the .256 Winchester, operate on the same set of basic principles. First, to gain greater velocity per grain of bullet weight, we must add more granules of powder fuel, burn more gas to get greater horsepower.

Hence in order to drive a 150-grain .30-caliber bullet at 3,400 feet per second, as is the case of the .300 Winchester Magnum using a 26-inch barrel, instead of at 2,970 as from the 24-inch barrel of a .30-06, we must use some 78 grains of a powder like Dupont 4350 instead of about 59 grains. This is an increase in charge weight of roughly 32 percent.

Second, any enlarged charge of slow-burning powder, if we are to pack it all in and fire it without dangerously increasing pressures, requires a cartridge of higher volume, either of greater length or, as is the case with modern compact Magnums, of fatter diameter. And note that today's Magnums like the .300 Winchester do not operate at significantly higher pressures than certain of their smaller-cased counterparts. Both get up a head of steam somewhere between 50,000 and 55,000 pounds per square inch.

A third basic point is that the principle of diminishing returns sets in as we continue to increase case volume and add powder to gain bullet speed. At some point the curve of velocity gain per grain of powder must flatten sharply. In the instance above, we used over 30 percent more powder to get less than 15 percent added velocity—just as in a car we may need 50 extra horsepower to get 10 more miles per hour. The Magnum must be balanced off at some optimum point. Necking down a 37mm anti-tank shell to shoot .224 bullets as some sort of ultra-super woodchucking Magnum would get us absolutely nowhere with today's propellants. This is no real disadvantage, however, since that point of peak efficiency is directly responsible for the reasonable size of our present hunting Magnums.

And finally, if desirable for hunting heavy and dangerous beasts, we can use a bigger case and more powder in a Magnum, not for more speed with a given bullet but for greater bullet weight at the same speed. The .458 Winchester is an example. Its ballistics, calling for a 500-grain bullet at 2130 feet per second, actually duplicate those of double-gun cartridges like the .470 and the .475 No. 2 and such that the English cooked up two generations ago.

But this modern cartridge does not need a special action. The round is destined seldom, if ever, to be fired at game more than 50 or 100 yards away, and long practical experience has proved that just about that combination of bullet weight and velocity will drive through the bony armor of an elephant's brain case, and provide proper medicine for toughies like buffalo and rhino. Pure poison it has been on the several elephant and dozen or so Cape buffalo I've taken with this modern Magnum. The .458 is a most reassuring tool to have in hand when crawling through jungle greenery in order to look up at tusk ivory or sweeping black horns.

There are inevitably some drawbacks to the Magnum idea. Big powder charges wash out rifle barrels faster than lesser ones, especially in the smaller calibers. Yet this is small cost compared to the price we pay for getting ourselves into range of those animals at which we may aim the rifle. Modern high-pressure Magnums also lose velocity more rapidly when the barrel is shortened to gain hunting handiness than what we might term the standard cartridges. A .300 Magnum, for example, might shed some 35 foot-seconds for each inch of barrel cut off as opposed to some 25 foot-seconds per inch for the .30-06, but the Magnum will always retain much of its original advantage.

Big loads admittedly mean more noise, but cotton or ear plugs will take care of blast on the range, and whoever heard muzzle noise when a critter with hair and long horns stood in the sights? And Magnums inevitably kick harder per pound of rifle weight; they must, unless Newton was fibbing when he set forth the Third Law of Motion. But until bullet weights pass 200 grains, this added recoil is more sound than real fury. Most Magnum rifles run somewhat heavier than their standard-chambered counterparts; every hunter or rifleman must someday come to a realization of his own tolerances with respect to recoil, and he must select calibers accordingly. In cartridges as in cars, we don't acquire performance benefits for free.

And there can be no doubt that Magnums have an edge when the chips are down. Karamoja Bell undoubtedly slew hundreds of elephants with items like the 6.5 Mannlicher and the 7x57, cartridges effective in their field but puny by today's standards. But Bell was shooting selectively, he hunted under conditions of terrain, game habits, and cover quite different from those encountered by a present-day safarist; and who among us claims Bell's knowledge of pachyderm anatomy? The average hunter visiting Africa today is better off with two and a half tons of energy and 500 grains of hard-jacketed slug capable of going in one elephantine ear and out the other!

One mountain-state outfitter friend of mine makes no bones of the fact that over the years he has killed a carload of elk with loads like the .243, even the .219 Zipper, and has often started mule deer on the way to the freezer with a Hornet bullet into the neck vertebrae; yet he would be the last to make a flat recommendation that these loads are right for Tom, Dick, or Harry on an expensive and long-planned hunt. A highly skilled rifleman, he was executing these animals for meat, firing at short range and only when he had them dead to rights. When he is packing dudes back into the high country, both his rifle scabbard and that of the customer are likely to carry Magnums.

The trophy hunter of today has gener-ally accepted the fact that the Magnum caliber suited to his game offers a percentage distinctly in his favor. He seldom passes up the tough chance on a tremendous bull moose or elk in favor of the tastier and easier cow that stands nearby. He may very likely have to take his trophy the hard way, at extra yardage or in difficult cover, but his Magnum gives him an extra edge.

There can be no doubt that when we move into the Magnum velocity levels, say above 2800 feet per second at the muzzle, the shocking violence and tissue-destroying effect that kills game quickly is carried further out. A modern 7mm Magnum, for example, will exert at 300 yards the sudden-death effect of a standard 7x57 at 100 yards. A big .30 like the .300 Winchester will do at 350 or beyond the damage we expect of a .308, say, at 150. In short, the properly designed Magnum should extend the effect of its standard counterpart by 150 yards or even more.

If the Magnum bullet is itself properly designed, it will have a much broader spectrum of useful effective distance, and even of impact conditions—the type and density of flesh, bone, and tissue in which it will expand and properly penetrate—so as to put to practical use its built-in bonus of speed. And commercial Magnum bullets today are not mere duplicates of the types of the same weight used in standard calibers.

In developing the .264 Winchester Magnum, Winchester-Western started with the premise that no ordinary bullet of 6.5mm dimension could stand the high impact speeds generated by 3200 foot-seconds of muzzle velocity without smashing up. A 140-grain projectile with far better control of expansion was needed, and after

Winchester .264 Magnum Model 70 is
sighted-in prior to hunt that
brought one-shot kill of mule deer at
about 150 yards and javelina at
more than 300 yards. Penetration
and expansion were excellent.

Warren Page and companion grin
with understandable elation
over record-book trophy. Alaskan moose
are big and tough, but this one was
no match for 175-grain bullet
from Page's 7mm Mashburn Magnum.

exhaustive trial and error it was worked out.

All this sounds highly academic, but it does in fact pay off to the practical hunter, especially to the selective hunter. In Colorado several seasons ago, careful searching among at least 200 mule deer a day finally produced the one master buck I wanted. But he had also spotted us and was moving upslope through snow-covered cedars. Nailing that massive rack on the wall meant a stern shot or nothing, at 250 paces.

Most bullets and most calibers would have produced only a smashed ham and a nasty job of trailing up a wounded animal. But the Magnum I was using drove its bullet through ham, abdomen, and diaphragm far up into the lungs, so that the tall-antlered buck, a handsome entry for the Boone & Crockett listings, was down and out in a couple of jumps. The Magnum's 30 percent velocity bonus and its Magnum-designed bullet made the difference. It usually does. That's why we have our Magnum breed.

Shotgunning Secrets

by Pete Kuhlhoff

15

"What's the secret of shotgun shooting?"

"Actually," I answered. "There is no great secret involved in perfect shotgun shooting. Practically anyone can shoot a scattergun well. All you have to do is find a safe shooting area, load the gun and pull the trigger. The problem is in pointing the gun so the target will be hit."

"Don't try to be funny," my friend said in utter disgust. "I really want to learn to shoot a shotgun. What's the scoop?"

There truly is no mystery to effective shotgun handling. Yet, there are a number of salient and essential elements to be considered—some probably a bit subtle or downright obscure to the person who recently has acquired that beautiful first shotgun.

Undoubtedly, the most important element in competent shotgun handling is practice, but certain preliminary requirements must be met before the shooter begins to gather practical experience.

When a beginner visits a store or gun shop with the idea of buying a shotgun, he undoubtedly has his eye peeled for the type of gun he desires—automatic, slide-action or double-barreled. He knows what he wants—it's a matter of personal prefer-

ence. The type of shotgun makes little or no difference in learning effective handling.

The fit of the gun, and perhaps its balance, *can* make the difference between consistently hitting targets and missing them. On the other hand, proper gun fit certainly will not guarantee accurate shooting. But it is a fact that without reasonably good fit, the gunner definitely is shooting with a disadvantage.

Modern shotguns are made with stock measurements to fit the average shooter. Today, in most instances, stocks are straighter (slightly less drop at the comb and heel) than they were not too many years ago. This is a plus factor because most individuals can adapt more easily to a straighter stock than to one with too much drop.

The approximate average measurements of today's standard field guns are based on length of pull and drop at both comb and heel. Length of pull (14 inches on a "stock" gun) is established by measuring a straight line from the face of the trigger to the center of the gun's butt. Drop is calculated by laying a straightedge or ruler along the top of the receiver or barrel rib and extending it back above the stock; the distance from this line to the top of the comb is the drop at comb (1½ inches for standard measurements); the distance from line to butt top is drop at heel (2½ inches on standard guns).

With these measurements in mind, how can a prospective shooter manage a rough check for shotgun fit?

Let's say that you are examining a new shotgun for the first time. If it's a double, you have checked the chambers and if it's a single-barreled repeater, you have looked into the chamber and magazine to make certain it's unloaded. Now you look at a small object that is some distance away and mount the gun as if you intend to shoot the object. If you are looking directly over the barrel (called the line of sight) with the bead at the bottom of the small object, the comb is correct in width and height and, in shooting, the shot pattern will be about centered on the target.

If you are looking directly over the barrel, but see its full length, the comb is the correct thickness but too high and the shot pattern would travel above the target.

If you are looking below the line of sight and can't see much except the hind end of the receiver, the comb is too low and maybe low at the heel. If the gun were to be fired, the shot pattern would be delivered low or under the target.

If your eye is lined up over the barrel, but to the left of the line of sight, the comb is the correct height but too thick for a right-handed shooter and the shot pattern would go to the left of the target. Reverse for the southpaw shooter. Conversely, if the eye is directly to the right of the line of sight, the comb is too thin and the pattern would go to the right.

The comb is the most important element in the fit of the shotgun, and some-

The late Pete Kuhlhoff is pictured holding shotgun he used with skill derived from long experience. Among his last writings was this chapter on scattergunning which remained unpublished until now.

times a very slight change in stock dimensions can result in greatly improved pointing for the individual. However, before making any changes in a butt stock, it is of utmost importance to practice mounting the gun to make sure the diagnosis is correct, and it would be smart to consult an expert.

Now that we know what to look for in shotgun fit, it must be said that most anyone, regardless of his or her physical makeup, can do very well in adapting to the configuration of the modern shotgun. There are exceptions. A short-armed person requires less length of pull so the heel of the stock will not catch in the coat during the fluid motion of mounting and pointing the gun. With a stock that is too long, the tendency is for the right-handed gunner to shoot to the left, and vice versa for the left-hander. On the other hand, a tall person with long arms may need a longer stock than standard, not only for comfort but to overcome a tendency to shoot to the right.

Most persons begin their shooting career with the rifle, usually as a youngster with the .22 rimfire. It has been said that an expert rifleman, more often than not, is a poor shotgun handler. This is not necessarily true. It is a fact that rifle shooting requires severely exact control of the arm and precise aiming. A rifleman, grooved in this concept of action, has to change his mental approach somewhat when shooting the shotgun. The scattergun requires fluidity of movement in pointing the gun rather than precise aiming—smooth coordination and control!

You can practice mounting a gun almost anywhere—even at home during the evening. Any small object can be used for an aiming point. The unloaded gun should be brought to the shooting position each time with the eye exactly at the line of sight. When the action of mounting is so well grooved it is almost automatic, it is time to begin actual shooting.

Here are some points to remember: The head should be held upright. As the gun rises and the barrel comes into line, the head moves slightly forward (not downward or to a tipped position) so the comb meets the cheek at the instant the butt plate firmly meets the shoulder. The cheek must contact the comb of the stock without variation in position or pressure to insure constant position of the master eye at the rear of the sighting plane. To shoot with the eye in any other position results in a miss. The swing in following the target is best accomplished by pivoting the body with a relaxed, fluid movement.

The majority of shotgun shooters keep the left arm fairly straight, with the hand well out on the forearm, for better control of the gun. Actually, an extended arm contributes to steadiness and uniform control of swing. If there is a tendency to shoot behind the target due to slowness of swing, bringing the hand back on the forearm can result in a faster swing at the muzzle because the hand travels in a relatively shorter arc of travel. This problem has to be worked out by the individual.

The trigger is not pulled with a steady squeeze (as with rifle-trigger pull, which is too slow for shotgun shooting), but with a sharp pull or slap. Pull may be described as a contraction of the muscles that manage the index finger, with the finger already in light contact with the trigger. Most game-bird hunters I know do not pull the trigger but slap it. They carry the gun with the trigger finger across the trigger guard. When a bird flushes, the safety is put to the fire position while mounting the gun, then when the gun is pointed according to the individual's particular way of shooting, the trigger is slapped. The finger is not in actual contact with the trigger when the sharp movement is started.

How is the gun pointed so that the fast-moving cluster of pellets will intercept the slower-moving target?

The very first shooting should be at a stationary target. And now is the time to pattern the gun to make sure the pellets are hitting where you are pointing. Put up a piece of heavy wrapping paper, 40 or more inches square. Put a black spot at its center for an aiming point. Now step off 40 yards, carefully mount the gun to insure that the eye is in the correct position, and pull or slap the trigger. Examine the paper. If the center of the shot pattern is quite some distance from the aiming point, the chances are that after mounting the gun, you moved your head one way or another. Put up another piece of paper and try another deliberate shot. With the pattern well centered on the black spot, you know that the gun shoots where you point.

Next, at the same safe shooting place, stick a pole into the ground and hang up a regulation clay target. Move back about 20 yards. Be sure you are standing with your feet fairly close together and with most of your weight on the left foot, which is forward with the right-handed shooter, and with the toes pointing slightly to the right of the target. Load your gun, deliberately mount it, and fire.

So far, what you've been doing is mainly getting the feel of your gun and the feel of the shot going off—and learning how the sight picture looks when the gun is pointing at a target. But the target has been stationary, and all this practice may seem like child's play. Well, admittedly, this part of the learning process really *is* pretty easy, but that doesn't make it any less important to become accustomed to the look and feel of mounting and pointing the gun and pulling the trigger properly.

After that, it's time to work on moving targets, practicing with a hand trap and a couple of cartons of clay pigeons in some safe location. This is more fun if you work with a partner, and it's also easier because one gunner can toss up targets while the other shoots. By taking turns—switching after, say, five shots—both gunners can get plenty of practice. Another very effective and enjoyable way to practice is to visit the nearest trap or skeet field, and I'll say more about that in a few moments.

But first, let's look at the problem of hitting a fast-moving target. What you're trying to do, of course, is to make the pellets in the shot charge intercept the target; that is, the pellets and the target must arrive at the same place at the same time. But you have control only over the gun—not over the shot charge once it leaves the muzzle. This means you must direct the charge effectively at the instant of pulling the trigger (and even afterward, in a way, because if you swing the gun past the target smoothly, with the kind of "follow-through" that golfers talk about, your shooting will quickly improve). No one can tell you exactly the right distance by which to lead a moving target. Every person's reflexes, coordination, and eyes are different; every person takes a different length of time—the so-called reaction time—to move the gun and pull the trigger, so the correct lead for one person would be incorrect for another. When you've practiced sufficiently, the correct lead will begin to be part of your natural reaction.

Meanwhile, concentrate on the obvious: The gun has to point above a rising target, below a falling one, and in front of a crossing one. That's the way to put the shot charge not where the moving target is but where it will be when the pellets reach out there.

Experienced shotgunners will tell you that there are three ways of accomplishing this feat. First, the "snap-shot" is made by shooting directly at a point ahead of the target so that the shot and the target arrive at this point simultaneously. The snap-shot technique usually is used as an emergency measure on grouse or other game fast flushing in thick cover.

Second, "pointing out" means swinging the gun muzzle ahead of the target at exactly its apparent speed, and far enough ahead to allow for the time of flight of the

Skilled shotgunner keeps his cheek against comb, butt snugged into his shoulder as he works pump-action—ejecting spent shell, cocking gun, chambering fresh load, and swinging ahead in one smooth motion for follow-up shot.

shot charge to the target, which averages about .12-second for #4 shot at 40 yards. A mallard duck, with a full head of steam, can fly about 10 feet in that length of time.

Last, "swinging past" is best with close-to medium-range shooting (20 to 35 yards), as encountered with a large portion of upland hunting—as well as on the skeet field, where targets are taken at 15 to 20 yards. The swing of the gun muzzle is accelerated from behind the target and the trigger pulled as the muzzle swings past the target, pointing on the target itself. How come, no forward allowance? Because there is built-in lead with this technique.

For the averge person, the time it takes to pull the trigger after the brain has willed the action—the reaction time mentioned above—is approximately 1$5 of a second. To this must be added the lock-time (mechanical delay time of the gun's firing mechanism), ignition, and barrel time, and the time of the shot charge in flight. The total time averages over ¼ of a second on a target at 25 yards.

During ¼ of a second, a black duck, mallard, or bobwhite quail, sizzling at 40 miles per hour across the front of a hunter, will move almost 15 feet. That is quite a forward allowance! But remember, with the swinging-past method of shooting, the acceleration of the gun muzzle is in relation to the speed of the target—the faster the target is moving, the faster the gun muzzle is moving as it overtakes and passes it. On a quartering target, the apparent speed of the target, at a right angle to the line of sight, is less—so the acceleration of the gun muzzle in its swing is less. Ordinarily, the automatic lead is built up enough for the shot charge to whack targets in stable flight.

The swinging-past method probably is the best technique for the beginner—bearing in mind that "follow-through" is a must. However, with experience, it is natural for a hunter to almost automatically use the method that is most suitable for the conditions at hand.

But regardless of the shooting technique,

after you have reached the point where you regularly powder quartering and crossing clay targets, you will do much better in the field than your pals who have not engaged in this kind of practice!

If the hunting season is closed in your area when you want to try your mettle on game, then shooting preserves may be the answer to your quest for good hunting. And there is nothing better than skeet and trap shooting for year-round practice. Skeet, after all, was developed as a substitute for field shooting. For good sport and to maintain top-level shooting proficiency, just keep that shotgun swinging all the year round!

Young shooter "smokes" clay target. After novice has learned to mount gun well and center pattern on stationary targets, author recommends hand-trap sessions—and year-round trap or skeet practice even for experienced gunners.

Sighting-in at Short Range 16

by Jack O'Connor

A generation ago, a cynical guide of my acquaintance told me that when his dudes arrived to hunt at least half of them brought rifles so poorly sighted-in that the best shot in the world shooting from a steady position could not hit a standing deer with them at 150 yards. Many, he said, brought rifles so poorly lined up that they could not hit a deer at 100 yards.

Hunters are better informed today, but many still believe that sighting-in a rifle is a matter requiring expensive equipment and a great technical knowledge. Many turn the job over to gunsmiths and to dealers that fit telescope sights. I remember one very sad story of a hunter who thought he had hired an expert to do his sighting-in for him. He was a busy executive, the president of a famous company. He regarded the desert bighorn sheep as a handsome and prestigious trophy and made arrangements with an outfitter I knew who took out sheep hunters in northwestern Sonora. For the occasion, he had a famous gunmaking firm build him a handsome .270 on a Model 70 Winchester action. It was a lovely rifle with a French walnut stock and a 4-power scope. Now this chap was pretty high-powered. He was used to giving orders and having them executed. He told the gunsmith to see that the rifle was sighted-in with the 130-grain bullet at the point of aim 250 yards.

The executive spent most of three weeks climbing around in some of the roughest, rockiest, most difficult mountains on earth, bumping into cactus, twisting his ankles, skinning his shins. In the process he turned down some fair rams. He wanted a real buster.

Then one day as his hunt was drawing to a close, he saw the ram of his dreams—a skinny old-timer with a pair of broomed and massive horns that seemed too heavy for his skinny neck and bony body. After a long and well-executed stalk, the hunter and his guide lay just under a rocky ridge peering through thin brush at the ram. He lay in his bed not much over 100 yards away across a narrow canyon. The hunter crawled up, took a solid rest over his hat against a stone, put the top of the post reticle in the scope right behind the ram's shoulder and squeezed off his shot. The astonished ram jumped to his feet and stood there. The hunter shot again. This time the ram got the message. He bounded over the ridge and disappeared.

Hunter and guide went gloomily back to camp. When they got there, the guide

took his client's rifle, rested it on a bedroll and shot at a spot on a giant cactus about 100 yards away. Instead of being three inches high as planned, the bullet was well over a foot above the point of aim. I wish I could say that hunter and guide resighted the rifle and pulled a nice ram out of the hat at the last moment. They did not. The executive went back to New York without a ram.

The moral of this depressing tale is that no one should depend on anyone else's word that his rifle is properly sighted-in. A further lesson is that the first thing anyone should do when he gets to the hunting area is to shoot his rifle from a known distance at something that will retain the bullet hole to see if the point of impact has changed during shipment. Good improvised targets for checking are a blaze on a tree, a conspicuous mark on a rock, a bull's-eye drawn or pasted to a box. Our executive took the gunsmith's word that his rifle was sighted-in and he failed to check when he got to his first sheep camp.

The gunsmith who builds a rifle or the dealer who mounts a scope or a receiver sight seldom has facilities for sighting-in a rifle by shooting. Instead he aligns sights and bore by putting the rifle in a vise and adjusting the sights so that they rest on an object seen in the center of the bore when looking through the breech. This is called bore-sighting. It is by no means a complete and satisfactory method of sighting-in, but it assures that the first shot will be on the target. The rifle owner can cut a couple of notches in a box to rest his rifle in, remove the bolt, and line up his sights by bore-sighting. Today most gunsmiths have collimators—optical gadgets used to line up the axis of the bore with the scope. Obviously, if the axis of the bore and the aiming point of the scope reticle coincide at the same spot, the bullet is going to strike nearby.

The simplest method of all for sighting-in a rifle is to shoot at short-range against some safe backstop. To use this method one needs no collimator, no vise to hold the rifle, no box with "V's" cut in it. This method of sighting is based on the fact that a bullet fired from a properly sighted-in rifle crosses the line of sight twice: once at short range and the other at the distance for which the rifle is said to be sighted-in—at from 150 to 250 yards, in the case of big-game rifles.

Most hunting-type scopes are mounted from 1¼ to 1½ inches above the line of bore. When the rifle is sighted in for big game the bullet rises until it crosses the line of sight for the first time at approximately 25 yards from the muzzle. The bullet continues to rise above the line of sight until the top of the curve of trajectory is reached. In the case of the popular .30-06 with the 180-grain bullet at about 2700 fps, this is at about 125 yards, where the bullet will be slightly over 3 inches above line of sight. The bullet then starts to drop toward line of sight. It crosses it at about 200 yards (the distance at which the rifle is said to be sighted in), drops 9 inches below line of sight at 300 yards, about 24 inches at 400 yards.

Knowing this, I decided about 30 years ago that shooting at the distance where the bullet first crosses the line of aim and adjusting the sights to hit the point of aim at that distance would be a quick way to make preliminary sight adjustment. This short-range sighting method has many advantages. It needs no elaborate equipment and it enables the shooter to get on the target with his first shot. Many a man has tried to sight in a rifle with a newly installed scope at 100 or 200 yards and has found it cannot even hit the target. No one can make a sight adjustment until he knows where his rifle is shooting.

So let us take our rifle with its newly installed scope. We go to some spot where we can fire against a safe backstop. We put up a target at 25 measured yards. At 25 yards the scope will be somewhat out of focus, but this makes no difference. We fire three carefully squeezed-off shots. At 25 yards they should be quite close together. Taking the center of the three shots as the point of impact, we measure the distance from it to the spot we aimed at. Let's say that our bullets are striking

two inches left and 1½ inches high. Since a minute of angle is one inch at 100 yards it is ¼ inch at 25 yards. Therefore our group is eight minutes left and six minutes high. Hunting scope sights have dials for windage and elevation adjustment graduated in minutes of angle. Some dials give off clicks as they are moved. The Weaver K2.5 and K3 click in half minutes, the K4 and the K6 click in quarter minutes. Supposing our rifle is mounted with a K4, we turn the dial in the "Right" direction eight minutes or 32 clicks and the elevation dial six minutes or 24 clicks in the "Down" direction.

We now shoot another shot or two at 25 yards for verification. Possibly we need a few clicks one way or another. The rifle is now fairly well sighted-in, but it should be checked and refined at 100 yards from a padded rest or from a steady prone position. Probably a little refining will be necessary to see that the group is centered and three inches high. Remember that any error made at 25 yards is multiplied by four at 100 yards and by eight at 200 yards.

This method of sighting-in at 25 yards and checking at 100 was first written about in my department in *Outdoor Life*. The W. R. Weaver company reprinted an article of mine on the subject and distributed tens of thousands of the reprints with new scopes. The company also sold a plastic sighting-in gadget that could be moved to show the point of impact of various cartridges when the bullets first crossed the line of sight at 25 yards. Such a gadget is useful to have.

The following table has been calculated to show the effect of trajectory over practical ranges when the rifle's sights have been zeroed for 100, 200, and 300 yards. For low-velocity cartridges an iron sight height of .8 inches is assumed. For modern high-velocity rounds the table assumes use of a telescopic sight mounted approximately 1.5 inches above the bore.

WINCHESTER-WESTERN CENTER FIRE RIFLE CARTRIDGE BALLISTICS

Cartridge	Wt. Grs.	Type	Muzzle	100 yds.	200 yds.	300 yds.	Muzzle	100 yds.	200 yds.	300 yds.	100 yds.	200 yds.	300 yds.
	Bullet		Velocity (fps)				Energy (ft. lbs.)				Mid-Range Trajectory		
218 Bee Super-X and Super-Speed	46	OPE(HP)	2860	2160	1610	1200	835	475	265	145	0.7	3.8	11.5
22 Hornet Super-X and Super-Speed	45	SP	2690	2030	1510	1150	720	410	230	130	0.8	4.3	13.0
22 Hornet Super-X and Super-Speed	46	OPE(HP)	2690	2030	1510	1150	740	420	235	135	0.8	4.3	13.0
22-250 Super-X and Super-Speed	55	PSP	3810	3270	2770	2320	1770	1300	935	655	0.3	1.6	4.4
220 Swift Super-X and Super-Speed	48	PSP	4110	3490	2930	2440	1800	1300	915	635	0.3	1.4	3.8
222 Remington Super-X and Super-Speed	50	PSP	3200	2660	2170	1750	1140	785	520	340	0.5	2.5	7.0
225 Winchester Super-X and Super-Speed	55	PSP	3650	3140	2680	2270	1630	1200	875	630	0.4	1.8	4.8
243 Winchester (6mm) Super-X and Super-Speed	80	PSP	3500	3080	2720	2410	2180	1690	1320	1030	0.4	1.8	4.7
243 Winchester (6mm) Super-X and Super-Speed	100	PP(SP)	3070	2790	2540	2320	2090	1730	1430	1190	0.5	2.2	5.5
25-20 Winchester High Velocity Super-X	60	OPE	2250	1660	1240	1030	675	365	205	140	1.2	6.3	21.0
25-20 Winchester	86	L, Lead	1460	1180	1030	940	405	265	200	170	2.6	12.5	32.0
25-20 Winchester	86	SP	1460	1180	1030	940	405	265	200	170	2.6	12.5	32.0
25-35 Winchester Super-X and Super-Speed	117	SP	2300	1910	1600	1340	1370	945	665	465	1.0	4.6	12.5
250 Savage Super-X and Super-Speed	87	PSP	3030	2660	2330	2060	1770	1370	1050	820	0.6	2.5	6.4
250 Savage Super-X and Super-Speed	100	ST(Exp)	2820	2460	2140	1870	1760	1340	1020	775	0.6	2.9	7.4
*256 Winchester Magnum Super-X	60	OPE	2800	2070	1570	1220	1040	570	330	200	0.8	4.0	12.0
257 Roberts Super-X and Super-Speed	87	PSP	3200	2840	2500	2190	1980	1560	1210	925	0.5	2.2	5.7
257 Roberts Super-X and Super-Speed	100	ST(Exp)	2900	2540	2210	1920	1870	1430	1080	820	0.6	2.7	7.0
*257 Roberts Super-X	117	PP(SP)	2650	2280	1950	1690	1820	1350	985	740	0.7	3.4	8.8
264 Winchester Magnum Super-X and Super-Speed	100	PSP	3700	3260	2880	2550	3040	2360	1840	1440	0.4	1.6	4.2
264 Winchester Magnum Super-X and Super-Speed	140	PP(SP)	3200	2940	2700	2480	3180	2690	2270	1910	0.5	2.0	4.9
270 Winchester Super-X and Super-Speed	100	PSP	3480	3070	2690	2340	2690	2090	1600	1215	0.4	1.8	4.8
270 Winchester Super-X and Super-Speed	130	PP(SP)	3140	2880	2630	2400	2850	2390	2000	1660	0.5	2.1	5.3
270 Winchester Super-X and Super-Speed	130	ST(Exp)	3140	2850	2580	2320	2850	2340	1920	1550	0.5	2.1	5.3
270 Winchester Super-X and Super-Speed	150	PP(SP)	2900	2620	2380	2160	2800	2290	1890	1550	0.6	2.5	6.3
284 Winchester Super-X and Super-Speed	125	PP(SP)	3200	2880	2590	2310	2840	2300	1860	1480	0.5	2.1	5.3
284 Winchester Super-X and Super-Speed	150	PP(SP)	2900	2620	2380	2160	2800	2290	1890	1550	0.6	2.5	6.3
7mm Mauser (7x57) Super-X and Super-Speed	175	SP	2490	2170	1900	1680	2410	1830	1400	1100	0.8	3.7	9.5
7mm Remington Magnum Super-X	150	PP(SP)	3260	2970	2700	2450	3540	2940	2430	1990	0.4	2.0	4.9
7mm Remington Magnum Super-X	175	PP(SP)	3070	2720	2400	2120	3660	2870	2240	1750	0.5	2.4	6.1†
†30 Carbine	110	HSP	1980	1540	1230	1040	955	575	370	260	1.4	7.5	21.7
30-30 Winchester Super-X and Super-Speed	150	OPE(HP)	2410	2020	1700	1430	1930	1360	960	680	0.9	4.2	11.0
30-30 Winchester Super-X and Super-Speed	150	PP(SP)	2410	2020	1700	1430	1930	1360	960	680	0.9	4.2	11.0
30-30 Winchester Super-X and Super-Speed	150	ST(Exp)	2410	2020	1700	1430	1930	1360	960	680	0.9	4.2	11.0

Cartridge	Bullet Wt. Grs.	Type	Velocity (fps) Muzzle	100 yds.	200 yds.	300 yds.	Energy (ft. lbs.) Muzzle	100 yds.	200 yds.	300 yds.	Mid-Range Trajectory 100 yds.	200 yds.	300 yds.
30-30 Winchester Super-X and Super-Speed	170	PP(SP)	2220	1890	1630	1410	1860	1350	1000	750	1.2	4.6	12.5
30-30 Winchester Super-X and Super-Speed	170	ST(Exp)	2220	1890	1630	1410	1860	1350	1000	750	1.2	4.6	12.5
30 Remington Super-X and Super-Speed	170	ST(Exp)	2120	1820	1560	1350	1700	1250	920	690	1.1	5.3	14.0
30-06 Springfield Super-X and Super-Speed	110	PSP	3370	2830	2350	1920	2770	1960	1350	900	0.5	2.2	6.0
30-06 Springfield Super-X and Super-Speed	125	PSP	3200	2810	2480	2200	2840	2190	1710	1340	0.5	2.2	5.6
30-06 Springfield Super-X and Super-Speed	150	PP(SP)	2970	2620	2300	2010	2930	2280	1760	1340	0.6	2.5	6.5
30-06 Springfield Super-X and Super-Speed	150	ST(Exp)	2970	2670	2400	2130	2930	2370	1920	1510	0.6	2.4	6.1
30-06 Springfield Super-X and Super-Speed	180	PP(SP)	2700	2330	2010	1740	2910	2170	1610	1210	0.7	3.1	8.3
30-06 Springfield Super-X and Super-Speed	180	ST(Exp)	2700	2470	2250	2040	2910	2440	2020	1660	0.7	2.9	7.0
30-06 Springfield Super-Match and Wimbledon Cup	180	FMCBT	2700	2520	2350	2190	2910	2540	2200	1900	0.6	2.8	6.7
30-06 Springfield Super-X	220	PP(SP)	2410	2120	1870	1670	2830	2190	1710	1360	0.8	3.9	9.8
30-06 Springfield Super-X and Super-Speed	220	ST(Exp)	2410	2180	1980	1790	2830	2320	1910	1560	0.8	3.7	9.2
30-40 Krag Super-X	180	PP(SP)	2470	2120	1830	1590	2440	1790	1340	1010	0.8	3.8	9.9
30-40 Krag Super-X	180	ST(Exp)	2470	2250	2040	1850	2440	2020	1660	1370	0.8	3.5	8.5
30-40 Krag Super-X	220	ST(Exp)	2200	1990	1800	1630	2360	1930	1580	1300	1.0	4.4	11.0
300 Winchester Magnum Super-X and Super-Speed	150	PP(SP)	3400	3050	2730	2430	3850	3100	2480	1970	0.4	1.9	*4.8
300 Winchester Magnum Super-X and Super-Speed	180	PP(SP)	3070	2850	2640	2440	3770	3250	2790	2380	0.5	2.1	5.3
300 Winchester Magnum Super-X and Super-Speed	220	ST(Exp)	2720	2490	2270	2060	3620	3030	2520	2070	0.6	2.9	6.9
300 H&H Magnum Super-X and Super-Speed	150	ST(Exp)	3190	2870	2580	2300	3390	2740	2220	1760	0.5	2.1	5.2
300 H&H Magnum Super-X and Super-Speed	180	ST(Exp)	2920	2670	2440	2220	3400	2850	2380	1970	0.6	2.4	5.8
300 H&H Magnum Super-X and Super-Speed	220	ST(Exp)	2620	2370	2150	1940	3350	2740	2260	1840	0.7	3.1	7.7
300 Savage Super-X and Super-Speed	150	PP(SP)	2670	2350	2060	1800	2370	1840	1410	1080	0.7	3.2	8.0
300 Savage Super-X and Super-Speed	150	ST(Exp)	2670	2390	2130	1890	2370	1900	1510	1190	0.7	3.0	7.6
300 Savage Super-X and Super-Speed	180	PP(SP)	2370	2040	1760	1520	2240	1660	1240	920	0.9	4.1	10.5
300 Savage Super-X and Super-Speed	180	ST(Exp)	2370	2160	1960	1770	2240	1860	1530	1250	0.9	3.7	9.2
303 Savage Super-X and Super-Speed	190	ST(Exp)	1980	1680	1440	1250	1650	1190	875	660	1.3	6.2	15.5
†303 British Super-Speed	180	PP(SP)	2540	2300	2090	1900	2580	2120	1750	1440	0.7	3.3	8.2
308 Winchester Super-X and Super-Speed	110	PSP	3340	2810	2340	1920	2730	1930	1340	900	0.5	2.2	6.0
308 Winchester Super-X and Super-Speed	125	PSP	3100	2740	2430	2160	2670	2080	1640	1300	0.5	2.3	5.9
308 Winchester Super-X and Super-Speed	150	PP(SP)	2860	2520	2210	1930	2730	2120	1630	1240	0.6	2.7	7.0
308 Winchester Super-X and Super-Speed	150	ST(Exp)	2860	2570	2300	2050	2730	2200	1760	1400	0.6	2.6	6.5
308 Winchester Super-X and Super-Speed	180	PP(SP)	2610	2250	1940	1680	2720	2020	1500	1130	0.7	3.4	8.9
308 Winchester Super-X and Super-Speed	180	ST(Exp)	2610	2390	2170	1970	2720	2280	1870	1540	0.8	3.1	7.4
308 Winchester Super-X and Super-Speed	200	ST(Exp)	2450	2210	1980	1770	2670	2170	1750	1400	0.8	3.6	9.0
32 Winchester Special Super-X and Super-Speed	170	PP(SP)	2280	1870	1560	1330	1960	1320	920	665	1.0	4.8	13.0
32 Winchester Special Super-X and Super-Speed	170	ST(Exp)	2280	1870	1560	1330	1960	1320	920	665	1.0	4.8	13.0

Cartridge	Bullet Wt. Grs.	Type	Velocity (fps) Muzzle	100 yds.	200 yds.	300 yds.	Energy (ft. lbs.) Muzzle	100 yds.	200 yds.	300 yds.	Mid-Range Trajectory 100 yds.	200 yds.	300 yds.
32 Remington Super-X and Super-Speed	170	ST(Exp)	2120	1760	1460	1220	1700	1170	805	560	1.1	5.3	14.5
32-20 Winchester (Oilproof)	100	L, Lead	1290	1060	940	840	370	250	195	155	3.3	15.5	38.0
32-20 Winchester (Oilproof)	100	SP	1290	1060	940	840	370	250	195	155	3.3	15.5	38.0
32-40 Winchester	165	SP	1440	1250	1100	1010	760	570	445	375	2.4	11.0	28.0
†8mm Mauser (8x57, 7.9) Super-Speed	170	PP(SP)	2570	2140	1790	1520	2490	1730	1210	870	0.8	3.9	10.5
338 Winchester Magnum Super-X and Super-Speed	200	PP(SP)	3000	2690	2410	2170	4000	3210	2580	2090	0.5	2.4	6.0
338 Winchester Magnum Super-X and Super-Speed	250	ST(Exp)	2700	2430	2180	1940	4050	3280	2640	2090	0.7	3.0	7.4
338 Winchester Magnum Super-X and Super-Speed	300	PP(SP)	2450	2160	1910	1690	4000	3110	2430	1900	0.8	3.7	9.5
†348 Winchester Super-Speed	200	ST(Exp)	2530	2220	1940	1680	2840	2190	1670	1250	0.7	3.6	9.0
35 Remington Super-X and Super-Speed	200	PP(SP)	2100	1710	1390	1160	1950	1300	860	605	1.2	6.0	16.5
35 Remington Super-X and Super-Speed	200	ST(Exp)	2100	1710	1390	1160	1950	1300	860	605	1.2	6.0	16.5
351 Winchester Self-Loading (Oilproof)	180	SP	1850	1560	1310	1140	1370	975	685	520	1.5	7.8	21.5
358 Winchester (8.8mm) Super-X and Super-Speed	200	ST(Exp)	2530	2210	1910	1640	2840	2160	1610	1190	0.8	3.6	9.4
358 Winchester (8.8mm) Super-X and Super-Speed	250	ST(Exp)	2250	2010	1780	1570	2810	2230	1760	1370	1.0	4.4	11.0
375 H&H Magnum Super-X and Super-Speed	270	PP(SP)	2740	2460	2210	1990	4500	3620	2920	2370	0.7	2.9	7.1
375 H&H Magnum Super-X and Super-Speed	300	ST(Exp)	2550	2280	2040	1830	4330	3460	2770	2230	0.7	3.3	8.3
†375 H&H Magnum Super-Speed	300	FMC	2550	2180	1860	1590	4330	3160	2300	1680	0.7	3.6	9.3
38-40 Winchester (Oilproof)	180	SP	1330	1070	960	850	705	455	370	290	3.2	15.0	36.5
44 Magnum Super-X	240	HSP	1750	1350	1090	950	1630	970	635	480	1.8	9.4	26.0
44-40 Winchester (Oilproof)	200	SP	1310	1050	940	830	760	490	390	305	3.3	15.0	36.5
†45-70 Government	405	SP	1320	1160	1050	990	1570	1210	990	880	2.9	13.0	32.5
†458 Winchester Magnum Super-Speed	500	FMC	2130	1910	1700	1520	5040	4050	3210	2570	1.1	4.8	12.0
†458 Winchester Magnum Super-Speed	510	SP	2130	1840	1600	1400	5140	3830	2900	2220	1.1	5.1	13.5

†—Winchester Brand Only
HSP—Hollow Soft Point

PSP—Pointed Soft Point
PP(SP)—Power-Point Soft Point
FMC—Full Metal Case

SP—Soft Point
HP—Hollow Point
L—Lubaloy

OPE—Open Point Expanding
ST(Exp)—Silvertip Expanding
FMCBT—Full Metal Case Boat Tail

RANGE TABLE FOR WINCHESTER-WESTERN CENTER FIRE CARTRIDGES

Cartridge	Bullet Weight (grs.)	Bullet Type	Muzzle Velocity (fps)	Sight Height Above Bore (in.)	Path of Bullet Above or Below Line of Sight (in.) 50 yds.	100 yds.	200 yds.	300 yds.	400 yds.	500 yds.
218 Bee	46	H.P.&O.P.E.	2860	1.5	0.0	⊗	-5.8	-24.5		
22 Hornet	45	S.P.	2690	1.5	0.0	+2.9	⊗	-7.2	-16.0	-29.5

Path of Bullet Above or Below Line of Sight (in.)

Cartridge	Bullet Weight (grs.)	Bullet Type	Muzzle Velocity (fps)	Height Above Bore (in.)	50 yds.	100 yds.	200 yds.	300 yds.	400 yds.	500 yds.
22 Hornet	46	H.P.&O.P.E.	2690	1.5	0.0	⊗	−7.2	−29.5		
220 Swift	48	P.S.P.	4110	1.5	−0.5	+3.6 / +0.7 / +2.2 / ⊗	⊗ / −1.5 / +3.0	−18.5 / −6.7 / −4.4 / ⊗	−18.0 / −15.0 / −9.2	−41.5 / −36.5 / −26.5
222 Remington	50	P.S.P.	3200	1.5	−0.1	⊗ / +1.7	−3.4 / ⊗	−14.5 / −9.4		
225 Winchester	55	S.P.	3650	1.5	−0.4	+1.0 / ⊗ / +3.0	−2.1 / +4.0 / −2.2	−9.1 / −6.0 / ⊗		
243 Winchester	80	P.S.P.	3500	1.5	−0.3	⊗ / +1.1 / +3.0	−2.2 / ⊗ / +3.8	−9.0 / −5.8 / ⊗	−21.5 / −17.5 / −9.6	
243 Winchester	100	P.P.(S.P.)	3070	1.5	−0.2	⊗ / +1.5 / +3.8	−3.0 / ⊗ / +4.6	−11.5 / −6.9 / ⊗	−26.0 / −20.0 / −11.0	
25-20 Winchester	86	Lub. Lead (S.P.)	1460	0.8	+2.2	⊗	−24.0	−79.5		
25-20 Win. H.V.	60	O.P.E.	2250	0.8	+0.8	+3.9	−11.5	−49.0		
25-35 Winchester	117	S.P.	2300	0.8	+0.6	+1.7 / +4.3	−7.8 / ⊗	−30.0 / −18.0		
250 Savage	87	P.S.P.	3030	1.5	−0.2	⊗ / +2.1 / ⊗	−3.4 / ⊗ / +5.3	−13.0 / −7.9 / ⊗	−32.0 / −25.0 / −14.5	−53.0 / −45.5 / −33.5
250 Savage	100	S.T.	2820	1.5	−0.1	+3.3 / ⊗	−4.2 / ⊗	−16.0 / −9.5		
256 Win. Mag.	60	O.P.E.	2800	1.5	0.0	+1.5 / +3.3	−6.6 / ⊗	−26.5 / −17.0		
257 Roberts	87	P.S.P.	3200	1.5	−0.2	⊗ / +1.5 / +3.9	−3.0 / ⊗ / +4.9	−12.0 / −7.3 / ⊗	−27.0 / −21.0 / −11.0	
257 Roberts	100	S.T.	2900	1.5	−0.1	⊗ / +1.9	−3.8 / ⊗	−14.5 / −8.9		
257 Roberts	117	P.P.(S.P.)	2650	1.5	0.0	⊗ / +2.5	−5.1 / ⊗	−19.5 / −11.5		
264 Win. Mag.	100	P.S.P.	3700	1.5	−0.4	⊗ / +0.9 / +2.6	−1.8 / ⊗ / +3.4	−7.7 / −5.1 / ⊗	−18.5 / −15.0 / −8.4	−36.0 / −31.5 / −23.0
264 Win. Mag.	140	P.P.(S.P.)	3200	1.5	−0.3	⊗ / +1.3 / +3.3	−2.5 / ⊗ / +4.0	−9.8 / −6.0 / ⊗	−22.5 / −17.5 / −9.7	−42.0 / −36.0 / −26.0
270 Winchester	100	P.S.P.	3480	1.5	−0.3	⊗ / +1.0 / +3.1	−2.1 / ⊗ / −4.0	−9.2 / −6.0 / ⊗	−22.0 / −18.0 / −9.8	−43.0 / −37.5 / −27.5

Cartridge	Bullet Weight (grs.)	Bullet Type	Muzzle Velocity (fps)	Sight Height Above Bore (in.)	Path of Bullet Above or Below Line of Sight (in.)					
					50 yds.	100 yds.	200 yds.	300 yds.	400 yds.	500 yds.
270 Winchester	130	P.P.(S.P.)	3140	1.5	-0.3	⊗	-2.7	-10.5	-24.5	-45.5
						+1.3	⊗	-6.5	-19.0	-39.0
						+3.5	+4.4	⊗	-10.5	-28.0
270 Winchester	130	S.T.	3140	1.5	-0.2	⊗	-2.7	-11.0	-25.0	-46.5
						+1.3	⊗	-6.7	-19.5	-39.5
						+3.6	+4.5	⊗	-10.5	-28.5
270 Winchester	150	P.P.(S.P.)	2900	1.5	-0.1	⊗	-3.5	-13.0	-30.0	
						+1.8	⊗	-7.9	-23.0	
						+4.4	+5.3	⊗	-12.5	
284 Winchester	125	P.P.(S.P.)	3200	1.5	-0.3	⊗	-2.7	-10.5	-25.0	-48.0
						+1.3	⊗	-6.7	-20.0	-41.0
						+3.6	+4.4	⊗	-11.0	-30.0
284 Winchester	150	P.P.(S.P.)	2900	1.5	-0.2	⊗	-3.5	-13.0	-30.0	
						+1.8	⊗	-7.9	-23.0	
						+4.4	+5.2	⊗	-12.5	
7mm Mauser	175	P.P.(S.P.)	2490	1.5	0.0	⊗	-5.8	-21.0		
						+2.9	⊗	-12.5		
7mm Remington Magnum	150	P.P.(S.P.)	3260	1.5	-0.3	⊗	-2.5	-9.8	-23.0	-43.0
						+1.2	⊗	-6.0	-18.0	-36.5
						+3.3	+4.0	⊗	-9.7	-26.5
7mm Remington Magnum	175	P.P.(S.P.)	3070	1.5	-0.2	⊗	-3.3	-12.5	-29.0	
						+1.6	⊗	-7.5	-22.5	
						+4.2	+5.0	⊗	-12.5	
30 Carbine	110	H.S.P.	1980	0.8	+1.0	⊗	-13.5	-49.0		
30-30 Winchester	150	P.P.(S.P.),S.T., O.P.E.&H.P.	2410	0.8	+0.5	⊗	-7.4	-26.5		
						+3.7	⊗	-15.5		
30-30 Winchester	150	P.P.(S.P.),S.T., O.P.E.&H.P.	2410	1.5	+0.1	⊗	-6.7	-25.5		
						+3.3	⊗	-15.0		
30-30 Winchester	170	P.P.(S.P.),S.T. &F.M.C.	2220	0.8	+0.8	⊗	-8.3	-30.0		
						+4.1	⊗	-17.5		
30-30 Winchester	170	P.P.(S.P.),S.T. &F.M.C.	2220	1.5	+0.4	⊗	-7.6	-28.5		
						+3.8	⊗	-17.0		
30 Remington	170	S.T.	2120	0.8	+0.7	⊗	-9.6	-34.0		
						+4.8	⊗	-19.5		
30-06 Springfield	110	P.S.P.	3370	1.5	-0.2	⊗	-2.9	-12.5	-31.0	
						+1.4	⊗	-8.0	-25.5	
						+4.1	+5.4	⊗	-14.5	
30-06 Springfield	125	P.S.P.	3200	1.5	-0.2	⊗	-3.0	-11.5	-27.0	-51.5
						+1.5	⊗	-7.1	-21.0	-44.0
						+3.9	+4.7	⊗	-11.5	-32.0
30-06 Springfield	150	P.P.(S.P.)	2970	1.5	-0.1	⊗	-3.6	-13.5	-32.0	
						+1.8	⊗	-8.3	-25.0	
						+4.6	+5.5	⊗	-14.0	

Cartridge	Bullet Weight (grs.)	Bullet Type	Muzzle Velocity (fps)	Height Above Bore (in.)	Path of Bullet Above or Below Line of Sight (in.)					
					50 yds.	100 yds.	200 yds.	300 yds.	400 yds.	500 yds.
30-06 Springfield	150	S.T.	2970	1.5	−0.1	⊗	−3.4	−12.5	−29.0	
						+1.7	⊗	−7.6	−22.5	
						+4.2	+5.1	⊗	−12.0	
30-06 Springfield	180	P.P.(S.P.)	2700	1.5	0.0	⊗	−5.0	−18.0	−42.5	
						+2.5	⊗	−10.5	−32.5	
						+6.0	+7.0	⊗	−18.5	
30-06 Springfield	180	S.T.	2700	1.5	−0.1	⊗	−4.5	−15.5	−35.5	
						+2.2	⊗	−8.7	−26.5	
						+5.2	+5.8	⊗	−15.0	
30-06 Springfield	180	F.M.C.B.T.	2700	1.5	−0.1	⊗	−3.8	−14.0	−32.0	
						+1.9	⊗	−8.5	−24.5	
						+4.7	+5.7	⊗	−13.0	
30-06 Sprg. Wimbledon Cup and Super-Match	180	F.M.C.B.T.	2700	1.5	−0.1	⊗	−3.8	−14.0	−32.0	
						+1.9	⊗	−8.5	−24.5	
						+4.7	+5.7	⊗	−13.0	
30-06 Springfield	220	P.P.(S.P.)	2410	1.5	0.0	⊗	−6.1	−22.5		
						+3.0	⊗	−13.0		
30-06 Springfield	220	S.T.	2410	1.5	0.0	⊗	−6.1	−20.5		
						+3.0	⊗	−11.0		
30-40 Krag	180	P.P.(S.P.)	2470	1.5	0.0	⊗	−5.8	−22.0		
						+2.9	⊗	−13.5		
30-40 Krag	180	S.T.	2470	1.5	0.0	⊗	−5.5	−19.0		
						+2.7	⊗	−10.5		
30-40 Krag	220	S.T.	2200	1.5	+0.2	⊗	−7.2	−25.0		
						+3.6	⊗	−14.0		
300 Win. Mag.	150	P.P.(S.P.)	3400	1.5	−0.3	⊗	−2.2	−9.2	−22.0	−42.5
						+1.1	⊗	−5.9	−17.5	−37.0
						+3.1	+3.9	⊗	−9.8	−27.0
300 Win. Mag.	180	P.P.(S.P.)	3070	1.5	−0.2	⊗	−2.8	−10.5	−24.5	−45.0
						+1.4	⊗	−6.5	−19.0	−38.0
						+3.6	+4.4	⊗	−10.0	−27.0
300 H&H Mag.	150	S.T.	3190	1.5	−0.2	⊗	−2.8	−10.5	−25.0	−46.5
						+1.4	⊗	−6.4	−19.0	−39.5
						+3.5	+4.3	⊗	−10.5	−29.0
300 H&H Mag.	180	S.T.	2920	1.5	−0.1	⊗	−3.2	−12.0	−28.5	−52.5
						+1.6	⊗	−7.3	−22.0	−44.5
						+4.0	+4.9	⊗	−12.0	−32.5
300 H&H Mag.	220	S.T.	2620	1.5	0.0	⊗	−4.6	−17.0		
						+2.3	⊗	−10.0		
300 Savage	150	P.P.(S.P.)	2670	1.5	0.0	⊗	−4.8	−17.5		
						+2.4	⊗	−10.5		
300 Savage	150	S.T.	2670	1.5	0.0	⊗	−4.8	−16.5		
						+2.4	⊗	−9.5		
300 Savage	180	P.P.(S.P.)	2370	1.5	0.0	⊗	−6.9	−24.0		
						+3.4	⊗	−13.5		

Cartridge	Bullet Weight (grs.)	Bullet Type	Muzzle Velocity (fps)	Sight Height Above Bore (in.)	Path of Bullet Above or Below Line of Sight (in.)					
					50 yds.	100 yds.	200 yds.	300 yds.	400 yds.	500 yds.
300 Savage	180	S.T.	2370	1.5	+0.1	⊗	−5.9	−21.0		
						+2.9	⊗	−12.0		
303 Savage	190	S.T.	1980	0.8	+0.9	⊗	−11.0	−39.0		
303 British	180	P.P.(S.P.)	2540	1.5	0.0	⊗	−5.2	−18.0		
						+2.6	⊗	−10.0		
308 Winchester	110	P.S.P.	3340	1.5	−0.2	⊗	−3.1	−12.5	−31.0	−53.5
						+1.5	⊗	−7.7	−25.0	−45.5
						+4.1	+5.2	⊗	−14.5	−33.5
308 Winchester	125	P.S.P.	3100	1.5	−0.2	⊗	−3.1	−12.0	−28.0	
						+1.5	⊗	−7.3	−22.0	
						+4.0	+4.9	⊗	−12.0	
308 Winchester	150	P.P.(S.P.)	2860	1.5	−0.1	⊗	−3.9	−15.0	−34.5	
						+1.9	⊗	−9.2	−26.5	
						+5.0	+6.2	⊗	−14.0	
308 Winchester	150	S.T.	2860	1.5	−0.1	⊗	−3.9	−14.0	−33.0	
						+1.9	⊗	−8.2	−25.0	
						+4.7	+5.5	⊗	−14.0	
308 Winchester	180	P.P.(S.P.)	2610	1.5	0.0	⊗	−5.4	−19.5		
						+2.7	⊗	−11.5		
308 Winchester	180	S.T.	2610	1.5	0.0	⊗	−4.4	−16.5		
						+2.2	⊗	−10.0		
308 Winchester	200	S.T.	2450	1.5	0.0	⊗	−5.8	−20.0		
						+2.9	⊗	−11.5		
32 Win. Spec.	170	P.P.(S.P.)&S.T.	2280	0.8	+0.6	⊗	−8.6	−31.0		
						+4.3	⊗	−18.0		
32 Remington	170	S.T.	2120	0.8	+0.7	⊗	−9.2	−32.5		
						+4.6	⊗	−18.5		
32-20 Winchester	100	Lub. Lead, &S.P.	1290	0.8	+2.8	⊗	−30.0	−97.5		
32-20 Win. H.V.	80	O.P.E.	2100	0.8	+1.0	⊗	−16.5	−58.5		
32-40 Winchester	165	S.P.	1440	0.8	+2.0	⊗	−21.5	−70.5		
8mm Mauser (8x57; 7.9)	200	P.P.(S.P.)	2320	0.8	+0.6	⊗	−8.0	−27.0		
						+4.0	⊗	−15.0		
338 Win. Mag.	200	P.P.(S.P.)	3000	1.5	−0.2	⊗	−3.3	−12.5	−29.0	−54.5
						+1.7	⊗	−7.6	−22.5	−46.0
						+4.2	+5.0	⊗	−12.5	−33.5
338 Win. Mag.	250	S.T.	2700	1.5	−0.1	⊗	−4.4	−16.0	−37.5	
						+2.2	⊗	−9.5	−28.5	
						+5.4	+6.4	⊗	−16.0	
338 Win. Mag.	300	P.P.(S.P.)	2450	1.5	+0.1	⊗	−6.0	−21.5		
						+3.0	⊗	−12.5		
348 Winchester	200	S.T.	2530	0.8	+0.3	⊗	−6.4	−21.5		
						+3.2	⊗	−12.0		
35 Remington	200	P.P.(S.P.)&S.T.	2100	0.8	+0.8	⊗	−11.0	−39.5		

Cartridge	Bullet Weight (grs.)	Bullet Type	Muzzle Velocity (fps)	Sight Height Above Bore (in.)	Path of Bullet Above or Below Line of Sight (in.)					
					50 yds.	100 yds.	200 yds.	300 yds.	400 yds.	500 yds.
351 Win. Self-Ldg.	180	F.M.C.&S.P.	1850	0.8	+1.2	⊗	−14.5	−52.0		
358 Winchester	200	S.T.	2530	1.5	0.0	⊗	−6.0	−21.0		
358 Winchester	250	S.T.	2250	1.5	+0.2	+3.0	⊗	−12.0		
375 H&H Magnum	270	P.P.(S.P.)	2740	0.8	+0.3	⊗	−4.7	−17.0	−35.0	
				1.5	0.0	+3.5	−4.0	−9.8	−27.0	
						+5.2	+6.3	⊗	−14.5	
						+2.3		−15.5		
						+2.0		−9.5		
375 H&H Magnum	300	S.T.	2550	0.8	+0.4	⊗	−5.9	−19.5		
				1.5	0.0	+2.9	−5.2	−11.0		
								−18.5		
								−10.5		
375 H&H Magnum	300	F.M.C.	2550	0.8	+0.4	⊗	−6.4	−22.0		
				1.5	0.0	+3.2	−5.7	−12.5		
						⊗		−21.0		
						+2.8		−12.0		
38-40 Winchester	180	S.P.	1330	0.8	+2.7	⊗	−29.0	−94.0		
38-55 Winchester	255	S.P.	1320	0.8	+2.5	⊗	−25.0	−18.5		
44 Magnum Super-X	240	H.S.P.	1750	0.8	+1.4	⊗	−18.5	−64.0		
44-40 Winchester	200	S.P.	1310	0.8	+2.8	⊗	−29.5	−95.5		
45-70 Government	405	S.P.	1320	0.8	+2.5	⊗	−25.0	−81.5		
458 Win. Mag.	500	F.M.C.	2130	0.8	+0.7	⊗	−9.0	−29.5		
				1.5	+0.3	+4.5	⊗	−16.0		
						+4.1	−8.3	−28.0		
						⊗		−15.5		
458 Win. Mag.	510	S.P.	2130	0.8	+0.7	+4.6	−9.3	−32.5		
				1.5	+0.3	⊗	⊗	−18.5		
						+4.3	−8.6	−31.0		
							⊗	−18.0		

*Since this target was shot at
25 yards, minute of angle equals
¼ inch. Aim was taken at
center of upper left black square,
so group is centered ¾ inch
right and about 1¾ inches high.*

*Using pedestal and sandbag rest at
shooting bench, rifleman has
lined up scope and bore by bore sighting
and then fired a couple of 25-yard
groups to adjust scope. Now he
checks and refines sighting at 100 yards.*

Commonsense Gun Care

by Jim Carmichel

Several years ago I knew a fellow who had the best collection of fine guns I had ever seen. Winchester 21's, Parkers, and a host of other expensive models lined the walls of his gunroom and dazzled the eyes of everyone who came to see them.

Yet nearly every gun in his collection was in a state of almost total ruin! Not from lack of care, mind you, but *too much* care! Oil literally dripped from the mechanisms, and the beautiful stocks, many of them custom-made from the finest Circassian walnut, were blackened beyond beauty and weakened beyond use as a result of the steady soaking with gun oil.

Whoever opened one of his doubles and allowed the ejectors to snap back got a faceful of flying oil and his clothes well spotted. This was gun care at a terrible extreme.

At the other terrible extreme are the fellows who never give any thought or care whatever to their guns, allowing rust, powder fouling, grime, and dust to accumulate until the inevitable moment arrives, usually at the worst possible instant, and the gun ceases to function altogether.

Actually, modern guns require very little care to keep them in top working order. They're designed that way. In addition, they are designed so that the parts that need special attention on a fairly regular basis can be opened or removed quickly and easily. The trigger mechanisms of most pump and autoloading shotguns, for example, can be dropped out of the action simply by pushing out one or two large pins. Likewise, most shotgun barrels can be removed with little effort in order to get at all the areas that need cleaning and lubricating.

Proper gun maintenance requires only a cleaning rod, a soft wire brush, some powder solvent, a stiff brush such as a toothbrush, oil, and a fistful of clean rags. And here's how you go about it.

Shotguns are more easily cleaned if they are partially disassembled. This means taking the forearm off and removing the barrel from the receiver. In the case of single-shot or double-barreled guns, this is quick and easy. Pumps and autoloaders are a bit more trouble to take down, but not much. Also, with pumps and autoloaders it may be necessary to remove the trigger unit. Usually this means pushing out a couple of large, loosely fitted drift pins, or with some models, only taking out a single screw.

Small, stiff-bristled brush is
ideal for cleaning narrow recesses
and other hard-to-reach parts
of gun mechanisms. You don't have to
buy this kind of brush, because
any old toothbrush will serve nicely.

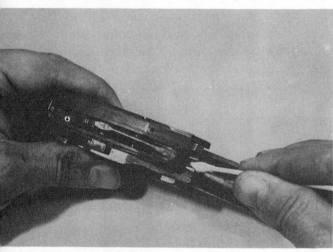

Another handy gadget for getting
into hard-to-reach crannies
is ordinary cotton-tipped swab. Just
take care not to leave bits
of cotton in mechanism. To probe even
tighter spots you can use toothpick.

You may need to give shotgun
barrels thorough scrubbing with either
bronze- or copper-bristle bore
brush in order to loosen lead fouling.
Then use clean patches to wipe
all loosened matter out of barrels.

The trigger mechanism doesn't require further disassembly, and in fact it isn't wise to do so. The idea here is to brush or wipe away all of the dirt and powder particles clinging to the trigger parts. A toothbrush works fine for the job. For the really narrow crevices a small probe such as a toothpick might be needed to pry loose the accumulated crud. A favorite cleaning tool of mine for scrubbing out delicate areas is a cotton-tipped swab such as a Q-Tip.

If the layer of grit and grime is especially heavy, you'll probably notice that it got that way because it had lots of oil and grease to stick to. So here you see firsthand one of the reasons why too much oil can cause trouble.

On some models of pumps and autos the bolt easily drops out once the trigger assembly is removed. If this is the case give it a good brushing and set it aside until later. Now brush out the inside of the receiver shell or give it a thorough wiping. But don't make the mistake of wrapping a thin cloth around your little finger and using this as a scrub brush. There are some sharp edges along the rail slots and other internal contours, some of which are worn to razor sharpness. Instead, use the old toothbrush or at least wrap a rag around something less precious than your pinky.

For cleaning the barrel, run a clean patch, well wetted with solvent, through the bore. This will soak into the fouling and loosen it up a bit. Next run a dry patch through the bore. If all the fouling comes out, you're mightly lucky. Usually there is some fouling and leading that appear as long, dark streaks. These require a bit more elbow grease to remove. Give the bore another wetting with the solvent and then have at it with the copper- or bronze-bristle bore brush. Usually, after a few

passes with the brush, followed with a clean patch or two, the bore will be bright and clean.

Now move on to cleaning the outside surfaces of the barrel. Pay particular attention to the locking surfaces and/or threads. Any grit will cause damage, and old oil should be carefully removed too. Stubborn gunk is easily dissolved with a rag dipped in the solvent. Also, if the barrel has a ventilated rib, run a lightly oiled patch through each of the open spaces. This is especially important if the gun has been exposed to rain. The vented rib is a perfect hiding place for droplets of water which will soon cause rust. If the shotgun has a gas-operated mechanism, be sure to clean the area around the gas ports and the piston. A hard fouling collects in these areas but is easily wiped away when softened with solvent.

Now, with the shotgun thoroughly clean, you're ready for oiling and reassembly. First of all, keep in mind that a thin film of oil offers as much protection as a heavy coating. A good technique for getting the correct amount of oil on your gun is to wipe it on with an oiled patch. Three or four drops of oil on the patch go a long way. Just give the metal a thorough rubdown with the patch. If a spray-can type oil is used, allow only a fine mist to settle on the metal parts; not so much that it streaks and runs—this will be much too much.

If you oil the trigger mechanism at all, make sure it is only a light spraying or wiping with the oily patch. If you apply oil directly from the can you will almost certainly use too much. Oil the contact areas of the moving parts only, so that there is enough there to see but not enough to run off. Any "runny" oil is going to run into the trigger mechanism and gunk things up good, and also soak into the wood and make it dark and ugly.

Finally, run an oily patch through the bore(s) and reassemble the gun. If the stock is dirty or water-spotted, give it a good buffing with a soft, clean cloth. An occasional waxing with a good grade of furniture wax will keep the stock looking new a lot longer.

Cleaning a rifle, either centerfire or rimfire, is much the same as cleaning a shotgun, except that you're dealing with a smaller bore size and, usually, much more stubborn fouling. For cleaning a centerfire barrel start off by giving the bore a good wetting with solvent. Let it soak for a few minutes and then scrub it with a *clean* bronze-bristled brush. Run the brush completely through the bore before reversing direction and make about ten round-trip passes. If the rifle is a bolt-action model, it is a good idea to clean from the breech end. This way there is little chance of the cleaning rod damaging the bore at the muzzle and causing any loss of accuracy. However, if your rifle is a lever, pump, or autoloading model you will have to clean from the muzzle end. Just be very careful to keep the cleaning rod from rubbing too hard against the side of the bore. In this respect be sure to use a cleaning rod with a slick surface, and by all means *keep it clean.* You can ruin a good barrel with a gritty cleaning rod!

After the brushing run two or three clean, dry patches through the bore and give your work a critical inspection from both ends, if possible. If the bore appears bright and shiny, you're all through, but keep a sharp lookout for any dark flaky-looking patches. These might be strips of copper-wash which have built up on the surface of the bore. Sometimes they ap-

pear only as small shiny lumps (especially if they've been brushed over a lot), only a thousandth of an inch, or less, high. These deposits play hell with accuracy, so get out the solvent and start all over. Keep on with the brush until the bore is cleaned to your satisfaction.

As a rule, a rimfire barrel requires little if any brushing. A solvent-soaked patch followed by a clean patch or two will almost always leave the bore nice and clean. If the bore should require brushing, however, do the job with a soft nylon or natural-bristle brush. Rimfire barrels are made of milder steel than are centerfire barrels and may be harmed by a harsh scouring with a stiff wire brush. Also, be extra careful to keep your rod clean.

After a bit of shooting, a fair amount of powder residue and related trash accumulates around a rifle bolt. All you have to do here is remove the bolt, wipe it off with a solvent-wetted rag, and wipe dry. And now is as good a time as any to wipe out the inside of the receiver with a dry cloth. If necessary, use a toothbrush to clean out thoroughly the various slots and contours. The chamber is best cleaned with a properly fitting chamber brush, but if you don't own one just wrap a clean cloth around a wooden dowel and wipe out the chamber as well as you can manage.

Now rub a light coat of oil on the bolt and run an oily patch through the bore. A spot or two of oil in the receiver at the operating points (where the metal surfaces rub together) is a good idea, but don't let any oil get into the trigger mechanism. Modern rifle trigger mechanisms are fairly complicated and work best when they are absolutely clean and dry. Oil begets crud, and pretty soon the trigger-pull is rough and inconsistent.

A final note on storing your guns is in order: Keep them in a dry, well-ventilated place and out of harm's way. Gun cases sometimes create and hold condensation, which can cause rust and corrosion. Likewise, the old-fashioned notion of sealing the barrel with a cork stopper is nothing more than a good way to trap damaging moisture in the bore.

The secret of good gun care is nothing more or less than good old-fashioned commonsense (which is said to be quite uncommon). The idea, simply stated, is to get the dirt and fouling out without doing any harm in the process. Too much oil or haphazard use of cleaning tools can, and often does, cause considerable harm.

Jim Carmichel's gun-cleaning tools and accessories include solvents, oil, patches, swabs, rods, and assorted bore and chamber brushes. He also uses furniture wax occasionally to protect stocks and keep them looking new.

The Muzzleloading Hunter 18

by B. R. Hughes

According to the National Shooting Sports Foundation, muzzleloading is the fastest-growing shooting sport in the United States today. Not only do a lot of folks try it; in most cases they get hooked for life!

There are a number of reasons why people turn to muzzleloaders for hunting. Perhaps the first of these is the challenge offered by such hunting. Whereas a person equipped with a flat-shooting centerfire rifle and a telescopic sight may take shots from 300 yards and beyond, the nimrod carrying a muzzleloader must try to get within 125 yards or so of deer-sized game—closer if possible—and he must make that first shot count, because with a front-loader that's probably all he is going to have.

It has been suggested frequently that sportsmen have turned to black powder in order to take advantage of special seasons offered by many states for front-loaders. This may be so, but personally, I'm opposed to special seasons for special arms. If a man has the faith and confidence in a muzzleloader, or a bow or what-have-you to use it in the field, he should have no qualms about hunting with it during the regular season. On the other hand, if he feels that his equipment or his skill is inferior, then he should either stick to more conventional arms or pass up hunting altogether.

There is no denying that many have turned to muzzleloading because of the sheer romance. We are on a national nostalgia kick, and while the black-powder movement may be related to this, the interest in muzzleloading is more than a passing fancy.

Another reason for the growth in popularity of muzzleloading hunting is the cost: A man can outfit himself for a very reasonable outlay of cash.

Since we are concerned with hunting, we will confine this discussion to long guns with rifled bores and shotguns. Handguns are interesting, but I don't think anyone should hunt with a front-loading revolver or single-shot pistol. Neither can I recommend a smoothbore musket for hunting. Also, if you are just breaking into the game of hunting with a muzzleloader, I believe you should shun flintlocks—quality flintlocks are expensive, and cheap ones are a

For black-powder buffs, half-stocked .50-caliber plains rifle makes fine match or hunting arm. With sensible loads at reasonable ranges, muzzleloading guns provide more than enough accuracy and power for deer-sized game.

waste of money. Moreover, I find them more temperamental than a percussion gun.

For small game such as rabbits and squirrel, there is a great deal of pleasure to be derived from the use of a .31 or .36 rifle. Unfortunately, while most people associate the use of a longrifle, which is generally termed a Kentucky, with such sport, there is not a single factory rifle of this type on today's market that I can recommend. The person desiring a quality Kentucky should either purchase a custom rifle or pay approximately $175 for a good kit and devote about 40 hours of dedicated labor to turning out a satisfactory longrifle.

Conversely, there are a number of quality half-stock muzzleloaders, generally called "plains rifles," as well as acceptable Civil War replicas. For small-game hunting, my recommendation would have to be the Thompson/Center Seneca in .36 caliber. This gun retails for less than $210. For hunting larger game such as deer, black bear, elk, caribou, and moose, you'll need a rifle of at least .50 caliber, and there is something to be said for larger bores. In

my estimation the best buys available today for the man wanting to hunt big game with a factory muzzleloader are the T/C .50-caliber Hawken, the Green River Lemans in either .50, .54, or .58, the Parker-Hale 1861 .58 Enfield, and the Navy Arms Zouave, also a .58. These are priced from approximately $140 to $225. Should Lyman elect to offer its Plains Rifle in a caliber larger than .45, it could be added to this list.

While lesser replicas that I have tested have not proved to be dangerous to use, many of them were inaccurate, possessed very soft inner parts that wore out quickly, and had extremely low-quality locks.

If you wish to compete seriously in muzzleloading target competition at the state or national level, you should know that it is necessary to spend as much as $400 and more to purchase a "ready-made" rifle that will win for you, but such an expenditure is not required for an accurate hunting rifle.

In addition to a good rifle, the muzzleloader will need black powder, percussion caps, a few pounds of lead, a mold of the proper size, some patch material, some type of lubricant, a ball starter, and some means with which to throw the desired charge of powder.

For any muzzleloader with a bore larger than .45 caliber, FFG powder may be considered proper, and there is no need to use the ultra-heavy charges of powder recommended by many. For target shooting, try one grain of powder "per caliber"—in other words, use 50 grains of FFG in a .50 caliber, 54 grains of powder in a .54, etc. For hunting, when using patched round balls you can double such loads, but when using Minie balls these loads should be increased by only about 1½. Hence, a suggested hunting load with a .54-caliber rifle using a patched round ball would be about 110 grains of FFG; with a Minie, the same rifle should be loaded with approximately 80 grains of powder. If such loads are incapable of handling the task, you should either (1) get closer to the game; (2) learn to place your shots more accurately; (3) get a bigger bore; or (4) forget about black-powder hunting.

The desired charges of powder may be premeasured and carried in small plastic containers, or a measure can be taken and used afield. A friend has discovered that a fired .45-70 case will throw just the right amount of powder for an accurate load in his .50 Hawken. A little searching should produce something equally inexpensive and acceptable for your rifle. I prefer to carry my powder in a flask; some hunters use small powder horns, and I have seen more than a few use the factory can. Under no circumstance should you ever use anything other than black powder in a muzzleloading gun.

When selecting a mold, you can generally obtain the correct size, if you do not know it, by informing the manufacturer or supplier of the make and caliber of your rifle. The best molds that I have used were made by Lee, Ohaus, and Lyman. Never use anything other than pure lead for casting either round balls or Minie balls. For most of my shooting I use a .490″ ball in my .50 Hawken and a .527″ ball in my Thompson/Center .54.

When shooting round balls, proper patch material must be used. The best is pure cotton, and synthetics should be avoided like the plague, as should old tee shirts, sheets, towels, etc. The fabric should be tough and closely woven, such as pillow ticking or blue denim.

The patch must be lubricated, and there are a number of good commercial preparations available as well as water-pump grease and Crisco. For hunting purposes do *not* use saliva, as it will dry in a relatively short period of time. This not only plays a role in rusting the lower portion of the barrel, but you'll find yourself shooting a non-lubed patch.

Shooting a muzzleloading rifle is not at all complicated. First, clean it thoroughly. Then you're ready to dump in the correct amount of powder. Next, place the lubed patch material over the muzzle, and position the ball in the muzzle. Push the ball down just below the level of the muzzle with the aid of a "short starter," which can be made or purchased for less than $3. Then cut the excess patch material away with any knife you have available and seat the patched ball over the powder with your ramrod. It should require firm but not excessive pressure to seat the ball. If a hammer must be employed, the ball/patch combination is too tight. If you are using a Minie, forget the patch and simply seat the lubed Minie ball over the powder.

Only at this point may you place a percussion cap on the nipple. Never load a muzzleloader with a live cap in place. The Civil War replicas will use a musket cap, while the others generally use a #11 cap.

Before going hunting, get plenty of practice, just as you should with any new rifle. When firing extended sessions at the range, you'll discover that loading will be easier and accuracy will improve if you wipe out the bore at least once every three shots or so. A patch soaked in Hoppe's on the end of a good cleaning rod, followed by a couple of clean, dry patches, will suffice.

Good-quality shotguns can be purchased for a bit less than rifles of comparable quality. A number of acceptable double-barreled percussion muzzleloaders are available at prices ranging from about $100 to $150. While single-barreled guns are available at lower prices, I much pre-fer the two-shot guns for wingshooting.

Loading and shooting a muzzleloading shotgun is simpler than a rifle. Some "experts" make a great fuss over proper wad selection, but paper toweling has proved perfectly acceptable in my experience. If you simply remember that the powder, wadding, and shot should each take up about the same amount of room in the barrel, all will be well.

One of my pet loads features 80 grains of FFG powder, a wad of paper toweling, one ounce of shot, and more toweling atop the shot to keep it in place. Not very scientific, perhaps, but out to 25 or 30 yards it will bring down the game. Since many front-loading scatterguns do not possess any choke, there is little advantage in loading more powder or shot in such guns. Should your muzzleloading shotgun have

At top is reasonably priced .50-caliber T/C Hawken, one of several good hunting choices. Rifle at bottom is .58 caliber; with lead ball and better than 100 grains of black powder, it will handle any American game at modest ranges.

This whitetail buck fell to .58 Texas Carbine. Projectile was Minie ball, which takes lighter powder charge than round ball. Hunters who use single-shot front-loaders understand importance of clean, one-shot kills.

choked barrels, a bit more powder and shot could extend the effective range a few yards.

Regardless of whether you're shooting a rifle or shotgun remember that black powder is highly corrosive, and a gun should be cleaned as quickly as possible after use. Boiling water with a touch of soap will do the job. Take the barrel from the stock and remove the nipple. The latter chore is performed with a nipple wrench, standard equipment with most quality guns. If you don't have a wrench you'll need to buy one, but they are very inexpensive. Now take the boiling water and pour it down the barrel until the metal is much too hot to touch with the bare hand. Set the barrel aside to cool, and clean the lock, wood, and nipple. Next run several dry patches down the barrel followed by a lightly oiled patch or two. Carefully clean the nipple hole and replace it with your wrench.

That should do it. Before shooting again, the barrel should be wiped with a clean, dry patch. With proper care a good muzzleloader should last a lifetime.

Should you wish to learn more about muzzleloading, you might consider subscribing to *The Muzzleloader,* published bimonthly by the Rebel Publishing Co., Inc., Box 6072, Texarkana, Texas 75501 ($6 a year) plus *Muzzle Blasts,* the official monthly publication of The National Muzzleloading Rifle Association, Box 67, Friendship, Indiana 47021 ($8 a year).

After you really get into muzzleloading, you may find yourself wanting to purchase such items as a buckskin jacket, moccasins, a tomahawk, flint and steel, and a lot of other equipment. On the other hand, only that described previously is essential for a lifetime of enjoyment. Whichever trail you travel, I'll wager you'll never regret venturing into the muzzleloading field.

Welcome to Bowhunting

by Fred Bear

19

Archery is perhaps man's oldest sport, and hunting with the bow goes back in history nearly 50,000 years. When primitive man realized that his physical strength, unaided, was insufficient to throw spears great distances, he made arrows (small spears) and, by stretching sinew or vine between the two ends of a stick, made the first bows.

Today, archery equipment is much more refined, but the hunting styles haven't changed very much. Man still needs some stalking and tracking ability, patience, perseverance, and, at times, even courage. But most of all he has to like hunting—not necessarily taking game—but hunting itself. For there is no thrill quite like that which comes from pitting your skill against wildlife in its own environment and getting within bow range. To me, that is the real sport, the true thrill of hunting with bow and arrow. I trust that you will find the same quiet enjoyment in bowhunting that I do, the pleasure of being outdoors, being in, and one with, nature, and the memories that grow with each passing season.

However, you first need an idea of how to approach the sport, so let's take it step by step, starting with your equipment or, as archers call it, tackle.

Many states have minimum bow weight requirements for the deer hunter. Generally, the minimum is 35 pounds, but ideally, if you can handle it, your bow weight should be between 40 and 50 pounds. With practice, most men can handle these weights rather quickly. The type of bow you buy depends pretty much on your personal preference and pocketbook. My choice is a 60-inch take-down model, but many hunters prefer a shorter 48- or 52-inch bow for brush shooting. While glass-and-wood laminated bows are faster and more accurate, many beginning hunters get excellent results with the less expensive solid-glass bows.

Your bow comes to you with the proper string for that particular model. A good idea when hunting is to carry an extra string which you have already used on the bow and on which you have established a nocking point. Your bowstring will last longer if protected with a good grade of string wax.

Hunting arrows are available in wood, fiberglass, or aluminum. My personal choice is an aluminum arrow with a screw-

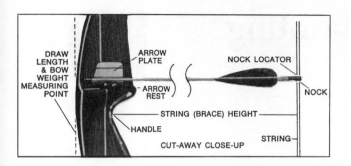

Diagram shows bow-and-arrow setup and indicates one method of measuring your correct arrow length: At full draw, point of your nocked arrow should reach to front of arrow rest above handle.

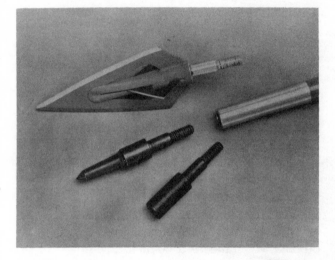

Interchangeable "Converta-Points" screw into this Bear arrow quickly and without tools, so one arrow gives you big-game Rasorhead, small-game blunt point, and tapered practice point. All three points are matched in weight.

Fred Bear prepares to draw arrow in hunting bow. Note that additional arrows are kept handy in attached bow quiver. Bear is noted for expertise in taking big game with a bow; he holds six world bowhunting records.

in head. A set usually consists of six broadheads and six field points, all the same weight and thus interchangeable. It is much better to practice with a head the same weight as your hunting head. Note: Be sure that your arrows are spine- (stiffness-) and weight-matched to your bow. Never use an arrow that you can draw beyond the front of the arrow shelf.

I prefer a broadhead hunting head with a disposable insert. I have found it to be the most effective, most humane hunting head available, for it causes more hemorrhage and has more cutting action. Any hunting head, however, must be kept sharp. Factory-sharpened hunting heads should always be touched up a bit before using. The steel in my favorite broadhead is of the finest grade, tempered to just under file hardness. The heads leave the factory ground with a wide bevel, but should receive additional attention before they are used on game.

A very satisfactory cutting edge can be obtained with a medium, single-cut mill file. File toward the point of the main blade with the insert removed. Try to get a long bevel like that of a knife, and continue to stroke the edges from all four sides. Finish this sharpening with light strokes toward the cutting edge to remove the wire edge that results from your filing.

Special attention should be given to the very tip. It should have a rather blunt, chisellike point, not a long slender point, as this may turn and curl when hitting hard bone. Serrated edges on a broadhead should be avoided. While they look wicked, the teeth fill with hair, tallow, and tissue and thus impede clean cutting and penetration.

Except for practice, never use broadheads without the insert blades. The insert blade is purposely thin, designed to cut like a razor and yet fold or break off if heavy bones are struck, allowing greater penetration. The inserts are designed to be expendable but can be sharpened, if necessary, in the same manner as the main blade. Care should be taken not to dull the insert blade when fitting it into the head.

Do not make the mistake of dulling sharp broadheads by letting them jostle together in a leather quiver, sticking extra arrows in the ground at a stand, or even snipping off stems as you walk along. The head must be razor sharp at the instant it hits the game. Wiping the heads with an oily cloth will not only keep the edges free from rust, but will also aid penetration.

There are a few basic accessories every bowhunter needs. First is a quiver. I like the type that fastens on the bow, either the snap-on, screw-on, or tape-on style. By all means, it should have a protective shield that covers your hunting heads, yet leaves your arrows ready for instant use. If your bow does not have camouflage paint, the limbs should be covered with slip-on camouflage sleeves so that reflection from the bright finish won't spook your game. Another good idea is brush buttons, which slip easily onto the string and prevent your bow from snagging on the brush. I would also suggest string silencers to dampen the hum when you shoot.

An armguard will help protect your arm and keep your sleeve from interfering with the bowstring. What you wear on your string hand is a matter of personal choice. The field glove or the bowhunter's glove are both adequate for the job. Lastly, I would recommend camouflage makeup cream to hide the bright shine of your face and back of your hands. Camouflage clothing is also recommended, but any clothing that blends in with the area you are hunting will do.

Practice is essential, both to tone up the muscles used in archery and to become used to your equipment. A good idea is to start your practicing several months before you plan on hunting. Shoot just a few arrows a day, or until you have trouble holding the bow at full draw. Shoot at varying distances from your target, and use the same arrow and point weight you will use in hunting. Don't just shoot *at* a target, always pick a particular aiming point.

It is a good idea to begin planning a hunt several weeks before the season opens. If possible, visit the intended area and look for deer trails linking feeding areas, drinking spots, shelter areas and bedding places. A little research on the favorite foods and cover of the species of game to be hunted is necessary. Check for sites where you can get broadside views of deer trails. Maybe the area has distinctive wind patterns. Which way will you enter? How will you cross or skirt openings? Travel the few extra miles necessary to get into rougher country, even if you don't know it very well.

Go into your hunting grounds against the wind if you can. If there is little wind, remember that air flows up the slopes when it's warm and into low places during the cool hours of the day. Since the best times for still-hunting are in early morning and late afternoon, when the game itself is on the move, stick to high ground most of the time. Always move against or quartering into the breeze. Seldom can deer be approached downwind to within arrow range. Remember that when a deer is about to bed down he will travel into the wind for a short time before choosing a spot. When he does lie down he will face his back trail. Thus he relies on scent or hearing to check his back trail and trusts his eyes to spot danger in front of him.

When stalking, remember this cardinal rule: never step on anything you can step over. Secondly, take several steps and stop. After some experience you will be able to train your eyes to pick several steps ahead at a glance. No game will ever be sighted if all attention is paid to where you step. Applying the first rule will aid in noiseless approach. The second gives you the advantage of seeing the animal before it sees you. Thus you can take advantage of the fact that, while game is quick to see movement, it does not seem to be able to pick out motionless objects from the rest of the scenery. If deer do not smell you and you remain motionless, even in the open, your presence will often go unnoticed by feeding or passing deer. The advantage then reverts to the hunter; he can plan the pursuit instead of hunting by luck and hope.

And there is a third rule: Don't look in open places for deer. Look at small openings between trees and through brush, and try to single out a piece of deer—maybe his ears, his head, legs, or rump. Don't make the mistake of only watching in front of you. Allow your eyes to rove from side to side, over every single bit of cover. And don't just look—*see* what you are looking at. If you spot an object which might be a part of a deer, study it closely. Look for patches of color that are out of place in their surroundings, and be especially alert to any movements, no matter how small. A flick of an ear or a movement of the tail may focus your attention on a spot, and suddenly the entire outline of an animal will take shape.

Dry leaves, twigs, and gravel are murder, and shortcuts of any variety are usually fatal mistakes. Once you lose sight of your quarry after beginning a stalk, you must always assume the animal is still there. Never doubt that for a moment or you will find yourself doing things you shouldn't, like taking shortcuts. That tremendous temptation to hurry must be curbed. Never relax vigilance for a moment. When necessary, get down on your hands and knees to see under tree limbs. A bowhunter, like animals, should always use every available particle of cover, for it helps break up that telltale silhouette.

Great attention should be paid to items you wouldn't otherwise give a thought to. Trousers must be of soft material which will not rustle. Loose objects allowed to jingle in pockets are out. Extra equipment carried should be strapped securely to your body. A soft arrow plate on your bow and silencers on the bowstring are "musts." A camouflage suit, or at least clothing of dull neutral colors, is a big help.

Don't stay in camp during wet or stormy weather. Such times provide excellent opportunities for a silent approach. On such a day the animal has to rely chiefly on sight for protection and this is sometimes dimmed by raindrops on its eyelashes.

The hour after dawn is the very best time of all for stalking deer. After feeding undisturbed most of the night deer are much less wary, are on the move toward bedding grounds, feeding slowly as they go, and keep their heads down more than at any other time of the day. If you can find an area with trails or old logging roads running through the travel zones, along which you can silently progress, your chances of getting a shot are good. Another trick to remember is that a browsing deer usually switches his tail just before raising his head to look around. If you are trying to close the gap on a feeding deer, watch his tail and freeze when you see it move. When a deer is located and a stalk begun, keep a sharp outlook for other deer that might be standing unnoticed nearby.

Many chances are lost because of an unseen deer warning the trophy the hunter is after. If a deer has discovered you before you are ready but is within range, slowly work yourself into position, draw, and shoot.

There is little doubt that the method of bowhunting offering the greatest chance of success is to stay in one place and let the game come to you. However, you can't just pick a spot at random. You have to find an area frequented regularly by the animals and be there at the right time of day, properly hidden and immobile.

Again, preseason scouting of your intended hunting territory is helpful. Fresh game sign in the form of tracks, droppings, beds, pawed areas and brush or tree rubs are the indications to be looked for. Trails mean little without fresh tracks. Runways that were good last year may not be in use this year because of a change in feeding and bedding areas. By close examination it is easy to determine how fresh the various signs of game are.

Your blind should be built overlooking either a frequented feeding area or travel routes between feeding and bedding grounds. As the blind is a hiding place from which to ambush approaching game, it must be situated so as to blend with the background. Do not build a blind right alongside a trail, but pick a place 20 to 30 yards to one side. It must also be situated in accordance with the prevailing wind direction. It does little good to sit in a blind with your scent blowing toward the area from which game is most likely to appear. If a really hot spot is found it sometimes pays to build two blinds, one on either side, so that no matter which way the wind is blowing you can wait with it either coming toward or quartering across your position.

Now as to the blind itself, there are several varieties you can employ, depending on the region you are hunting. But certain rules apply no matter what type you use. The blind must be large enough to let you swing your bow in any direction. It should be rather dense below head height so that your bow can be picked up and directed without being seen. Do not make holes in the blind to shoot through and do not impair your vision. Again, you must see the game before it sees you. Your head and shoulders must not provide a silhouette. Background material behind you is required. Approach your blind from a direction where deer are not expected. Do not walk on the game trails nearby. The telltale human scent will alert game and you may not get a shot.

Perhaps the most important rules in constructing a blind are these: Always use material coinciding with that found in the immediate area and, it is more important to have good cover behind you than in front. Do not haul logs, limbs, or brush and pile them up in a wall. This is an easy way to get material, but a wary buck instantly recognizes such an edifice as being out of place. The bowman who cuts a bunch of evergreen limbs and sticks them up in a grove of aspen or brush thicket is advertising rather than concealing his presence.

It takes patience to wait for two or three hours in a blind, and the only way to stick with it is to be comfortable. This usually means a sitting position. Therefore, if your blind is built on ground level, you need a piece of log or stump to sit on so you can remain almost motionless for long periods without strain. Also, leave enough room between you and the edges of the blind so that you can turn in any direction without getting a bow limb hung up. Game often

has a disconcerting habit of appearing from the least-expected direction.

In order to shift position without noise it is necessary to remove all leaves and twigs from the floor of the blind, and to check for overhanging limbs or twigs which might catch a bow tip. Two forked sticks, a foot or so in length and stuck upright in the ground, make a good rest for the bow. The two most effective forms of blinds for any game are those that get the hunter below or above the animals' "alert zone." A ground blind can be greatly enhanced by digging a hole waist deep for the legs, with a sitting shelf at the rear and about a foot below ground level. The blind can then be less tall and conspicuous than would otherwise be the case. Shots can be made by slowly rising as the bow is drawn, or from a kneeling position on the edge of the hole.

Undoubtedly, the most effective blinds of all are those elevated 10 to 15 feet above ground level, in trees or on platforms. They have the unique advantage of being out of the game's normal visual range, of carrying the human scent out over the heads of approaching animals, and of requiring almost no concealment for the hunter's body. Elevated blinds of any kind are illegal in some states, however, so check your game laws before trying this method.

The best times to hunt from a blind are the two or three hours after daylight and the last two or three hours before dark, as game is moving about more during these periods of the day. A good hunting method is to use a blind in the morning, still-hunt during midday, and retire to a blind again late in the afternoon.

A lot has been said about where to shoot large game with an arrow to get the best killing results. It is general knowledge that a hit anywhere in the chest cavity makes for the quickest and cleanest kills. Lung shots are the easiest and most effective of all for the archer. The lungs fill the front part of the chest cavity and so form the largest fatal area available. Heart shots are almost always fatal in short order. Shots have a tendency to go high for most archers, and any shot aimed at the heart which goes a bit high will get the lungs. A large arterial system serves all parts of an animal's body. When any one of these vessels is cleanly cut it is quickly fatal.

A hit in the liver is much like a lung shot. It can be almost instantly fatal. However, if you don't cut the large arteries which serve the liver and spleen, the deer may travel some distance before succumbing. But don't give up the trail. A shot through the rear quarters, which severs the large femoral artery, will also cause death before very long.

Regardless of where you think your arrow hit, do not follow the quarry immediately. Mark the line of flight by sight and sound. After a few minutes walk quietly to where the game was standing when the arrow hit. Look for blood signs. Light frothy or bubbly blood means a hit in lungs or in windpipe or carotid artery. Bright red blood without froth indicates arterial bleeding—also fatal. Greenish or yellowish matter mixed with blood means a hit far back in the stomach or intestines. A shot in the intestines is a poor one and calls for more waiting time and more patience in tracking. There are arteries serving this area, and if one of them is cut, your chances of finding the game quickly are good. The blood trail, however, will be poor. The one exception to this waiting would be if a heavy snow or rain threatened to obscure the trail.

It is one of the cardinal rules of sportsmanship that you follow an animal up as far as humanly possible, regardless of the circumstances. Much game is lost each year which, with a little more effort, might have been recovered. The man who goes afield with a bow (or a gun, for that matter) must, above all, be a conservationist as well as a taker of game. That is what we call a sportsman, in the best sense of the word.

Take-down bows like this Bear '76er have become popular among hunters. This model comes apart quickly so you can pack it conveniently, and you can buy interchangeable limbs—one set for target shooting, one for game.

Part III: Small Game

The Mightly Cottontail

by John Madson

20

The greatest game animal in North America isn't grizzly or moose, but the mighty cottontail rabbit. Hotfoot throws a very long shadow—he's been the hunting standby of millions of gunners and an all-age favorite for generations.

No one knows how many cottontails are shot each year, but the total runs high into eight figures. Yet in spite of this huge harvest, there are plenty of rabbits to go around. That's the big reason for the cottontail's popularity: He thrives in nearly all cultivated and wild areas and he's available in numbers to everyone. He's here, he's fun to hunt, and he has no peers in a hot skillet. Who could ask more?

Where is the *best* place to hunt rabbits? Find a lazy farmer and you'll probably find good cottontail hunting. Prime rabbit country is often farmland that's half asleep, with overgrown fencerows, old orchards, and plenty of grass, thickets, tangles, and food.

Cover is all-important. There may be plenty of waste corn exposed in winter fields, but if there is no escape cover nearby, the rabbits will not use those fields. During winter in most farm areas,

cottontails hang around weedpatches, farm dumps and buildings, windbreaks, and weedy fencerows. In clean-farmed countryside with skimpy field cover, most of the rabbits may be concentrated in the 40 acres around the farmstead with its buildings and shrubbery, rather than in open fields and naked fence lines.

Orchards, if they have thick clumps of grass and heaps of prunings, are excellent hunting areas. So are abandoned farmsteads with their ramshackle buildings, old fruit trees and patches of sumac, and rank grasses. Broken foundations provide hiding places, and grassy cover along old fencerows is used as "forms" for resting.

In deep winter, valley cornfields and other croplands may give you fine shooting, particularly after a wet season that has choked fields and fences with lush growths of weeds, grass, and young brush. Such lowlands may be the best places for midwinter rabbiting. After a siege of very cold weather, try little hard-scratch farms along creeks and rivers—weedy havens that lie under the wind and shelter rabbits that drift in from the barren uplands.

When the mercury really dives, hunting

may be poor. Rabbits, especially does, make some use of woodchuck dens all winter but mostly during cold snaps. So if you want to stay home because of the weather, rabbits probably will, too. But when a warming spell follows a cold snap, grab your gun and cut out for the weedpatch. The rabbits will probably be moving.

Grassy roadside ditches are often good bets. Places with long grass, plenty of woody shrubs along the fence line, and maybe cornfields beyond. Some hunters search out abandoned county roads that have either reverted to private ownership or have been forgotten by everyone but a few farmers and the county engineer. Such thickety roadways, bordered by open fields on each side, are ideal wildlife coverts that can often be located on county plat maps.

Piles of logs and brush are always interesting, so don't overlook any woodlots that are being cleared or thinned, especially if they adjoin food patches. Weedy waterways that extend from fields down into timber may also hold rabbits.

During deep snow, work into stands of young trees. Willow thickets may be very productive; they can carry heavy rabbit populations during snow when willow bark is the best and most available food, and shooting may be fabulous.

A few hunters along the Missouri River play a shrewd game in the vast willow bats of the river islands and sandbars. During deep snow they hunt from folding stepladders! These hunters look for areas where young willows about six feet high are laced with rabbit trails, and set up their light, compact folding ladders near the junctions of major rabbit "runs." While they sit on these ladders—eyes nine or ten feet above the ground—their companions walk through the area and stir things up. This trick might also be useful

Tennessee hunter rests on stump while he congratulates his beagle on smooth work with morning's first cottontail. Abundant nearly everywhere, rabbits rank as most popular game animals throughout this nation.

in alder bogs and young pine plantations where a gunner wants to rise above his environment.

Grassed waterways in fields may pay off in good shooting, and margins of potholes and farm ponds that aren't heavily grazed may have scads of cottontails. And don't overlook the centers of land sections where farmers may not take as much pride in "clean farming" as along the roads.

In many parts of the country there are still long strips of virgin wildlife cover—the rights-of-way of rural railroads. These are often rank with long native grasses, sedges, and shrubs, they lie beside woods and croplands, and they're perfect rabbit country. But such areas are private property and you should learn if hunting is permitted. Also know the state shooting laws; it may be illegal to hunt along your railroads.

Hunting probably won't be permitted along your major rail lines, but there are many little-used trunks where hunting will be allowed or tolerated, as well as some spur lines that have been abandoned altogether. Here again a county plat map is handy; it may reveal old railroads that are omitted from larger maps.

Above all, check with your state fish and game department on the locations of *all* state-owned hunting areas. There may be hundreds: lake and river access areas, recreational or botanical preserves, waterfowl and upland game areas, forest areas, state-owned lakeshores, riverbanks and islands, old gift properties that have never been "improved," and small farm-game habitat plantings that are open to private hunting. Every state has little-known public hunting areas, and they're worth exploring.

If it can be shot from the shoulder, it has been used to shoot rabbits. Anything goes in rabbit hunting, from .22 shorts to 12-gauge Magnums.

The most widely-used rabbit gun is undoubtedly the full-choke, 12-gauge shotgun throwing number 6 shot, simply because this is America's standard work gun. The number 6 pellets are excellent for cottontails, but the full-bored barrel may overgun a rabbit. Cottontail shooting is usually done at moderate ranges, rarely over 35 yards, and a tight shot pattern can wreck a rabbit's meaty haunches. For average rabbit hunting a modified boring or even improved cylinder is excellent.

A repeating shotgun is best; the cottontail can be a tough target and is often missed, for real rabbit hunting is a sort of low-level wing-shooting. A fast second or third shot may be needed.

Although the 12-bore gun is a gauge suitable for any farm game, 16- and 20-gauge guns are superb for rabbits—fast,

light, and capable of flipping a cottontail at surprising ranges. There are mixed opinions about the .410. Many hunters believe it's too light for rabbits, either mangling a cottontail within its limited range or only crippling them farther out. It does not have the latitude of a heavier gun and doesn't throw a dense pattern on longish shots, but it is ideal for a small boy on his first hunts *if* dad carefully prescribes the effective ranges and calls the shots.

Many hunters—particularly eager greenhorns—center their shotstrings on a rabbit's bouncing rump and pulverize the choicest meat. But some gunners have mastered the trick of shooting just far enough ahead or over the rabbit so that the fringe of the pattern catches the foreparts of the little speedster. It takes practice and a mental picture of pattern diameters at various ranges, but it pays off in satisfaction and undamaged meat.

If you can't do this, at least wait out your shot if the rabbit is flushed underfoot. Let him get out there 30 yards or so. There's plenty of pellet energy left at that range, and the pattern will be wide enough to compensate for any fancy footwork on the rabbit's part and still won't be so tight as to ruin good meat.

The .22 rimfire is a fine rabbit outfit, providing sport and a lightly-marked carcass. Maybe you like the autoloader, a fast pump, or a little tack-driving bolt action equipped with a scope. All are precision tools for the job of rabbit hunting.

Standard velocity ammo is probably best; hollowpoints are definitely not needed. The tender cottontail can be stopped with a .22 bullet anywhere in the body, for he's our most easily-shocked game animal, large or small.

Some expert riflemen use autoloaders with iron sights for the ultimate in fine riflework taking cottontails on the run. The shooter may not even be conscious of using his sights. He simply "feels" for the rabbit until he finds it.

But most rifle hunters like their rabbits slow, and a good method is to hunt a dense weedpatch or other heavy cover after a fresh snow. While the rifleman is on a stand, preferably a high position, a companion works slowly through the cover below and moves the rabbits along their runways. The rabbits hop leisurely with frequent stops and make sharp targets against the snow. With such a system, of course, you must always know exactly where your companion is and never move from your stand without telling him.

Or try ambling through lowlands with a scoped rifle on sunny, quiet winter days. Hunt country where grassy slopes and hillsides drop away from cultivated uplands and scan these south-facing slopes carefully for rabbits that are sunning themselves. It's most productive after a lengthy cold snap, and most fun if you take the rabbits at 50 yards or so.

Some riflemen like to just "injun" along a fencerow or field border, watching for rabbits crouching in their forms and plinking them at close range. Maybe it's potshooting in a sense, but it calls for sharp eyes and alert hunting and is how many of us got started in this hunting game. Sometimes it's fun to be a boy again.

In that regard, an ideal gun team is a father-son combination—the old man heeled with a 12-bore and the boy with a .22. Both will have shots the other can't take, and their two guns can meet any situation. A perfect team with young legs and wide-eyed enthusiasm on one side and experience and old, rekindled memories on the other.

Like any hunting, rabbit hunting is at its best with a good dog, and the finest dogs for the job are the beagles—lovable little hounds that live only for coursing rabbits.

Dense cover can be most effectively worked with a beagle, and this is particularly true before snowfall, when a rabbit is nearly impossible for a dogless gunner to hunt in thickets or deep brush.

And if one beagle is good, more are better. Hound music should always be sung in chorus and the merry tongues of several beagles will turn a routine rabbit hunt into a weedpatch symphony.

When started by dogs, a cottontail will usually follow established runways. Take position on a stump or knoll and keep your eyes peeled: The dogs will often push the rabbit within gun range. Better yet, head for where the rabbit was jumped and wait for him to circle back. He usually will, for rabbits aren't happy about leaving their home neighborhoods.

Good beagles will stay with a rabbit until it takes cover or is shot, and older dogs may be difficult to call in as long as there's action. Your best chance of catching the dogs is just after you've shot a rabbit and before they can pick up a new trail. Some hunters like "islands" of isolated cover where their beagles are restricted to a limited range and are easier to call up.

Whenever you work your dogs, they should bear your name and address on metal collar tags. Not that hounds get lost. Hounds are never lost. It's the owner who goes astray, and a tagged beagle will enable someone to find *you*.

The beagle is a work dog, a friendly little cuss that makes a splendid pet as well as a hunting companion. He's sturdy, intelligent, and warm-natured, and improves with use. It is almost impossible to give a beagle too much rabbit hunting, and some former field champions have had little training other than routine hunts. Usually, however, a young beagle will come along faster if he's run with an older, seasoned dog.

Now and then, dog experts to the contrary, small farm mongrels develop into really remarkable rabbit dogs. They're usually lowslung feists in a vast variety of colors and patterns, poking happily through the densest cover and trying hard to please the boss. Such dogs are inspired at the sight of gooseberry thickets, road culverts, and old farm dumps. At their best, they're alert, durable little tramps with a bawdy sense of humor. At their worse, they are far better than no dogs at all.

But if you want the best, you'll save time and temper by getting a dog bred to the job—a little rabbit-rousting hound that loves to hunt and sings with the joy of it.

Half-grown cottontail streaks across meadow in early fall. Natural causes eliminate large percentage of young, but long breeding season and high birth rate combine to provide surplus of rabbits by hunting time.

In high gear, cottontail bounds across open, snow-blanketed field as gunner swings ahead of erratic target. Full-choked 12-gauge is most popular gun, but rimfire rifle is also great, especially after fresh snow.

Jacks and Chucks— Tune-up for Big Game

21

by John Jobson

You may be a big-game hunter with scant interest in off-season shooting—but if you'd like to improve your trophy chances afield by becoming a cool and deadly marksman, then this is for you. There is no mystery or hard work involved. We sportsmen are blessed with a duo of made-to-order, animated field targets (needing harvesting) that consistently elevate so-so centerfire-rifle shots to lofty echelons of lethal precision.

It is a long-accepted and established fact among the hunting cognoscenti that the greatest big-game shots are those providential few who regularly shoot off-hand at running jackrabbits, and the topmost stars of open-country, long-range shooting are confirmed chuck hunters. These are the folks who collect trophies with consistency.

The training one gets while hunting these little rascals is highly *concentrated.* If a skeet shooter zeros in on fresh limes sizzling along at 200 miles per hour he isn't going to have much trouble hitting watermelons at 50 miles per hour, and if you counsel an aspiring long-range marksman to faithfully practice hitting walnuts at 300 yards he is going to be murder on coconuts at 100 yards.

Errors on jacks and chucks are easier to make than they are on big game. The rabbit twists and dodges like a deer could only dream of doing, and the chuck hunter's acquired skill at range estimation, wind, shooting positions, and delicate, precise trigger letoffs make him such a maestro that his hitting a big-horn ram in the chest at 275 yards would be like Einstein totaling a gin rummy score. The habitual centerfire pest/varmint shooter is always in good form. And if he gets in a few days of condensed rabbit/chuck practice shortly before departing for Africa, Alaska, or wherever, his skills are honed as keen as a boxer's reflexes.

Conversely, there are countless stories of the guy who plans and saves for years to make that hunt of a lifetime. Then when his long-coveted chance comes at last and he's facing that regal Dall ram, he shoots *and misses*—all because he didn't give himself adequate practice.

The fact is that in this country no man can any longer become a crack shot by shooting solely at big game, because there are just not that many opportunities. Fortunately, we do have jacks and chucks, which, by divine hunter's providence, are ample in number and actually are superior to big game for the purpose of making us accomplished marksmen.

No two rabbits dart over the landscape precisely alike. They bound, twist, go flat out, vary pace, and afford every conceivable chance to focus sharply into one supreme millisecond effort such assorted necessaries as safety off, mounting the rifle and accurately using the scope, lead estimation, muscles-and-joints response, trigger letoff, plus confidence—lack of which is called "buck fever." Incidentally, it's not vital to cosh every running rabbit, because an inch-or-three miss on them is a centered lung shot on big game.

There are two sorts of jackrabbits—whitetail and blacktail (though each has subspecies). The varying whitetail of the north-central plains (like South Dakota) is the larger. A good way to hunt both is with two or three buddies spread apace, like driving a cornfield for ringnecks. Whites usually hold well and when flushed, gallop and bounce until a near-miss turns them on to a gait as smooth as that of a whippet.

In comparison, the lean and hungry blacktail is smaller and inhabits an area so vast you might say it's the whole West. Ranging far and wide, high and low, he's our primary target jack and you'll find him in cactied Mexican deserts near sea level, mountain sage flats above 7500 feet, the interminable grass-rich plains, and points in between, including the runways of the Los Angeles and Salt Lake City International Airports. Spooked, they tear purposefully away, and their even pace while attempting to put landscape between them and you makes them the kings of moving rifle targets.

It does no harm to scrag all the blacktails you sportingly can. They have gargantuan, insatiable appetites, and a jack population can eat tons of food, polishing off an occasional alfalfa stack. One rancher told me that one memorable winter jacks put away 30 tons of his alfalfa. Besides, if they're not checked, the dreaded poisoner with his ghoulish bag of tricks depletes their ranks from 100 percent clear down to $99\frac{99}{100}$ percent, getting, alas, other wildlife too. When not harassing landowners, blacktails gorge on feed more suited to pronghorns and such. Sportsmen with rifles can never greatly affect jackrabbit population because these animals are incredibly stupid and nature's way of protecting them is to grant them extraordinary breeding powers.

My pet rifles for offhand jack shooting include a tiny .257 Roberts with a 6X scope and a 6mm with 6X (this one a .220 Swift until the barrel wore out and my friend P.O. Ackley rebored to 6mm). With the main magazine filler plate judiciously yanked out, this is one good 6mm. Sometimes I fetch a little 7-pound .270 sheep rifle with 3X. Other regulars are a .22/250 with variable and a .222 Magnum with 4X.

If the running jackrabbit is the queen of training aids for big game going flat out, the king of assists for the long-range shooter at relatively still and slow-moving big game is the ubiquitous little rifleman's pal known colloquially as woodchuck, rockchuck, or marmot. He can teach you the fundamentals of game spotting, stalking, range estimation, shooting positions, and trigger squeeze. Succeed with him and you are a Rocky Mountain hunter who can repeat on grizzly, moose, caribou, sheep, and goat. You've learned binocular use and how to "see" wildlife. In hitting chucks, bear in mind that (again) his size compared to big game is enormously shrunken and he's most often shot at longer range.

You're seldom far from some kind of chuck. Sportsmen's club secretaries can arrange meetings with local chuck gurus, and so can game wardens and live-wire sporting-goods establishments. To find their habitats yourself, search the rocky outcroppings off highways, near lush forage of wild grass or hay, or better, some busy farmer's alfalfa patch. Permission is usually granted to polite, responsible-looking characters. East or West, strategy and tactics are much the same, but with more climbing for rockchucks.

My favorite rifles are a heavy 29-inch-barreled .270 with 10X, a .270 Weatherby with 8X, .25-06 with 12X, and 6mm 40XB with 15X. Because it is such a joy and gives me great pleasure, I often take my beautiful .257 Roberts.

In playing this game it's advisable to use the same action as that of your big-game rifle; and the same scope reticle, a good type being four heavy wires ending in fine crosswires. Efficiently versatile, this reticle.

Upstream to popular opinion, long experience has taught me that for me, neither the heaviest nor the lightest bullets available are best all-round for either jacks or chucks. I use 52- or 53-grain slugs in the .22's, 130 in the .270's, 100 in the 25's, etc.

Here in the mountain states we ole apple knockers have our frequent expeditions organized. While by no means essential, one fellow brings a motor home (else a trailer or coach), another a 4-wheel-drive. We sequester the motor home strategically

Blacktail jackrabbit tenses his powerful hind legs before taking off across Texas desert. Author cites jacks as furnishing top practice for any rifleman who may have to take shots at moving big game.

Just as jacks can improve your shooting at moving big game, chucks can hone your marksmanship on stationary big game at longer ranges. Here, two sportsmen use scoped bolt-actions on distant rock chucks in Utah Hills.

in some halcyon dell as a command post for eating, reloading, and resting. The 4-wheel-drive gets us in and out of remote spots to hike around in. We tote canvas coin sacks of ammunition, canteen, raisins, candy, and peanuts.

It comes to me here that once upon a time I carried away my little bride to Colorado on a three-month camping trip. There it came to pass that I fired several thousand .270 rounds at jacks which were peak-cycle that year and absolutely out of hand. I entered the big-game season that fall with the best shooting skill of my life, and near Salida, at the Buffalo Peaks Reserve, a gigantic gray, glossy, beginning-the-rut mule deer with spreading, highly polished antlers came barreling over an aspened crest 150 yards away, his magnificent nostrils flaring clouds of vapor. One

glorious unforgettable instant he was like that, the next he had, to my immense satisfaction, four feet in the air—the only movement in sight a few hairs floating downwind.

Out of Gunnison (near there) a trotting bull elk took one 130-grain .270 in the heart and went down within 100 yards. We cut over Rabbit Ears Pass on dirt roads into Wyoming and got sleek mule deer near Encampment, elk out of Dubois, and antelope out of Lander. From there we hastened to Oregon's Wallowa country for deer and late elk, and only the Wyoming elk took two shots, one not needed.

The experience made a true believer out of me, and I conceived a powerful adage which is known as "hunter's law," and goes: "To shoot big game, first shoot rabbits."

In rolling Eastern pastures and fields, woodchucks provide fine summer hunting, particularly at long range with heavy-barreled rifles. Chucks love clover and alfalfa but are also found among many other farm crops.

Squirrel Strategy

by John Madson

22

More than most other wildlife, the huge animal order *Rodentia* has lent color, romance, and humor to the American tradition. Our best-known rodents are, of course, the squirrels, and to hunters, the best-known squirrels are the gray squirrel and the fox squirrel. For generations these rugged and nimble rascals have been the first targets of American hunters.

There's a proper squirrel rifle for every hunter. To a soft-stepping farm boy, a mail-order .22 with iron sights is perfectly adequate. It doesn't lend itself to 80-yard shots, but most of the kid's squirrels are probably taken at 20 yards. On the next ridge you may meet a hunter with a target rifle that's mounted with an 8-power scope. The boy likes to injun up on his squirrels and pop them at 20 yards; the man likes to snipe his squirrels at 70 yards with slide-rule precision. Both have fun. Both take squirrels.

High-powered telescopic sights are neither necessary nor desirable for light .22 hunting rifles. A gilt-edge target rifle can exploit a scope of as much as 10-power, but a 2½X scope is ideal for the average squirrel rifle. This little glass has a large field of view and excellent light-gathering characteristics. A 4X scope is not objectionable—it's just a bit more than is needed.

Many purists prefer the bolt-action rifle for squirrel hunting. The basic design lends itself beautifully to a telescopic sight, and this rigid action has high inherent accuracy. Yet, many fine squirrel hunters prefer slide-action, autoloading, or lever rifles. All are quite accurate, and any is much faster than a bolt rifle.

In any case, expensive rifles and shotguns aren't necessary for squirrel hunting. The dedicated squirrel man doesn't need a vent rib or a $75 scope. He does fine with a work gun that's hauled in the back of his pickup truck like a shovel. But fine guns add to sport. A slick, fast-handling shotgun or a tack-driving little .22 with a fine scope can produce more squirrels and more enjoyment.

Although squirrels may be incredibly rugged, any shotgun or rifle cartridge will drop them within range. Many hunters prefer .410's, or take even the biggest fox squirrels with quiet, lethal little .22 CB caps. But everything else being equal, squirrel hunting is a job for heavy shot shells and .22 Long Rifle cartridges.

Among continent's game species, only fox squirrel (left) and gray squirrel
rival rabbits as top favorites. Fox squirrels love small cornbelt
woodlots; best hunting for grays is in stands of big old den-riddled hardwoods.

There are a few cut-and-dried guidelines for finding squirrels. For either species, timber areas with big, acceptable den trees are always good, especially when they are in conjunction with nut trees such as hickory, walnut, and white oak. The best hunting for either species is often on forest edges rather than in heavy, unbroken blocks of timber.

In the second-growth timber of large modern forests such as those of the Ozarks and Appalachians, the best gray squirrel hunting is often in small pockets of original hardwoods that were overlooked by the old lumbermen. Surrounded by a sea of uniformly-aged oak and hickory, such pockets of huge, den-riddled trees are ideal gray habitat.

Fox squirrels may be hunted anywhere within small corn-belt woodlots. In larger timber, the best hunting may be in trees that border cornfields, or in narrow groves that connect large woodlots or woodlots and cornfields.

Some of the most successful hunters are those who amble easily into the woods and determine what nuts the squirrels are cutting. They attempt to learn feeding habits and pinpoint activity. Early in the season squirrels will probably be working on mast, and caching nuts and acorns. At the peak of the nut season, the smart hunter watches hickory and pecan trees if they're bearing crops, or white oaks and walnuts. A fruitful hickory stand may swarm with squirrels.

But when most of the nuts have been cached and eaten, the hunter may have to change his tactics and search out food pockets of wild grape, dogwood, or redhaw. In large forests a man may be foolish to sit in a randomly-selected area after mid-October. Squirrel activity has probably focused on concentrated food supplies. In late fall and early winter, food holds the key to good squirrel hunting.

Leaf nests can be a general index to squirrel abundance. Generally, there is about one squirrel per good nest in an area. Fresh shells of nuts and acorns are hopeful signs. And when autumn color is at its peak, it is sometimes possible to scout a forest from a distance. Count the colors of foliage. The more colors, the more varied the forest composition. Highly-varied forests are usually more attractive to squirrels.

It isn't always easy to spot top squirrel country. But with experience you will absorb certain subtle truths on successful and unsuccessful hunts. You can't define these truths, but with time you'll learn to sense the best squirrel situations.

The best squirrel hunter we ever knew had moss on his north side. A hermit thrush built a nest in his hair, and one day his gunstock sprouted suckers and took root.

In other words, most top squirrel hunters are very stealthy, lazy men. They will move, but you must look twice to tell it. Mostly, they just sit.

Like many wild creatures, squirrels are most alarmed by unusual motion. However, if an alien movement ceases for a time, the squirrels usually calm down and resume their business. Meanwhile, the hunter must become part of the forest.

While he's waiting-out squirrels, the hunter should choose an easy place to sit—such as the base of a big tree—that commands a good view of the woods. It should not be obscured by low bushes or woody tangles, although a thin screen of foliage will help conceal the hunter.

Once in position, make necessary movements slowly and deliberately. Watch from the corners of your eyes as much as possible and if you do move your head, take plenty of time to do so. Many squirrel hunters smoke while they still-hunt, and it apparently makes little difference. But the

With pump shotgun ready, hunter stands still as he scans trees. Often he'll spot quarry by a flicker of tail or grayish bump where squirrel has flattened itself against bark on upper or far side of branch or trunk.

key to success is vigilance and immobility.

If possible, sit on the shadowed side of the tree where light is in your favor. Your targets are well lit and handicapped by looking toward you into the low morning sunlight.

It's usually smart for the gray squirrel hunter to be in the woods at the literal crack of dawn, but it isn't necessary for the fox squirrel hunter to be abroad so early. For years we would be in our favorite fox-squirrel timber before it was light enough to shoot. With time, we realized that the hunting was often better at 8 a.m. than at dawn. But even so, we're still usually out at first light for fox squirrels—partly because of personal tradition but mostly because it's a revelation to wake up with the forest.

Once in the woods, begin studying the trees in your hunt area. Scan the trunks, and follow out the major limbs through the forks. Take each tree in turn and study it limb by limb. You are not looking for squirrels. You are looking for the unusual and out-of-place—suspicious knobs and rounded bulges on limbs, or small tufts of orange or gray fur beneath branches. With experience, your eye will be drawn to a small knot on a tree limb that somehow looks softer, smoother, or fuzzier than a tree knot should look. This may be the curve of a squirrel's rump or back. Watch for any small movements. The swaying of a clump of foliage when there is no wind, or a movement along the backside of a tree's shadow on the ground, may indicate a squirrel's presence. Above all, keep your ears turned. More often than not, squirrels are located by sound—especially late in the season when they are working a great deal in the ground litter.

Don't spend too much time in one place unless it's a travel lane or a key squirrel area such as a complex of den trees or a small hickory grove. If you approach the usual hunting station carefully and don't raise a fuss, you will be able to see about all there is to see in 25 minutes of careful sitting. If your approach drove a squirrel into a den, you might make this a little longer. But don't invest too much time; a denned squirrel in late morning may go to sleep and forget all about you.

If you do see the squirrel's head within the den entrance, watching you, don't chance a shot. He'll almost always fall backward into the den. And even if you can climb up to the den, there's the problem of getting him out. The writer once reached into a den after a "dead" squirrel and learned a Great Truth: not to reach into dens after "dead" squirrels. It's like grabbing a fistful of broken razor blades.

A wooded site that contains one squirrel usually contains several. This is especially true of grays, but also applies to fox squirrels. So when you shoot a squirrel, stay put. Reload immediately with as little fuss as possible, and remain motionless. In the right setup, a man can shoot his entire limit without standing. The slight crack of a .22 disturbs squirrels very little if the hunter stays put, and even a 12-gauge blast doesn't disturb them as much as it should. Sometimes a gun shot will actually stir the squirrels up and improve hunting. But if a squirrel falls to the ground where you can't see it, it may be wise to retrieve that squirrel at once. A stricken squirrel may fall limply from a tree, hit the ground with a sodden thump, and appear to be thoroughly dead. But now and then such squirrels will come to life and steal away without making a sound.

Still-hunting is the classic fundamental. But in certain places at certain times, stalking is more productive. Especially when squirrels are working on the ground in numbers.

One good technique involves two men hunting about a hundred feet apart. In this way an alerted squirrel can't slide out of sight on the opposite side of a limb. But when you stalk squirrels, they usually see you long before you see them, and are often flattened on limbs and tree forks as you pass them. This calls for incredibly sharp eyes on the hunter's part. It's a highly sporting way to hunt, and a good way to get from one still-hunting area to another.

Stalking should be a silent, slow affair. Some old-timers even hunt squirrels barefooted. This isn't as silly as it sounds. A barefoot man is mighty leery of where he plants his feet and he soon learns a lot about sharp dry sticks. Even in dead leaves he eases his feet down carefully to avoid sharp objects, and he is able to "feel the noise" and move with amazing stealth.

Some hunters, if they see squirrels feeding and active in the distance, will not try to stalk them. They walk boldly into the area, driving the squirrels into hiding, and then sit down in a motionless vigil. The squirrels will usually begin to reappear after 15 minutes or so. Squirrels can be very cute about vanishing at a hunter's approach. They seem to neither stay in the trees nor run away; they simply evaporate. But devote some quiet waiting to those squirrels and they will often materialize as if by magic.

One of the most exciting and maddening aspects of stalking is trying to sneak on a barking squirrel. A squirrel usually begins its feverish barking because it has been alarmed—often by the hunter himself. Such barking may be an attempt to lure the hunter into showing his intentions. Those intentions become clear when the hunter moves toward the animal, and the squirrel will usually vanish. More often than not, a hunter may be better off to let the squirrel cool down; this can often result in a better chance for a shot than by trying to "pull a sneak." But it's mighty hard to ignore a raging squirrel. You may know better, but who can resist the temptation to move just a little closer?

Most hunters stalk squirrels too fast. A hundred yards in 15 minutes is a good pace. It is a highly-critical way to hunt, and can demand more care and alertness of the hunter than almost any other form of American hunting. For this reason, many hunters lose patience. Frustrated, they often begin shooting squirrel nests.

Squirrel nests are big, obvious, easy to hit, and the few squirrels that are shot out of nests are enough to encourage the practice. But for every squirrel that is blasted from a nest, many others are wounded and unknowingly left to die.

Come December, squirrels have squirrels on their mind. It's mating time, and bushytails may throw caution to the winds during their hectic courting chases. As many as eight or ten squirrels may be involved, making a tremendous racket and running aimlessly through the trees. This can make for easy shooting, but it doesn't pay to head directly toward a party of courting squirrels. Try to position yourself at a likely place and wait for the lovers to arrive. If you're in a small woodlot, just stay put. Sooner or later, they'll probably be all around you.

The best hunters mix up their methods. It all depends on the situation and the season.

Down Texas way, some hunters combine stalking with flushing. In the dense gray squirrel range of the Big Thicket, they move among vine-covered trees, shaking the vines to flush grays from their hiding places. Since this always involves highly-mobile squirrels, it's a lively shotgun sport.

In many parts of the country a popular method of stalking squirrels is by canoe or boat, floating easily and soundlessly down small rivers. Squirrels are frequently seen on the banks and in trees overhanging streams, for creekside nut trees·are exposed to a maximum of light and moisture and may bear some of the heaviest nut crops. Canoeing for squirrels is common on many Ozark streams. On some southern creeks, the hunters simply wade quietly along in hip boots.

Some of the writer's most fruitful stalking has been along sandy creek beds in early autumn. In dry years the forest floor is quite noisy, but it is possible to follow a deep, empty creek bed through the heart of splendid squirrel habitat without making a sound. The hunter can hear squirrels in the dry leaf litter far away, yet he can hardly hear the whisper of his own feet.

In some northern squirrel range the earliness or lateness of the first killing frost is probably the most important single condition determining whether the hunter will take his share of the squirrel crop. Frosts coming early in the season will open up the woods and increase visibility well beyond accurate gun range. If frosts are late, and oak leaves are not shed until late October or November, the squirrel harvest may be sharply reduced.

Yet, we once had a fine hunt on a clear, warm day when the wind rose to gale proportions. It was mid-September. The foliage was heavy, and the wind was blasting out of the southwest. Conditions were quite dry. We found, while walking along the crests of steep, wooded ridges, that we could look down into wind-whipped oaks and see squirrels clinging to large branches. Those fox squirrels were most reluctant to climb or run and were revealed as the wind blew aside leaf cover that otherwise would have hidden them. We didn't limit out, but did better than conditions warranted.

So only one thing is certain; the worst weather for squirrel hunting is the weather that keeps you at home.

Bushytails are harvested by stalking, calling, waiting on stand in early morning, drifting streams, and occasionally by hunting with dogs. Many hunters use shotgun (above) while others carry rimfire rifle (right).

'Coons, 'Possums, and 'Taters

23

by Russell Tinsley

There's a story about the farm boy who invited a city friend on a coon hunt. The moon was full and silver light shone in puddles between the trees. They were standing on a ridge, waiting, while somewhere below the hound pack was trying to unravel a cold track along the river bottom.

Suddenly a muffled, high-pitched voice rose from the distant eerie darkness, followed shortly by another, then another. Soon the dogs' voices mingled in a frantic chorus.

"Just listen to that music," the country boy swooned.

"I'd like to hear it," his city friend interrupted, "if those damn dogs would just quit barking."

Well, to each his own. For the hound-dog man there is no music quite as sweet as that of a cooner on a hot trail—no matter whether the dog is a Bluetick, a Black and Tan, a Redbone, Treeing Walker, or maybe just a talented cur. The sound rings through a clear night, echoing off ridges, oscillating back and forth in the dark and sullen timber.

Some purists claim that a hound pack is the *only* way to hunt the ubiquitous rac-

coon. There is a certain romance and excitement to the chase—agreed on that point—but to pursue a coon with hounds you must first have access to trained dogs. Urban life has made it increasingly more difficult for many hunters to keep dogs; others, not so fanatically enthusiastic about the sport, have found that training and maintaining hounds is simply too much of a bother.

The modern lifestyle has discouraged many. As big chunks of land are being cut into smaller and smaller parcels, the cooner can't go far in a straight line without encountering a fence, and some owners don't take kindly to strange dogs and hunters trespassing through their lands. Free-wheeling dogs obviously don't realize that a fence is some sort of taboo, and many without proper training turn their attention to domestic stock and deer. So in many places the traditional sport of chasing coons with hounds is a vanishing pastime.

But it is exciting and fascinating. If you get a chance to join a coon hunt, don't miss the opportunity. Sitting by a cheerful campfire, you wait for the hounds to hit a track. Then each hunter, listening intently, tries to identify his dog or dogs by their telltale barks, the staccato of one rising above the chorus, then fading as another distinctive voice takes charge.

"That's Old Sam. . . . Listen, Blue's on the trail. . . . Go get 'em, Joe!"

Occasionally the excited dogs get a bit carried away and run an innocent bystander—a 'possum—up a tree. When this happens most hunters cuss the mentality of their hounds and disgustedly pull them off the treed 'possum and order them back to the job at hand. "Go find a coon, damitt!"

Let it be known, however, that they are walking off from some very fine eating. A roly-poly 'possum, if the excess fat is removed and the meat is cooked properly, is very similar to domestic pork in texture and taste. Bake a 'possum with "sweet 'taters" and you'll have everyone coming back for seconds.

But now let's talk some more about the main attraction. A hunter doesn't have to own hounds to pursue coons. There are alternatives. Like calling, for example. A raccoon readily will respond to the sound of a bird in distress. I have seen eager animals swim into a lake and try to climb into a boat from where the bird cries were originating. Some callers can imitate a bird by trilling their tongues as they blow on conventional dying-rabbit predator calls, but a mouth-blown call designed primarily for duping coons is preferred.

Bird distress cries also are available on eight-track tape cartridges, cassettes, and on records, and they can be played with battery-powered machines to attract coons. (Check your laws and be sure such electronic devices are legal for hunting in your state.)

While the best times for calling coons are late summer (when the young of spring are susceptive to the call, yet still not wise to the facts of life) and the so-called "hungry season"—late winter when food sources, flora, and fauna, are scarce—the critters will come most any season of the year if you are calling at the right spot. The most common mistake most callers make is that they are calling in an area where there are no coons. Learn something about your quarry's habits, where you will find it at various times of the year.

The raccoon is scientifically classed as carnivorous, but anyone who owns a fruit orchard or grainfield knows better. There are not many things a coon won't eat, although the species does have a sweet-tooth fondness for water and anything that resides therein. In one study, stomach and fecal analyses revealed that acorns and crayfish constitued more than half their yearly diet. So any area where there is adequate food and water—a lake, river bottom, or even farm pond—would be a likely place to call coons.

When a coon answers a call it waddles right in, almost as if hypnotized, oblivious of any danger, this being especially true at night when the animal feels safe and is therefore most gullible. It isn't uncommon for one to try and scramble up the caller's leg to get at the sound. Unless spooked the animal doesn't move around with fast, quick movements like the fox, and there is ample opportunity to pinpoint a shot to a vital area (this also applies when a raccoon is treed). A .22 rimfire rifle with Long Rifle cartridges is plenty adequate, as is a .22 handgun.

You can hunt coons with a big-game rifle or a shotgun if you choose, but such firepower isn't necessary. Despite its squatty bulk—a typical adult will weigh between 15 and 25 pounds—a coon isn't difficult to kill.

*To traditional purists, "coon-hunting" means treeing raccoon with pack of
keen-nosed, strong-voiced hounds. Raccoons are outstanding game animals whether
taken in that manner or by any of several other effective techniques.*

Some hunters rebuke their dogs for running possum up a tree when pack is supposed to be concentrating on coon. But possum and "sweet 'taters" can be delicious hunting bonus— and well prepared raccoon is also tasty.

Some nondescript dogs are as talented and enthusiastic as traditional hound breeds. Here, dog gets taste of coon knocked from tree with .22 pistol during night hunt. Gunner wears head lamp that leaves both hands free.

Coons are most easily duped at night, when they are active and prowling. An ordinary headlight is sufficient illumination. But if it is illegal to hunt in your state at night with a light, try calling coons sans any artificial light, utilizing nothing more than the moon. The coon is one critter that will respond to a call even on the brightest moonlighted night. Pick an area with high contrast, such as dead or dry grass or a bleached river sandbar, where you can spot the animal coming toward you. A shotgun loaded with #4's is the logical weapon.

Where legal, coons also are hunted at night with lights. This is uncomplicated sport; just walk through likely country and sweep the beam across timber, searching for eyes. Such hunting has become more popular in recent years for a couple reasons: An increase in fur prices has made the hunting of coons for their pelts financially profitable; and in many areas a coon population explosion has led to destruction of domestic crops and the critters are hunted as unwanted pests.

But no hunter merely shoots at eyes; he approaches close enough for proper identification. Nowadays it is easier to creep near to an unsuspecting coon, thanks to a revolutionary red-lens hunting light. Wild animals seem to ignore the reddish beam; because black and red are essentially the same to color-blind animals, the theory is that a coon or other wild critter can't see the light. Whatever the reason, field tests have proved conclusively that while a conventional white light will frighten a wild creature, the red light will not.

Getting close to the quarry also has an obvious advantage other than just identification. The shooter can pinpoint his bullet into a vital area with less margin for error. And a quick and humane kill is what the sport of hunting is all about.

Even when hunting without dogs, you may sometimes come upon opossum—especially during very early morning—near persimmons or at daytime denning sites such as hollow logs, old chuck burrows, woodpiles, etc.

Proper calling in good locale can often bring raccoon in close enough
for handgunning, and sport has also become popular among skilled archers. Coon
is apt to respond, even in daylight, to call imitating bird in distress.

During early morning and late evening, raccoons are often found in or at edge of water. When not raiding farms or subsisting on vegetation, they prey on fish, frogs, crawfish, insects, small rodents, birds' eggs, and even young muskrats.

Outfoxing the Foxes

by Leonard Lee Rue, III

24

The fox has always had the reputation of being highly intelligent, sly, crafty—in a word, foxy. This reputation is well deserved, as anyone who has ever hunted foxes will readily attest. My intimate knowledge of foxes comes from a lifelong association with them.

As a boy, raised on a farm in the last years of the Depression, I learned to trap because it was about the only source of money available to a farm boy. I trapped all the furbearers of my area of northwestern New Jersey but I specialized in foxes because of the bounty money and the challenge that trapping foxes presented. And I got to be a good fox trapper, taking 93 foxes, both red and gray, in a period of six weeks while trapping only part-time. I studied foxes, I kept foxes in captivity, I read about foxes, I spent every spare waking moment thinking about foxes and even tried to think like a fox. But most of my knowledge was gained by following foxes, following them for miles and for hours, across the snow-covered hills, fields, and woodlands. It is still the best way to learn about fox habits. I honestly believe that no one can become really knowledgeable about foxes without following them, to learn what they do, where, how, when, and why they do whatever they are doing. I admire foxes. I love them and I love to outwit them. And it can be done.

When I talk about foxes I'll be referring to either the red or the gray fox; for all practical purposes we can forget about the kit, swift, and Arctic foxes. The red and the gray have many things in common but they also have a great many differences.

To follow foxes, snow is needed, preferably slightly wet and from one inch to eight inches deep. A powdery-dry snow will show where the fox went but most of the details will be lost. A wet snow records everything.

The gray fox is native to the southern two-thirds of the United States. It has gradually extended its range northward until it is now found along the border of Quebec and Manitoba, and up into Washington state. It is absent from most of the Rocky Mountain states and the neighboring high plains areas of North Dakota, South Dakota, and Nebraska.

The red fox is a northern species that inhabited Alaska and all of Canada except the Arctic areas, south to the northern fringe of the United States. During the mid-1700s many red foxes were imported from England and released in New York, New Jersey, Maryland, Delaware, and Virginia. Gradually the red fox from Canada pushed its range southward while the imported red fox pushed north, south, and west. Eventually the two strains met, interbred, and went on to populate all of the contiguous 48 states.

The difference in the ranges of these two foxes is immediately apparent in their tracks in the snow. The gray fox, being a southern animal, has larger toes and exposed pads so that body heat can be lost. This heat loss through the pads may well be the factor that will eventually limit its northern expansion. Its exposed toe pads do not give a good grip on ice and the pads may be cut by sharp ice or snow crust.

The red fox has a much larger foot but much smaller pads and these are hard to see because of the long, stiff hairs that grow between the toes, covering them and offering a grip on ice and excellent insulation. Both foxes have five toes on each front foot although only four toes and the pad show in the track. The fifth toe, corresponding to our thumb, is the dewclaw up on the side of the foot. Each hind foot has four toes and a pad. When you are tracking a fox that is walking or trotting, you will see only the tracks of its hind feet because each hind foot is placed precisely on top of the spot just vacated by the front foot. Because foxes have very narrow chests, their feet are placed almost directly under their bodies when they walk, leaving tracks that look almost like a dotted line; their usual stride while trotting will print the tracks about 12 inches apart. Fox tracks may sometimes be confused with house cat or bobcat tracks. However, a house cat's tracks are smaller and the stride length is about eight to ten inches. The bobcat has a larger foot than either of the two foxes although its stride length is about the same. The positive identification is that the claw marks of the foxes always show in the tracks while the cats, having retractable claws, never leave claw marks.

Although red and gray foxes both weigh from eight to twelve pounds, the red fox has longer legs and larger lungs. The red is a runner and prefers open country, although it may be found in the mountains or woodlands. In fact, some red foxes seem to exult in running, often deliberately leading dogs on a merry chase. The gray fox prefers dense cover such as is found in swamps and in heavily wooded areas and mountainsides. If pursued, it lacks the stamina for a prolonged chase and prefers to escape if it can by going into an earthen burrow, a rocky crevasse or den, or it may climb up into a tree.

Except for the period when the female is giving birth, or for short periods of extremely bitter-cold weather, red foxes just do not den up. They prefer to sleep out in the open even in a snowstorm and are often completely buried by the time the storm passes.

There are several ways to hunt foxes on snow without a dog, but you can't hunt them if the storm did not stop before dawn. During a snowstorm almost all wildlife remains sequestered in whatever shelter can be found before the storm started. If the storm stopped in the late evening or through the night, you are in luck. If the storm was of several days' duration, every hungry predator will be on the prowl, leaving tracks galore.

When hunting by yourself, either walk out to a good fox area or drive your car along the back roads till you find where a fox has crossed the road. If the snow is deep and dry, you may have difficulty telling which way the fox was heading. The toe marks should show on the plowed road to give you the right direction. If you are on foot in the open fields or woodlands, just follow the tracks into the prevailing wind. Foxes almost always hunt into the wind so that the scent of game or danger is borne downwind to them.

In my state we have to hunt with shotguns only, and a 12-gauge is preferred. I have an old, reliable Winchester Model 12 pump gun that is plugged to hold the legal three shells and fitted with an adjustable choke which I keep set on full for long-distance shooting. I prefer #4 shot in 2¾-inch Magnum shells.

Following a fox on foot is hard work, so although the weather is cold you'd better dress lightly. I usually wear Norwegian fish-net underwear under wool trousers and shirt with a leather vest and a light windbreaker. My windbreaker has a hood that can be used when I stop to rest or if it gets very windy. For footwear I prefer hunting pacs with felt liners over sweat socks and wool socks. I like a knitted hat such as a toque which comes down over the ears. The knitted hat allows the perspiration to escape from the head. I may wear a down mitten on my left hand to carry the gun but I wear a fine wool glove on the right hand so I can get it inside the trigger guard when the action starts. I wear a light nylon rucksack to carry apples, dried fruit, raisins, nuts, and protein

wafers, a candle for firestarting if need be, a small hatchet, and an emergency "Space Blanket"—they weigh very little and can prove invaluable. A heavy wool sweater and an extra pair of socks are carried, and I wear sunglasses and binoculars.

If the snow is very deep, I wear snowshoes. That *is* hard work but if the snow is soft it is doubly hard for the fox because it sinks in and tires easily.

I do not follow the track exactly but stay off to one side. Foxes will usually begin to zigzag a bit before picking out a spot to sleep. They invariably circle and always walk into the wind for a good distance before they lie down. Then, with the wind blowing from behind them, they rely on their keen noses and ears to warn them of anything upwind while they can watch their back trail with their eyes.

By walking off to one side of the track you may not be detected by the fox and perhaps can approach close enough to get a shot as it leaves its bed. As you are not on the track, the fox may be fooled into thinking that you are not aware of its presence and will remain hidden, hoping you will walk by while it remains undetected.

(If you come to the fox's bed without seeing the fox go out, make a large circle and cut the trail.) The fox usually does not go far before bedding up again.

Your best chance of success in walking up on a fox is to work with two companions. Then you walk in a huge V-formation. One hunter follows the track directly while the other two are at least 300 feet ahead and 300 feet apart from each other. All of the hunters should try to keep each other in sight. The fellow following the track makes noise; some hunters even clang a cow bell fairly constantly to focus the fox's attention. When the fox is started

After prolonged snowfall or extremely cold spell, predators are very active,
leaving plenty of tracks as they search for prey to alleviate their
hunger. Above, gray fox has fed and is walking into wind before bedding down.

Below, red fox has curled up to rest atop slight elevation from which
it can watch back trail. Hunter who wants shot at bedded fox
should walk to one side of tracks or he will probably be detected prematurely.

from its bed, there is a very good chance that one or the other hunter on the wing-points will be in a position for a shot.

A much easier method of hunting on snow is to drive the backroads looking for fox tracks and stopping every so often to look for the fox itself. In states where a rifle may be used, a sleeping fox is sometimes spotted from a road and picked off with a good scoped varmint rifle. The reddish coat of a sleeping fox can be seen for a tremendous distance against white snow. Foxes prefer to sleep on elevated areas, so every hay stack, straw pile, or mound of dirt should be glassed thoroughly and, if possible, checked from the sunny side.

Because I cannot use a rifle in my state, I have to do this type of hunting with a companion. After a fox is spotted, we drive on and then one hunter gets out and attempts to reach an area where we think the fox will run when disturbed. While he tries to get into position, the driver takes the car back and attracts the fox's attention by making noise. But do *not* get out of the car or the fox may be out of its bed and away before your companion is in position. If we guess wrong, and the shooter is in the wrong spot when the fox does go out, we know where to be the next time we locate the fox in the same area.

Hunting foxes with a good dog or dogs is a lot of fun, and no snow is needed. Until the price of fur skyrocketed in 1973, the value of fox pelts had dropped so low that very few hunters had kept their dogs, but now fox hounds are again bringing premium prices.

Fox hunting with dogs can be very productive for a single hunter who has good hounds and knows the area intimately. In an unfamiliar area, a better chance of success is assured if several hunters participate.

Foxes are creatures of habit. They know every path, trail, old wood road, gate, bridge, fallen trees across streams, etc., in their area and they use them. A good hunter knows that if a fox is able to fool the hounds one day by some trick, it will invariably do the same the next time it is hunted. So if you miss the fox or are in the wrong place but see the fox cross elsewhere, just get into the proper place the next time. Here again, snow helps if you don't actually see the fox, but if your hounds are open-mouthed you should be able to tell about where the fox went even without snow. Most hunters prefer open-mouthed dogs because they constantly let you know where the action is taking place. A slow-moving dog is better than a fast one because there is less chance of pushing the fox right out of the county.

In my area there are a lot of gray foxes and a lot of hilly and mountainous country with lots of talus slopes and crevasses. Most of the gray foxes usually hole up before the hunter has a chance for a shot. Many fox hunters carry a small fox terrier with them. When the hounds put the gray fox to earth, the terrier is slipped into the hole. Soon all hell breaks loose, and if the terrier is a good one that fox is coming out. Of course, it may not come out the hole you thought it would use—and then the hounds are used again.

Some hunters who don't have hounds keep a terrier and concentrate on the gray foxes by walking the ridges till they find where a gray has denned up. If the hunter has explored the area before, it does not take long to locate most of the fox dens. Then the terrier flushes the foxes from the dens.

Calling foxes has become extremely popular in the country today and it is a thoroughly challenging way to hunt. A good time to call foxes is from daybreak till about one-half hour after sun up. An even better time is from an hour before sundown till dark. Some states allow night-hunting with calls and spotlights but most states do not. Too many unscrupulous people have taken advantage of the situation to poach deer and so have spoiled it for all hunters.

It is best to call on a calm evening so that the sound can be heard for a long distance. There are many good calls available on the market today. In some states it is legal to use a tape-recorded call of a dying rabbit, in other states no electronic equipment may be used.

In calling, it is important that the hunter be able to see in most directions.

Red fox brings ground squirrel to den to feed litter of young. Except when raising their pups, red foxes seldom den up as grays do. But both varieties of fox can be hunted with hounds or lured into range by calling.

There is no point in watching downwind because *no* fox is going to come upwind to the hunter. You should use camouflage clothing or be well hidden and it is very important to keep from being silhouetted. All canines are able to recognize a man as a man, even if the hunter is motionless.

Foxes are curious creatures and if they can hear the call and have not heard the hunter move in and cannot smell him, they will come to investigate. However, they are also cautious creatures and are not going to dash wildly into what may be trouble. So when the fox comes to the call, it will probably be with all the stealth usually associated with bobcats.

Although calling is very successful in many areas, it is not overly productive in mine. In my section of the country, due to the high human population, the foxes are exceedingly wary.

I don't know which of the hunting methods I've just described will work for you in your particular area and I do know that you won't get rich on the money from all of the fox pelts you hope to take. I will guarantee, however, that you will have a lot of fun hunting when the season is closed on most other creatures. Fox hunting is one way of extending your hunting season legally. In the process you should learn a lot more about foxes, and that could enrich your life as it has mine.

Hound has helped this shotgunner bag one red fox and one gray. Body coloration can be confusing but red fox always has white tip on tail, while gray's brush invariably is tipped with black.

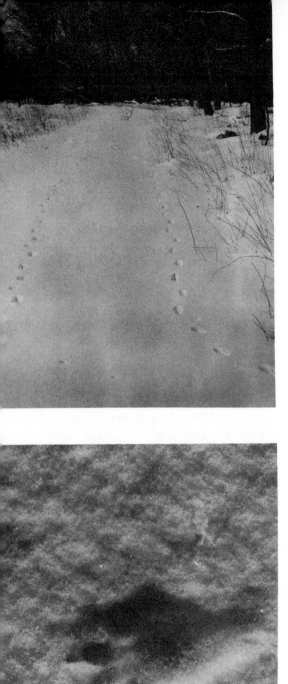

*Here are two sets of red-fox
tracks. In deep, powdery snow, claw
marks may not show and prints
may be so blurred you can't tell
direction of travel; in that
case, trail probably heads upwind.*

*This track was left by front foot
of gray fox. Red fox would
make smaller, less distinct pad
indentations because of
long, stiff hair between toes, but
overall print would be larger.*

El Coyote—Game Animal

25

by Ed Kozicky and John Madson

Call him "brush wolf," "song dog," or "coyote," it adds up to the same thing—one of the smartest and most colorful game animals that any hunter could want.

Coyotes today are widespread and prosperous, our largest abundant predators. They're on the rise in the upper Midwest and Northeast and are plentiful in most western states. So we have coyotes to enjoy or destroy—a choice between hunting and poisoning. And *El Coyote* deserves something better than poisoning.

One way of enjoying coyotes, and also keeping their number within bounds, is by bringing them to the hunter with predator calls. Coyote calling is probably most productive in September and October at the peak of the year's coyote crop, but it has special appeal during the bleak winter months when most game seasons are closed and you have a bad case of cabin fever. This is also when coyote pelts are in prime, either as trophies or for the market.

The best way to break into this game is to wangle an invitation from a good caller. Study his actions, listen to his calling sequence, ask him questions. Check with your local library for books about coyotes. Two of the best are *The Clever Coyote* by Stanley Young, and *Voice of the Coyote* by Frank Dobie. Learn to recognize coyote sign and how to tell coyote tracks from dog tracks—it's easier than you might think.

The beginner's biggest obstacle is lack of confidence. If there's no action in the first hunt or two, he may quit in disgust. But for reasons that no one can explain, calling may be fruitless for days on end and then, for no apparent reason, the hunter may call up four coyotes at once. So hang tough, and have faith. Most experts feel that coyote calling isn't as difficult as crow or duck calling.

The main thing is to move into an area without letting coyotes know it. If ever silence is golden, it's when you're taking up position to call coyotes. They rank near the top in animal intelligence, with faculties to match. Their eyesight is at least as good as man's, and their senses of smell and hearing are keen beyond our comprehension.

Despite war on coyotes waged by ranchers and farmers in some regions, species remains plentiful and has spread eastward, perhaps filling environmental niche left when wolves vanished. This well-fed specimen was taken in New Jersey.

The last two hours before sunset and the first two hours after dawn are usually the best calling periods. Coyotes are active then, and there's likely to be little wind. Coyotes can be called any time of the day, and even at night, but most hunters don't hunt at night. Anyway, the big thrill comes from watching a coyote approach over open ground from a great distance—a sight guaranteed to give you the willies.

Coyote calls simulate the screams of an injured cottontail or jackrabbit. Coyotes hear such sounds many times during their feeding activities, and it means an easy meal. The more pain, fright, and urgency you can put into your calling, the more likely a response. Imagine a rabbit struck by a horned owl—there is the first loud scream of terror and pain, and then a series of short, gasping cries. But the rabbit isn't dead. In a moment or two, the owl shifts his talons and the rabbit squalls again—but less loudly.

Coyotes usually respond within five minutes, but it pays to wait for up to 15 minutes in a choice location. When you leave, move at least a mile away. Always call into the wind—preferably from knolls or hills (but not on the skyline) which give a clear view in several directions. Mouths or heads of draws and gullies are good spots. Experienced callers prefer to sit in shadows or lie in front of some natural cover. Don't stand; El Coyote knows about critters that stand on their hind legs.

Before starting to call, take a few moments to study the lay of the land. Don't move. And if you have a partner, it may be well for him to be 25 to 30 yards away from you. When a coyote responds to a call, his attention is riveted on the caller and he comes in a beeline.

A predator caller can never be sure what he'll invite to dinner. Depending on region, you may bring in eagles, foxes, skunks, badgers, raccoons, antelope, deer, elk, mink, bobcats, or even mountain lions. Predator calling isn't reserved for shooters. You may want to use a camera. It's a fine way to get rare photos of predators from a rabbit's-eye view—and that's a pretty dramatic angle!

When rifle-hunting in open country, never shoot at a skylined coyote. The bullet should be of such a design and velocity that it breaks up on impact, which eliminates the .22 rimfires. A Winchester Model 70 in .22-250 or .243 is an excellent coyote rifle, as are the .270 Winchester with a 100-grain bullet, or the .30-06 with a 125-grain bullet. By all means, use a scope sight such as the Weaver 4X or 2X-7X variable. Fine optics are especially useful at dusk and dawn. Coyotes aren't hard to hit—they're just easy to miss.

If you use a shotgun, the coyote should be called to less than 40 yards. A full-choke 12-gauge, with No. 2 shot in the Super-X or Double-X Magnum, is excellent.

Coyote hunting has been criticized by some people who are concerned about the future of the little wolves. We share that concern. But it is not possible to wipe coyotes out of an area by still-hunting or calling, for the odds are strongly tilted in the coyote's favor. It is unfortunate that most states classify the coyote as vermin, and treat it accordingly. Coyotes have been almost eliminated in some parts of their range by 1080 (sodium monofluoroacetate), an insidious poison that does not break down chemically and can be passed along the entire food chain. The stuff is frightfully deadly, and less than one ounce of 1080 is needed to poison a 1,000-pound

In open country on snow, white camouflage outfit is excellent for hunting coyotes or foxes. Kneeling on rubber crib sheet, hunter wears white knit cap, ski mask, and dairyman's coveralls. White tape covers rifle and scope.

horse carcass for use as a coyote bait station.

Some states, such as Kansas, prohibit the use of 1080 and depend on trapping and sporthunting to keep coyotes in check. Carrying this a step further, we feel that the coyote should be elevated from pest predator to game animal—as has been done with the mountain lion and fox in many states. If designated as a game animal, the coyote would be managed. As a pest species, the emphasis is likely to be on control by poisoning—with side effects on many other animals.

Coyotes, like other predators, respond to calling. Sounds that imitate screams of injured rabbit will awaken animal's hunger and bring it to investigate, though it's usually too cautious to approach as close as this Alaskan coyote.

Bob Henderson, Extension Specialist of Wildlife Damage Control at Kansas State University at Manhattan, teaches trapping methods to ranchers and farmers with coyote problems, but he also promotes sporthunting of the animal. Bob is one of the best coyote callers in the nation. His booklet, *How To Call Coyotes,* is a well of knowledge, and is available without charge from Kansas State University. Bob is also willing to direct hunters to parts of Kansas where coyotes are numerous.

Like many other hunter-conservationists, Bob regards the coyote as a game animal instead of vermin, and the thought of poisoning coyotes is repugnant to him. As a biologist, he knows that some coyotes are needed on the range to keep rodents, jackrabbits, and smaller predators in check. And as an outdoorsman, he dreads the silent emptiness of a prairie without coyotes.

A Short Course in Predator Calling

26

by Russell Tinsley

It's a common failing. A hunter buys a predator call, carries it into the woods, blows on it a few times as he looks about, and if something doesn't immediately show, he complains that the blasted contraption won't work. It's almost as if he expects some sort of magic.

Well, there is no magic involved, but if you have all the pieces of the puzzle in place—right spot, right time, right call—it will indeed work. I've seen literally hundreds of different creatures beguiled by the distress cries of a rabbit or bird. But certain rules and fundamentals must be followed. There is no shortcut to success.

Murry and Winston Burnham are among the foremost predator callers in the world. These Texas brothers have called at one time or another just about every animal and bird that can be called. For some they have had to develop special sounds when the old reliables wouldn't produce. Here is the Burnham Brothers' quickie course for successful predator calling:

1. Don't take your quarry for granted. A predator possesses a super amount of cau-

tion. Your strategy should be aimed at counteracting its basic line of defense.

Most predators depend on their noses as their primary warning system. A whiff of human odor is one danger signal that no crafty predator ignores. The one exception is the bobcat, which uses its eyes more than its nose for detecting danger.

Because of the scent problem, the best time for calling predators is during calm weather or when only a very mild breeze is blowing. In windy weather the sound carries in the direction you don't want it to go, downwind, and a predator that hears it will simultaneously sniff your human odor.

If there is any breeze, use some sort of scent to mask your own. There are many on the market. Perhaps the best is skunk musk. A small bottle of this malodorous liquid is set, uncapped, downwind from the caller. The scent sometimes confuses the predator just enough to permit a shot before he spooks.

And speaking of shots, a predator is a lean and muscular animal, difficult to kill. For foxes the Burnhams recommend a

This exceptionally large coyote presented clear shot after brief period of calling. Hunter was hidden in well-chosen area, where tracks and droppings indicated busy predator trails near waterhole.

shotgun for close shooting or a .222 rifle; for larger predators, bobcats and coyotes, they use something in the .243, 6mm, or .25-06 class. With smaller calibers there is too little assurance of a clean kill.

Although a predator depends greatly on its nose, we cannot ignore the ears and eyes. Wear camouflage clothing, anything that might blend you into the background (conventional "camo" usually, but white if there is snow). Cover your face with grease paint or a camouflage headnet. With a bobcat, concealment is doubly important. Make as little noise and movement as possible, both while approaching the hunting site and while actually calling. A predator that detects an unnatural sound, such as the slamming of a vehicle door, will become suspicious and much more difficult to fool. No woods-wise predator will completely let its guard down.

2. Don't get too hung-up on the call and ignore other, equally important factors. Few successful callers use exactly the same technique and sound. In fact, some are downright weird. Instruction records are available which will teach you the proper pitch and tone. Electronic devices—tape recorders, phonographs, etc.—have taken much of the guesswork out of calling. Authentic tapes and records of live animals and birds in distress have been made, and while these sounds are very effective in beguiling predators where electronic devices are legal, they are no more productive than a mouth-blown call if the hunter knows how to use it.

If you do prefer the manual call, the Burnhams nevertheless recommend that you get a tape of a rabbit in distress and listen to it. This gives some inkling as to the sound you are trying to imitate with your call.

3. A common mistake made by many callers is to hunt the same area time and again. Often this is by necessity rather than choice, as few of us have access to un-limited hunting territory. We must make do with what is available.

Hunting the same country regularly has an obvious drawback: Once a predator has been fooled by a call it wises up in a hurry. It associates the sound with danger and is reluctant to respond again soon. One way to counteract this is to change sounds. Maybe the first time you call an area you'll use the dying-rabbit cries; the next time try bird-distress cries. This change of pace might fool the predator into answering a second time, even if it has been called before.

Usually when a predator is going to come to a call, it does so *muy pronto*. Foxes and coyotes normally will show up within 10 to 15 minutes. The bobcat, how-ever, is much more deliberate, sneaking and stalking toward the caller rather than running in. Sometimes it takes 20 to 30 minutes before a bobcat appears on the scene. Most callers never have seen cats simply because they quit too soon. If you've hunted deer by waiting quietly and patiently on stand, you know that half an hour takes much longer to pass than most people would imagine. Check your watch and stifle the impulse to quit prematurely, especially if you are calling an area where bobcats are known to roam.

4. Now we come to the single most im-portant rule of all: The most meticulous preparation and planning is for naught if there are no predators present where you are hunting. Predators are not found everywhere. Generally they are isolated in a few scattered spots dictated by habitat and available food.

Fox, like coyote, is apt to approach caller soon or not at all; this one was taken after hunter tried several different locations. Good site has cover and plenty of rodents on which foxes can feed.

Predators have such keen eyes that concealment can be crucial. This caller's camouflage includes head net, and he stays low behind screen of brush and cactus. Scoped rifle can be either light sporter or heavier "varmint" type.

While predators are very adaptable, they nonetheless prefer some sort of cover where they can hide and build dens and raise their young. But this is a secondary consideration. A coyote, for instance, can exist on an open plain where there isn't much more than tall grass to hide in, but it stays there because there is an abundance of food, mostly rodents. Available food is the foremost consideration. While predators will eat things like wild berries and fruits at times, they prefer meat. The bulk of a predator's diet is small mammals such as rabbits and rats, and maybe a bird occasionally if it can catch one.

When you locate an area that has such food, look for signs like droppings and tracks. This is the only sure way of determining whether predators are present, unless of course there have been visual sightings.

Predators are fairly predictable in their habits. They travel trails and country roads. Search along these transit avenues and around waterholes for tracks and droppings. Learn the signs that different predators leave. The preponderance or absence of these signs will give an accurate reading of what the predator population is in any area.

Scouting potential hunting terrain before you actually call always pays off. It serves a twofold purpose, enabling you to ascertain whether or not predators are present and giving you a chance to learn the country. You can pinpoint the best calling areas and formulate some sort of plan. Under ideal conditions the sound of a call will travel half a mile or more; so the caller should move at least this far between stops. By scouting there is less chance that you will wander around and call the same country over and over. Which, obviously, is just a waste of time.

Bobcat is more cautious than fox or coyote, and may take 20 or 30 minutes to appear. Where night hunting is legal, red-lensed head lamp can provide enough visibility without discouraging approach of quarry.

Javelina Country
by Byron W. Dalrymple

27

The javelina might be classed as a "little" big-game animal. It is a piglike desert creature weighing from 30 to 50 pounds. Many years ago it was hunted for hides, which make beautiful thin leather. It was considered a pest and killed on sight by many ranchers in the Southwest. Land clearing also put heavy pressure on the animal. Finally it was in rather precarious supply, gone from its northerly range in Texas and from original range in southwestern New Mexico, restricted to southern and western Texas and southeastern Arizona.

It is a most intriguing desert character, a desirable trophy, and good eating when properly cared for. But because of early lack of attention by sport hunters it never had much popularity until the last decade or so. Arizona was first to give the javelina sound protection and management, and consequently its greatest hunting popularity has been there. The Arizona season is brief, generally in February or March, with several thousand special permits offered at a stipulated fee via application and drawing.

There are javelina guides available in Phoenix, Tucson, and other cities within their range. For a hunter who is unfamiliar with the area a guide can be most helpful. Javelina are gregarious animals, running in droves large or small. Thus, on a whole mountain most of the javelina population may be in one spot, and difficult to find. Guides do preseason scouting, know javelina habits, and for a first-timer are well worth the cost.

The prime Arizona javelina range is in the foothills and on the desert floor in the numerous small mountain ranges of the southeastern quarter of the state. Chief among these are the Santa Teresas, Galiuros, Grahams, Santa Ritas, and Chiricahuas. The Superstitions near Phoenix, and the desert area between Phoenix and Tucson are also good.

In New Mexico, hunting is rather restricted. There the animal was re-established a few years ago on a small scale. Most years of late, a season has been offered for residents only. It also falls in February or March. The Animas and Peloncillo Mountains in Hidalgo County have

Hunter examines javelina's tusks, which are impressive but much smaller than those of wild boar, and are straight rather than curved. Javelina, also known as collared peccary, can be hunted in several Southwestern states.

the largest population. Other good locations are Steins Pass and the Pyramid
Peaks, out of Lordsburg. There are a few
animals also in Grant, Catron, and Luna
counties.

In both Arizona and New Mexico, public lands are so vast that there is no difficulty finding a place to hunt. But in Texas,
which has the largest javelina populations,
almost all lands are in private ranches, and
private-land hunting for a fee is the tradition. Presently the javelina is becoming
more and more in demand in Texas. A few
ranchers now offer package hunts—guide
and transport—for an average of $100. A
few furnish meals and lodging at extra
cost. Most of this hunting is from a four-
wheel-drive vehicle, cruising ranch trails,
glassing, walking. A few offer hunts using
dogs. Texas hunter success is high.

Although a scattering of javelina can be
found in about 100 counties in Texas, there
are two concentrations of population. One
is throughout most of the Brush Country
south and west of San Antonio. This is a region of undulating cattle lands, with dense,
low thornbrush and cactus for cover. Much
of this is leased by deer hunters, and it is
difficult to set up a hunt here unless you
know someone. In Val Verde County there
is one ranch, Dolan Creek, that offers
guided package hunts. There are also
guides at Hondo and Pearsall who take
hunters out, and there is a drawing on the
state-owned Chaparral Wildlife Management Area occasionally.

The second prime area is the Big Bend
Country west of the Pecos River, in far-
west Texas. Most counties here have at
least some javelina. Presidio and Brewster
counties usually have high populations.
This is a land of huge ranches. A few offer
javelina hunts for a fee. Both here and in

the Brush Country the best way to find a
place is to contact Chambers of Commerce in the area for assistance.

At one time numerous Texas counties in
the prime range had no closed season. But
that has changed. Nowadays only a very
few counties fail to protect the javelina. In
most javelina counties the season runs
from early October to the end of the year.
In a few it is shorter.

Hunting methods are generally similar
in Arizona, New Mexico, and west Texas.
This is because most of the hunting is done
in the valleys, draws, and foothills of
desert mountains. Where there are trails
passable to a 4WD, most hunters slowly
cruise them, keeping a close watch on the
slopes and stopping often to glass carefully. A binocular is as important as the
gun. If there are no trails, one simply has
to hike. But glassing is still important.

A band of pigs seen distantly can be
stalked to within easy range by a careful
and knowledgeable hunter. The javelina
has a keen nose, fair hearing, but extremely poor eyesight. If you move quietly, slowly, and into the breeze commonly you can move to within short range.
If the animals seem nervous, raising
hackles and popping their teeth, just pause
and stay still a few seconds. Occasionally a
group is very wild, but usually this is because they have got your scent. It pays to
glass long and carefully and to watch for
movement in catclaw or other low brush
in draws. Javelina are low to the ground
and unless they're in the open they can be
difficult to spot.

As in deer hunting, early and late are
the best times of day to find bands moving.
On cool, overcast days they may forage at
any time. But if it is warm at all, midday
finds them up in the rimrocks or in the

Taken by surprise and cornered at short range, bedded
javelina backs up against rock and pops tusks in anger as hunter
squeezes off fast shot with open-sighted rifle.

Best way to hunt peccary in some areas is to walk and search for sign
or wait at feeding or watering spots, but on open desert flats
you can sometimes cruise and scout with four-wheel-drive vehicle.

shaded brushy places near a waterhole, bedded down. You can often flush javelina by walking the rims during midday, or working through the higher cover that usually surrounds ranch tanks or other water places. Walking deep washes with brushy edges also is a good method during the bulk of the day. In late afternoon especially, bands move out onto the slopes to feed; often they are easily seen and not especially wary.

The southern Texas Brush Country is quite different hunting. Cover is dense. Here there are many ranch tanks for cattle, however, and the ranches are gridded with ranch trails and also seismograph trails due to oil exploration. A popular method is to take a stand on one of these, on a crossing ridge, so a draw can be watched on either side, as well as the ridge top. When roaming bands cross the trails, an open shot is offered. More are bagged that way in the brush than by any other method. Curiously, javelina will occasionally respond to a coyote call. This gets a few in the brush.

It pays to check for sign: prickly pear cactus ripped to shreds, lechuguilla torn up on hillsides (these are favorite foods), tracks near waterholes or in dry washes (they're small and blunt-toed), shallow rootings, wallowing spots near a waterhole. It also pays to keep your nose alert. Javelina musk is strong and distinctive, not pleasant. They use the scent to keep in touch with and to alert each other, and also when frightened. Walking the rims slowly at midday, or upwind in a dry wash,

Javelina makes good eating if you shoot fairly young animal and take care to get no musk on the meat. Musk is exuded from skin gland located high on rump. When you dress trophy, cut off this patch of skin.

it is not at all unusual to catch the scent before you see or flush out the quarry.

Archery hunting for javelina has become popular, and is very sporty, indeed. For gun hunters the choice of rifle is not crucial. Most use whatever deer rifle they are used to. The flat-shooting .243 is a good choice, especially in desert mountains where long shots may be presented. But any rifle from an unscoped .30/30 to the .30-06 is all right. A scope on any rifle, however, is recommended. Shots should be carefully placed, preferably in the rib cage if you intend to have the head mounted. The target is rather small. It is not easy to distinguish boars from sows and it makes little difference, except that you should be sure an animal does not have young fol-lowing it. Javelina may be born at any time of year, never more than two in a litter.

After the kill, if you intend to use the meat, and especially if you must carry your trophy out, remove the musk gland. It is a simple skin gland located high on the rump. Just cut a patch of surrounding skin and peel it off. Musk on your hands or clothes, or on the meat, creates an un-pleasant and long-lasting annoyance.

The javelina is not a true swine, but belongs in an ancient family of its own. It is perhaps the most unusual of North American trophies, and deserves much more respect and attention than past history has generally accorded it.

Byron Dalrymple is shown checking for javelina sign in desert country. He points to ripped and chewed prickly pear cactus on which game has fed. Also look for lechugilla, torn up on hills.

Part IV: You and Your Dog

All (Well, Almost) About Hunting Dogs

28

by Ed Zern

No one knows when man first domesticated the dog, but we find sculptured records of coursing dogs used to run down antelope and hold lions at bay as early as 2500 B.C. Probably prehistoric man found it easier to spear a wild boar when he came upon one already besieged by wild dogs; it must have been apparent even to his primitive mind that a pack of half-tamed dogs could make his hunting more productive.

Although modern man has perfected hunting weapons that bear little resemblance to his first crude clubs and spears, he still frequently relies on dogs to help him cope with cottontails, coons, cougars, and a number of other game species. And just as man has become more specialized in his own work, so his hunting dogs have been bred for theirs, until today there are specialized breeds for scenting, trailing, coursing, treeing, flushing, pointing, retrieving, and often a combination of these jobs.

Today's sportsman, if he's at all serious about hunting small game, birds, or wildfowl, and if he's eager to enjoy these gun sports to the full, will almost certainly own a dog, perhaps several. For as land available for shooting sports decreases and the ranks of sportsmen increase, he learns that without the help of a good dog—his own, his companion's, or his guide's—he stands little chance of finding top sport with such species as bobwhite quail or ringnecked pheasants. Without a dog he also loses wounded or crippled waterfowl and upland birds which by rights should be in his bag.

He finds, too, that without a dog in the field he misses out on much of the satisfaction that field-shooting offers: the thrill of seeing a high-spirited setter quarter a field at a gallop, then slam stiff-legged into a rigid point, and the nerve-tingling tension of walking up to the squatting covey—the pride in watching a spaniel puppy he trained himself work a pheasant covert and put a cagey old cockbird into the air (and into his game pocket)—the joy in

*For hunters who want "utility dog" but are interested primarily in
wildfowling, Ed Zern recommends Labrador retriever—a breed that also does well
in uplands. Lab in photo has just delivered eider after long retrieve.*

seeing a well-trained retriever hit the water with a mighty splash and return to deliver a fat mallard to hand.

Since I have a big topic and very little space, I'm going to try to answer some of the most often-asked questions about the scattergunner's best friend.

"I hunt for a few months of the year, during the legal season. Should I have a dog? It doesn't seem like good business to keep one all year just to use it a few short weeks."

If your hunting is a business proposition, forget a dog. And forget hunting, too, because you'll do better buying your meat at the supermarket. But if you hunt for sport, pleasure, and all the satisfaction that a day in the woods, fields, or marshes can give to the wingshooting sportsman, then a gun dog may be one of the best investments you'll ever make—and one in whose dividends your whole family, especially the kids, will share. Granted it will cost you a few dollars a month to feed your dog even when there's no legal hunting, but you'll get a hundred dollars worth of love and affection in return, every day of his life.

"I hunt ducks and geese sometimes, upland birds other times, and occasionally bust a bunny. Is there such a thing as an all-purpose pooch for a guy like me?"

No. But there are some breeds that come closer than most to being "all-purpose dogs," and you should consider one of them. If I were primarily a duck hunter (which I am), I'd want to own a Labrador retriever (which I do). The Lab can't be beat as a cold-water retriever, and can also be trained to work reasonably close to the guns in pheasant or ruffed grouse country. (I let my three Labs work the partridge or woodcock covert ahead of me, keeping them as close as I can, and while they flush a few birds out of gun range, they also over-run some birds tha flush back toward me for a relatively easy shot.) When I drop a partridge into heavy ground-cover, I know the dogs will find him whether he's stone-cold dead or a runner.

The golden retriever (not to be confused with the light-colored yellow Lab, a color variation that may occur in the same litter with black puppies) is another breed that can double in brass, but the golden doesn't take to cold water like a Lab, and its long coat can pick up a bushel of burrs in a pheasant field.

If I were chiefly a pheasant hunter, with ducks and geese as a sideline, and I wanted an all-purpose dog, an English springer spaniel from good hunting or field-trial stock would be my first choice. The springer is a great pheasant finder, and a good working retriever even from a duck blind or sneak-box. I've also seen and shot over Brittany spaniels that could find woodcock and pheasants, hold a point, and "fetch dead" as nicely as anyone could ask.

But if I had my druthers, which most of us don't, I'd own a retriever for ducks, an English springer for pheasants, a pointer for bobwhite quail, and a setter for grouse and woodcock. (I'd also have a matched set of Winchester Model 21's in 12, 20, and .410 gauges, plus a shooting estate in Spain.)

"I can't afford a professionally trained dog, and don't have much spare time. Could I buy a puppy and train him myself?"

Almost anyone with a little time and a lot of patience can train a dog—but be sure the puppy's from good working stock rather than a strain bred chiefly for bench shows and fancy looks. Insist on "papers" certifying his breeding, and have an expe-

Pointing breeds are obviously best for quail, grouse, and woodcock, as well as several other upland species such as chukars and Huns. Good pointing dog like this one can also perform outstanding job on ringneck pheasants.

rienced dog man (or woman) look the papers and the pup over carefully before you finalize the deal. Don't ever buy from a pet shop with a window full of cute puppies! When you get your pup—preferably when he's about eight weeks old, and in any case before he's six months—establish the twin facts that you're (a) his best friend and (b) his boss, to be obeyed at all times. You can do this without either bribing him with food (as any youngster, what he mostly wants is love) or terrorizing him with blows (a few loud but painless whacks with a folded newspaper are all the force-and-violence you'll need).

There are some excellent books on gun-dog training on the market; get one, or several, and *read them through carefully before you start training.* If you can devote just 15 minutes daily to this pleasant chore—and if you'll have patience, keep your temper, and follow the books' instructions—you should have yourself a well-trained gun dog within a year. Naturally he'll need a few seasons of actual field work under hunting conditions to back up his book learning before he'll be a finished product. The more experience he has with actual game, the faster he'll develop. And if he won't ever win the Grand National, at least he'll give you more pride and satisfaction than if you had paid a professional

*Noted hunting-dog authority John R. Falk is shown with outdoor photographer
Lennie Rue's springer, Freckles, and ringneck cock bagged on preserve. Ed Zern
believes springer spaniel is finest possible choice as pheasant specialist.*

trainer a small fortune to do the job for you.

"What about field trials? Do they have any relation to actual hunting?"

You can compound the fun and satisfaction you get from your gun dog—whether he's a trailer, a retriever, or a pointing breed—by running him in field trials, and the things you (and he) learn when competing with other dogs and handlers will make you a better hunting team. It's true that some bird-dog trials put more emphasis on speed and ground coverage than makes sense in northern covers, and some-

times the discipline of retriever trials seems a bit remote from the realities of duck-shooting (I want my retrievers to drop the duck and shake all the water off their coats *before* they come into the blind, and not after, and if a Lab of mine swam across a cove instead of running around the shoreline when running would be easier and faster, I'd consider him a mental case). But by and large the good field-trial dog is an equally good performer in the shooting field.

Today, too, there's a growing trend toward "fun trials" or "training trials" and the less ferocious forms of competition, so if you own a dog it's a good idea to join your local field-trial group and make your gun-dog fun a year-round proposition rather than seasonal.

"Should I get a dog or a bitch?"

There are good reasons for preferring either one. Males usually have more drive, courage, and stamina, and of course they don't come in season; bitches aren't as likely to fight or roam, and are usually easier to train because they're more anxious to please their master. I prefer dogs; a lot of experienced dog men prefer bitches; you pays your money and you takes your choice (or you evades the issue by getting one of each).

"How is it you haven't mentioned my favorite breed, buster? If you weren't in the pay of the Labrador retriever trust you'd have had at least a few paragraphs on vizsla (or Plott hounds, or Rottweilers, or Rhodesian Ridgebacks)."

There's not room in a brief chapter to cover all the great breeds of hunting dogs. If you're buying one, the important thing is to know what kind of shooting you'll be doing, and then to match the specialized, bred-in instincts and talents of a particular breed to your own particular needs.

And remember, there's almost as much difference between puppies and their potentials as there is between kids—there are bright ones, stupid ones, bold ones, craven ones. Even in the same litter it's sometimes possible to find a pointer with a full-choke nose and one that couldn't scent an upwind billy-goat. But generally you'll get a puppy that—with love and patience and a little pleasant work—you can transform into a good gun dog and a good friend. Go to it.

Teaching the Basic Commands

by Jerome B. Robinson

29

Every hunting dog, regardless of breed or purpose, should be totally obedient to the four basic commands: *come, heel, sit,* and *no*. In addition, a pointing dog must stop and stand still when ordered to *Whoa*, and a retriever must know that he may not leave the blind until he is sent with the command *get back*.

Training begins with those basics.

Come is the command that keeps your dog under control. It's been said, "If you can call him, you've got a hunting dog." Having a hunting dog is not that simple, but it is true that if you can't call him, you haven't got a hunting dog—or any dog at all.

Heel is the command that keeps your dog from getting hit by a car when you are crossing a road and keeps him out of trouble when curious farm dogs come out to the hunting field with threatening intent. It brings him to your side.

Sit makes it possible for you to take your hunting dog into a house and have him behave like a gentleman. Furthermore, it keeps a retriever still while in the blind

and allows a bird hunter to take a break without having to keep up a running conversation with his restless bird dog.

No is the magic word that well-behaved dogs of any breed have learned means "Stop whatever you are doing NOW."

A bird dog that does not *whoa* on command probably will not back a bracemate, and will be unstoppable when he wants to break and chase. Even if you don't demand steadiness to wing and shot, you'll want your dog to hold his point until you either walk up his birds or send him in for the flush (not a field-trial standard to be sure, but practical at many times under actual hunting conditions). A dog that has been trained to *whoa* is more controllable under the stress of the moment.

Get back is the proper command used to send a retriever. Until he hears those words, a retriever's job is to stay steady in the blind and mark the falls of the birds you down.

Assuming that your dog has plenty of hunting instinct, a good nose, and an intelligent makeup, you can do a large meas-

Writer-photographer-outdoorsman Lennie Rue reinforces basic training with his dog Freckles. Dog must learn to Sit and Stay until owner sends him to fetch bird. Rue is using retrieving dummy to practice voice and hand signals.

Dog can't be expected to understand hand signals or voice commands until you show him what's wanted and let him master lessons through repetition. Here, voice is combined with manual positioning as dog learns to sit attentively.

ure towards preparing him for a successful hunting season by a lot of summertime schooling on those basic commands. Insist on the right response every time. Ten minutes of this kind of yard work every day will do wonders.

Here's how:

If your dog needs brush-up lessons to make him come every time you call him, take him out with a long checkcord attached to his collar. When he's at the full length of the checkcord, call his name and order him to *come*. If he doesn't respond immediately, give a sharp yank on the checkcord and haul him to you, repeating "Come" or "Here," whichever command you use.

When you have drawn him to your feet give him praise and repeat "Come, come." After a few sharp yanks, the dog will need only a flick of the checkcord to make him come streaking to you. Repeat this lesson

In brush-up session, Freckles is reminded of proper response to command, "Heel." Dog is controlled—guided to walk at master's side—with aid of leash, but if discipline is combined with fun, leash can soon be put aside.

for 10 minutes a day until the dog will stop whatever he is doing and come to you instantly when you call.

Teaching a dog to heel is simple, and it is imperative in certain situations to be able to order your hunting dog to walk at your side calmly. To teach a dog to heel you need only a leash and a strong stick five feet long. Repeating "Heel, heel," walk at a brisk pace, holding the dog at your side with the leash. If he forges

ahead, tap him on the chest with the stick, pulling him back with the leash at the same time. If he drags behind, simply pull him up beside you, repeating "Heel, heel."

After several 10-minute sessions of this sort the dog will know he must walk at your side when you say "Heel"—at least while he's on a leash. Now it's time to eliminate the leash. Before you start this lesson, fill your pocket with pebbles.

Now start him off on the leash, making

Good retriever remains seated until commanded to "Get back!" and fetch bird.
As with pointing breeds, therefore, training includes steadiness to wing and shot.
Dog must be accustomed to gunfire, and blank pistol is useful training tool.

sure he stays right beside you. Stop and take the leash off him and immediately start off, ordering him to heel. Tap him with the stick if he moves ahead and keep a handful of pebbles ready in case he bolts or swings wide to one side.

If he does run ahead, realizing that he is free of the leash, fling the handful of pebbles at him. He'll be very impressed. He didn't know you could reach out and administer discipline that way. Now he'll remember.

Once he gets the idea and is willing to heel, make it fun for him. Have him heel beside you as you run. Heel him in circles, stopping and changing direction. He'll like that and quickly learn to fall in step with you no matter what the pace or direction. Practice this the year round.

To teach a dog to sit, you merely force him into a sitting position, say "Sit, sit," and return him to the spot and make him sit again every time he gets up to leave. Admonish him, "Ah-ah." Repetition gets the job done quickly and without discipline other than the firm insistence that he sit and stay seated until you release him. Make him sit and walk around him. Tempt him to break out but insist that he stay seated anyway.

No is simply a loud command that is followed by punishment if the dog fails to stop whatever he is doing. He learns this from puppyhood, and if the command is always followed by punishment when the dog fails to respond, the dog will learn to respond very quickly and will not forget the lesson.

Teaching a gun dog to whoa goes hand in hand with teaching him to heel. When he's heeling well, stop and say "Whoa." Make him stand still for a moment, and repeat "Whoa"—then heel him ahead. With a pup under a year old, you should probably go no further. Just get him to stop and stand still when you whoa him at those times when he is walking at heel.

But as the dog gets into his second year and is confidently bird hunting, his whoaing lessons should progress.

Walking him at heel, order the dog to *whoa*. Then drop the checkcord and step off to the side, repeating "Whoa" and cautioning him with an upraised hand or pointing finger. Move around in front of the dog, insisting that he stay put. If he does jump or creep toward you, admonish him, saying "Whoa" sternly. Slap him in the chest between the front legs with your hand, firmly but without anger. Pick him up and carry him back to the spot and set him down, insisting, "Whoa." When he does stand still on command and lets you walk ahead of him or off to the side for a few seconds, go to him, pat him, and heel him forward. Keep repeating this in daily 10-minute sessions until the dog has progressed to the point that he will let you walk around him in circles without moving.

Now whoa him and begin walking farther and farther away from him, insisting that he stay put until you come back and give him a pat and move ahead with him at heel. When the dog has become content to let you walk around him, away from him and back without moving, begin tempting him to break, insisting all the while that he stay perfectly still until you pat him and send him on.

Walk in front of him making noises. Fire a blank pistol in front of him. Throw a handful of straw in the air and fire the pistol. Make your yard lessons progress toward the eventual time when you will whoa him even as live birds flush in front of him.

He is not a steady dog at this point, but he does know what *whoa* means and he will be easier to steady because of it. Keep him in practice by making him whoa several times a week. Tempt him to break, but don't allow him to do it.

Similarly, if your dog is a retriever, your yard-training sessions should be forming a base towards later field training for steadiness in the blind. Hence, you should insist that your retriever stay seated at your feet until you send him to retrieve upon the command, "Get back!"

Once the pup's first birthday is past and his retrieving instincts have surfaced fully, you can start restraining him without damaging his spirit. Make him sit with a checkcord attached to his collar. Now throw a dummy, saying nothing. When the dog breaks, yank him over backwards with the checkcord and haul him back to you. Make him sit and insist that he stay sitting for a few seconds. Then put your hand next to his muzzle, point out the line to the fallen dummy, drop your hand and say "Get back" simultaneously.

Daily repetition of this lesson is necessary. Never let the dog break, insisting that he stay seated beside you until you send him for the retrieve. If your dog is particularly hard-headed and doesn't seem to care how hard you yank on his neck, tie the end of a 20-foot checkcord to a tree or firm post and attach the dog to the other end. Seat him at the base of the tree and throw the dummy. Don't say a word. Let him hit the end of that anchored checkcord at full tilt. Then bring him back to your feet, seat him and repeat the performance as many times as it takes until the dog gives up charging out each time the dummy is thrown.

When that point is reached, begin over, making him sit and insisting that he stay seated until you signal him to make the retrieve by dropping your hand next to his muzzle and saying "Get back."

Once your dog has learned his basic yard-training lessons, you should keep him in practice by testing him the year around. During the last six weeks before gunning season, yard practice should be extra-emphatic. The dog that is kept in practice the year around will be a manageable dog in the field.

Preseason Conditioning

by Jerome B. Robinson

30

The seasonal extremes are potentially the most hazardous and least cordial to your dog's general health and comfort. During summer and winter the gun-dog owner should be alert to the need for providing the extra care so important to his dog's physical and psychological well-being.

For the neglected gun dog, summer can be purgatory. Left to the mercy of sweltering sun and stifling humidity, hounded by flying insects and badgered by crawling parasites, the kennel dog, especially, can only look forward to a summer in abject misery. His indoor counterpart, though somewhat better off, might also wish for a more considerate owner.

Properly providing for his summertime comfort will take a little initial sweat and elbow grease on your part. But, if the effort can't be dispensed as a labor of love, it can at least be chalked up to practical necessity, as good insurance against poor condition that will be a detriment to your dog come hunting season. The recipe for summer comfort is hardly complex, but it

does take in numerous ingredients, principally involving cleanliness and grooming, feeding and exercise.

Whether your dog is housed in a kennel or shares the family quarters, one of the first steps toward his summer comfort should be a haircut. For the shorthaired breeds—German shorthairs, vizslas, etc.—this will be little more than a good session with stripping comb and brush to eliminate dead excess hair from the coat. The longhaired breeds—setters, spaniels, goldens, and the like—will need a light overall trim, taking about a quarter of an inch of coat length in the process. A stripping comb will do, but electric clippers are the ideal tool for the job.

The folks who argue that a haircut has no cooling value to a dog are right. The pores of the canine skin differ considerably from those of humans. Unlike ours, the dog's skin pores release only minute amounts of body heat through evaporation; most of the dog's sweating is done through his tongue. But the canine haircut provides comfort in other ways. Princi-

Whether kenneled or housed indoors, dog and his quarters should be thoroughly disinfected to rid both of insect pests and parasites. After summer trim, dog should be soaked in commercial dip; then his quarters should be sprayed.

pally, dispensing with superfluous coat during a time of year when that coat is least needed enables an owner to spot more easily the presence of skin irritation or parasitic infestations. Not only can they be detected more readily, they can also be treated more expeditiously when the coat is sparse.

Moreover, the removal of excess coat makes less of a task out of the more frequent groomings the dog should receive during the summer months. The combined effects of a light trim and regular brushings help stimulate the growth of a healthy new coat by the time the fall gunning season rolls around.

The trim and brushing should be followed by thoroughly soaking the dog in one of the commercial dog-dip mixes designed to rid him of all external parasites. Sold in highly concentrated form, these solutions are made to be mixed with water and are easy to prepare. Dipping is quick and simple when done properly. The best utensil for the purpose is a 50-gallon steel drum or clean G.I. can of sufficient proportions to dunk the dog right up to his neck or shoulders. When placed in the prepared mixture, the dog is able to stand on his hind legs and place his forepaws over the edge of the container's rim for support.

Taking care to protect his eyes, nose,

Light summer trim with stripping comb or electric clipper won't significantly cool dog's skin but will help you spot any skin irritations or parasites and, if combined with regular brushings, will stimulate growth of new fall coat.

and ear canals, you can then scoop the solution over the head, neck, and outer ears
and give the submerged portions of the
dog's body a few brisk rubs to make sure
the coat is thoroughly soaked. The entire
procedure takes no longer than six or eight
minutes.

After dipping, it's not necessary to dry
the dog; simply let him shake—he will anyway—and walk him around in the sun for a
few minutes. When his coat is dry, follow
up with a quick brushing, and he'll not
only look and feel clean and refreshed but
will also give off a pleasant odor.

In fact, the aroma, which lasts for a
week to 10 days, will repel fleas, ticks,
mosquitoes, and other insect pests during
that period.

Kennel dogs should be dipped approximately every other week for maximum
comfort and freedom from parasites; house
dogs need be dipped only every three or
four weeks during the warm months. Incidentally, the dip solution can be saved
and reused, often for the entire summer, if
a lid is kept over the container to prevent
evaporation. Before each dipping session,
the solution should be stirred briskly and a
few more drops of concentrate and water
added, if necessary, to replenish the
mixture.

On the same day the dog receives his
trim and first dip, his quarters should be
thoroughly cleaned and sprayed with a
suitable disinfectant and tick-and-flea
killer. Take care in reading the labels of
any sprays before using, to determine that
they contain no ingredients harmful to
pets. Obviously, it does no good to dip the
dog and skip disinfecting his sleeping and
living quarters, or vice versa. If fleas and
ticks are eliminated from one and not the

other, the dog will quickly become re-in-
fested.

Extra care must be given to cleaning the
doghouse and kennel run. A cement run is
the best type, since it is easiest to keep
clean, disinfected, and sweet-smelling in
hot weather. However, if the dog is kept in
a pen with plain earthen or gravel surface,
the run should be soaked down with a
strong solution of salt water at least once a
week. The saline mixture discourages fleas
and kills their eggs as well as those of parasitic worms. For most effective results,
earthen runs should be turned over and
graveled runs raked prior to sprinkling the
salt water.

Besides cleanliness, shade is one of the
most important considerations for the
comfort and well-being of the kennel dog
in summer. If his enclosure has the advantage of natural shade from a nearby tree,
the problem has been solved. But if his run
is out in the open, some form of artificially
provided protection becomes a must.

A drape of heavy duck canvas placed
across a portion of the top and one side of
the fence will serve as well as anything. It
is not necessary, or even advisable, to
shield out the sun entirely. Some sunlight—
preferably that of early morning and late
afternoon—should be available to the dog.
So adjust the width and placement of the
canvas in accordance with your kennel's
dimensions and east-west exposure.

An adequate supply of fresh, cool water
is as much a comfort as a necessity for both
the kennel and indoor dog during the
warmer months. Diet, or rather the
amount of food given, is significant, too.
Generally speaking, a reduction of about
25 percent of the winter volume of food
given the kennel dog will adequately sus-

tain him during the summer. Cutting down on the fat content of his rations by about a third will keep him from gaining more weight than he should. Remember, though, that every dog is different, and it is up to you to watch your dog's diet carefully while making appropriate adjustments.

No less important in summer than at any other time of year is the matter of providing the dog with proper exercise. The major difference, however, is that in warm weather the dog should be exercised in the cool of early morning or late evening. Additional exercise, for dogs who naturally take to water, can be obtained by swimming, one of the best of all possible summer conditioners.

A word of warning for the gun-dog owner in summer. A car parked in the direct rays of the sun, with windows rolled up tight, will become a death-trap for a dog in amazingly short order. Always leave all car windows open at least an inch and a half to two inches from the top and park in a shady spot. Don't forget, the sun moves and so does the shade; never leave your dog in a parked car any longer than a half-hour without checking on him.

Going from one extreme to the other,

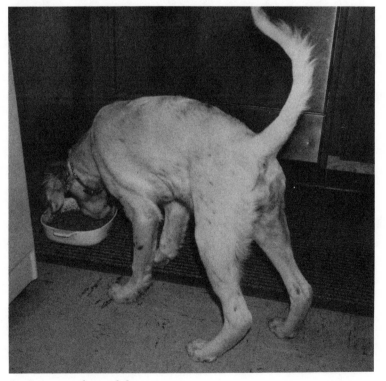

In winter, your dog needs larger quantities of his regular ration, plus supplements of high-energy foods, because he'll burn energy just to maintain body heat. This applies especially to kennel dogs but is true of house dogs, too.

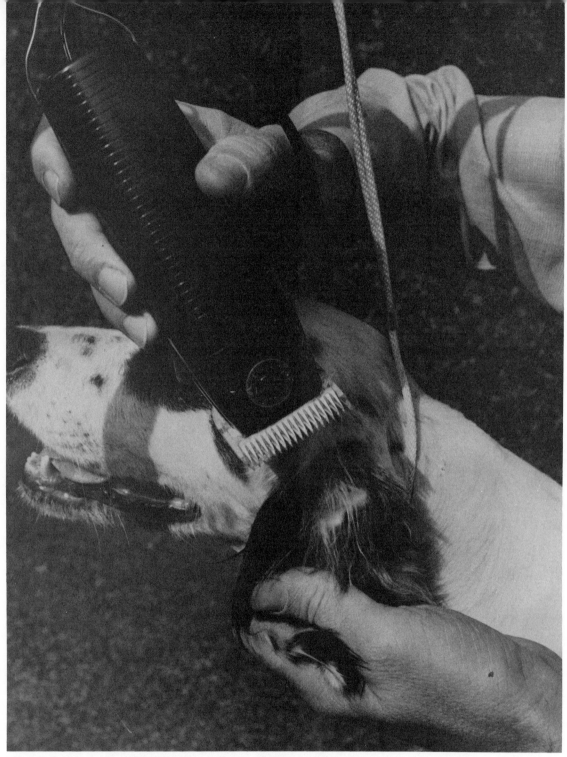

Electric clipper is very handy for removing excess coat and keeping your dog handsomely groomed. Depending on how fast hair grows, you may not have to repeat summer trimming, but dipping and house-cleaning are needed periodically.

winter is, of course, a time for buttoning up, fortifying against the elements. For the kennel dog, the cold months are potentially the dreariest and loneliest of the year. During no other season does he receive so little companionship, attention, or exercise.

Properly winterizing the kennel dog consists first of providing him with adequate shelter. It should be draft-free, large enough for comfort but small enough to be kept warm by the dog's own body heat. Many doghouses, especially the homemade kind, are constructed of wood. Since wood can rot, split, expand, and contract, cracks are bound to appear. These should be filled with plastic wood compound and painted—with a non-leaded paint—to seal out cold air.

The base of the doghouse should be elevated several inches off the ground, so that air can circulate beneath the floor and prevent dampness. A brick placed under each corner of the house is the most common method of providing elevation. A double floor, with a two-inch air space between it and the exterior flooring, offers adequate insulation for the base of the house.

At the entrance, either a two-way swinging door or some sort of breeze-break should be installed. The simplest form of baffle is a slab of plywood catercornered across the inside front of the entrance, and extending a few inches above the doorway's highest point. The most practical and efficient baffle arrangement consists of a detachable entrance extension. Even the dog owner who complains of being "all thumbs" can build one in a couple of hours. In design, it is essentially like a box with one end knocked out and an opening cut in one of the sides near the closed end. By means of hooks-and-eyes—one at the

top and another at the bottom on each side—the open end can be secured to the doorway of the doghouse for the winter. In effect, the extension provides a sort of closed porch, the end and sides of which prevent any drafts from blowing directly into the regular entrance port. An old piece of carpet, or a double thickness of burlap, tacked over the outside entry point of the extension serves to block out chilling breezes.

In severe winter climates, an insulated doghouse is distinctly in order. Most of the modern varieties now available are made of metal or plastic compounds that include built-in insulation. But even the less expensive plywood types can be insulated by a handy and ambitious owner who is willing to rebuild the interior.

You can give your kennel dog extra protection from howling winds and driving snow in two ways. The first involves the simple precaution of facing the doghouse entrance in the opposite direction from the prevailing winds. The second is to attach a tarp or strip of heavy canvas around the outside of that portion of the kennel fence that the doghouse entrance faces.

The inside of the doghouse should contain fresh, dry bedding of the sort that your dog can snuggle into to keep warm on the coldest days and nights. Ordinary straw makes about the best winter bedding obtainable. It has the proper consistency for burrowing and its peculiar body-heat-holding qualities are unequaled by any other material grown or manufactured. It's both economical and generally available.

After seeing to his primary requirement of protective shelter, the next most important consideration is your dog's winter diet. Generally speaking, the colder the climate, the greater the percentage of food energy he'll require to maintain body heat. He'll need larger quantities of his regular ration, in addition to supplements of higher-energy-producing foods.

Animal fat in either liquid or solid form must be included in the dog's daily diet. A good feeding rule for the kennel dog in winter is a 25 percent increase in his portions plus the addition of two tablespoons of rendered fat daily. Since climactic factors must be considered, along with the normal variance in the needs of individual dogs, you obviously should not hew to a hard-and-fast rule on winter feeding.

Adequate amounts of fresh water, too, are no less important to your dog during the cold months. Unless an electrically heated bucket is used, there is no easy solution to the problem of avoiding freeze-up of the dog's drinking water, with the resulting necessity of making three or four trips to the kennel each day to replenish his supply.

A possible alternative is to attach the water bowl or bucket, by means of a sturdy bracket, to the inside wall of the doghouse, where freezing will be prevented or at least slowed considerably. Every precaution must be taken, however, to insure against spillage, for soaked bedding would constitute a far greater health hazard to the dog than would temporary thirst.

The kennel dog's daily exercise should not be neglected. Turning him out to stretch his legs and flex his muscles is just as necessary to his mental state as to his physical condition. A brief exercise period twice daily will tend to break the monotony and loneliness of kennel life during the long cold spell.

Grooming a kennel dog in the dead of winter would be regarded as sheer idiocy by some folks. Yet much of the practical merit in its practice is purely psychological. Bringing the dog into the kitchen, basement, or garage for a nightly 10-minute grooming where it's warm and cheerful gives his spirits a tremendous lift.

Not only is the change of scene from his kennel beneficial, but the idea of spending a little time with his owner will mean more to him than a hefty chunk of beefsteak. Even these few minutes of personal contact each night will prove sufficient to instill in him the sense of belonging that every dog must have, but which is most often lacking in the kennel dog, especially during the winter.

Actually, that's about all there is to providing proper winter care for the kenneled gun dog. If most people are willing to go to as much or more trouble winterizing a car to keep it serviceable, you can hardly mind some extra effort to do the same thing for your own gun dog.

Your Dog's Summer and Winter Health

by John R. Falk

31

A good bird dog, like a well-mannered child, is the product of continuous, day-in, day-out attention. No matter how well trained your dog was once, the maintenance of that training is a matter of regular reminding. He must be taught to be on his best behavior at all times—hunting season or not.

Don't expect a dog to remember to hunt for you rather than for himself in bird season if you have treated him as a kennel cast-off the rest of the year. The best way to insure that your dog will want to please you in October is to be his friend and companion all year long—and let him be yours. You probably cannot work him on birds the year around, but you can let him know that he is respected by taking him in the car with you as often as possible, bringing him in the house often and letting him share your other outdoor activities: vacations, fishing trips, family picnics, and romps in the yard. Make him enjoy his times with you by asking him to do things, thereby letting him show you that he has

not forgotten what he has been taught and that he still wants most to please you.

Put him through regular reviews of the lessons he knows. Call him often and be sure he comes. Have him sit still while you walk around him. If he's a retriever, keep him in practice. Teach him that he has a place in the car and in the house, and insist that he stay quietly in that place when sent there.

Don't get the idea that you can make your dog happy by letting him run loose. Running without supervision is the quickest route to failure. The dog will learn only bad habits, not good ones, and he's likely to start hunting for himself instead of for you. What any dog wants most is your attention, your affection, and your praise. Remember that and help him to earn those rewards by regularly asking him to demonstrate that he is a cut above the street bums and neighborhood nuisances that get their kicks from running free.

You can't reason with a dog, but you can show him what action you demand when a

command is given. Praise him when he responds properly and correct him when he fails. Dogs understand such lessons and quickly learn to seek the reward of praise by proudly responding to your commands.

If you are planning to hunt your dog in October, you must begin preseason conditioning and refreshing his bird-handling manners by mid-August. This means field exercise and contact with birds should begin at least six weeks before opening day.

When hunting season opens, you'll expect your dog to be able to work all day without being exhausted—and you'll want to be able to keep going yourself. This demands physical conditioning for both of you. A dog keeps in fair physical trim by running and jumping in his kennel. But before the hunting season opens he must build up leg muscle. Exercise is the only thing that will replace summer flab with the hard muscle that he must have in order to run all day.

If you have no open country handy where you can run the dog for two hours several times a week, try roading him with a bicycle. Work him in the cool of early morning or in the evening—not in the midday heat.

Put the dog in a roading harness and attach it to the steering column of your bike with a 15-foot checkcord. Dogs naturally tend to pull against the harness. Let him pull you along the flat stretches of road and help him by pedaling up the hills. A half hour of this several times a week will tone up both of you.

If gun dog is allowed to run loose often, without supervision, he's apt to start hunting for himself instead of for you. Preseason refresher course includes work on checkcord, hunting birdy-looking cover and planted game.

To staunch dog on point, it helps to stroke ridge of his back, against the grain of hair. If he seems ready to break point, "whoa" him gently while pressing his hindquarters forward; resisting pressure, he'll get steadier.

Three times a week, and more often if possible, get your dog out in the country and work him in open fields with a 40-foot checkcord attached to his collar. Work him with the same enthusiasm you will have when you carry a gun behind him in hunting season. Show him you are interested. Begin with 15-minute runs and work up gradually to runs of two hours or more. Gradual lengthening of the running time will avoid muscle soreness which will otherwise cramp the dog's hunting style.

If native birds are not easy to find, use pen-raised birds for refresher training. Plant a dizzied pheasant or quail in a large open field. With the dog dragging the 40-foot checkcord, work him for 5 or 10 minutes, letting him hunt out birdy-looking spots, then swing him upwind into the area where the bird has been planted.

Keep yourself in position so that when he hits bird scent and flashes to a point you can get to the checkcord quickly. If he's going to break, this is the time he'll do it, and it's important for you to have the cord in hand before he makes a mistake.

Steadying him gently by repeating, "Whoa," work up the checkcord to his side, and get your hands on him. Calmly raise his chin with one hand and stroke the ridge of his back against the hair with the other. Raise his tail and stroke the underside of it until the dog holds his flag high and stiff. Then gently press his hindquarters forward, softly whoaing him if he acts nervous or seems about to break. He will resist this forward pressure, not wanting to be pushed into the bird. His point will become intense.

Now, stepping away from him with the checkcord in hand, work around in front of the dog, cautioning him with an upraised hand and whoaing him if he seems inclined to break. If you are satisfied that he is going to hold, increase your distance from him, indicating that you trust him. (Don't call him "good boy" at this time. To do so will probably make him wag his tail or look up at you and lose the intensity of his point.)

During early refresher lessons, don't hold him on point too long. A minute or two is plenty. Then move in and either kick the bird out or pick it up and throw it in the air—but get it out of there.

If the dog makes a hesitant break, jerk him back into place with the checkcord and speak the word "whoa" abruptly. If he really tears out after the bird with full intention to chase, brace your feet and let him go the full length of the cord. When he hits the end of the line, yank him off his feet and over backwards, the harder the

better. No word is needed. No one has ever broken a dog's neck doing this, but many dogs miss the full intent of the lesson because their handlers fail to realize that one good hard jolt can do more than any number of halfway measures.

Having yanked him over backwards, there is no need to show anger. Bring the dog back to the point of his misdeed, set him up on point with your hands and whoa him, holding him in place for several seconds. Then give him a pat and send him on.

A dog that has been trained will not need much of this to make him remember that points are to be held until he is touched by your hand and sent on.

Work for relocations of the same bird and, if your state's laws permit, shoot a blank pistol or shotgun over him when the bird is flushed. Two or three points in each training session are sufficient. More will make the session seem too artificial to the dog and he may become bored.

Remember that the training field is no place for a display of anger. If the dog infuriates you, put him back in the kennel until you have cooled off. Then go about correcting his mistakes in a constructive manner. Make every training session end on a happy note by commanding the dog to do something he does well and praising him for it when he obeys.

Preseason conditioning puts extra drains on your dog's energy. He needs to be fed more now than during his lazy summer

Preseason polishing includes repetition of basic voice commands and hand and whistle signals. For some of this training, checkcord will be helpful, but drop it after you're getting good responses.

If dog isn't steady or stylish enough on point, raise his tail and stroke its underside until he holds flag high and still. When you step away, do it slowly and, with your hand raised, caution him to prevent breaking.

months. A steady regimen of exercise will work off fat and replace it with muscle. Don't try to starve the fat off an overweight dog; this will only weaken him when he needs his strength the most. Exercise, exercise, exercise!

If you customarily hunt on foot and at a slow pace, it will be necessary to train your dog to check back with you at frequent intervals to avoid his getting too far ahead. Teach this by calling him back to you whenever he exceeds what you consider maximum range. This is not field-trial strategy but will do much to assure that your dog hunts with a pace and pattern that suits your own hunting speed. With repetition, the dog will soon adjust his ground pattern to include frequent check-backs that will keep him well within range and under control at all times.

If he insists on breaking out ahead and fails to heed your calls, run him down, shouting "NO," and thrash him. Then send him on and insist that he come to you when you call him back a minute later. Always correct the dog's mistake and discipline him immediately. Catch him and punish him at the point of his misdeed.

Don't call him to you and then give him hell or he's likely not to come next time you call him.

Once you have reaffirmed the dog's steadiness, it is important to work him with another dog, insisting that each honor the other's points. In the field you will often hunt with a friend who wants to run his dog, too. If neither animal has been trained to back, one will surely steal the other's point with the inevitable result of wildly flushed birds and the distinct possibility of a dogfight to add to your headaches.

Backing, like other training responses, is effected through repetition. When one dog establishes a point, bring the other in on a checkcord. The moment the pointing dog is sighted, whoa your dog and steady him with your hands. Then have your partner flush the birds from in front of the pointing dog. Do not lead your dog in to where he can smell the birds. He must learn to stop when he sees another dog on point, not wait until he confirms the point by smelling the birds himself. Repeat this lesson frequently until your dog automatically stops when he sees the other dog pointing. Then begin testing his responsibility by working him with a freely dragging checkcord and later with no checkcord at all. Stay near the dog so that you can stop him with your voice should he fail to back the moment he spies the pointing dog.

Preseason conditioning and refresher training are absolutely necessary for an enjoyable hunting season, regardless of how well your dog may have behaved the previous season. So assess your situation carefully. If you do not have time or do not feel enthusiastic enough to take the time to get your dog ready for hunting season, admit it to yourself early and make arrangements for your dog to spend at least six weeks with a professional trainer who can do the job for you. The cost will be negligible compared to the frustration and disappointment that an unprepared dog will cause once opening day is upon you.

Part V: Upland Birds

Hitting Upland Birds

by Charles F. Waterman

32

The fine wingshot who is also a good instructor is a rare treasure, for most good shots have forgotten how they do it—if they ever knew. Take an expert who has studied coaching *as well as* shooting and you're getting somewhere, but if a man's only qualification is the ability to kill 10 quail with 11 shells, his well-meant instruction may do more harm than good.

Watch him? Heavens, yes, man! Watching him may be an education—but take his words with salt.

For example, he may tell you he sees only the bird and never the barrel or bead. He's honest. He *thinks* he doesn't see them because that part has long been subconscious with him—the way you never consciously feel the accelerator when you want to drive faster, but if he never saw them he couldn't hit with a gun that didn't fit him—and the chances are the true expert can do fairly well, even with an oddball gun.

And there are some time-honored rules about upland guns that should be examined. The upland gun is supposed to be open-bored and lightweight, thus easy to carry, quick to point, and able to throw a broad pattern at close range. But not all upland game is at close range, and the best dove shot I know uses a Model 12 trap gun when the shots are to be long. If they're apt to be close, he takes an open-bored double or over-under. If he's uncertain, he's likely to lug both of them to his stand, by gosh.

And one of the best tight-cover gunners I know uses a stubby riot gun that's heavier than most experts would want. It's a load to carry all right but the weight is between his hands and he's fast as a cat with his load of 1¼ ounces of Number Nines. A longer barrel would change the balance and his speed would be gone. These are extremes, but think about them. In general, the short, light barrel is better for quick shots at slight angles. Muzzle weight helps in smooth swings when time isn't so limited.

Perhaps the improved-cylinder choke is nearest to an all-around uplander in anything that throws ⅞ ounce of shot or more.

Whitewing hunter, operating in desert brush of Mexico, demonstrates good gun position. Doves are among hardest winged targets; author knows expert who takes along trap gun for long shots plus open-bored double for close shots.

The 12, 16, and 20 are fine. The 28 and the .410 are expert's guns to be used only by keen judges of range, and they're cripplers in the hands of those who are occasionally overcome by enthusiasm especially on days when chances are few. They demand tighter choking than the bigger guns if anything but a very short shot is tried.

There's a tendency to use a gun that shoots too tight a pattern. Ruffed grouse, woodcock, and bobwhite quail gunners are often well served by skeet or cylinder boring. Once the range gets out to 25 yards and more the improved cylinder is better.

There's a simple rule about shot sizes: The more open the boring, the smaller the shot. Skeet is handled with #9's, and most skeet guns scatter too much for anything much larger than 8's if the shot is long enough to require the penetration of something bigger. Only solution is a very heavy load, which creates an awkward situation.

The "close-shooting" gun still has an aura about it. A thoughtful soul will buy an improved-cylinder weapon, go out and pattern it, and come back in ecstasy if the blamed thing throws a modified or full-choke pattern. If that's what he wanted, why didn't he order it?

Okay, with repeaters the skeet or improved cylinder should do for bobwhite quail, woodcock, or ruffed grouse. With

Outdoor photographer Bill Browning holds up morning's take of Hungarian partridge. Average flush of Huns is 14 yards or so from gun—nearly trap range— but rise is slower than clay target, and too much choke can handicap you.

doubles, skeet and improved cylinder or improved cylinder and modified should fill the bill. If you're willing to spend a little money at a gunsmith's and a little time at the pattern board you can get your barrels on the tight side and have them opened to suit—except with chrome tubes, where reaming isn't recommended.

Pheasants holding before a dog or in thick brush are good improved-cylinder targets. Generally speaking, modified boring will handle most pheasant situations, including cornfield shooting. Most of the western birds like sharptails, prairie chickens, sage grouse, and chukars are good modified-choke targets and the scaled, valley, and Gambel's quail often get up a far piece out too.

There have been volumes written about the three forms of wingshooting—the sustained lead (establishing a lead and swinging the gun at the same speed the bird is moving as the shot is fired), spot-shooting (firing with a stationary gun at the point you think the bird is going to be when the shot gets there), and the swing-through method (putting the bead on or behind the bird and swinging it through faster than the bird is going).

Most of the expert feather shooters use the swing-through method although they may subconsciously modify it to fit a situation. When a bird is going away at a narrow angle they spot-shoot just a little to the proper side. The aforementioned dove expert with the trap gun uses a swing-through on short shots but a sustained lead at long range, taking plenty of time.

The swing-through method comes very naturally when you're at short range and in a hurry. Your speed in coming up and past the target is almost automatic. Don't let yourself be bothered by the slide-rule facts—just swing through him, touch 'er off, and follow through. Most shooters with moderate experience shoot better when they have to hurry just a little. Watch a cock pheasant coming for a hundred yards, track him with the muzzle, take great care to do everything just right, and you'll miss him sure as hell.

For neurotic people like me the best way is to wait until it's time to shoot before I put the gun to my shoulder. The main thing in all upland-game shooting is to make the gun mounting, the swing, and the letoff all a part of the shot. Thinking of them one at a time is disaster.

Every shot begins from some kind of a gun carry, and regardless of how you tote it you should have your trigger hand on or nearly on the grip of the stock. The hand that will support the forend (lightly) can generally be brought to bear in time, even from your pants pocket, but the right hand (for right-handers) should be close to the operating machinery. You can carry the gun on your shoulder (trigger up), across your chest with the muzzle high (most common position when a shot is expected momentarily), pointing toward the ground, or across your left arm (forend in crook of elbow), or even pointing straight forward the way you're walking. The last isn't good if you're not hunting alone.

Of course you have to choose the position with regard to safety of any other nearby hunters and you should spend a moment figuring where your gun's going to be pointing if you stumble. Most of us have peered into a few muzzles from time to time, a 28 appearing remarkably like an 8-gauge on such occasions.

The correct moves are easily described. You begin to track the target with your muzzle as the butt heads for your shoulder.

You release the safety while you mount the gun. Your right shoulder lifts and your face moves to come down on the stock but if the gun fits well the shoulder and cheek motions are slight. The butt may brush your clothing as it nears firing position but some gunners automatically push it out a little as it comes up, then back to battery.

That's a good practice if you may be using stocks of different lengths. Once the gun is up, don't dawdle. Go ahead and shoot.

The classic pose, if terrain permits, is to have the left foot slightly forward, the left knee slightly bent and the body leaning into the shot and onto the left leg. The swing is made with the entire body, not

This one-man practice setup utilizes lanyard-activated trap and long pull cord that can spring it from any position. Since shooter has to mount gun after pulling, such clay-bird shooting improves field technique and reflexes.

the arms alone. The swing might be upward for a higher incomer and a little downward for a high outgoer. You blot out the incomer. You hold a little under the overhead outgoer.

I've made a lot of pictures of game shooters in action and many of them squat with their feet wide apart. This doesn't make for the "easy swing," but it's a controlled swing, even though it may be forced. Don't put it down, because some of these squatters are deadly. The same guys will be more relaxed at trap or skeet and most are surprised to see pictures of themselves squatting while shooting game. At trap or skeet there is so much shooting that the squatting pose would be tiring.

"Face the shot" is the rule. Try to have all of your physical apparatus lined up in the right direction, but don't worry if it won't work in a hurry. Just remember to follow through, even if it's awkward to do so. Lots of birds are killed with bad form and you may be better off to shoot instead of prancing around for a classic pose while a grouse bores through the willows.

Straightaway shots look easiest of all, but the straightaway and the very slight angle are responsible for what some call the "expert's miss." If there's more angle he can definitely ascertain the target's direction and be sure of his elevation as well as swing and lead. The straightaway may be rising a little or just leveling off, sometimes difficult to judge.

There's one common miss in which the shooter swings up fast on a straightaway, thinks he's stopped the gun as it's aligned, but actually "swings through" and misses high. Because flushing birds are *usually* rising there are some who say an upland gun should shoot high, something accomplished by a straight stock or reduced

pitch. This is a matter of the individual shooter and I know one good quail popper who says he wants more stock drop in his bird gun than in his duck gun. Says the upland shot is quick and it takes more cheek adjustment to get located on a straight stock. So it's a personal thing.

In shooting over dogs you can make an educated guess as to where the game will go when it flies. A woodcock veteran studies each point carefully, assuming that if the cover is thick the bird will go toward the most daylight and he prepares to shoot that way. Chukars can be expected to go downhill. The quails nearly always head for thicker cover and if they're close to it you may not be happy if you try to cut them off. I do not shoot well when their beady little eyes are coming right at me. Better to approach them from the open side where the shots won't be arm-length confrontations.

Beware of hard and fast rules but you might say there are three phases to a bird's escape from the ground. There's the steep upward climb as he gets flying room, there's the leveling off, and there's the high-speed getaway once he's established direction. This is especially noticeable in pheasants rising from thick stuff.

When walking up to dogs you should focus your eyes somewhat above the ground and a little farther out than the spot where you expect the rise—and don't try to see the birds on the ground as it's a psychological noose. Timing is the mark of the master and the temptation is to shoot too soon on noisy covey rises. You bang out two or three hasty misses and then stand and watch the birds, still within easy range and seemingly flapping off like buzzards. I know a few covey shooters who fire just as the birds leave the grass, using open guns.

Brittany spaniel delivers bobwhite to Charlie Waterman during Southern quail hunt. With covey birds like these, he points out, it's best to focus your eyes beyond where you expect the rise; then stay cool and pick one target.

Sometimes they kill a lot of game but it's a specialized method. Most of them use repeaters and figure there's still time for two carefully pointed shots after the rise. You can say it isn't sporting but it's not as easy as it sounds. Takes a cool head.

On any covey rise you should select a single bird, of course, and if you tend to flock shoot, make a practice of following one somewhat out of the main crowd.

Most prairie and desert birds tend to rise far out, even when pointed by dogs. I figure the average Hungarian partridge flush is about 14 yards from the gun. That's trapshooting range but they don't *leave* as fast as a clay target, and if you want a perfect gun for that I believe a double with improved cylinder and full choke is hard to beat. Make the first shot quick and take your time with the second after they level off. In a repeater I think modified is better than full choke. Sharptail grouse and sage grouse often take off at considerable distance as do western quail. Although there doesn't *seem* to be the urgency of a bobwhite quail flush, there's actually more need for hurry.

For these western birds, high-brass loads of 7½ shot will work, but for the sage grouse, 6's or 4's are better. You need at least 1⅛ ounces of shot.

Most of us could never get enough practice on game these days to develop into the class of the old market gunners of a century ago. The obvious substitute is clay targets, which may lack some of the elements of game but will give you the basics.

There are still a few places—even today—where the shooter can fire all the ammunition he can carry at live game. In Latin America there are dove shoots where the supply of birds is seemingly endless and the bag is used by local residents. If you wanted to spend the time and money you can get just as much live practice as the old market gunners. But these days, few can manage that.

How to Be a Better Bobwhite Hunter

33

by Lamar Underwood

It had been a tough day with bobwhite quail—long slogging walks between coveys and tough chances on swamp-loving speedsters that always seemed to be in the bad places. I had already watched three bunches fade into woody sanctuaries and then, for the fourth time, missed neatly with both barrels as a dozen vague brownish blurs exploded through the trees. I did not enjoy telling the pointer dog, Mack, "Sorry, boy!" again.

Where, I wondered, *were those obliging coveys we used to pin in cornfields and weed patches, that scattered so predictably into those gallberry swamp fringes where single-bird shooting could be taken seriously?*

By the end of that frustrating foray through Georgia's best quail country, I had learned the answer. It's quite simple, actually: Quail have smartened up. Letters I swap with bobwhite hunters here and there so frequently contain the same lament that the problem seems to be a national experience. Except for isolated lodes of open country and populous coveys

the bobwhite game has come down to a choice between plunking down the greenbacks for preserve shooting, gaining an occasional passport to the plantations of the heavy hitters, or learning to cope with the tougher conditions and wiser birds that characterize public gunning.

My experiences (mostly misfortunes) have taught me how to deal (or try to deal) with this modern version of Mr. Bobwhite. On the chance that you are about to travel the same dreary paths, I'd like to share a few observations that may help put more quail in your hunting coat.

The bobwhite behavior pattern approved by the Outdoor Writers Association of America is that the covey awakes leisurely in the a.m. and strolls to the feeding area closest at hand. After an unhurried meal, the gang walks on to a patch of semi-open cover where they loaf and dust until the late afternoon, when they repeat the same pattern.

Unfortunately, the quail I stalk have learned that such rigid patterns of behavior can be read by the enemy. They often

*Here's Mr. Bob, one smart bird that's grown still smarter under hunting pressure
and changing farm practices. When quail aren't where they "should" be
at a given time of day, Lamar Underwood suggests hunting areas of thicker cover.*

fly directly to the field and out again. This is especially true in areas of thick cover where the birds have become wise to the fact that those long walks in the thick make them more vulnerable to predators.

One pattern I see often works like this: The birds roost in a heavily grassed flat well away from thick woods but close to the corn or bean field. They leave the roost very early, running quickly into the field to feed, then fly all the way into the nearest woods. At dusk they fly out again, feed, and hole up in the roosting patch.

Certain coveys are more likely than others to be flying to feed. You can expect a good deal of aerial travel from birds that are located within striking distance of a farmhouse where house dogs run loose. When hunting such areas, be ready for unpredictable birds that are harassed to extreme wildness. Even when you find them, they probably will not hold for your dog, because they've learned to associate the sound of his approach with real trouble.

Flying to feed is also common among birds that have been hunted heavily. This makes it doubly important to know more than a *few* good places to hunt. Give those spots a rest between bouts. If you hit the same areas hunt after hunt, you're training the birds to be super-smart.

Birds that have to cross a road between their holding cover and the fields will invariably fly rather than walk. Sure, you'll see an occasional bunch leg it across a road. But don't count on the habit, even on back-country dirt roads.

Finally, expect some flying from birds that use loafing areas deep in the fieldside woods.

Very often, the birds will spend both the roosting time and midday hours well back in the woods. Most fieldside forests seem like impenetrable walls next to the fields, with tangled briers and screens of second-growth bushes beneath the taller trees. But chances are that deeper back these areas contain many open, amphitheaterlike patches where the birds will have low grass for protection and yet be in a position to get the jump on sneaking predators. This is why serious rabbit hunters flush so many coveys of quail. These boys are used to busting through the kind of cover that often turns back bird hunters—and their dogs. With a little determination and a solidly controlled, slow-working dog, you'll find a lot of coveys in the fieldside areas. When the birds have gone away to feed, Old Sport may be able to trail them into the field. If you're not reducing a pair of hunting trousers to rags every season, you're just not working these areas hard enough.

However, dealing with these unpredictable coveys requires you to cover all the bets. You need to work the fieldside woods, the fields, and even those smallish patches that sometimes escape attention—brushy ditch banks, bulldozed brush piles, weed-grown layout land, and brushy fencerows.

Keep in mind also that top-drawer quail country will contain enough wild seed-bearing plants for Bob to have a decent meal without ever going into a corn or soybean field. Acorns are a good bet, and I'm always amazed at the way many southern hunters ignore those numerous low-oak ridges where the birds have good cover and food all in one spot.

In my opinion, most quail hunters today plan their hunts as though the bobwhite were the greatest glutton in the outdoors. The minor inefficiencies of modern crop-picking machinery leave so much grain spilled on the ground that coveys can feed

Whether in Georgia or Oklahoma, you may still find lots of old-fashioned field shooting if you know where to work dogs, but in many regions bobwhites have developed tendency to fly instead of walking to feeding areas and to roost.

in minutes. The days when they were forced to range widely, leaving a nice trail, are over, except in late season when thin table fare does force more movement.

Another popular notion that my personal experience has deflated is that we can linger over our coffee and breakfast until long after daylight because the bobwhite is a late riser and slow starter. Mebbe so when the weather turns sour with rain or locally extreme cold. But on most days I figure the covey to come awake at sunrise and whistle at least once. Some quieter chirping and whistling may follow, and shortly they'll be on their way off the roost. I'm convinced that many coveys have fed and retreated to deep-wood haunts by the time most hunters get afield. That habit of whistling at sunrise is also cashable when you're trying to get a line on the location of coveys while casing a new area.

Since most of us hunt whenever we get a chance, the question is academic. But if I'm fat with time and can have my druthers, I'd druther not hunt when the wind is carrying the scent into space and has the birds skittish (they know full well that the wind noise covers the usually reliable sounds of approaching danger); or during the morning when one of those bitter-cold highs has moved in, and the ground is like iron and a good breeze is whipping about; or during the rain (the birds seem to move less, and scenting conditions—judging from the performances of most dogs I've seen— are at an all-time low); or during those frequent early-season periods in the Deep South when the weather is unseasonably warm and dry.

My favorite time? It has to be a day that begins to turn dark while the temperature plummets every minute and heavy low clouds begin to spit a little snow or sleet,

Sensing the approaching storm, birds will be on the move all day.

Some quail hunters talk too much. These are the boys who are so flattered at their local reputations and prowess that they're willing to take casual acquaintances to their favorite spots. I've been burned on that one several times. Mr. Casual Acquaintance later shows up at *your* hunting spot with his buddies, sometimes taking it over and sometimes sending your farmer friend into a well-justified rage. Now I hunt with a couple of other quail addicts. We worked hard to find our good places, and we keep our mouths shut.

Surprisingly enough, some hunters talk too little, especially before the season opens. There's nothing wrong with strolling into a farmer's yard with your hunting clothes on and a car full of impatient dogs nearby, but the job of finding a place to hunt goes a lot easier when you seek out landowners *before* the season to obtain hunting permission.

Do extraordinary quail dogs make some men seem to be outstanding bird hunters, or do outstanding bird hunters make mediocre dogs look like champions?

The question has always intrigued me because I love bird dogs and the wacky, wonderful things they do more than any other aspect of quail hunting. Pointers, setters, Brittanies, shorthairs—I like 'em all, and the hours I've shared in the field with them have led me to the conclusion that they all need a lot of help and cooperation from the men who take them hunting. A great nose, desire, brains—these are the credentials for quail-dog greatness. But they cannot be developed or used properly by a poor hunter.

The best quail dog of my youth was a real ground-burner who could find birds as

though he had a map of their locations stamped on his brain. Were he alive today, I think he could be bringing in some hardware from amateur shooting-dog stakes. But I seriously doubt that he would get the job done in most of the areas where I hunt quail.

Throughout the South, the no-burning laws that result from the cultivation of pulpwood timber, combined with an absence of woods-roaming livestock, have resulted in forests that are often nearly impenetrable with undergrowth.

Give me a close-working dog that stays under solid control, and I'll be a happy man. I'd like to see him bend out a bit when we hit the more open areas, and he should seek birdy objectives constantly. When a cast takes him out of sight, as is inevitable sometimes, he should swing back reasonably soon.

When I can get it, steadiness to wing is an important plus. I do want my dog to break shot to retrieve, because a few seconds' edge is all some cripples need to become lost. Obtaining these qualities in a dog with a good nose is a real challenge that cannot be covered adequately here. Three books will make the job easier—*Training Your Own Bird Dog* by *Sports Afield* magazine's late Gun Dog Editor, Henry P. Davis (Putnam), *Gun Dog* by Dick Wolters (E. P. Dutton), and *The Practical Hunter's Dog Book* by John R. Falk (Winchester Press).

The help your dog needs from you in the field begins the moment you start your hunt. Plan your swings so as to take maximum advantage of the wind while in the hot areas. When scent problems develop with running birds or the trail of birds that have secretly flown, you'll want to give the dog plenty of time to work out the situa-

Brace of quail like this is often bagged thanks to close-working dog that stays under constant control, although there are still plantations and other hotspots suited to traditional pointers that range way out and cover ground fast.

tion. You're not helping him any by walking about and breaking up the lines of scent. (The same tip applies to retrieving problems, of course.) As the dog works, take a good hard look at the country and try to determine where the covey might have gone.

"A partridge is a throw shot."

This message, hammered at me by a southern quail-shooting mentor when I was at a tender age, has helped my score on quail somewhat but has pretty well reduced me to a shambles on doves, ducks, and the other speedsters that require a fast swing.

On days when things are working well,

the results usually stem less from marksmanship than my experience in sizing up the situation after a point. How far are the birds in front of the dog? What route will they take? What's the best way to approach the point to get a clear shot? When I'm coming up with the answers to these questions consistently, I get easier shots and score better.

Single birds that flush unannounced have always given me the heebie-jeebies and still do. The old grouse-shooting technique seems to help, though. You start mounting the gun at the sound of the flush and point in that direction. Now you're ready to fire the instant you spot the bird (assuming you know where your partner is at all times).

That old-timer I mentioned earlier had a favorite expression to chide me with whenever I blew an easy chance. He'd shake his head and say: "That's some mighty sorry gathering up of partridges." Even today I can't miss a simple shot without hearing that remark rattle in the back of my mind.

And I hear it often!

Western Quail

by Charles F. Waterman

34

The true desert is hostile, violent, unreliable, and often frightening to visitors, with quivering heat in summer. It bursts into sudden bloom at the touch of rain and contracts to apparently lifeless browns and grays when normal drought returns. It is strange that such a place is crowded with wildlife.

I list four kinds of birds as desert quail. The Gambel's quail is a dry-land equivalent of the California or valley bird. The scaled quail is a widely distributed ground racer, and the edges of its range get into country hardly ever termed "desert." The Mearns quail goes as a desert quail, even though it doesn't live at all in what would commonly be called true desert. Its home is grassy highlands, but they are within the desert's boundaries. I must list the masked bobwhite as a desert quail, although it is too scarce to hunt and may or may not return to huntable populations within the United States.

There are several things to be impressed upon new hunters of the desert. For one thing, there are many bird dogs that hunt a

lifetime in true desert without ill effects. There may be individual dogs that cannot adapt to the many piercing, gouging, and cutting things the desert quail live in, but there are others that learn to take care of themselves within a few hours. Almost invariably a dog has some troubles at the beginning.

The same goes for the hunters themselves. They need good footwear, and they must learn not to sit down on cholla balls or lean against saguaro cactus, but it is seldom in hunting season that they are in serious danger from the poisonous reptiles or from the much-maligned peccary, which is just a shy little pig despite its tusks.

The Gambel's quail has the same questionmark topknot carried by the California or valley quail. Like its relatives, it runs hard, sometimes flushes wild, and often holds tightly as a woodcock. It flies pretty fast but seems to lack the acceleration of a bobwhite. It will go a long way at times, especially when it can pitch down a desert mountain, and often forms large coveys.

They split up well, seldom holding together for a series of flushes, and their scattering is both helpful, when you can find a bunch of singles, and frustrating, when they sometimes land, run in all directions, and keep going.

I got my start on Gambel's quail with Steve Gallizioli of the Arizona Game and Fish Department, a research chief, biologist, and hunter. The Gambel's country Steve chose was very hilly, a part of the giant Sonoran Desert not far from Phoenix, and carried a vast variety of desert vegetation. The arroyos were brushy, and we saw some Coues deer and very frequent sign of javelinas. The footing was very bad in places. It wasn't the kind of country where you'd fall off a cliff, but it was easy to sit down hard on any one of a variety of cacti, a good place to turn an ankle or smash an elbow, and a place decidedly rough on fine gunstocks.

We were running two pointing dogs, but they didn't hold a large covey at any time. They would put up a bunch, well out of range, and then we'd mark the birds. Usually they would simply cross over into the adjacent draw, and Steve could tell you about where they'd be without even looking. All he seemed to need was their general direction. Once they landed, the dogs did pretty well until it got hot and dry late in the day.

Of course I'd heard the stories that a dog won't help on desert quail, but on the first covey we had a pretty good dog demonstration. The birds went up wild and drifted into another draw, and when we followed them up one of the dogs pointed near the bottom. I went over there and several quail went out, one at a time, not exactly where the dog was headed, evidently having moved after it stiffened

up. Those birds didn't seem very noisy as they left, each of them heading for the gully's rim, and I knocked down a couple in short order. When I went up the bank of the arroyo to encourage a dog that was pursuing a cripple, another dog pointed what I thought must be the wounded quail, but it was a healthy bird, and I got it as it skimmed the ground.

Later in the day we saw a large covey running ahead of us, hurrying along a high ridge with the dogs trying to point but continuing to move after a moment's hesitation. The accepted practice is to run at such birds, hoping to make them fly, but that can be an athletic endeavor and may not work anyway. When we lost track of that bunch our assumption was that they had walked off the ridge in the direction we last saw them, so we slid down off the top and hunted hard where they should have gone, to no avail.

It must have been an hour later that we clambered back to our ridge to head back where we'd come from and found that our covey was hidden on the slope opposite from the one we'd descended. They were no more than 50 yards from where we'd lost track of them. A single bird lost its nerve first, zoomed down into an enormous valley, was followed by half a dozen birds, and then the entire covey. They spread out broadly and began calling almost immediately. We found quite a number of individual birds.

Gambel's quail live in the desert lands of Nevada, Utah, Colorado, California, Arizona, New Mexico, western Texas, and northwestern Mexico. They roost in dense thickets and they're usually found near water. Undoubtedly the Gambel's quail might like some of the things eaten by its relative, the valley quail, but in the desert it shows a strong preference for mesquite and deervetch, primarily the seeds.

In some areas the scaled quail lives with the Gambel's quail. Some observers say that it can stay in more barren desert land than the Gambel's, but it also appears in what I'd call fairly arid country that certainly isn't desert. It's collected as far north as Kansas, but it doesn't live as far west as California.

It is also called blue quail and cotton-top, and this one is the track star as far as I am concerned. Scalies fly fast, generally tending to go higher into the air than the Gambel's quail. Steve Gallizioli pointed that out to me early in my desert-hunting career, and my experience certainly bore it out. I've seen scaled quail going some 150 feet high on occasions.

Sometimes they hold but they're more likely to flush wild, and you'll read that dogs are useless except to recover the dead and wounded. I think they're harder for the dog than Gambel's or valley quail, but I'll take the dog if I can control it. Even when they're whistling along the sand with their legs hardly visible in blur I'd like to have a dog, and after I've lost sight of the danged things I like to have someone with a nose to get them going again. And if the dog gets birdy it may even be wise to call it off and make a big circle, coming on the

Author and his dog Kelly hunt Gambel's quail in habitat where "scaleys" are also found. Some hunters won't take dogs into hot, dry, cactus-and-rattler country, but Waterman stresses that many dogs adapt to desert hunting.

Clockwise from top left, these birds are: Gambel's quail, mountain quail, scaled quail, and California, or valley, quail. Closely related Gambel's and California varieties have similar curling topknots, but in range and habits the latter is more like straight-plumed mountain quail. Mountain species is our largest quail—about 12 inches long and weighing more than eight ounces—but nevertheless it can be tricky to hit. Scaled quail is slightly bigger than bobwhite and rises less explosively but runs far out before flushing.

fugitives from another direction. It doesn't work very often, but nothing works very often on cottontops.

I have repeatedly found scaled quail in desolate country where there is little inviting vegetation, but there is a tendency for them to stay where the brush is just a little higher, the grass just a little denser, and the cactus just a little closer together, even though none of it looks thick enough.

As to the method of running at scaled quail—or any running bird for that matter—the best method is to gain gradually if you can. You see them moving along ahead of you, probably keeping the same distance, and by speeding up just a little you may gain appreciably, possibly getting within range before you ever make your break. Then when you go, go fast, and whether you yell or not is a matter of personal preference. What you yell probably doesn't make much difference either, but many of the things I yell at desert quail make me feel much better. Shooting into the air might help to get them airborne, but unless you're toting a repeater it can leave you short of ammunition when they do jump, if they do. If you have no dog and they scatter instead of flying, you have tough work ahead of you, for there's no telling how far the individuals will run. Once they do scatter, make a quick survey of the places you would hide if you were a scaled quail and kick the stew out of those places. They can go right up your shirt front sometimes.

Many scaled quail are shot on the ground while running, a practice frowned upon by most upland gunners. It sure isn't wing-shooting, but I doubt if it's much easier than shooting cottontails, which hardly ever fly. I don't shoot scalies on the ground but I won't help lynch someone who does.

In much of the desert bird hunting you can look upward and see a quick graduation from a true desert ecology to the mountain slopes, possibly grassy areas that grade into conifer timber and peaks, sometimes snowy in hunting season. Up there you might even find blue grouse in some of the northern parts of what we call the desert, but in the Southwest, near the Mexican border and on into Mexico, is a quail that follows the bobwhite pattern ahead of a dog and lives in a unique habitat.

It's the Mearns or harlequin quail, confined to a small U.S. range, and hunted by only a few gunners who use bobwhite methods and dogs that would be equally at home with bobwhites. You don't hear much about that sport because there isn't much of it. In Mexico it's the Montezuma quail.

The terrain is higher than the true desert, and in Arizona it's made up of hills carrying tall grass and scrub oaks. Nearer the equator in Mexico I understand the altitude is likely to be much higher. The Mearns quail is especially unusual in its food choice, for although it has adapted to grain where that's available, as have most other quail, it does a great deal of digging for tubers or bulbs, the chufa tuber being listed prominently as crop content. Where the harlequin has been digging, it leaves a gouged-up area that resembles squirrel excavations. The bird's feet are especially designed for it.

The Mearns quail has about the same silhouette as the bobwhite; it holds tightly and perhaps runs even less. On our first hunt for it, I walked away from our little van camper to exercise the dog, stepped into a covey of quail, and watched them whir away over the grasstops, looking and acting like bobwhites.

That afternoon we worked waist-high grass along some ridges, and when my dog disappeared I finally found him frozen in grass so tall and thick he was only a shapeless light area. When I went to him the quail went up from under his nose and I managed to wait until it had leveled off well above the grass tops and bagged my first harlequin. I did it again a few moments later, obviously having worked into a scattered covey along the ridge. Then I had another point and half a dozen birds went up, boring downhill for the oak clump in the draw below me.

I think that is typical of hunting Mearns quail. It acts like a bobwhite. The dogs should work it like bobwhites, and the gun that works for bobwhites should be perfect for the harlequin.

Valley quail hang around towns, stroll about under bird feeders in backyards, and stage military parades on the shoulders of main-travelled highways. Apparently they aren't very wild and not particularly afraid of people. My efforts at hunting them would indicate they needn't be afraid of me.

My very first experience with them was a forecast of things to come. Using a good pointing dog in Hun and chukar country, I put up a covey of valley quail in sagebrush that was about waist high. They got up like a swarm of big bees and pitched right back into the sage, possibly 30 of them, and I wasted no time taking after them for I'd heard they might scoot out of the country if I was slow. Apparently only part of the bunch had gotten up the first time. The little hilltop was swarming with them.

My dog pointed in front of me and five or six birds got up behind me, fluttering over the sagetops and in no hurry at all. Just as I got on one of them, they dropped to the ground and I shot too high. I actually saw them running haphazardly around in a little open place, evidently looking for the best spots to hide, so I rushed at the opening to make them fly, but nothing happened, and I looked wildly about to find my dog pointing staunchly 20 yards away. He had his head tipped downward as if the bird was right under his nose, which it was. When I walked up, the quail fluttered around a little at the bottom of a sage bush and disappeared again.

Then I almost stepped on a bird and it buzzed away to dive back into the cover. I missed that one twice, and the dog pointed again. I kicked and shook the sage, but nothing came out and I assumed the bird or birds had run. Then we put up a bird accidentally and I killed it before it could dive back into the sage. End of episode.

The California quail is also called the valley quail, but there are a number of races of very similar birds, all of them found in the West, and only a biologist with a library can really straighten out the Latin. Generally, it's California quail near the coast and valley quail inland. The Gambel's quail is quite similar in appearance and a close relative, but I consider it separately because it is primarily a desert bird.

Where they are found together, the valley quail (I like to call it by that name when it isn't in California) and the mountain quail behave about the same, except that the mountain quail doesn't form huge flocks as the valley quail does and has a somewhat different flight pattern.

Valley quail will sit in trees after being flushed from the ground and sometimes are in plain sight, a situation that has never contributed to my mental attitude. Like any other bird flying from a tree, they can get added speed in diving downward but are addicted to little 20- or 30-foot flights to other branches. Before putting this down as easy shooting, you should try it.

Valley quail and mountain quail have a very similar range, although the valley quail is found in a somewhat larger area. Both are found all along the Pacific coast from the Canadian border clear into Baja California, although the valley or California quail are found somewhat farther south of the Baja peninsula. Valley quail are as far east as Utah. Both birds are shot in Washington, Oregon, Idaho, Nevada, and California.

The mountain quail is the largest of our quails and wears a plume that sticks straight out of its forehead, whereas the various valley quails and the Gambel's quail have questionmark plumes that curve forward. The mountain quail is commonly found at higher elevations, but its range overlaps that of the valley quail so much that they're frequently hunted together. Mountain quail do not bunch into the huge flocks quite common with valley quail. Like the valley quail, the mountain model is quite willing to run instead of fly. When it does fly it is more likely to rise somewhat higher into the air before leveling off. Perhaps it's because the mountain quail is larger, but it doesn't seem to go quite as fast. It goes fast enough.

Hunters after these birds for the first time are surprised to find not many of their kills are the fully plumed and uniformed adults. Young birds of the year are likely to have abbreviated plumes and drab colors, and when you first shoot one you're likely to think you've bagged another species entirely.

It may be that both mountain and valley quail are capable of wide ranging, but they will often stay in a very small area, even when hunted. I've chased both kinds back and forth when the cover was right. Of course it's the same as with other birds. The more you harass a covey, the smaller it becomes as individuals walk away or find really secure hiding places.

Mountain quail are usually found in brushy draws if there are such places, but they seem to run or fly out into the open occasionally when hard-pressed. I get the impression that they have decided the hunt is going along the draw and it will be safer to get out of it. In Idaho I once worked a small and brushy draw thoroughly with the dog birdy all the way. Then the dog wandered out into the sagebrush and pointed. The only birds I killed were out in the wide open where the sage was only a couple of feet high. I am convinced they went out there because our hunting pattern was definitely following the draw.

Woodcock— Acrobat of the Alders

35

by Ed Kozicky and John Madson

Not many hunters really know the woodcock, which may be just as well. To know the timberdoodle is to become owned by him, and the avid woodcock hunter is probably flakier than even the avid quail hunter, which is saying a lot. For the woodcock is a strange bird, and casts a strange spell on the men who hunt him.

He's a chunky, almost neckless creature, his warm browns and buffs in a dead-leaf pattern. He is a little larger than a bob-white (4 to 8 ounces), with an extremely long bill and bugging eyes near the top of his head. As a bird, the woodcock is put together all wrong, with ears in front of his eyes. He looks like a mistake—until he takes wing.

Woodcock are strong migrants; inhabiting the eastern part of the United States, the range north in summer into southern Canada. Migrating at night, they fly south in early fall for as much as 2,000 miles, and for reasons known only to woodcock they tend to concentrate in Louisiana bottomlands. There are other wintering grounds in the South, but these are best known to woodcock and to a few men not eager to talk about them.

Woodcock are crepuscular by nature—meaning that they're most active during early morning and evening. Through the day they just lie low, but to date no one has caught one asleep.

They subsist almost entirely on earthworms. Their bills are highly adapted for extracting earthworms, and their digestive tract is designed to convert those earthworms into energy. The timberdoodle's tireless quest for earthworms is a guidepost to the hunter. You often find the birds in alder swales where the overhead canopy has shaded out the understory, and experienced hunters watch for woodcock probing in the moist soil and the telltale white splashings that the woodcock leave.

It is difficult to fathom why woodcock prefer one area and not another. But as they funnel south down the flyways, newcomers from the North replace their brethren who have moved on, and they somehow find the same coverts. Woodcock

Occasionally woodcock flush wild, but more commonly they hold, like this one, blending into ground litter; dogless hunter may pass birds he never sees. If you shoot and miss, try to follow flight, as woodcock won't go far.

hunters are careful, watchful men, constantly on the lookout for splashings and probings, and they can tell at a glance whether the signs are old or new. If the signs are fresh, they search the area carefully.

Hunting is best with a pointing dog. Woodcock hold well—so well that it's easy to walk past them without a good pointer. But getting a bird dog to retrieve woodcock may be another matter; there are many dogs that will not touch a woodcock. Even if they won't retrieve a downed bird, they can be trained to help locate the bird. Woodcock can be hunted with a flushing dog, but with less success and considerable frustration. We have used a Labrador retriever that's worked rather well, although at times he was surprised as we when a woodcock flushed. His real value was retrieving a downed bird.

We think the ideal shotgun for wood-

cock is a trim, fast Winchester 101 over and under, in 20 gauge with skeet barrels. Super-X shotshells loaded with 7½ or 9 shot are best, since they also have sufficient energy to down the occasional ruffed grouse—and partridge and woodcock are often found together. In fact, most woodcock are bagged incidental to grouse hunting.

One difference between shooting grouse and woodcock is measured in the extra second or two that one has with woodcock. They're a touch slower than grouse. But even though you may be aware of this slight edge, it is very difficult to keep from shooting a split-second too soon at woodcock if your nervous system is programmed for grouse. Result: You end up pruning the local covert and have the dubious pleasure of watching the woodcock twitter out of range.

When you have cleanly missed a wood-

*Whether you're hunting amid
New England alders or—as in this
case—Louisiana pines, cover is
apt to be thick and you have to get on
woodcock fast, but without
losing control and shooting too soon.*

cock, despair not. Get hold of yourself and carefully note the flight direction of the departing bird. After a few corkscrew turns, he'll settle down to a fairly straight line of flight. He won't fly far, and you may get another crack at him. But more often than not, after the second flush, he will decamp for parts unknown.

Even though woodcock are usually loners, it is quite common for more than one bird to flush from a small area. When looking for a downed bird, you may flush another woodcock. In a sense it is a cat-and-mouse game, much the same as grouse hunting.

One finds woodcock coverts through trial and error. Choice sites are alder swales 10 to 20 feet high with little ground cover, due either to grazing or shading by the overstory of alder branches. Pastures that contain hawthorns, crab apples, hazelnut, or aspen are also ideal, but the density of the vegetation six inches above the ground must be light for easy foraging. Some of the best coverts are temporary at best, and can deteriorate badly in fifteen to twenty years through plant succession, with such trees as birches replacing alders. During the fall migration, woodcock may be found in a variety of cover types but seldom in large concentrations. Good woodcock coverts are closely guarded secrets and shared only on invitation. In short, woodcock are where you find them— make the most of them when you do.

October is the best time to hunt woodcock in the northern tier of states. As a rule, the birds have departed after a hard freeze or two. Frozen ground is hard on their bills, and the earthworms usually burrow out of range—problems that are solved by a quick departure south.

Proper clothing is essential to the tim-

Like many woodcock and grouse hunters, authors Kozicky and Madson
favor open-bored, double-barreled guns in timberdoodle coverts. Skeet-choked
over and under is pictured with good warm-weather game vest.

Favorite woodcock dogs include Brittany spaniels, English setters, and German shorthairs. This Brit is belled so hunters can follow him in dense Michigan birches and alders, knowing that sudden silence usually means a point.

berdoodler, and one of the most important items is a hunting cap, coat, or vest of blaze orange. When a bird flushes, blaze orange helps to show where your companion is in heavy cover. In our opinion a gunner should wear blaze orange not only for his own protection, but as a courtesy to his hunting companion. Unless a hunter knows where his partner is, he should not shoot. Woodcock coverts are often wet underfoot, so be shod accordingly. Shoe pacs with rubber bottoms are generally good, but for the alder runs ankle-deep with water you can't beat a well-fitting, non-insulated rubber hunting boot.

Woodcock are an obsession with some hunters, and men have devoted their lives to the study of this grand game bird. We've known sportsmen whose interest

was year-round; they captured and banded woodcock in spring and summer months to gain more biological information about woodcock—knowing that the more information there is, the better the bird can be managed.

And if you've never witnessed the courtship ritual of the woodcock in late March or April, find someone who knows where woodcock perform this spectacular ceremony and enjoy one of the wonders of wild America. Even while hunting during the fall, keep your eyes and ears open for woodcock flying to and from feeding grounds in the gathering darkness. Shooting hours may have ended, but the thrill of seeing and hearing these birds on the move adds a memorable finish to an unforgettable day afield.

Ruffed Grouse ABCs

by Ed Kozicky and John Madson

36

The best way to learn any art is to study with a master and get plenty of practice—and that's as true of ruffed grouse hunting as it is of fresco painting.

Almost every town within good ruffed grouse range has one or more veteran partridge hunters who will share their savvy with willing apprentices and teach the ABCs of grouse hunting. If you get an invitation to hunt with such an individual, observe and learn, and count your blessings, but *never* usurp his favorite hunting areas! To do so is an unpardonable breach of confidence.

Anyway, there's plenty of grouse hunting to go around. Grouse covers are generally abundant and easy to get into; extensive state and federal forests and state-owned public hunting acreage assure most hunters of a place to shoot. No other game bird in the upper Midwest or the Northeast is found on so much land that's generally open to hunting. Even on private property, the grouse hunter has access for the asking, since such land is brushy and wooded, and is not planted to crops.

Good grouse hunters learn to read cover. They know where partridges are likely to be found at any given time of day or season. They know that food, more than any other factor, governs the location of grouse. Grouse are opportunists when it comes to filling their craws, and seek the best available foods as they appear: wild grapes, dogwood, thornapple, apples, acorns, beech nuts, wild cherries, aspen buds, and, usually, some green vegetation such as white clover. Examine the crop contents of each grouse brought to bag, and hunt accordingly.

Most grouse hunters are firmly convinced that late afternoon is the best time to go after grouse, since this is the time of day they are busy feeding. Grouse are birds of the cover's edge—or where two or more cover types meet. They are not migratory, and tend to congregate and remain in a given area as long as it provides an abundance of food and cover.

Grouse prefer young forests where the trees seldom exceed 30 feet in height and there is a good stand of brush cover, pref-

*Ruffed grouse is pecking about forest floor in typical autumn cover
combining young aspens (whose buds are very important grouse food) with brushy
patches and conifers for roosting or hiding, plus clear spots for dusting.*

*Being nonmigratory, grouse stay in one area as long as it has food and
cover, so hunting remains good late in season. Autumn foods are
supplemented in winter by such plants as hawthorn, greenbrier, and wintergreen.*

erably in patches, as opposed to a solid stand of eye-level undergrowth. Evergreens, pines, fir, and spruce are never far off—and provide good refuge cover when the birds are threatened by man or predator. The edges of fields, swamps, roads, and clearings are favored for gravel, dusting areas, and green vegetation.

The apprentice hunter would do well to keep within sight of tag alder, checking patches of dogwood, highbush cranberry, chokeberry, and hawthorn, as well as any small openings or evergreens. Other hotspots for grouse are windfalls, slashings, or bulldozed strips along swamp edges. Tag alder along stream drainages is also prime woodcock cover, and the timberdoodle is a delightful bonus on a grouse hunt. Woodcock must be got when the gettin' is good, for they are migratory and are here today and gone tomorrow.

Unlike most upland bird shooting, grouse hunting is not necessarily best early in the season. Flushing rates generally increase as the season advances—when leaves are off the hardwoods and the cooler weather makes walking more comfortable.

The local grouse hunter has time to prospect for them before the open season; he knows the better coverts (they call 'em "covers" in New England) and can check on the abundance of preferred foods. The out-of-state hunter can best be guided by writing to the state wildlife department.

Once within a specified grouse area, drive the back roads—especially in the late afternoon—and watch for grouse there. It's a quick way to locate grouse concentrations, but a poor way to shoot them. Road-hunting grouse with a car is akin to "ground-sluicing" quail or shooting ducks in the decoys.

Good grouse dog, if he's to be used for more than retrieving, must freeze like this setter at slightest whiff of scent, because "ruff" won't hold tight, in manner of woodcock. Setters, pointers, and Brits are top breeds.

If it's private land, check with the land-owner and obtain his permission to hunt, and know the location of his boundaries. We like to use county plat maps or topographic maps to mark the locations of good grouse coverts. Such maps show the smallest roads and creeks—and next season a carefully marked map can save hours of searching for good grouse coverts.

The two most important pieces of grouse-hunting gear are the shotgun and footgear. We both prefer the Winchester Model 101, over-under, 20-gauge, with improved-cylinder and modified-choke barrels. The Model 101 is a beautifully balanced shotgun that is fast to get into action, and a pleasure to carry "at ready" all day long. Whatever gun and gauge you use, stick to open chokes; on a single-barreled gun, the improved cylinder should be just about right.

Check the fit of any shotgun before going into the field. One of the best ways is to practice skeet shooting—and call for the targets with your shotgun butt at waist level. When you start breaking in the 20's, you're ready to go grouse hunting. We've also heard of men practicing with hand traps and clay birds in the woods. Number 7½ or 8 shot, in the Super-X load, are ideal for grouse and woodcock.

Grouse hunting is a walking game, so comfortable boots are a necessity. Buy the best and test them before the hunt. Some type of rubber footgear is mandatory to hunt lowlands and alder runs . . . unless you like walking with wet feet. Boots should have adequate soles to protect against stone bruises and should be high enough to provide support for the ankle, but avoid the extra weight of insulated boots. It also helps to have a change of wool socks available at the lunch break.

Wear a comfortable shell and game vest, preferably the suspender type, and a light wool shirt. Except on the coldest of days, pants just heavy enough to resist brush and briars should be adequate. A blaze orange cap is a necessity. Don't hunt grouse without wearing one, especially if you have a companion.

Because grouse hunting is done in brushy areas, glasses are needed for eye protection. Last fall, one of the authors forgot his shooting glasses and was blinded in his "master" eye for several hours after being slapped with a branch. It spoiled the best time of the day. Light buckskin shooting gloves are also recommended; brush is hard on the backs of hands and wrists. You may as well prepare for brush-busting before you start—for the brush is where the grouse are.

A compass is handy. It is easy to become confused in the woods on a cloudy day. More than one grouse hunter has spent some anxious moments getting back to his car as twilight faded into darkness.

Shooting grouse requires fast gun pointing; one's reflexes have to be razor sharp. Fatigue dulls those reflexes, and an empty stomach is not conducive to concentration. A sack lunch and a long noon break make good sense; so does a high-energy snack late in the day. (Blessed is the hunting buddy with an extra candy bar!)

Don't wait until the grouse season to get your leg muscles in shape—stay in condition throughout the year. And should you be on an extended grouse-hunting trip, reserve one morning to rest.

Good grouse dogs are few and far be-

*Dog and his best friend congratulate
each other after good point
and productive flush. Gun is light,
fast-swinging 20-gauge double,
bored improved-cylinder and modified,
an excellent grouse combination.*

tween. Grouse are touchy; compared to woodcock they do not hold well, and are likely to run. The best dogs are setters, pointers, and Brittany spaniels. However, a dog's greatest value is to retrieve birds which might otherwise be lost. We have used Labrador retrievers that not only helped find birds, but retrieved both woodcock and grouse that we'd never have found.

A grouse-hunting survey showed that men using any kind of dog averaged 15 birds for the season, as opposed to ten birds for those without dogs. Dogs may not be necessary to successful grouse hunting, but they're a big asset.

Most grouse hunters are dogless, and depend upon a knowledge of bird habits to find their annual quota. A good hunter uses his ears almost as much as his eyes. If you hear one grouse flush, there's a good chance that another is close by.

The hunter who rushes through grouse cover will end the day battered, brush-whipped, and disappointed. *Ease* through grouse cover and, to the best of your ability, always be in position to shoot! It's a cat-and-mouse game, and it pays to stop for a few seconds every 25 to 50 feet. If a grouse is near, your stop will undo him and he will take to the air.

When a grouse flushes, note the direction of his flight. He probably won't fly far, and you may be able to put the bird up again by walking in that direction. If you hit one, mark the fall with the eye of an eagle and make a beeline to that spot. Drop your hat there and start searching the cover in a thorough and systematic manner.

Grouse hunting is best done alone, or

with one companion, because it maximizes flexibility to investigate likely coverts and eliminates the necessity to stay on course. When hunting as a pair, know your buddy's location at all times. If you are not sure where he is, and a grouse departs at a low angle, don't shoot.

It's a gentleman's sport, best taken at a leisurely pace. Still, grouse hunting is a tiring game. Every nerve and muscle must be cocked for hours on end, ready for that sudden, muffled explosion of brown feathers. And no matter how alert you are, you will hear more grouse than you ever see.

How do you measure hunting success? Well, it depends on how you feel about grouse hunting. You will earn every bird brought to bag, and you'll remember the misses as well as the kills. Surveys indicate that you will hunt an average of five hours for each bird bagged, and you will get a chance to shoot at only about half the flushes. It's best not to count your fired shells—but if you must, and if you're averaging one grouse per three empty hulls, you're doing some great shooting.

Prairie Grouse Boom Again

by Bert Popowski

37

As long as there are prairie grouse in this country—ranging from the historic prairie chickens, through their sharptailed cousins and up to the largest of the clan, sage grouse—they'll put on bizarre spring shows. They'll gather at ancient "booming" or "dancing" grounds to prance and flutter and fight, sing their chuckling and reverberating love songs, and select mates for another annual grouse crop. Their posturings are preserved in many dance steps of plains Indians.

As is usually the case with avian forms, it's the males who put on the show. The hens come to the party but they stroll about pretending vast interest in imaginary bits of food. Nonetheless, they are ready for pairing off to complete the annual cycle. The cocks bob and shuffle around with outspread wings and lowered, threatening beaks and occasionally rear back to sound variations of clucking to booming love songs. These dawn assignations culminate in the breeding of a few hens. When the sun is fully up, the birds disperse, flying to break the scent trail, un-til the next dawn summons them to an encore. After all the hens commence nesting, the cocks still gather, on the chance that some lonely female has been overlooked.

All grouse are short-legged, hence their favored mode of travel is by flying. Since prairie grouse live in spacious country, where the distance between roosting and feeding areas is measured in miles, they're often seen on the wing. Also, if observers watch for them near dawn and dusk, their favorite times to move, they are often fully exposed on favored feeding grounds. It is when they have fed and moved to their midday loafing and dusting areas that they're often infernally difficult to find and flush. Successful grouse gunning depends on knowing the birds' habits.

Over 60 years ago, my father took me to see how market hunters operated on grouse. I never forgot that dawn show. Three hunters strung out about 80 yards apart, spread long sheepskin coats at their stations, and dumped burlap sacks of handloads on them. Then, with their three dogs, they settled down to await the morn-

*In spring, male prairie grouse stage
strange "dances" to court mates.
Here (from top) are sharptails
threatening one another; sage grouse
puffing, leaping, and strutting;
and prairie chicken booming and bowing.*

ing feeding flight from the rushy lake where the birds (prairie chickens in this case) spent the nights.

When the grouse came flying out in continuous flocks of a dozen to a score, they were no more than 15 yards off the wheat stubble. If they swerved to avoid one hunter they were within shotgun range of two flanking gunners. Estimating a killing range of 40 yards, the three gunners thus blanketed a flight corridor some 240 yards wide. Shots were taken both in the approach and departure angles, with crossing birds often producing two or more kills in each calculated shot pattern. Dad later told me that morning's shoot produced about 300 birds, bringing 25 cents a brace.

This era of the early 1900s saw the transition from double to pump-action shotguns, of which the Model 97 Winchester hammer gun was an outstanding favorite. Some semi-automatics were introduced but they were anathema to sportsmen, who called them by various game-hogging names. It was a time of transition, with extension magazine tubes to allow loading with up to seven or even nine shotshells. North Dakota then had only six game wardens, a 25-bird daily limit, and no defined possession limit.

Dad expertly used a Model 97, which was also the shotgun on which I cut my bird-hunting teeth. When charged with Dad's stout handloads it recoiled like a kicking mule on my skinny 10-year-old shoulder. But growing up in those days taught everyone that all projects and skills had their price. If you wanted to play the game, you followed the rules.

Prairie chickens and sharptails were unbelievably abundant during my boyhood. When their numbers dwindled it was because intensive cropping robbed them of

Five members of South Dakota Game Department check in with morning's bag of pinnated grouse—better known as prairie chickens. Like many Midwestern wingshooters, they lean toward tightly choked pumps and autoloaders, usually in 12 gauge.

the virgin sod needed for nesting and for both nocturnal and year-round cover. For a time, as both species were supplied with abundant small-grain food, they prospered. But when the needed grasslands went under the plow, the prairie grouse suffered a recession. The National Grasslands Act of the last 25 years created a kind of living memorial to the original Great Plains era. And these two grouse forms are again booming.

The native flora which this act saved also provided natural habitat for many forms of plainsland fauna, including all prairie grouse. While they are nowhere as abundant as I remember them in the early 1900s, they're plentiful enough to provide excellent hunting on some parts of their ancestral range.

The mechanics of such hunting haven't changed. This is still full-choke country (or the equivalent in pattern density with shot-protecting cup wads). Residents often own only one shotgun and use it for all game, from quail and cottontails to honkers. Some of them also use very few sizes

of shot, sometimes only one, which isn't dense enough for top performance on plainsland grouse. I feel that chickens and sharptails should be taken with nothing coarser than #6 shot. I prefer 7½'s and 8's since these birds will come down easily if properly hit with small shot. Since sage grouse are so much larger, 6's perform very well on them but 4's are only very rarely justified. I believe in the dense patterns of small shot.

The great majority of plainsland bird hunters do not use dogs. A prairie-hunting dog is occasionally in danger from rattlesnakes and may be almost constantly bedeviled by needle-sharp cactus spines and stickery seeds from bootjacks, burdocks, and sand burrs. But hunting these three grouse is much simpler when using pointers or setters.

Pinnated grouse (prairie chickens) and sharptails subsist chiefly on seed foods, which is why they got along so well for a time while grain farming was on the increase. But sage grouse have rudimentary gizzards, unsuited for grinding up hard

Author's son, professional game manager
John Popowski, shows photographer
Dale Jensen prairie chicken and sharptail
while setter rests. Above, Brit
fetches sharptail—a species that has
adapted to modern agriculture.

grain or weed seeds. Their main food consists of sagebrush tips, from which they get their common name. Only in areas where such tender-leafed crops as alfalfa and clover have been introduced do they benefit from man's intrusion. Even then, since sagebrush provides a much higher protein content than the legumes, such cultivated food is only marginally and temporarily adequate in nourishment.

It thus follows that sage grouse are best hunted in proximity to sagebrush growth, or domestic plantings of legumes, and near water. Like all grouse, they often fly between food and shelter but, because of their weight, such flights are usually limited to less than a mile. If they weren't protected by short seasons and low bag limits they could be readily extirpated. If hunters kept following them up for repeated flushes, they could seriously thin entire flocks.

Sage grouse should be drawn as soon af-

ter shooting as possible. When they're feeding on sagebrush tips, the pungency of such fare readily permeates the meat if any shot pellets pierce the digestive system. But if quickly dressed out, their meat makes fine eating though it is somewhat coarser in grain than that of other grouse.

All prairie grouse tend to band up late in the season, or shortly after the first frosts strike their range, whichever comes first. So the gunner who wishes to minimize his hunting problems should go out for early-season birds, while they are usually in family-sized flocks. He can then pick out the younger birds—by their somewhat smaller size and less speedy and more laborious flight—and harvest a reward of tenderer eating. I never eat grouse without thinking back to the days when pioneers often subsisted on the three forms of prairie grouse. Big game was then in short supply but the grouse fed high on the croplands and settlers and travellers fed high on grouse.

Reflections on Huns and Chukars

38

by Steve Ferber

The Canadian lifted his hand-made whistle from the breast pocket of his shirt, clamped it between his lips, and cast his brace of dogs out ahead of him along a hedgerow. He stooped over for a few seconds and pulled four or five burrs from his knickers, dropped a pair of shotshells into the action of his hammer-gun, and watched his dogs work. They came up with nothing and he gestured to them with a sweeping motion of his right arm. The dogs immediately turned away from the hedgerow and began working in some standing timothy.

To one side of the man were the two judges, on horses, sitting perfectly erect in the saddles, attired in the club colors, watching the pointers dart in and out of the grass. Several yards behind the judges another man and two boys were lifting a crate of Hungarian partridges from a wagon to the ground. The man flipped open the door of the crate, reached in with gloved hands and carefully removed two of the brown-gray birds.

One partridge in each hand, he walked about a hundred yards behind the judges, rocking the birds as he walked, keeping their heads tucked under their wings, and placed them both in some scrub weeds on that Saskatchewan prairie. When he stood up and faced the far-off wagon again, he was in time to see the man in knickers walk in behind his dogs, flush a pair of Huns, and bag them both.

Moments after the shooting, another man walked his leashed dogs toward the registration table near the game wagon, secured the leather leads to a ring on the corner of the table, lifted a waiting pen, and wrote in the open book: "John McClintock, September 4, 1912. Sandy, a bitch pointer & Salty, a bitch setter."

Until the beginning of the First World War, when importation of that European gamebird was all but halted, the field trial—Canadian and American—was responsible for the establishment of Hungarian partridge populations throughout many cold-climate sections of North America. The birds which weren't located by competing dogs escaped, to thrive in their new habitat. Coupled with this grow-ing "accidental" partridge population, game-management agencies and sports-men's groups imported the birds from the grassy plains of Hungary specifically for re-lease here to bolster the gamebird popu-lation in general. It worked.

Ernest and Mary Hemingway used to shoot Huns in Idaho—she still does—and she told me that her husband used to put his guests in the best possible position for the shot. A Hun shooter knows what this means: way out in front. The average covey of Hungarian partridges—or gray or English as they're often called—numbers from half a dozen to 20 birds. They don't hold particularly well for a dog and unless the animal freezes the instant he whiffs them, they'll flush well forward of the shooter—totally unlike bobwhite quail, for example.

There are those times when we, almost to a man, do not shoulder our guns, pass through the target, and pull—fair shot or otherwise. We can't explain why, but we know it may happen with any game, from partridge to deer. We have our private reasons that sometimes allow the white tail to sail over a fence unscathed. We let the grouse zoom up and away and wait for it to perch high in a spruce . . . it never does. We let the lone honker—close enough to see its bill open, the tongue flut-ter—fly right on by.

About 10 years ago, in California, I was jump-shooting pintails with some success along a narrow rivulet that served to irri-gate adjacent wheat and lettuce fields. About 10 o'clock that morning I saw per-haps half a dozen Hungarian partridges pecking away in some stubble, 75 yards off. I walked up toward the covey and a larger section of the birds, which I hadn't

seen, flew off to my right. At almost the same instant, another pile of Huns, located on the same side of the foot-wide water ditch where I was located, took flight. Fi-nally, the six birds I had spotted initially soared off, low to the ground like the oth-ers, these mixed with still more in the same area. I was only 25 yards away when they began taking to the air and they ac-complished their combined exit in under 10 seconds. I had never then, nor have I seen to this date, so many wild gamebirds together at one time. There were more than 125 Huns in the sprawling covey, and that funny little time came again. I didn't shoot. Some minutes later I did walk up and bag a few singles.

But I think if *you* had been witness to the sight and staggering sound of 100 pounds of fast-flying gamebirds taking wing in a bunch, shattering the absolute stillness of a big California farm for 10 su-perb seconds, your own don't-shoot-this-time-private-reason might have left you staring past a pair of unfired shotgun bar-rels, too. I haven't the foggiest notion why the Huns were having a regional meeting that morning.

Besides Idaho and California, the Hun-garian partridge—which is about twice the size of a quail and has the same general configuration—is found in at least four other Western states. There's also a good population of Huns extending just north of Iowa, reaching into Canada, and there are a scattered few in upper New England. Huns are a tremendous delight to shoot be-cause when they take flight they approx-imate closely the speed of quail, but unlike the bobwhite and several other varieties, Huns don't give you the opportunity to lit-erally walk over them. They're almost al-ways located in reasonably open country.

Above, Hun rises from draw between
farm fields. Shot is long but dog seems
confident retrieve will be needed.
Left, bird in hand is Hungarian partridge—
quail-sized species but apt to flush
much farther out than bobwhite.

Occasionally chukars venture away from their wild, rocky or hilly habitat. Here they're shown gleaning stubble field. At such times, they're nervous; unable to escape by running uphill, they'll flush far ahead.

Gunner and dog search typical chukar cover. Hunters often walk canyon rims and slopes. Rocky outcroppings like this one are particularly productive at midday, when birds settle down to sun themselves and rest.

Even though chukars seek rocky roosts and need no cultivated land, they sometimes visit crop fields and end up in mixed bag with pheasants. And, like ringnecks, they're excellent preserve birds, readily bred and raised.

But because the shot will almost always be made between 25 and 35 yards away, marking the bird is particularly important whether a dog is used or not. It's far easier to mark the fall of a quail, or find a cripple of that species, simply because it touches earth closer to the shooter.

The chukar partridge—likewise an import—is rarely found in open country. Though roughly the same size as a Hun, the chukar is far more colorful. Whereas the Hun is essentially brown and gray, the chukar has a black and white face, red legs, and a black, white, and bluish body. Our chukar partridges are descendants of birds brought to this country 50 years ago from the Himalayan foothills and released first in Washington, Oregon, and California.

At first the Asian chukar was considered a lost cause by game managers because the imported birds soon appeared to have died out. Management people underestimated the hardiness of the birds—they had simply moved to rugged wilderness country resembling their own high-altitude homeland, subsisting on insects and wild plant food.

Hunting chukars in the wild is no easy business because their preference of habitat is high, hilly, rocky ledges (except when they sometimes walk many yards downhill to feed) and they'd rather run than fly. When pressed hard, they'd rather fly than hide. Springer spaniels and Labrador retrievers are probably the best chukar dogs, but both dog and man had best be in condition for the hardy climb necessary to locate them.

Coveys are generally small, and the birds sometimes just pair up. Like the Huns, they fly more or less in the manner of quail—though not as fast initially—and since they'll be uphill when they're flushed, they'll fly downhill for escape. At close to 50 miles an hour, flaring right or left!

Chukar have become very popular preserve birds because they're bred and raised as easily as ringnecked pheasant, retaining their wild characteristics. They rely on their crazy red legs more than their wings to carry them to safety, and when they do flush, they're not easy targets.

Homage to the Ringneck

by Bob Bell

39

It was late in the season, late in the day. I was cold and wet. A week of the golden days that grouse hunters love, with the maples catching the sun on the hillsides and the smell of crushed grapes in cool hollows, had given way to typical pheasant weather—a bone-chilling rain that had filtered down all night and into the morning, soaking weedfields, building moisture layers and drops on every bush and branch and evergreen, turning cornstubble fields into red grease. I'd been cold in the jackpine-studded corner, I became colder when I worked out onto the weed- and sumac-covered sidehill. Even on the lee side of the low ridge the wind found me, and I hunched my shoulders and tried to snuggle my chin inside the collar of my old pigskin shirt. For a moment I paused to gaze through the slanting rain toward the thick swale below, to study the scraggly fencerow and standing corn beyond. The gray sky dominated everything. It was heavy, dismal. "Bell, you gotta be crazy," I said aloud. I blew a raindrop off my nose, shivered, and with an effort started zigzagging slowly down toward the swale. I'd been cold and wet for more than three hours now, I was getting hungry, and my old Jeep with its sack of sandwiches and thermos of coffee waited a mile and a half away—in the opposite direction. Well, I'd get there eventually. Meanwhile, there was that chunk of cover in the bottom.

I was just well into it, getting wetter with every step, when a half-strangled *Cuk-cuk-cuk-cuk!* sounded near my feet and a waterlogged bird struggled skyward from the greenbriers that were tearing at my pants. And just as suddenly I wasn't cold any more. For that big, loud, PO'd bird was a ringneck—so wet he looked black, but his white neck ring, his splendid tail, and his angry, coal-down-a-chute squawk instantly identified him—and I was a pheasant hunter!

Maybe a half second later that long form buckled, its beautiful streamline crumpled by my load of 7½'s centered on its upper back and head, and thumped to the ground, tracked by the muzzle of my old M21 Winchester. Years of dogless hunting

Cock and hen pheasant poke about in front of tall, thick ground cover
where they can skulk or run ahead of gun instead of flying. But when walking them
up without dog, you'll sometimes panic them into flushing if you simply stop.

as a boy had conditioned me to send in the second shot on almost any falling rooster—more than a few big ringnecks that looked dead as a withered oak leaf in the air turned into greyhounds on the ground. But this was an easy chance, with the vulnerable thin-boned meatless back as the target, so I held the second barrel. And my decision proved correct, for the bird had died in mid-air.

I reloaded, laid the little 20-gauge on the ground, and picked up the pheasant. I folded the wings, smoothed the wet-copper body feathers, straightened the long tail. Soaked and chilled as I was, I couldn't help but stand there in the rain, feeling a moment of kinship, maybe even love, for this short-winged, powerfully built immigrant from a far-off land.

Descendant of maybe a hundred generations, the pheasant is an ancient and venerable bird. I rarely hold one in my hand without being touched by his mystery. Oh, it's easy enough to say that Judge Denny managed to get a few dozen Chinese pheasants from the Shanghai region to Oregon's Willamette Valley back in the '80s and that their population exploded, or

that others arrived on our East Coast from England and the Continent. Or even that stocking was attempted as far back as George Washington's and Ben Franklin's time. There's good documentation for most of this. But what is a century or two to a bird whose image was woven into Chinese tapestries more than 3,500 years ago, a bird that the Greeks knew before the time of Christ, a bird that the Roman legions took into then-uncivilized Europe?

The American hunter who downs a pheasant should take a moment to ponder this bird's background, the endless stretches of Asia which this gaudy creature calls home, from the banks of the River Phasis near the Black Sea (from whence came his name), clear across the middle-southern reaches of this world's greatest land mass, from sea level to dizzying Himalayan heights, and on through India, China, and the East Indies to Japan. The pheasant has survived unknowns which no white man yet understands, and I think it behooves hunters like us, whose instincts trace back to the beginning of our species, to show a moment of respect when we down such a bird.

It's easy to underrate the pheasant. He found a home in this country, multiplied fantastically, and is now seen in numbers ranging from fair to incredible almost everywhere except in our Southeast and extreme Southwest. He's common, and, therefore, in the minds of some, of lesser ranking than a gamebird such as the grouse, say. That's a strange attitude, seems to me, but perhaps it's human nature to value something simply because it's scarce.

Personally, I prefer pheasants. To put it plainly, I think the ringneck is the greatest gamebird we have. I don't like sounding opinionated about it, but after spending much of my life listening to guys make a living preaching the glories of the grouse and simultaneously shuffling off the pheasant as a third-rate cousin, I've had it. This is not to say the grouse isn't a great gamebird. It is. A lovelier creature never flew. However, it's not the impossible target some hunters make it to be. The typical roaring blastoff freezes many hunters, and in the dense cover favored by this species any hunter hesitation can be fatal—to the gunner's chances, not the bird. But the hunter who uses the grouse's thunder as a stimulus and reacts by swinging and shooting will kill grouse about as well as pheasants. Neither actually flushes very fast.

The pheasant is a far tougher bird to drop. He's much bigger, which makes it harder to get those high-velocity 6's into his vitals, he's "shingled with galvanized feathers," as John Madson once put it, and at times he's just too dang ornery to die. I've centered an old rooster at less than 20 yards, shredded his near wing and put a pellet into practically every square inch of his near side—and then had to wring his neck to keep him in my game vest. Grouse just don't do that. One or two pellets in the body will usually lay them on the forest floor, reflexive wing action often leading you to them.

It doesn't always take that much to kill a pheasant, of course. Four or five #6 pellets in the body almost always do the trick. But there are enough exceptions to this rule to make many experienced retrieverless hunters drive a second load into a falling rooster, just to increase the chances that he'll be found when they run up. That's something else that pheasant hunters learn early—get to a downed bird on the double. Given a few seconds to recuperate, many fatally wounded but not disabled birds vanish. And despite their gaudy colors, they can disappear on a putting green. Where? Nobody knows. Down the cup, probably. That Jacob's coat is actually an excellent camouflage in most types of fall cover.

The casual hunter believes pheasants are easier to bag than grouse because he does most of his hunting on the opening day. At this time ringnecks, which have spent thousands of years in proximity to man, are still close to farm buildings in easy cover—cultivated fields, fencerows, weedfields, etc. They're so used to humans that the season's opening hours shouldn't be called hunting at all, but more properly shooting. In the same cover, grouse also would be simple to down. But within a few hours, a day or two at most, the easy chances are gone. The pheasants have vanished—been shot out, the average hunter will tell you, and demand stocked birds from his game department.

He's wrong. Admittedly, many roosters have been bagged and some cripples have died wastefully, but there's still a lot of 'em left. They're just not in traditional pheasant cover anymore, but rather in the thickest, most tangled messes in the area. Tree-grown ravines smothered in honeysuckle, briar-covered creekbanks, choppings, overgrown farm dumps, head-high weedfields interspersed with sumac clumps—this is where you'll find them, if you're hunter enough.

Unless you have an unusual dog—a birdy beagle, small enough to squeeze through thick stuff that would wear down a big brush buster is probably best for rooting birds out of such places—you have to go in after them yourself. To do this hour after hour and day after day, tromping and squeezing, circling and smashing, ignoring the briars that rake your wrists and ears and neck, the sweat and dust that blind you on dry days, the mud and chill that get you on the wet ones, takes a mental attitude so determined it's more accurately called bullheadedness. But these thick places are where the roosters are as soon as the season is a few days old, and that's why hunting them is as challenging as grouse gunning. They're as tough to find as that smaller brown bird, harder to flush because they prefer hiding or running to flying. A rooster will often squat motionless and invisible until you almost literally stomp on him, or else scuttle silently around you in the thick stuff. If flushed here, ringnecks are as hard to hit as grouse, because of the cover and the way it restricts gun handling. And they're always harder to kill. As a reqult, after the first day or two, the average hunter has a hard time collecting a couple of pheasants despite the fact that there are enough ringnecks that in total they offer far more sport to a greater number of hunters than grouse do. So, from any objective standpoint, this big

This situation favors rooster under point. He will almost certainly run or else fly deeper into tangle beyond field. Though pheasant doesn't rise as fast as other upland birds, quick shooting is needed here.

bird from the Phasis has to be the top gamebird in this country.

Despite the efficiency of beagles in extremely dense cover, for all around use I prefer a good retriever such as the Labrador. Trained to work close to the hunter as a flushing dog, it eliminates the biggest problem with pheasants—losing cripples. It's easy to break a rooster's wing, even at long range, but awfully hard to find him without a good retriever, as these birds run like racehorses even when they're not hurt. So far as I'm concerned, a retriever is the top pheasant dog.

Going into thick cover after pheasants necessitates tough clothing. Low leather boots, leather-faced pants, a heavy pigskin pullover shirt, buckskin gloves, a light game vest, and a hat with a brim to protect the eyes and ears are my preferred outfit. Underwear is chosen to match the temperature, fishnet for cool clear days,

Sometimes ringnecks will fool you, remaining still and unseen until you walk past, then rocketing into air with loud cackle. Bird got up behind this shooter but he heard it and twisted around fast enough make good shot.

Springer pushes up cock and hen in Nebraska field. Changes in agriculture have brought about slow decline of ringnecks since 1950s, but pheasant hunting remains very good in this and other corn-belt states.

"itch-scratchy" wool longjohns for the miserable wet ones so typical of late pheasant season. Nylon-reinforced wool socks are the best choice. Shooting glasses, amber or green according to the weather, are good protection for the eyes in briar thickets, though perspiration can make them a nuisance.

The gun is a personal thing. To gun-cranks, and I guess I'm one, its selection can be almost a mystical thing, based on legends and traditions stretching back to the time when fur-clad hunters crouched around tiny fires lost in endless gloom and grunted their way through arguments on flint-tipped spears vs. hand axes. When it comes to a choice of weapons, all hunters are a bit tetched.

The truth is, any shotgun is a good pheasant gun, if . . . It's that *if* that complicates life. But at bottom it comes down to two things: (1) If it handles enough shot to put four or five pellets of acceptable size into a rooster's body at the maximum range you'll be using it, and (2) if you can hit with it.

Before we get too involved with guns, though, some thought should be given to the ammo, as that's what actually does the killing.

Unless you hunt such a specialized area that all shots are at extremely short range, or you're willing to pass up more shots than you take, the .410 bore won't cut it; this load is about a 22–25 yard outfit on pheasants. And unless most shots are well beyond the 50-yard mark, which is an awful long shotgun shot when each of those yards has three genuine feet in it, you don't need a 3-inch, 12-gauge Magnum. Most pheasants are taken between 18 and 35 yards, with a small percentage at lesser ranges and a fair number farther, say to 45 or 50 yards maximum. Many so-called 60- and 70-yard shots are actually about 50— and that's still a very long way. At such ranges, shot charges of 1, 1⅛, or 1¼ ounces will do from a properly choked bore, the heavier loads being better on the longer chances, of course. Such loads are available in 20-, 16-, and 12-gauge guns, though it takes the 3-inch Magnum to get the 1¼-ounce charge in the 20.

A few shooters have weird ideas about pheasant loads, but the majority seems to agree that 1⅛ or 1¼ ounces of 6's, usually in high-velocity loading, is top choice. Over 30 seasons of pheasant shooting have convinced me of the validity of this claim. It's an excellent compromise between pattern density and retained energy over average pheasant ranges. The same charge weight of 7½'s will serve even better for close-flushing birds, due to the denser pattern, but pellet energy is a bit chancy on the longer shots, as is penetration on a bird the size of a pheasant. It's a good choice for the open barrel of a double. Larger shot retains more energy per pellet, but the considerably few pellets available makes for sketchy performance out yonder.

For a couple of generations, long-barreled, full-choke slide actions and autoloaders were the top choices as pheasant guns. They still are with many hunters. But today there is a definite movement away from them and toward the double, for most hunters realize they have little need for a repeater's one big advantage, that third shell. A few generations back, when bag limits on many species were larger and there was still some market shooting, large-magazine guns made sense. For today's sport hunting, there's no real need for that extra firepower. This is not to suggest that the man with an auto is not a sportsman—his conduct is determined completely by the moral decisions he makes on every chance, just as with the man toting a $4000 Purdey or a single-shot Long Tom—it's just that current hunting situations tend to make the third shot unnecessary. Thus a lot of men buying new guns opt for doubles, primarily in over-under configuration, for many fine models are now available in the medium-price range, while the costs of top-quality side-by-sides are pretty hairy.

Good doubles of either design have many advantages. With a given barrel length, they're shorter than repeaters, thus handier and livelier feeling. They balance better, look better, and—we might as well admit it—have a bit of snob appeal about them. However, their biggest plus is genuine and not based on some mental attitude. The two barrels give the hunter his

Hunter shows good form as he swings smoothly ahead of rooster. Shooting behind or under pheasant may be most common cause of misses. Long tail adds to apparent but deceptive target, and flight is faster than it looks.

choice of two chokes. While mounting the gun he can select the boring that will prove most deadly on the shot offered—the open bore for close flushing birds, the tighter one for the long chance. And he can load different size shot in each barrel, which also affects pattern density. No single-barrel outfit can match this efficiency. The best a hunter can do with one tube is have a variable choke installed—a great advance, but still, once his choice has been made for a given cover, it can't be changed quickly enough to accommodate for an unexpected chance.

Unfortunately, most doubles are choked wrong for maximum field efficiency. The only combinations readily available are improved cylinder/modified or modified/full. Since IC will take birds to 35 yards and the full choke pattern is large enough to be practicable from that distance on out, and is the only sensible choice for the longest ranges, there's no valid reason for a modified choke in a double. Nevertheless, the double-gun buyer is stuck with it. Despite this, he's still better off than the single-barrel user.

For most pheasant hunting the IC/M combination will prove more effective than the tighter borings, as there are more short to medium range chances than extremely long ones. The hunter who needs the full choke fairly often might consider using "brush" or "scatter" loads in his modified barrel, as these in effect open it to about improved cylinder through the use of cardboard separators in the shot charge.

Being able to hit with a shotgun is largely a matter of getting one that fits properly and then practicing. All details are important to stock fit, but most problems can be solved by getting the proper length. If the stock is short enough that it can be shouldered easily when wearing hunting clothes and long enough that your thumb doesn't hit your nose when firing, it's about right. A recoil pad installed to an overall length that accomplishes these objectives usually takes care of fit. Then a few boxes of shells expended on crows, barn pigeons, or claybirds each week for a month or two prior to the pheasant season will get you into good shape for pheasants. And who can ask for more than that?

Turkey—the Biggest and the Smartest

40

by Frank T. Hanenkrat

A generation ago the wild turkey, North America's most magnificent game bird, was feared to be near extinction. But today, thanks to improved forestry practices, carefully controlled hunting pressure, and a spectacularly successful restocking and management program, this super game bird is back, back, it is hoped, to stay. The gobbler once more is legal quarry for an ever-growing number of hunters. In fact, today wild turkey is hunted in states where he was not found historically, but has been introduced by transplanting! This comeback has been one of the most heart-warming feats of the wildlife sciences.

There are four major subspecies of native wild turkeys in North America: the Eastern, found in the eastern deciduous forest range; the Ocellated, in Florida; the Rio Grande, of northern Mexico, Texas, and Oklahoma; and the Merriam's, found in the Rocky Mountains. As mentioned, the historical ranges of some of these races have been extended. Because they are subspecies, and not separate species, they interbreed where their ranges meet, and

intergrade subspecies are found. Representative specimens from each race can be differentiated from one another by differences in plumage and bone structure. The races also probably differ in physiological and behavioral details. But for the hunter these differences are mainly academic; all the North American wild turkeys can be hunted by essentially the same methods.

And the turkey is quite a quarry. For the hunter with little experience with turkeys, the greatest obstacle to success is probably the difficulty of realizing just how capable an adversary he is up against. With the exception of the Ocellated turkey, who is somewhat smaller, an adult gobbler of any of the races may attain a weight close to 20 pounds, and after the first year will seldom weigh less than 12. When he stretches to his full height, his head may be more than three feet from the ground. He can run up to 18 mph in strides over four feet long. His wingspread may exceed five feet. If frightened he can burst into a climb flight and clear the tops of 60-foot trees only 100 feet away, with an average speed

Vigilant, suspicious, ready to explode into flight at first sign of human presence, this big wild Eastern gobbler is fine specimen of America's largest game bird. Habitat is typical—open woods with plenty of mast.

of over 40 mph. In level flight with steady wingbeats he has been clocked at 55 mph. In a downhill glide he can attain speeds in excess of 70 mph. If forced into it, he can even swim with fair skill.

The turkey is constantly alert and suspicious, and cunning in the presence of danger. He can hear extremely well, and can pinpoint the location of a sound with almost unerring accuracy. His keenness of vision is hardly to be believed. One expert, a scientist, estimates that a turkey can see the movement of the minute hand of a clock as easily as an average human can see the movement of the second hand. If a turkey is spooked by a hunter's sudden movement, he will make as speedy an escape as possible. If he spots you sitting perfectly still, he may move slowly and easily behind a tree, stump, or bush; and you wait and wait, growing all the while more tense, waiting for him to step around

the obstacle and into view. Finally you can stand it no longer, and go over to investigate, only to find that he has disappeared as if by magic. How? By moving quickly and quietly away, all the time keeping, with uncanny accuracy, the obstacle between you and him so that you never see his exit. Meanwhile, he is over the ridge and about a mile away, probably chuckling to himself.

The turkey's gifts of supersharp vision and hearing, great speed and intelligence, and easily aroused suspicion, make him a formidable quarry, even for the person who has learned to locate turkeys and mastered the use of a caller. To cope with a turkey, the hunter has to have keen senses, an alert mind, absolute self-control, almost unlimited patience, and the ability to reach quick, commonsense solutions to immediate problems. Some of these things you are born with, and others you acquire

Turkey tracks are unmistakable.
Those pictured here measured almost
five inches wide and almost six
inches from heel to tip of middle toe.
In scouting for turkeys, look
for tracks on sand bars and mud flats.

by conscious effort and self-discipline. You cannot acquire any of them simply by reading books. However, if you do have these qualities, along with physical stamina and good marksmanship skills, you have the makings of a successful turkey hunter. About the only other things you need are a knowledge of the turkey's habits, some simple equipment, and the desire to bag a trophy gobbler.

The turkey's habits are well documented, and successful hunting is based on a knowledge of the turkey's behavior during the spring and fall, the seasons when hunting is usually allowed. (Some areas allow hunting in both seasons, others allow hunting in only one.)

Where laws permit, there are primarily three methods of hunting turkeys in the fall: still-hunting, stalking, and calling scattered flocks. Calling can sometimes be combined with the other two, as will be seen.

Still-hunting is essentially a game of patience. The hunter locates a range used by a gregarious flock, and positions himself near a spot he knows the turkeys have used

Where only gobblers are legal, surest
field marks are beard and spurs.
But young male may be hard to identify,
especially in dim light. In photo,
compare tiny first-year beard
with long, full beard of mature tom.

In spring, gobbler struts for hens, spreading and dragging his wing tips fanning his tail. In states that open spring season, this is when frequent calling, if properly done, will prod gobbler to respond and approach.

before. Such a spot is indicated by the presence of scratch marks which turkeys make as they feed—large, nearly round spots about the size of a dinner plate, with the ground-cover of fallen leaves or needles piled on one side. A feeding flock will leave a broad, highly visible path of these marks. Other signs are droppings and tracks. (Molted feathers are also an indication of turkeys, but because feathers are easily blown about by wind, this sign can be misleading.) The hunter who finds certain evidence of a turkey feeding area and waits there patiently enough will more than likely see the flock come back into the same area, for moving flocks tend to follow set cycles and return through the same area at regular intervals, usually of a few days or so.

If the turkeys appear at close range, the hunter can shoot, and will likely be able to scatter the flock as well. In this case he will have another chance if he is willing to wait a while and call. The techniques for this are discussed later.

Another method of hunting in the fall is to stalk a flock as it moves along. The only successful way to do this is to watch the flock from a distance without being seen. The hunter must determine the direction the flock is moving, then circle ahead of them, keeping completely out of their sight and hearing. The safest way is to keep a ridge or hill between himself and the turkeys. In this way he can set up a kind of ambush, and once again may be able to shoot and also to scatter the flock.

A third method is to locate and scatter the birds through the use of a trained dog or dogs. In this method, the hunter walks rapidly through a known turkey range, and the dog circles constantly in front of him, covering much ground and searching for the scent of a turkey trail. When a properly trained dog strikes a trail, he will follow it and rush into the flock and bark, surprising them and achieving a flush, and at the same time announcing to the hunter the location of the flush.

Calling a scattered flock is one of the highest arts in turkey hunting. The hunter conceals himself at the site of the flush, hiding behind some natural object; or, he builds a blind of materials found in the area. If a blind is built, it should be natural looking and inconspicuous. Calling should begin about an hour after the flush is made. But results should not be expected immediately. Sometimes turkeys scattered late in the day may not attempt to reassemble until first light of the following day. Birds scattered in the morning will frequently not reassemble until mid-afternoon, sometimes later. Calling is an art, and a hunter should expect to have to practice in order to master it. Many different designs of callers are on the market, with instructions for proper use.

In the fall and winter, the hunter should limit his calling, making calls only every 10 to 20 minutes, and then stopping altogether once he gets a response. A turkey who answers has almost surely identified the caller's location, and will come to it. He may be slow in doing so. Additional calls are unnecessary, however, and may make the bird suspicious if they are not rendered perfectly.

In the spring a gobbler announces his presence by calling vigorously and repeatedly from his roosting perch at the first moments of dawn. A hunter should move quickly and quietly through concealing cover toward the turkey's location, ap-

Author's father, Bill Hanenkrat, lifts 19-pound gobbler he took during spring season in Virginia. Beard and spurs are very evident on this mature bird. Its large size is obvious since hunter stands almost six feet tall.

proaching as closely as prudence allows—to within 50 or 75 yards, if possible. He then conceals himself and imitates the call of a hen turkey. The gobbler will respond with additional mating calls, and will eventually fly down from his roost, if he hasn't already. The hunter should at this time of year call frequently and regularly, keeping up a steady stream of calls with only brief intervals of silence. If they are delivered well, the gobbler will eventually approach, often coming to within a few feet of the hunter if the hunter is well concealed. The turkey will not, however, cross the boundaries of his territory to meet a hen, nor will he enter a thicket where he would be unable to see well in all directions.

Both rifles and shotguns are fine for turkey hunting. If a rifle is used, it should be equipped with a scope in the 4X to 6X range; a variable power model is also good. A model with an illuminated reticle is quite helpful, as much of the action in turkey hunting takes place in the dim light of dawn or dusk. The foot-pounds of energy delivered by the cartridge should be somewhere in the vicinity of the lighter .22 caliber center-fire factory loads. Loads in the .22 rimfire category are too light, unless a Magnum variety is used by a skillful marksman; loads that deliver too much power destroy the quality of the meat for the table. Light handloads in almost any reasonable caliber are suitable, but factory loads in the heavier and hotter cartridges usually cause too much destruction. Expanding bullets should be avoided in any caliber as they are entirely too destructive. A jacketed bullet will kill a turkey cleanly and not tear up the carcass. Excessive power and destructive ability are far less important than accurate marksmanship.

A shotgun of 12 or 16 gauge with a modified or full choke is an excellent turkey gun, with, of course, a more limited range than a rifle. With standard high-velocity loads, the modified and full choke can kill reliably up to about 40 and 50 yards, respectively; with Magnum loads, the ranges are extended five yards or so. Smaller gauges are effective, but within much smaller ranges. With any gauge shotgun, however, it's desirable to let the turkey approach much closer than the gun's maximum range, as this ups the odds of a clean kill. My preferred shot size is #4; other hunters like 5's or 6's on the lighter side, or, on the other side, 2's or BB's. Smaller shot than these will not penetrate a turkey's heavy feathers, and larger shot does not deliver a dense enough pattern. With a shotgun, shoot at the spot on the turkey's neck where the feathers end and the bare skin of the head begins. A good pattern of shot placed in this spot will kill a turkey almost instantly and will scarcely affect the quality of the edible meat.

After downing your turkey, run to it as quickly as possible and kneel on the body or wings to control the muscular convulsions that follow death; this will prevent the throes from destroying the beautiful plumage. Securing it immediately has another purpose as well: Many a "downed" turkey has got up and run off while an overconfident hunter stood amazed at a distance.

All turkey hunters should follow a few standard operating procedures. The first of these is to study the hunting regulations regarding turkeys in your state. They are often complicated and may vary from year to year. Follow them closely. The turkey can thrive only under close management requiring the cooperative efforts of land-owners, game management personnel, and hunters. Do your part.

Someday, learn as much as you can about the turkeys in your area—their habitat preferences, food preferences, breeding seasons, etc. Be aware that minor behavior patterns, such as length or pace of calls, may vary from one part of the country to another, and even from one flock to another in the same area. Your state game commission, local game warden, and nearby experienced hunters are all good sources of information.

Perhaps the key to successful turkey hunting is keeping the turkeys from being aware of your presence. Wear camouflage clothing; cover your face with netting or camouflage paint; wear gloves; make no movements within the turkey's range of vision. Line up your gun when the turkey is behind a tree or some other obstacle to vision. The closer he gets, the more likely he is to see you. If you're hunting with a shotgun and cannot move without his seeing you, let him get quite close, then stand up quickly and shoot at the moving target.

Finally, play it safe. Don't shoot at the sound of a calling turkey; it may be another hunter. If you're calling from a blind, be sure you're fully exposed to the view of anyone approaching from behind. Otherwise, *you* might be mistaken for a turkey.

Once you've bagged your first gobbler, prepare for a great eating experience. The meat of a wild turkey is to the meat of a domestic turkey what a good year of Lafite-Rothschild is to an ordinary domestic wine. Have your trophy properly cooked, and you'll learn that there's a lot more satisfaction to turkey hunting than merely outwitting America's biggest, smartest, and most challenging game bird.

Dove-Shooting Know-How

by Dan M. Russell

I witnessed only the last remnants of old-time dove shooting but, like most hunters in my part of the country, I've heard a lot about it. Big shoots were a tradition in the South, and they were lengthy "shootin', pickin', and partyin'" affairs. On several occasions I've participated in big dove shoots with, say, 300 people in the field and mourning doves coming in droves, shells popping like a string of firecrackers all up and down the line, birds falling, retrievers working, hunters yelling to each other, picking up birds, ducking low shots. It's quite a spectacle. In dove shooting now, the old country-style "Y'all come" party-sport is fast disappearing. The shooting is still frantic but more under control.

On opening day, hunters string out across a field early. Some just have to be there the first minute, some older shooters are not so eager. They take their stand. By and by some of the young doves begin to get hungry and drop in to feed. Shooting starts sporadically at first, then it gets so steady you can't draw a full breath between shots. Wings whistle and the hunters' calls of "low bird" and "let 'em come in" mingle with hoots and jeers and "I gotta go get some more shells," and "Mark 'em down, Junior" and "Fetch," and "How did I miss that one?"

Everyone wonders sooner or later just how it is that a "dead" dove can keep right on flying. You have a clean shot and your aim is dead on, but the dove just flies on past. I recall one shoot in a combine-harvested cane-sorghum field. About 30 hunters were present and the shooting was sporadic. During a lull, a dove slipped in at one end of the field before it was seen. It zipped through the middle to the far end with every hunter unloading at it. Then, as if to prove a point, it banked and bore right back through the same air and again outmaneuvered the shots as it powered into the sun and disappeared over the line of trees. No wonder doves make such a contribution—in the form of the tax on ammunition—to the Wildlife Restoration Fund.

In the more northerly states, most of the

Stationed in ditch where birds won't spot him until they're well within range, shooter scores on dove coming to farm pond. Some gunners wear camouflage, but most use shadows, hedgerows, and the like for partial concealment.

dove shooting is over quite suddenly. The first open weekend in September catches the bulk of the season's hunting pressure. After a cold snap and some heavy shooting the doves get so wild and wary that fast bag limits aren't too common, and a lot of the hunters then quit. But there is still much good dove shooting to be had—with a little more patience and, of course, a little less crowd.

Just about anywhere, the first week or two of the season is apt to provide good shooting, but in those southern states that open their seasons early the shooting remains good long after that. By October,

Shooter picks up bird he brought down at edge of water as doves came in for last drink before going to roost. Waterholes furnish good afternoon shooting, especially if they're near feed and haven't been hunted hard.

however, most of the field harvesting is done and there is plenty of food for doves everywhere, in every field, in any direction. The birds don't have to concentrate to feed then and a single shot might spook a flock of doves clear out of the country. At this time pass-shooting is about all you can expect; still, pass-shooting in a high wind is quite a challenge.

Favored shooting areas in early September are in harvested grain fields and around farm ponds. Once a flock of mourning doves has decided on a feeding ground—such as a wheat-stubble or sorghum field or corn cut for silage or a millet-bean hay field that has been cut and raked—they return regularly day after day. Doves gather on telephone lines and power lines and in trees near such fields. Hunters watch for these gathering places in order to locate the feeding grounds, and they usually have several such areas located by the opening date.

Hunters, ranging in number from one to a dozen or occasionally to a hundred or more, take their shooting stands at fence-corner posts, under trees, in brushy fence-rows or even in the middle of a field, using whatever cover is there. Some bring a portable blind. It takes several shooters in a large field to keep doves flying; otherwise the birds settle at the far end, feed, then pick up and leave. It doesn't take them long to finish feeding, once they get to it.

In September the weather is likely to be as hot as it was in August. Doves will "lay up" in the woods and thickets during the hot part of the day—until three or four o'clock in the afternoon. Then they fly out to feed, and after that to water and on to the roost.

Whitewings aren't basically very differ-

Lab brings dove to hand during afternoon shoot. Even in open-field dove hunting, many birds can be lost in ground cover without retriever. No single breed is considered best, and many types of dogs are used.

ent from mourning doves in their habits— or at least in those habits that influence a hunter looking for a good shooting station. As with mourning doves, the shooting is often very good in grain fields. However, whitewings in some regions depend more heavily on weed seeds and other wild foods. And they're so well adapted to arid country that the shooting can be excellent right out on the desert. One of their popular names, in fact, is "cactus dove." On the Arizona deserts where the strange-looking organ-pipe cactus grows, they often feed on the red cactus fruits that ripen at the time of the hunting season. Sometimes a shooter can stand in the shadow of a tall cactus and have fine sport as the doves come in.

Whitewings have a more deliberate style of flight than mourning doves and they don't appear to be travelling quite as fast, but that's probably an illusion. They can be tough targets, especially when they spot movement and flare. And they tend to fly high. At times maybe they're just pass-

ing through during migration and have no intention of coming down, but mostly it's just that they have to fly such long distances between roosts and feeding areas or watering spots. Some shooters like to station themselves on a hill or other elevation to get at least a little closer to the birds coming over. The sport is primarily pass-shooting, the same as with mourning doves.

Doves flock up at watering places, ponds, creeks, salt-water wells, and river banks. But hard, steady shooting will run them off in a day or two, just as it will in a feeding field. Doves seem to prefer scummy, dirty-looking ponds and brackish water. Possibly the attraction of minerals in the water has some connection with their physiological needs. But they do prefer clean, bare ground to land on and walk to the water. You will seldom if ever find them where the banks of a pond are grassy right to the water's edge. Where the water has receded or a pond has partially dried up, leaving a wide band of mud-flat

Ejected shell flies as shooter maintains swing for follow-up shot after missing on first try. Since misses are frequent even among old hands, repeaters are popular for pass shooting at doves; both pumps and autos are used.

around—that's a favorite drinking place for doves. If you find such a place and the doves are using it, you'll see small dove feathers that have collected around the edge of the water.

In the arid country of the Southwest, the area around a desert water tank is likely to provide good shooting. Both mourning doves and whitewings are attracted to water tanks.

Hunters quickly learn to identify doves in flight. These birds never seem to rest their wings or dip like a blackbird or a woodpecker. It is always a steady, powerful, rhythmical wingbeat that carries the bird along at a rapid clip. The speed and agility of the species is always amazing to a new dove hunter, especially one who has observed the hesitant, timid movements of cooing doves nesting in a backyard. Migrating doves probably cruise along at 35 or 40 miles an hour, but when they're flaring from gunfire as they cross a field—and especially if they have the benefit of a tailwind—a lot of shooters claim the birds hit 70. And while the wingbeats are steady, the flight path is often erratic, twisting, evasive. Anyone who averages two doves for four shells is definitely a good wingshot.

A dove in flight appears gray or graybrown on a bright day, but can look almost black in poor light, and the wings look darker than the body. The bird is much slimmer than a pigeon—more streamlined—with narrower wings that rake back more than a pigeon's and with a long, tapered tail rather than the pigeon's almost squared-off fan.

In some parts of the West a hunter can shoot mourning doves and whitewings both on the same day in the same area and in pretty much the same kind of habitat. The whitewing is a little plumper than a mourning dove and is easy to recognize by its big, white, sharply contrasting patches on the wing coverts and its shorter, blunter tail with broad white tipping at the corners. In flight it doesn't dip, rise, and twist quite as erratically as a mourning dove but it provides tough shooting, all the same. Incidentally, whereas whitewings don't make any flight sound, eastern shooters are familiar with the soft whistle of air through a mourning dove's primaries when a bird flies close enough.

I guess just about every make and model of shotgun is used to hunt doves. Singlebarrels, over-and-unders, doubles, automatics, pumps; 12 gauge, 28 gauge, 26-inch barrels to 32-inch barrels, open cylinders to full chokes—they all show up at the fencerows and water holes. All shot sizes are used, too, from No. 9 skeet loads all the way to high-brass No. 4's.

Probably No. 7½'s and 8's are most often used since small shot provides thicker pattern. Some hunters use field loads while others say they prefer high-velocity stuff late in the season, when birds have learned to fly high and flare promptly at the sound of gunfire. The most popular guns are 12 and 20 gauge, bored improved or modified. The birds may look small and fragile, but I'm told that for doves the 12 gauge continues to outsell any other bore size, North or South, East or West.

Before you take the field to shoot, if you can restrain yourself, watch the doves flying for a few minutes. Usually they'll follow a path if they're going on through. In a field they are using, pick a spot with the sun at your back, under a tree or in a fencerow. A depression in a hill, just below the crest, is a good spot. But don't hide so well you can't see to shoot. Once you get into position, sit still. Most doves won't notice you if you don't move. Then estimate your effective killing distance and keep your shots within this distance. If you don't get the hang of it quickly, don't let it worry you. The "experts" who tell you how don't always hit them either.

Decoys do work. Years ago, when I first heard about dove decoys, I didn't see much point in trying to decoy birds that just naturally drifted in over the shooters anyway. In most situations, maybe it is unnecessary work. But if you want to get by yourself, away from the crowded field, or pull doves in off a flyway or make them circle your end of a field or pond, then get some decoys. They work well in trees, on a fence or on the ground, depending on how you want to shoot. Often decoys will bring you birds that would otherwise stay away, and in the late season they're much more valuable. You can use silhouettes or blocks; both are effective.

Another thing to bear in mind is the "whistling wings." Whistling to imitate the sound of dove wings also attracts flying doves. It doesn't seem to make much difference early in the fall but later, during the winter season, I've seen it work with high-flyers passing over.

As for dove calls, I've never used them or seen them used very often. Because few doves are still calling during the hunting season, a call seems out of place and I don't have much faith in its ability to attract doves into shooting range. But then, admittedly, I was skeptical about decoys at one time, too, so don't take this as the final word on the subject. Perhaps, in your region, calling may be worth a try.

Hunters usually wear something drab— army color or dark green or any dark hue. The use of camouflage hats, suits, jackets, and netting is ideal. Netting material is now being made up into jackets more and more. It lets some air through to the skin and a September afternoon can be a real scorcher. At any type of shoot, dark clothes or at least a camouflage jacket will be of help.

Sometimes in mid-afternoon when the shooting slows and doves seem to have evaded the usual feeding area where you are, then you can try walking them up. Jump-shooting doves is not like the fast pass-shooting, but the birds do flush wild and make for sporty shooting this way, too.

You'll usually find them working in a field of standing corn, beans, sorghum grain, or such. Then again they may use a wheat-stubble or weed field. You might also flush them in a woodlot or thicket. The main thing to remember is that the cover is continuous and sometimes quite thick. In fact, the cover may be tall enough to limit your vision and thick enough to make your downed birds hard to find. Hunt and pick them up one at a time. This is one case where you really need a retriever.

Dogs work well with doves if you'll take the precaution to keep them cool and well watered, especially the long-haired breeds. Labradors readily retrieve doves. All bird-dog types do, though some owners claim their dogs can't stand the feathers. Dove feathers do come out very easily, so dogs often get a mouthful when picking up a dove and then have trouble getting them all spit out. Some dogs won't fetch other game than the type they are trained on, and there are dogs, with and without pedigrees, that simply refuse to pick up a dove. I guess only the dogs know why this is so. But I think it's safe to say that most dogs that retrieve will retrieve doves. Try it next time.

Crow Guns and Gunning

by Dick Mermon

42

I always shoot either by myself or with one other person. The reason is primarily for safety's sake. Sometimes there are four shooters, but only two in each blind. Each person can keep an eye on one other shooter in the same blind—it's that third man you can't see.

If there are to be three or four shooters, then two blinds can be used, a hundred yards apart in the same hedgerow. The decoys are placed between the blinds. When the birds decoy, the closest blind will take the shot first; if there are flaring crows, then the opposite blind will take care of them. Or there can be pre-arranged alternating shooting.

A caller can be in either blind, but there really should be one in each of the blinds. The crows will stool to the calling side more than the quiet. If there are two callers, then the crows will come to either one, and the flaring birds will be taken care of by the other blind. One thing to remember is that there must be no direct cross shooting. There must be an agreement that once a crow is past a certain

point, it will not be shot at unless it is overhead.

Three blinds are used if there are three shooters and each wishes to shoot in an individual blind. This is a triangle setup with the decoys placed slightly nearer the point blind. One or two shooters are placed in each of the blinds. The point blind should contain the best of the callers. This is where the crows will decoy to. The shooters in the side blinds should let the first of the birds come in close to the center caller. In this way the caller can get a crack at the birds as they decoy in and the others will take rear and flare-off crows as they try to get out of the situation. Remember always to have the wind coming from the back of the point blind. This way the crows will have to stool into the wind and come to the point caller first before flaring off to either of the sides.

Decoys are placed on the ground with some in the trees or low shrubs near the caller in the point blind. In the two-blind shoot all of the decoys are in the center between the blinds, or there can be a small

With decoys in corn-stubble field and in trees, hunter is ready in blind, visible at far left; Dick Mermon has used as many as 75 decoys to lure big flight between fields and roost. Note loudspeaker of electronic call atop fencepost.

scattering in the center, spreading out with a large group at each blind. Some decoys are placed in the trees or shrubs near the blinds on each side, with a few sucker decoys to the rear, to attract and distract the other crows.

With these two- and three-blind setups, caution is the word. It must be stressed that if there is any doubt as to whose bird it is, better let it go by than to cause an accident.

The type of gun that is used to shoot crows is basically up to the individual shooter. Most men I know use 20-gauge pump or autoloading shotguns. There are some crow shooters who stay with their trusty 12 gauges. I like the 20's for two reasons: They are light and they are less expensive to shoot. (On the expense angle, the steady shooters I know all reload their own shells, which is a big saving.)

When I first started to hunt crows I used a 12-gauge, three-inch Magnum pump gun, and was that ever a crow-buster! That is, when I hit them. I found the shells for this gun a little on the costly side, so I swung to a 16-gauge pump. From there I went to a 20-gauge pump with a full choke. I liked it so much that I bought two others like it to have in case of jam-ups. Several times I've been glad to have the other guns along. When things get hot in shooting, carelessness runs high. It's not easy to make repairs in the heat of battle. A swelled shell can jam the gun, for instance, and rather than trying to take care of it then, I prefer to set it aside and switch to another gun. It's safer that way, too.

Full or modified chokes are best for crow shooting, due to the number of distant shots. More than that, the shot patterns produced by full or modified chokes are very tight at 30 yards, and the tighter the pattern the less chance the crow has to get through a hole in the barrage. Skeet or open-choke guns are good when the crows will set in close early in the season, but after that the full choke to me is best.

Sure, there is more shot in a 12-gauge shell, but if the shooter knows what his gun or guns can do there is no problem. At the present time I use a 20-gauge semiautomatic with full choke. This is the fastest-swinging gun I have ever handled. It really does bust the crows out of the sky as well as reach up there and pull down birds that think they are out of range.

The shot size to use is the size that fits the gun best. I have found that the #8 shot produces the finest pattern with the full choke in my barrel. I have not patterned any 12-gauge guns with this particular shot because I found the right combination for my 20 gauges and let it go at that. In fact, several of us use this shot for all our shooting, from skeet to crows.

Early in my crow-shooting career I switched from a 12-gauge to a 16-gauge pump, figuring that since I had done pretty well with the 12, it was now time to start going smaller. Well, the first day I fired 19 shells at oncoming crows—easy shots—and never even nipped a feather. I just did not know what was the matter. I finally figured out that it was the lead I was taking on the bird, and the speed of my swing, that were off. The 12 gauge I had been using was a heavy gun that I had to fight to get ahead of the bird. The 16

Perched on tree limb, crow misses nothing that goes on in vicinity. Species has at least been granted status as a migratory game bird. Hunting is suspended during peak of nesting, so check your state's regulations.

Gunner in blind folds fast-flying "scout" crow that investigated decoys before flock would venture near. If you're not sure you can hit scout, it's best to hold your fire or he may warn his comrades and you'll get no more shots.

was a little lighter so I became lazy and was shooting behind the birds. I finally realized this and then had no trouble knocking out the crows I swung at.

An important point to remember is that the shooter will generally underestimate the speed at which the crow is flying. Whether he is travelling with the wind or against it, the bird is still moving pretty fast, and the sooner the shooter catches onto this the better. Lead is *very* important, so shoot ahead. One way I have found to tell whether I am shooting ahead or behind the crow is the way he acts after I fire the shot. If the bird veers back and up, the shot is in front of him; if he hightails it for the distant hills, the shot has travelled behind him. If he comes tumbling down, then you know you're on, and that is the way you want it.

There are additional reasons why I prefer pumps and autoloaders to over-and-under and side-by-side guns. They are safer to load, and they hold more shells than the others so they do not have to be reloaded as often as a double.

There's another factor. Loading a double in a tight blind is very hard, due to the fact it has to be broken open to load and unload and it has to be pointed down. The auto can be pointed up and out of the blind without danger to anyone if it should happen to go off. But to each his own.

The only problem I can see with the autos and some of the pumps is the ejection of the fired shells. The man on the right gets hit on the head occasionally by one of the ejected casings. They may be small but they hurt.

It's also possible to use a woodchuck rifle on an occasional crow. I position myself on a hill overlooking a large field empty of buildings or human inhabitants. It's a good crow-feeding area, and it doesn't take too long for me to spot a likely target 200 yards or so away through my binoculars. My .222 with 10X scope does a pretty good job on any crows that come within decent range. It goes without saying that the good hunter doesn't even think about shooting until he makes sure that the area in front of, at, or in back of

Author carries crows which he may prop up as extra decoys. Field stool employs
crow decoys alone—plastic or papier mache—but tree setup sometimes
uses owl decoy "under attack," prompting live crows to join attack on their enemy.

the target contains no one or nothing that might be harmed by the shot—except the crow.

No hunter can stress safety too much. Guns should always be held or placed off to the side or in front of the shooter, for safety's sake and for fast access. The safety on the gun is put there for a reason. Use it. Make especially sure that the safety is on when the guns are put aside after a quick volley.

Part VI: Vehicles, Boats, and Equipment

Driving Into Rough Country

by V. Lee Oertle

43

During the past five years American sportsmen have put behind them the notion that only all-wheel-drive vehicles can penetrate rough country. Cars, trucks, and station wagons have narrowed the gap between two-wheel-drive and four-wheel-drive vehicles in many respects. The much greater horsepower of cars and pickups is one factor. So are the new efficient automatic transmissions which provide tremendous torque multiplication.

However, the most amazing off-road improvement has been demonstrated in recreational vehicles. There was a time when travel trailers, motor homes, and pickup campers were driven just off the pavement and parked, and the hiking boots were donned. That situation need no longer be tolerated. For the truth is that camping vehicles driven with deliberation can go many places you'd never suspect. There are good and logical reasons for this new ruggedness.

First, consider dimension. The *height* of a camper affects its ability to sneak under low-hanging branches and rocky overhangs. The *width* of it will limit passage through narrow canyons and between boulders. The *length* of it affects the departure angle when traversing a sharp ravine or sudden incline. Learn those dimensions and when confronted by such places post an outside observer before proceeding.

Ground clearance between trail and undercarriage is greatest on motor homes, pickup trucks, and 4WD vehicles. Where the access problem is merely one of getting over mud ruts and occasional large rocks, such vehicles have a real advantage.

The turning radius of some small cars makes them extremely handy in back country. The wheelbase most affects this factor. Long motor homes will have difficulty when making U-turns and bending around sharp trails. So will the new 130-inch-wheelbase and 140-inch-wheelbase pickups. Cars towing trailers can use the old trick of disconnecting, turning the car around, then turning the trailer around by hand. It isn't that difficult, really. Reconnect and drive away.

Wide-footprint tires provide extra flotation and extra traction. Sportsmen plan-

Compact camping trailer can be towed into many hunting areas if you drive carefully. But even in smooth, level off-road spots like this, when turning around or backing up beware of holes, rocks, upthrust roots, and other obstacles.

ning extensive off-road travel should install such tires as optional equipment. They make an impressive difference in penetration ability.

Some extra equipment makes off-road exploration safer, more convenient, and is a backup to the emergencies which may crop up. On my list are the following: 25-foot towing strap (or chain), 50 feet of heavy rope, two large pulley-blocks, shovel, ax, chain-saw, extra jacks, come-along (rachet-type hand winch), auxiliary light, dropcloth for getting under, heavy work gloves, assortment of small tools, short length of chain (four feet) for securing come-along, a heavy-duty axle jack or hay baler's jack, wheel chocks, two-foot pry bar, and the usual camping supplies.

A great deal has been written concerning proper loading habits, and it *is* an important consideration. However, unless that gear is securely fastened, the rattles, squeaks, and thumping noises will make the road seem much worse than it really is. A spare water can grating against camper walls scratches the paneling. An outboard motor in the trunk can batter camp lanterns and portable stoves. Heavy tools in a pickup box can bounce loose and slam down on fishing rods. Much fishing tackle is ruined this way. I once lost a $60 fishing rod because I was too lazy to tie it up off the box. A heavy jack rebounded onto it and snapped it.

Inside an r-v the upper cabinets should be used only for lightweight items like towels, plastic dining utensils, dry packaged foods, and so on. Attach rubber bands around the hardware to keep the doors from flying open on rough roads.

Heavy canned foods and beverages should be stored on the floor under the sink, drainboard, or bed. For best results, carry most of your weight at a point slightly ahead of the rear axle. Remember not to mix heavy hardware with light and

Big motor homes can actually penetrate rough country better than some low-slung passenger cars because they have excellent ground clearance and plenty of weight on rear-drive wheels. Just watch out for low-hanging branches.

fragile sporting gear. Keep guns and fishing tackle heavily padded and *separated* from tool boxes, canned food, bait buckets, shovels, and so on. Clothes closets make good nesting places for fishing rods. Place your guns between mattresses or on bunk beds.

The fastest way to short-circuit a backcountry hunt is to drive along like a Sunday freeway tourist. On rough roads you *must* slow down to whatever speed is safe for your equipment. Sharp rocks can be crossed easily by driving at a crawl. But large rocks (bigger than a football) should be driven around, or the rocks should be rolled off the trail. Cactus is no problem to tough rubber tires. I've driven through 10-acre patches of cactus without incident. But some terrain will slash and puncture tires. Stay off stuff like volcanic tuff, sharp tree roots, old junk car parts like bumpers and bolts, and old trash heaps.

If you *must* carry spare gasoline and stove fuel, do so with great caution. Lash the cans so that they are in a permanent upright position. And *never* carry gasoline inside the living quarters of any camper, trailer, or motor home. Keep it outside the living quarters and firmly banded or strapped with leakproof lids.

Driving down through narrow, steep ravines usually causes the bottom of your car or camper to drag. Some outdoorsmen have welded small wheels, skid plates, or belly pans under their vehicles for protection. A careful driver can often get through such places unscathed by tackling the ravine at an oblique angle, the same technique used when quartering waves on rough water. The idea is to reduce the head-on impact and to twist the frame so that the rear end is not dragging. Incidentally, when driving on rough or steep trails, fasten your seat belts snugly. The belts will prevent your passengers from being bounced around, and the driver will be able to keep both hands on the steering wheel at critical moments.

The position of your hands on the steering wheel is also a big factor in control. Wear buckskin gloves for extra gripping traction. You'll be amazed how much difference gloves can make in wheel control. Keep your thumbs out of the steering-wheel spokes while driving. When a front tire strikes a chuckhole, the backlash may whip the steering wheel around and sprain or break a thumb. Sideview mirrors are a great help on paved highways, but they create problems when sneaking through dense brush and trees and between large boulders. The best types of mirrors will fold out or swing back as the need arises. Clamp-on mirrors with tension springs can be removed without tools. Just bring them inside the vehicle until the obstacles have been passed.

Carry a folding bow saw for trimming away stubborn branches that protrude along the trail. Thin-sided aluminum r-v's can't stand surface abrasion. However, if you do suffer a collision with a branch that punctures the coach sides, stop quickly. Saw off the branch before proceeding. Do not back away, because the end of the branch may tear out more metal.

Ground clearance is one of the key factors. Always consider the height of your towing vehicle. If you check a car-trailer combination from the side, it is apparent in most cases that though both frames ride horizontal, the trailer frame is higher off the road. Motor homes and pickup trucks have excellent ground clearance, an advantage that allows them to penetrate much farther into rough country than newcomers expect.

Another critical factor is tire width and tread pattern. Deep zigzag lugs will handle mud and snow best. Tires with lightly ribbed patterns or even no tread pattern at all are more efficient over sand. Since few sportsmen can afford to rig a vehicle strictly for back-country travel, a compromise is in order. Most tire companies sell a tread pattern called "extra traction" (or similar names) which produces very little of the objectionable "singing" that deep-lug patterns develop. Ordinary passenger-car tires are surprisingly efficient on dirt and moderately rocky terrain. That old maxim about letting air out of tires to cross sand is still viable, but do so only in emergency. Once back on the pavement drive slowly until you can inflate tires to proper levels again. Remember that letting out a *few* pounds of pressure is useless. The casing must appear pear-shaped or half-flat to really provide extra traction on sand. I would avoid this technique on any other terrain.

Carry a set of wheel chocks so that if your vehicle stalls out on a steep slippery trail you can block it while you restart the engine. The bouncing and steep angle frequently sloshes fuel out of the carburetor bowl, which kills the engine and terrifies passengers in that predicament. If the parking brake won't hold, then those wheel chocks will seem a mighty important asset!

Once stopped on a steep grade it is difficult to get going without spinning the wheels. It may be best to let the vehicle roll slowly back down the road and make a fresh start. When traversing sandy washes and beaches, keep your speed at about 20 miles per hour, if possible. The same is usually true when driving over snow and ice. Maintain 15 to 20 miles per hour, if possible, and stay off those brakes!

If you happen to slide into a ditch or snowbank, take it with good humor. It's a frightening prospect for women and city drivers, sometimes, but patience and a good jack will get you out again. It's a good idea to invest in a modest come-along if you intend much back-country driving. This is simply a double-pulley leverage device with a cranking handle and cables. The cable hooks are pulled out in opposite directions. One attaches to a solid object like a tree, rock, or post. The other end attaches to the stuck vehicle. You simply ratchet the crank handle and the device pulls the two ends of cable together, hence moving the vehicle.

When it comes to jacks, the one furnished with new cars and trucks is usually inadequate for rescue work. Carry at least one hydraulic jack in addition to the factory jack. The unsticking procedure is quite simple. Use the bumper jack to elevate the frame near the stuck wheel. Get it high enough to shove the axle jack somewhere under the frame. Then raise the tire high enough to push rocks, twigs, sagebrush, an old rug, or anything handy under the wheel for traction. Use the come-along after raising the stuck wheel. Crank the vehicle slowly out of the wheel depressions *before* applying power. In most cases a movement of only three or four feet puts the wheels on better traction. When the vehicle bogs down in a dense forest, it is sometimes possible to attach the come-along to an overhead projection and *lift* the front or rear end high enough to place sticks and stones under tires. Where a vehicle has slipped over the side on a steep

Where prairie or desert surface is mostly packed gravel, as at this deer camp,
a pickup camper or car with small trailer can negotiate tight, rough
spots if you go slowly, avoid rocks and stumps, and drive around sand dunes.

Pickup campers like this can carry enough supplies to serve as base camp, but care must be taken in loading. Heavy canned foods and beverages should be stowed at floor level, for instance, and guns and scopes should be padded.

slope, use the come-along as a holding method until help arrives. I've seen them used to prevent vehicle rollovers by attaching strong ropes around the roofline (through the windows) and clamping the come-along hook from tree to car roof. A $30 investment in one of the leverage devices (come-along, hay-baler's jack, or any kind of hand-operated winch) has proved invaluable to thousands of outdoorsmen. In addition to emergency uses, they're quite useful in lifting big game.

Fallen logs or boulders sometimes will block an access trail. Don't try to push them aside with your car or truck, or expensive damage may result. Instead, try to get a chain or loop around the end of the log or part of the boulder. Back away, exerting a steady pull. It may be necessary to try tugging from several directions. Eventually the object can be moved. Carrying a chain saw is added insurance. Cut fallen logs into manageable pieces and drag them aside. A chain saw can also be used to cut brush for placing under stuck wheels. In camp, it's handy to prepare firewood. Any way you look at it a chain saw is an excellent investment. The new compact models cost less than $150, complete with plastic carrying case.

There are several pitfalls in off-road maneuvering. For instance, making U-turns on soft or rocky ground traps many hunters. The secret is simply to keep looking until you find a wide spot. If the vehicle must be turned around in a narrow place, use ax and shovel to make a safe ramp. Backing and jockeying is tedious, but it's not as difficult as trying to get off a high-center rock after attempting a U-turn in the wrong place.

Occasionally, back-country travellers will get into discussions over right-of-way. Most common laws give the uphill driver priority, but commonsense should tell any woodsman that give and take is involved. Two drivers meeting on a narrow mountain road should stop and talk it over. Which way to the nearest pull-out? Avoid backing downhill and around blind curves. The driver nearest the turn-out should do the backing if it is safe to do so. I've encountered similar situations on long dikes and levees in waterfowl country. Again, it's a question of backing toward the nearest turn-out. Backing a trailered boat several miles along a dike is an experience most hunters long remember, especially when such a dike is swept by wind or pounded by high surf.

Carry plenty of auxiliary light sources—lanterns, 12-volt portable fluorescent lamps, flashlights, or pressurized propane lamps. Emergencies after dark will seem less frightening with plenty of light available. When passing another vehicle on a narrow trail, always take the high side if a choice is open. That way, if your own vehicle bogs down, it's less difficult to get back on the trail again.

When a *trailer* becomes stuck try this trick: Disconnect it from the towing ve-hicle and drive away. Then back up to the trailer from an *oblique angle* and attach a tow chain or rope. (Carry one of those handy new nylon towing straps, rated 10,000 pounds.) It's then possible to twist the trailer out sideways one wheel at a time. Repeat the process from the opposite angle to free the other wheel. Use the same technique for retrieving a bogged boat trailer in deep water.

Fording streams should not be done like the stunts you see in old movies. Ramming into the water at high speeds will simply flood the engine and get your crew into a worse predicament. Stop at the edge of the stream and scout it on foot. Use a long stick to prove the depth and footing. Gravelly stream bottoms are generally safe to cross. Muddy, slow-moving water and silty bottom will cause trouble. Rocky fordings provide a safe bottom but may damage equipment. Cross *very slowly*. Muddy lakeshores trap many vehicles, so stay off them. When crossing sandy shorelines remember to maintain speed.

Finally, when camping in back country remember the basic cautions: Park on high ground, never in the bottom of a wash or on a stream bank. Avoid camping under tall dead trees. High winds can drop a heavy limb through your coach roof. Park so that your car, camper, truck, or motor home is facing the quickest escape route. If a midnight storm arises, just that little advantage of facing the right way can eliminate bogging down while attempting to hitch up or turn around. If it starts to snow, leave before it gets over four inches deep unless you are equipped to stay. Carry emergency food, water, and heavy clothing. Provide your own tow-rope. And don't depend on others to solve your off-road problems.

Boats That Go Hunting

44

by Zack Taylor

When you talk about boats that go hunting, you have to separate them into two categories. The first group is comprised of specific boats for specific hunting purposes, and most of these boats are silent, unmotorized craft. Without a little canoe or johnboat, for instance, you simply can't have the fun of jumping ducks or floating a quiet stream in search of squirrels. The other group of boats is much broader and consists of non-hunting boats—most of them powered—that you press into service in the fall to enable you to hunt areas that are hard to get to—sometimes unaccessible—for boatless hunters.

Stalking the shoreline in a silent craft is an excellent way to hunt a wide variety of birds and game. Moose, which are extremely aquatic in their habits, never stray too far from a lake or bog, and it's often easy to surprise them by canoeing around a bend. A cruise through suitable cover with a scope-equipped .22 provides good squirrel hunting. Another float prospect occurs in spring and summer, when woodchucks become the quarry. But probably more people float for waterfowl than for

any other game. Both streams and rivers are the paths that ducks follow when migrating, and sneaking down on them in a boat is an exciting way to hunt. And when float-boats really shine is when ponds and lakes freeze yet the moving water keeps the streams open. Waterfowl are forced off these and they congregate in the unfrozen areas.

The main boat requisite for floating is lightness. You'll probably have to carry the boat in and haul it out up a bank. Canoes are traditional float boats but a johnboat or cartopper less than 200 pounds can also serve. Lash paddles to the boat, so you can drop them to reach for your gun. It's usual for just the bow man to shoot but when your teamwork develops the stern man can take side shots too.

Floats are a glamorous way to hunt. And the excitement is intense when you round a bend and a trio of squawking greenheads leaps for the sky. But another thing about floats most hunters don't realize is that you aren't a slave to time and weather as in other duck hunting. Even on bluebird days ducks will be resting on the streams. And if

Author pilots duckboat that transports him and his gear, and when grassed up and hidden also works as blind. Another type of access craft is shown on page 276, offloading rabbit hunters and beagles on North Carolina island.

your alarm clock doesn't go off at dawn, they'll still be waiting for you at ten.

If there's a road along your favorite stream you don't need two cars to float. Put the boat in and drive to your take-out point. Then hitchhike back. Here's the trick I use. I carry a canoe paddle and life preserver cushion while thumbing a ride. Motorists recognize instantly why you are out on the highway and give you a lift, usually to find out how you're doing.

One final word before we leave floating. Streams and rivers in fall and winter are usually at their highs and the water is cold. Take extreme precautions to avoid a capsize, and always scout any fast water for rapids or downed trees.

The same outboard you use for summer fishing can often become an important hunting tool, especially with today's proliferation of huge impoundments. On many of these, you can run easily to places that are roadless and tough for other hunters to hike into. Islands in lakes are often prime hunting areas, again you'll probably

have the place to yourself. Rivers often lead through areas that may be otherwise extremely difficult to gain access to. With your runabout it may be a snap for you to reach. The barrier islands of the North Carolina sounds are thick with cottontail rabbits. It's common to see boatloads of hunters, beagles barking, unloading on them. Deer, of course, swim well. Islands in rivers and lakes often can be hot spots for pheasants. The reason: The canny roosters know they get less hunting pressure there. Your boat can help change their attitude.

Of course, when you connect boats and hunting you think immediately of duck hunting. An increasing number of ducks and geese are being shot over field blinds today, but in many places it's take to the water or else.

Here, again, you have a division. Some boats are used only as access vehicles. You run to an area where you have a blind, you hide the boat by moving it a hundred yards or so away, and you gun from the blind. If you have a retriever, the boat stays idle the whole shooting day. Your summer runabout serves admirably for this purpose, provided you have a place to launch it and take it out.

At the other end of the waterfowl spectrum are boats used as blinds. Maybe you don't want to be tied down to one spot or go to the trouble of building a permanent blind. You might want to gun out of a little pram. I see plenty of hunters doing it with no more than a camouflage net to hide them.

You can build a coffinbox out of quarter-inch plywood in a day. This is just a coffin-shaped box with one end slanted so it will tow easier. Hauled to a good spot, the box makes for comfortable shooting, even in bitter-cold weather. You can disguise the box with grass or dig it down six or eight inches, which really makes it disappear. The boxes work well in field shooting too. They weigh only about 50 pounds. Cost is about $60.

I think two keys to today's waterfowling demands are mobility and adaptability. You must be able to go where birds are plentiful. More and more there is species management, special seasons you should be able to take advantage of. Today's hunter must be able to get in and get out and hunt a different area every day if necessary. More and more hunting is being done on public lands. If you build a permanent blind on public land, sooner or later someone will contest you for it. Who needs this kind of aggravation? Private land for leasing is more and more expensive, and there is less and less of it. While you'd need landowner permission to build a blind most of the time, you can slide a boat in a ditch and no one will bother you. You are here today and gone tomorrow.

Vandalism of permanent blinds is an increasing factor in many areas. You cross a local yokel and some night he pulls up to your blind in his fast outboard, sloshes some gas from the tank around, tosses a match and whoosh! In minutes there goes your blind and probably your hunting season.

All of this points toward waterfowling from a duckboat, a reasonably fast access vehicle that turns into a blind when you reach a good shooting area. I once made a survey of duckboats. Every Saturday for a whole season I sat at the toll booth of a major highway that leads to good waterfowling areas. What I learned about duckboats was that every boat—and even some that didn't deserve the name—is in active use to spook and harass ducks. I saw prams galore, canoes, johnboats by the dozen, and many boxlike runabouts that looked like recycled cement-mixers. While you can press almost anything that floats into service, any serious waterfowler will want a craft that is tailored to the demands of the sport. Every duckboat worthy of the name should fulfill the following functions:

1. It should be readily trailerable.

2. It should be reasonably light, to facilitate launching off ramps that range from bad to impossible, and to enable you to drag the boat into spots where you can easily hide it.

3. It should be strong and seaworthy.

4. It should have a deck (to keep you warm and dry) and a hatch with cover and lock. This allows you to lock the boat in the field and even in your backyard if you've got that kind of neighbor. And the hatch means you don't have to worry about water getting in the boat when you're trailering or when the boat sits on its trailer between ducking days.

*Canoes are valuable for several kinds of hunting, from waylaying moose
in Ontario (top) or Quebec (bottom) to jump-shooting ducks on
rivers or drifting quietly along wooded shorelines in search of squirrels.*

5. It should be rowable. Some dark cold night when the engine doesn't start you can still come home.

6. It should be reasonably speedy, say 15 mph as a minimum.

7. It *should* have decoy racks, though these aren't as important as the other considerations.

A boat like this becomes the focus of your season. It's always there, ready to go. All you need to add is your gun and personal gear, and you're off. When storms howl, your boat sits safe on its trailer. No vandal will harm it in your driveway. You can gun geese one weekend and ducks the next by merely changing decoys. Even in the harshest freeze, lanterns under the fore and aft decks keep you cozy and warm. When other guys are driven out of the field by winds or cold, you stick. And if you hang in there, you're going to score.

Boat-hunting techniques are the same as in all waterfowling. Basically you are looking for places where the birds are resting or feeding. You go there, set up your decoys, and wait for the birds to come. With the boat you utilize any and all natural cover. Covering it with grass or stalks, drawing it into a ditch, digging it into the ground, digging a slot in a bank where you can float it in out of sight—are all acceptable and practiced methods.

Another type of duckboat just coming into vogue is what I call the gunning barge. This is a large flat-bottomed sled-like hull with a high-horsepower motor to get it to the gunning grounds fast. Then two and even three men sit crossways in the boat behind grassed panels that fold up from resting places on the deck. Some duck hunters have fashioned gunning barges out of regular commercially sold aluminum johnboats. They bolt frames to

Here's how any small duckboat (in this case a "coffinbox") can be grassed up for waterfowling. With outlines disguised and broken by grasses, 18-inch-high sides of little vessel almost seem to disappear.

the boat's size, then bolt carlins to these to create about a 12-inch deck on either side. Grassed up panels fold up from this. Two end panels are placed. Two hunters sitting on the bottom of the johnboat are completely hidden. With the hull grassed up, even black ducks and Canada geese will be fooled by the rig.

Probably one reason more hunters don't use their boats as hunting aids is that they think that operating in the winter will somehow harm the boat. Aside from tracking a little mud on the deck, there is no way that ice, snow, or cold can do any damage, if proper precautions are taken.

You can run through ice with a plastic or aluminum boat. While a wood boat can go through ice a half-inch thick or more without problems, it must be protected from the sharp skim ice that will actually eat through the wood at the waterline. Traditionally, this protection came from galvanized or wooden sheathing, tacked into place. The more modern way is to fiberglass the waterline area. Water freezing inside a boat won't hurt it, nor will the boat be harmed if it is frozen in the ice. In

In summer these sportsmen use their outboard for fishing, and when duck season arrives they moor it in oblong berth whose light frame supports reeds to form natural-looking blind. Birds will decoy to rig if hunters keep low.

the latter case you probably won't be able to get it out until the first thaw, unless you want to do a lot of hard ice chopping. One plus about cold-weather boating is you don't need anti-fouling bottom paint. All the little plants and animals are hibernating.

Your outboard needs no special protection beyond not tipping it up or storing it on its side where water could be trapped inside to freeze. Stand the motor straight up so all the water can run out of it. I've never had any cold-weather starting problems with outboards, although I always make a point to feed them new spark plugs prior to the season. Even this is unnecessary if you have a capacitor-discharge ignition system. Motors take somewhat longer to warm up in cold weather. Keep the gas-oil ratio the same as the summer ratio.

If your boat is a sterndrive or conventionally powered craft, the block of the engine must be drained every night or even during a long freezing day unless you want to go warm it up every now and then. Draining isn't so bad if you set up for it. On one boat I had I put extension nipples

about four inches long into each of the four or five drain holes. Then I mounted good seacocks on the ends and painted them red. Open the cocks with the motor running so the water pressure will free the opening of any sediment that might be in the line.

Obviously you don't want to get wet in winter boat work. Good wet-weather gear is a must as are waterproof gloves. I use the plastic gloves most hardware stores stock. When it gets really cold or when I have to pick up decoys, I put on skin diver gloves. They keep my hands warm, even when I'm sticking them in the water or when the spray is flying.

Ice on a deck or cockpit sole has slipped many a duck hunter over the side. And I think it's fair to say that when the weather really gets cold all boating dimensions scale down somewhat. There's no question that cold makes the water a more dangerous opponent. So be extra careful when you're boat hunting in icy weather.

Add a boat or boats to your hunting and I'll bet you never regret it.

Hunting Knives— Selection, Use, Care

45

by David Petzal

In these days of unlimited progress, it is possible for a man to walk into a sporting-goods store with $20 in his pocket and emerge with a hunting knife of a quality almost unheard-of only a few years ago. Two factors are responsible for this. First is vast progress made in metallurgy and the production of fine cutlery steel. The second is the present boom in custom-made knives, which has pressured the big manufacturers into offering mass-produced cutlery that is superb by any standards.

Probably the two largest producers of fine knives at modest prices are the firms of Gerber and Morseth. Both offer a wide variety of models, the Gerbers ranging from $15 to $60 and the Morseths from $50 to $65. They are intelligently designed, tough, and will hold an edge with the best.

Western Cutlery has also entered the picture with its Westmark knives, which sell in the high 20's. These samples of the cutler's craft are not fancy, but they have blades of excellent steel, come with an edge that is really razor-sharp and are sheathed in scabbards that are among the best I have ever seen.

However, should your taste run to something more exotic, the picture becomes a bit more complicated. Fifteen years ago, when I began collecting custom knives, there were about five full-time craftsmen in this field. Today, you'd have no trouble compiling a list of over 100 names—and you'd probably be leaving some out.

While there are custom models that sell in the same price range as the mass-produced knives, you can pretty well expect to start at $50, and the stopping point is up to you. It is quite possible to spend $250 on a small hunting knife from a maker such as Loveless, the same sum on an engraved pocket knife by Frank, or $750-plus on a replica bowie by Henry.

This disparity in price between the factory and the custom product is due to the fact that a custom knife is almost invariably the result of one man spending hours and hours fashioning a knife with the skill of his own two hands. For all practical purposes, a $50 Morseth will serve you as well as a $250 Loveless, just as a good shot can bag as much game with a rifle that costs $150 as one that costs $1,050. (Note that the preceding sentence is regarded as high treason by many people conversant with the field, and is subject to considerable and heated debate. But I have yet to be convinced otherwise.) So, what you are paying for with that extra $200 is the fact that the custom knife is prettier to look at, will come to you with a sharper edge, and will not be found riding on the belt of every third hunter you encounter in the woods.

Do not get the impression that custom knives are a waste of money—far from it. It just depends whether you consider a knife a tool, or something to take pride in. You pays your money and takes your choice. Here, I cannot dictate for you, nor do I know how much you care to spend. However, when it comes to settling on a particular design, I have advice aplenty, most of it come by the hard way—through experience.

Probably the biggest debate in knife design concerns the question of big versus small: Is a large heavy knife more suited for the jobs a hunter has to do or is a small one superior? In order to answer this one, let's first define our terms. By a large knife, I mean one with a blade longer than five inches and/or thicker than ¼-inch.

Here, friends, I am for the smaller knife. Of all my hunting knives (and I presently own 16), not one has a blade over five inches long, and only one attains that length. Most measure four or 4½. The reasons for this are several, and good. First, at the end of a day you will feel every single ounce you are carrying, and who wants to lug around a small sword of half a pound when he can carry one that weighs half that? Second, a long blade is an abomination to wear. Like my cat, it is perpetually in the way. Last, and most important, for the majority of jobs it will be called on to do, the big knife is far inferior to the small one.

There is a simple reason for this. The knife is a cutting tool, period. Not hacking, chopping, or prying. The largest piece of cutlery you can reasonably wear on your belt is barely equal to a small hatchet. I have yet to see the hunting camp that did not include an ax, a wood saw, and a hatchet, so why carry a samurai sword?

I have also found that as the hunter's experience increases the knife he carries grows smaller. Many men of great experience in the game field prefer large pocketknives or folding knives with blades that lock open. These are more than equal to any task you'll require of them.

In choosing a correct blade shape, I have only a few words of advice. You'll need a certain amount of straight cutting edge (or very gently curved edge) and a reasonably acute curved edge toward the point. Many good hunting knives have the point dropped somewhat toward the center of the blade so that you will not cut too deeply while removing the guts. Many custom-knife makers offer designs that are weird and wonderful to behold. Some of them work, but most are a pain in the neck. You'll notice that most of the knives in the accompanying pictures are not the results of flights of fancy and overworked imagination—but they all work well.

Handles are another thing to look at with care. When using a knife in the game field, you hands will probably be sweaty, bloody, wet, cold, or several of these simultaneously. So what you hang onto must not slip. The handle should be long enough to go completely across your hand diagonally; if it won't it's too short to give you good cutting leverage. The best handles

These half dozen knives are all excellently designed for sportsmen. First three, from left, are skinning models with blades of 4½ inches or less—Randall Yukon Skinner with micarta handle, Loveless small hunting knife with micarta handle, and T. M. Dowell knife with staghorn handle. At center are two general-purpose models with five-inch blades—Seguine knife with finger-grip cocobolo handle and Ralph Bone knife with rosewood handle. At right is completely hand-made, elegantly engraved folding model by Heinrich Frank.

seem to be slab-sided. This design shows great resistance to turning and slipping in the hand.

Once you have a knife, caring for it is pretty simple, and rule number one is: Use it as a knife—not as a crowbar, ax, hammer, or hacksaw. And shades of the late Jim Bowie, don't throw it! Even the toughest hunting knife cannot long survive repeated crash-landings. Second, don't let it rust. This means never returning the knife to its sheath wet or bloody, and carefully wiping it off after use. High-quality tool steel has a marked tendency to rust merely from damp atmospheric conditions, so store your knife out of its scabbard, and give it a light coat of oil if it's not to be used for a while.

And finally, keep it sharp. For this,

you'll need a sharpening stone. Do not get a stone made of artificial abrasives; they are too coarse for what you want and can wreck a good knife. Instead, purchase a Washita/soft Arkansas stone. You can get them from sporting-goods stores or by writing to A. G. Russell, 1705 Highway 71 North, Springdale, Ark. 72764. The basic stone is the soft Arkansas, which will give you an excellent edge, but if you want a real razor, you should also invest in a hard Arkansas. This is a much finer grit, and will give you a blade you can dissect hairs with. You will also need a supply of honing oil, which is sold by Buck and by Russell.

There are probably as many ways to sharpen a knife as there are people who own them, but the following is more or less the standard method, and gives excellent

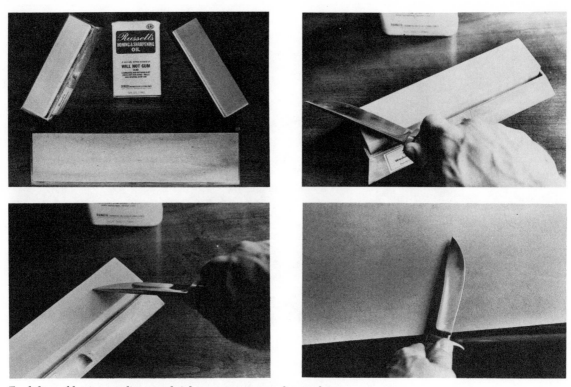

Top left, good honing supplies are soft Arkansas stone in non-slip stand,
mineral-base honing oil, finer-grit hard Arkansas stone, and larger soft Arkansas.
Top right, at start of sharpening stroke, blade is held diagonally on stone
and raised 20 degrees. Bottom left, at finish of stroke, handle is
raised to keep blade's curved cutting edge in contact with stone. Bottom right,
as final touch, blade is drawn backward across piece of cardboard.

results with a little practice. First, cover the stone's surface with a fairly thick coat of oil—don't be stingy, the stuff's cheap. Now, lay the knife diagonally (point rearward, hilt forward) on the stone and raise the back of the blade 20 degrees. Using a fair amount of pressure (only experience will tell you how much is fair) sweep the blade diagonally across the stone and, as you come to the curve that leads to the point of the blade, raise the handle upward so that the edge stays in contact with the stone on its circumference.

Give the blade about ten swipes on one side, then turn it over and repeat the process. Depending on the hardness of the steel and how sharp the knife is to begin with, you'll need about 50 strokes on each side before it really starts to get sharp. The sharpening process will go much faster if, at fairly frequent intervals, you wipe the accumulated oil and grit off the stone and re-oil it.

Your job at the stone is done when the edge will shave hair off your forearm. Now, if you want a real razor edge (you don't really need it) put the blade on the hard Arkansas stone and repeat the process. If your ambitions are more modest, lay a shirt cardboard on the edge of a table and sweep the cutting edge backward over it, ten strokes to each side, with the blade held nearly flat. That's all there is to it. As the ad used to say. "Feel sharp, *be* sharp."

One Man's View of Scopes

46

by David Petzal

Any hunting guide worth his nightly snort of Old Scramble-brain can regale you with tales of human folly that would bring tears to the eyes of an income-tax auditor. Here is one from a Montana guide who led his sport on an unsuccessful moose hunt.

"The guy showed up here with a .300 Magnum and an 8X scope. I begged him to replace that glass with something sensible, but he said it suited him just fine, and he was gonna hunt with it. Anyway, we humped the mountains for five days, and finally, near sunset, we got within 70 yards of a big bull in a lodgepole pine forest. The light was bad, the dude was shaking from the climb and the excitement, and all he saw was black hair. That critter was as big as a barn, but he missed it clean, and we never got another shot."

I guess it's part of our national character to be fascinated with gadgets and to be impressed by fancy figures (of the numerical variety). If you take into account some of the scopes that you see on big-game rifles each fall, this theory is borne out handsomely. If it's big, expensive, computes range, and offers great magnification, it's got to be good. Right? Well, ask the guy who missed his moose.

The truth is that the ideal big-game scope is the most compact, simple, and lightweight model you can find, and that you almost never need more than 4X for any big game you'll shoot on this continent. Once in a while, you'll come upon a situation where 6X or 7X would be helpful, for instance on a long shot at an antelope, but for the most part, you just don't need a lot of magnification.

Not only is high magnifying power unnecessary, but it can be a handicap as well. Until somebody succeeds in revoking the laws of optics, when you build a scope that has a high X-rating, you lose an appreciable part of your field of view. For example, a 4X scope has a field of view at 100 yards of 30 feet, while the next step up in power, 6X, takes in only 18 feet. When you're trying to put the crosshairs on something that's clearing out of the neighborhood as fast as possible, the loss of nearly half your field hurts.

*At target range, Dave Petzal tests scope rigged on Griffin & Howe side mount.
He distrusts many detachable mounts, but this type—which locks with
dovetails and levers—is very solid and keeps scope properly low and centered.*

*Advantage of detachable side mount is that scope can be quickly removed,
and when rear aperture sight is inserted in its place, view is uncluttered. Mount
locks to permanently installed sideplate, pinned and screwed to receiver.*

On hard-recoiling rifle, forward end of scope's ocular-lens bell should be no more than half-inch to rear of bolt. Otherwise, sudden rearward movement as rifle kicks can give you nasty cut or bruise over your eye.

And that isn't all. When you up the power of your scope, you get a larger, more detailed image, but at the same time, you magnify every tremor that goes through your hands, the repeated jerk of the rifle from your heartbeat, and the sway of your breathing. These factors are annoying enough on the range, and when you're excited and/or bushed, they can make it nearly impossible to hit what you aim at.

Last, but by no means least, you lose brightness as your power increases. The only way an optical designer can compensate for this is by adding a large objective, or front, lens. Thus, you can have a 6X scope with the same brightness as a 2¾X, but where the lower-powered glass has a one-inch objective lens, the 6X must employ a 1.825-inch lens, nearly twice as

big. Such a scope is bulky, and worse, it is heavy.

The magnification of the target is only one of the functions a scope performs. Probably the most important advantage to be obtained from the glass sight is not magnification, but the placement of the reticle (or aiming point) and the target in the same optical plane. This means that instead of having to try to focus on a front sight, a rear sight, and the target, which is impossible, you look *at* a sight picture, and everything is in focus. This is accomplished whether your scope is a 1X or a 30X, and high magnification need not enter into it.

The best rule for choosing a scope, as far as magnification is concerned, is to pick the *minimum* amount of power needed for

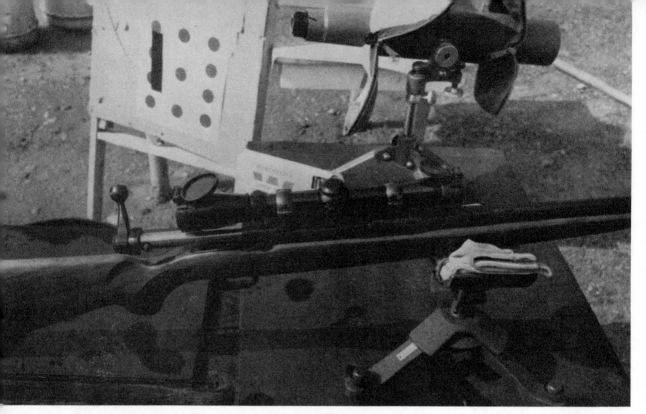

Rain, snow, or dust can hamper sighting disastrously, so lens caps are valuable accessories, especially in bad weather. There are all sorts of makeshift covers, but flip-up caps like these are handier and more effective.

the job at hand. If you're an eastern deer hunter, you can expect that most of your shots will be taken quickly, often at a moving target, and at close yardages. Thus, the logical choice is a scope of 2½, 2¾, or 3X, which will be compact and will offer a bright image and a wide field. Better than any of these is one of the newer variables that range from 1X to 4X. At their lowest setting, these glasses offer an incredible field of view—82 feet at 100 yards. You can see the whole world through them, and I would wager that there is nothing faster to use in the way of sighting equipment, not even open iron sights. If you'd like one glass to do everything, there's no reason why a 4X won't suit you fine. You can use it in the woods without feeling handicapped, and it offers sufficient magnification for any big game at any reasonable range.

My nomination for the top all-around glass is a 2X-7X variable. You can crank it down to take in the field of view of a low-powered model, or boost the magnification way up to get a good look at a set of horns or antlers. The glasses being built in this bracket nowadays are the same size as 4X models—some are even a bit smaller—so their size is no objection. You pay a few bucks more, but they're worth it.

Reticles have come in for some elaborate redesigning of late, and I am not sure that all the effort involved has been worth the results. Two of the more recent are the rangefinder reticles and one with a little light that you can switch on at the center of the image.

If buying either of these will make you happy, go ahead, except that using such gadgets runs contrary to practical hunting and its problems. Ideally, the reticle should be the aiming device you center on the target—nothing more, nothing less. Calculating range is something you do in your head, and the less conscious effort you have to spend on the matter, the better.

Almost all your big-game shooting will be done at ranges of 25 to 300 yards, with the rare shot at 400. No one has any business shooting at this last distance more than once in a decade, and it doesn't take much practice to learn to estimate range at the more common distances in the 100- to 250-yard bracket.

The best reticle for a big-game scope is one that is fine enough to allow for precise aiming, yet coarse enough to be seen quickly in dim light. When all the shouting dies, the medium crosshair is still a good choice, but the design that seems to be an overwhelming—and deserving—favorite in recent years is the tapered crosshair. Different makers list it under a variety of names, but basically it is a reticle that is very thick at the outer edge of the field and tapers toward the center, where each of the four crosswires terminates in a fine point.

This is a fine design indeed. The wires can be made very heavy to show up well when the light is poor, and yet they allow fine aiming, even at long range. In addition, the taper of the crosshairs seems to lead the eye automatically toward the center of the image. I use nothing but this style in my big-game scopes.

Rifle scopes are, for the most part, marvels of efficiency and ruggedness, but not so the mounts that attach them to the gun. There are a lot of mounts on the market, but very few are really simple or permanent or strong. The trouble starts because nearly all scope bases rely on three

or four lousy little 6/48 screws to hold them to the receiver. Quite often, they do hold, but quite often they work loose from the repeated vibration of recoil or rough handling, and then the unexplained misses start.

One manufacturer brought out a rifle a few years ago that utilized 8/40 screws, which are a lot heftier than the 6/48's. It was, and is, an excellent idea, but there has been no rush by anyone else to follow suit. The best solution of all is that adopted by two foreign manufacturers and one domestic maker of rifles—design the receiver with integral scope bases. This completely eliminates one source of trouble, so that all you have to worry about are the rings. Again, it is a splendid idea that no one else has picked up on.

But all is not lost. With a little diligence, you can attach a scope solidly to a rifle and have it stay that way forever— well, almost forever. When you mount the bases, you can keep the screws from working loose by putting a fraction of a drop of Loc-Tite (a commercial "liquid washer" that you can purchase at gun stores), shellac, iodine, or even epoxy cement on the screws before you drive them home. Put the gun in a padded vise and use a screwdriver that fits the screws exactly. When they seemingly won't turn any more, tap the handle of the screwdriver with a hammer and try again. You'll get another half-turn, and they'll be in there solidly. If you really want the bases to stay put, you can have a gunsmith sweat them in place. No way will they ever come loose, but if you decide you'd like to change bases and rings, you'll have a problem.

Speaking of rings, the same applies to them: Use a screwdriver that fits, tighten the screws until they scream, and use some

Author is shown sighting through variable-power scope. For big-game rifles, he recommends fairly low-power variable or—for most uses—4X. High magnification increases tremors in your sight picture.

kind of screw glue to make sure they don't work loose. And don't let matters rest here. One of the essential items for any hunter is a screwdriver(s) for the screws in his mount bases and rings. Check the rig every two or three days when you're hunting. It's a small step that can save you a lot of disappointment.

Once you have the scope in place, leave it. Do not go whipping it off the rifle every time the mood strikes you. It will not return to the same point of zero when you replace it, and if the mount is one that relies on metal-to-metal friction to hold it in place, you could eventually wear the thing loose. There are many claims for detachable mounts, and I advise you to take them with a cellar of salt. There is a lot of difference between theory and real life.

Despite the undeniable ruggedness of a good, modern scope, some shooters cannot be happy unless they also have access to iron sights. If you happen to be one of these people, let me remind you that it is the consensus of the most experienced hunters that iron sights on a scoped rifle are a waste of time. The odds that you'll ever need them are infinitesimal. You are as likely to encounter a broken firing pin or a broken extractor as you are a busted scope, so if you're heading far from civilization, you're probably better off taking two rifles.

But if you're still not happy, I have a suggestion—invest $50 or so in the Griffin & Howe side mount and know true tranquility. This mount has been around since the '30s, and has proved itself on a worldwide basis. It consists of a sideplate (which is screwed and pinned to the receiver), the top of which is a male dovetail. The other half of the mount is a bracket containing double locking levers, a female dovetail, and the rings for the scope. In use, you swing the levers apart, shove the scope and bracket forward onto the sideplate, and, when it comes to a stop, swing the levers upward. Although you can get the scope on and off in a second or two, that rig is as solid as the Hoover Dam.

The best arrangement for a scope and iron sight setup is to combine the glass with a front bead and a rear peep, such as the Lyman 48. All you have to do if you want to change sights is remove the scope and insert the 48 sight staff with the peep. It's quick and efficient, and you'll probably never need it.

One really invaluable accessory that every scope user should have is a set of lens caps. The one great drawback of the scope is the fact that when there is dust, rain, or snow on the lenses, sighting becomes difficult if not impossible. But you can leave your caps on until the moment before you shoot and avoid the whole situation. The cheapest lens protection available consists of a strip of old inner tube, cut to size like a giant rubber band and stretched over the scope. When you want to get it out of the way, just pull back on the rear end and let it snap forward.

But the caps that I favor are those made by E. D. Vissing Co. of Idaho Falls, Idaho. They consist of short soft-plastic tubes fitted with spring-loaded lids that seal tightly when closed. In use, flick the lid with your finger; it flies out of the way and stays there. I've used these caps in all sorts of repulsive weather, and they work to perfection.

That's about all you need to know. Remember, the simpler, the better. Don't be swayed by gadgetry or awed by high power. And buy quality, since expensive scopes are better than cheap scopes. Anyway, that's one man's view.

Part VII: Waterfowl and Shorebirds

Where Will Our Wildfowl Be in a Decade?

47

by Norman M. Strung

Although the waterfowling prospects for this or any season might look bright, a hunter worth his gunpowder knows that migratory wildfowl are extremely sensitive to changes brought on by both man and nature. Factors as diverse as the weather in Canada and the bag limit in Mexico regularly result in radical changes year after year. So a sizable crop last year or this year does not, of necessity, indicate good hunting in years to come.

What, then, lies in store for future duck and goose populations? Can satisfactory numbers of birds be maintained, perhaps even increased, or will the continued encroachment of civilization remove substantial numbers of birds from the skies?

Well, we've got a little bit of good news, and a little bit of bad news. First, the good.

Several factors point to at least a stable population of waterfowl in years to come. Perhaps most significant (yet difficult to measure) is the impact of a sudden national awareness of those much-used words "ecology" and "environment." In the past, only the active sportsman was concerned with nurturing and maintaining substantial populations of wildlife. Now more people than ever before seem to be getting involved.

While some of these new wildlife buffs are mistakenly opposed to hunting, they're at least a part of a new national conscience that looks before it leaps, and thinks before it acts in terms of preservation and conservation of the outdoors.

Builders and developers are forced to consider the impact they might have on fish and wildlife when they decide to fill a swamp, dredge a channel, or build an airport in the Everglades.

A city no less than New York saw fit to designate the sprawling Rockaway Swamps a wildlife preserve . . . at a time when New York sorely needs another airport, a function to which this Jamaica Bay location would have been perfectly suited.

On a smaller scale, but one with equal impact, individuals are realizing the esthetic and real pleasures to be derived by leaving small patches of woodlands "as they are" in lieu of turning them into lawns, parks, and baseball fields. Cities are experimenting with green belts; rural residents are waking up to the fact that wild-life makes desirable neighbors, economic-ally as well as esthetically. The net result seems to be a slow turnabout from the "plow-it-under, cement-it-over" mentality prevalent for the last three decades.

Entwined with this concern for the land and the things that live on it are new, rigid pollution controls, and bans on dangerous chemicals—pesticides in particular. Pollu-tion from oil spills, especially tankers "blowing" water ballast (now illegal), was especially hard on waterfowl. When they landed, their feathers absorbed so much oil they could no longer fly, and they either starved or drowned. Ducks, as much as any other animal, are part of a natural food chain. When they ingest chemically treated grain or fish that have fed on in-sects sprayed with DDT, they absorb these toxic substances into their systems, directly affecting their chances for survi-val, and indirectly, the survival of their fu-ture offspring.

All these concerns and controls, then, are bound to increase wildlife popu-lations—ducks included—in both subtle and significant ways.

Another attitude that appears to be changing for the better involves something more closely aligned with wildfowl water. In the past, it was commonly thought that the best thing you could do with water was to get rid of it. Dig trenches and drainage ditches in swamps; straighten streams to increase the volume of water they would carry. The notion served two ostensible purposes: to avoid flooding and reclaim land.

Recently, however, people have begun to realize that in terms of flooding, chan-nelization had the opposite effect. While it spared upstream residents from mild,

Barring catastrophes such as long droughts, this scene will be repeated in future, thanks to sensible limits and seasons, modern game management, and conservation programs of government agencies and groups like Ducks Unlimited.

predictable, yearly flooding, it sent tor-rents of water cascading downstream to plague the people who lived there. It was further noted that water is becoming a precious resource, and retaining it within private property boundaries or state bor-ders makes a lot more sense than losing it to the marginal farm lands.

No less an influence than the United States Department of Agriculture, through the Soil Conservation Service, responded to this new approach in water manage-ment. They instituted a "water bank" pro-gram, patterned after the soil bank. This is essentially a contract whereby landowners agree to preserve wetlands in return for subsidy payments. The total effect of changes in public attitudes and governmental policy is bound to be beneficial to waterfowl.

Although it's difficult to ascertain at this time, the new look in duck seasons and regulations appears to be exerting a positive influence, too. The so-called "point" system, by encouraging a harvest of previously ignored species and setting a premium on those ducks that are down in numbers, provides closer control over and management of the waterfowl trading back and forth across this continent. To a large extent, however, the success of this venture is up to the hunter. He's got to take the time to learn how to recognize species if the system is to work.

In more direct ways, two other developments bode well for the ducks and geese of North America.

Ducks Unlimited, a nonprofit organization of waterfowlers and wildlife buffs, has been leading the way toward increased waterfowl populations for four decades. They achieved this end by preserving and controlling the important "pothole" nesting areas in Canada.

This organization is undertaking a crash program in the '70s. Their aim is to increase the 2,000,000 acres of Canadian "duck factories" they manage by another 2,500,000. Since 80 percent of the waterfowl on the North American Continent nest and hatch their broods in Canada, this is bound to have a profound effect on populations.

It should be pointed out, however, that the establishment of these drought-proof wetlands isn't an accomplished fact, just a hopeful projection. To get the job done, Ducks Unlimited needs money and membership (they're a purely private organization, devoid of any connection with the U.S. or Canadian government, and government monies). So here's a very sincere plug: Join Ducks Unlimited and you'll be doing something personal and direct to improve waterfowling over the next decade. The address is: Ducks Unlimited, Box 66300, Chicago, Ill. 60666. All contributions are tax-deductible.

One other important move Ducks Unlimited has made in recent years is the establishment of Ducks Unlimited de Mexico. This means a lot more than just another branch of the organization; while 80 percent of the waterfowl we Yanks shoot at nest in Canada, approximately the same number of birds winter in Mexico. The presence of DU south of the border is bound to mean better management, and as a result, more birds up North in the spring, the time when numbers really count.

There are, however, a few clouds in this otherwise rosy picture. Lead poisoning is becoming an increasingly prevalent factor in waterfowl mortality.

The problem is roughly this: In certain heavily hunted areas, so much shot is slung around that rather large amounts of the stuff end up on lake and bay bottoms; #4 to 6 shot is just about perfect size for grit in a duck's gizzard, so he ingests the lead balls. As his gizzard grinds food, it breaks down the lead into fine particles that are absorbed into the bird's system. When a sufficient amount of lead is present in its system, the bird dies, poisoned by the metal.

The government has been considering a ban on the use of lead shot (and has already experimented with its exclusion in certain areas) but at the time of this writing there is no really satisfactory replacement. Soft iron pellets are not nearly as ef-

Canadas loaf at refuge in Illinois, a state where Frank Bellrose and other noted researchers have studied wildfowl habits. Studies continue elsewhere, too; among recently established projects is wildlife-disease laboratory in Wisconsin.

ficient as lead, since they lack the weight to make them effective at the long ranges required by waterfowling. Poor ballistics could well lead to the replacement of lead poisoning by equally destructive crippling, so there is a continuing program of research, development, and experimentation to find a suitable substitute for conventional lead pellets.

Another negative factor influencing duck populations is subtle and difficult to assess. It's anti-hunting sentiment.

Since its infancy, the concept of conservation, management, and preservation of game has rested in the capable hands of the sportsman, and his state fish and game departments, which he supports and finances through license fees and taxes on sporting goods. Little if any "public" money is spent in this area.

Should anti-hunting sentiment reach a point where it becomes an accepted pol-

icy, "marginal" hunters, the people who buy a license, a gun, and use both only once or twice a year, are bound to dwindle in numbers—and so will the important fees they contribute. People who fit this category constitute a major source of wildlife revenue—some estimates run as high as 50 percent.

Without sufficient money to operate, fish and game departments would have to cut back their habitat improvement, wetlands purchases, and general operations, and ducks are bound to be hurt in the process.

The final cloud on the waterfowler's horizon (or perhaps I should say the potential lack of one) is rain. No one can predict what the weather will be like in Alberta, Manitoba, and Saskatchewan during the next decade. If rains are heavy, duck populations will increase markedly because of the corresponding increase in available

North Carolina hunter prepares to "pick up" at end of day. Seaboard states are
heavily industrialized and urbanized, but new laws and public pressures
now force builders and speculators to consider environmental impact of development.

breeding areas. If severe drought strikes, populations will go down, though they probably won't plummet to the depths known during the very dry years of the past, thanks to Ducks Unlimited for a cushioning effect. Even in very dry years, their water-control facilities are capable of artificially maintaining essential breeding habitat. While such a stopgap measure can't be expected to produce a bumper crop of waterfowl, it will provide a population large enough to bounce back strong the next wet year.

Coupled with the other encouraging signs, this "insurance policy" tips the scales to the sunny side. Waterfowl population won't be without its ups and downs in the next decade, but in general, we can all look for better things to come.

Mallards, teal, and coots feed at pothole in Manitoba. Establishment and maintenance by Ducks Unlimited of "drought-proof" wetlands like this in Canada's "duck-factory" provinces should help to insure future of waterfowl.

How to Shoot at a Duck—and Hit It

48

by John O. Cartier

I've always remembered a little dissertation I received as a lad from the best wingshot I've ever known. This old man recently picked up his last decoy and passed on to his eternal open season. Back in the days when the limit was 15 ducks per day I watched him in action with an envy bordering on worship. Many was the morning I watched ol' Harry and three or four partners tumble up to 50 divers from a point blind.

This may sound like a sin today, but it was perfectly legal then. The point, of course, is that a hunter with that kind of experience knew a lot about pointing his gun. I mustered enough courage one day to row up to his blind with the hope of talking duck shooting. He was as gracious as he was proficient, and he asked me to stay awhile and kill some bluebills.

After I'd missed a few he grinned and laid a hand on my shoulder. "Sit down and relax, son," he said, "you'll never hit nothin' all tensed up. That's no charging elephant you're shooting at, just a harmless duck. You'll never kill him any deader by wanting him so bad. Good shotgunning and nervous pressure don't mix."

I noticed things about Harry's gun handling that were revelations. I saw, for instance, that he never moved his gun until ducks were well within shooting range. When he finally did shoot, it was in one continuous flow of movement. He snapped to a standing position, the gun came to his shoulder and the shot went off all in one smooth sequence. His reasons made sense.

"First place," he began, "I get a rhythm of swing when I do everything all at once. If I pointed the gun out there, picked up the duck, and tried tracking him I'd be all out of coordination. Same thing as in throwing a ball. You find your target first, then wind up and follow through. If you don't, you won't hit much. With a shotgun you have to be loose and liquid. Never try to get into aiming position first.

"There's two really big factors a man must be conversant with if he's a great wingshot. He has to know what his shotgun *can* do, and what his target *will* do.

"A shotgun is no cannon. Truthfully, it's a mighty short-range killer. Ninety percent of all kill shots are made at less than 40 yards. Pace off 40 yards sometime, it's a real short distance. Long-range shooting is plain silly; all the ballistic odds are against you. If shotgunners truly accepted this fact, they'd cut down their misses tremendously."

Harry told me about targets, too, and experience has proved that he was right.

The wise duck hunter is aware that a decoying mallard will tower straight up when he discovers gunners, reaching an almost stationary point before leveling off. Know this point and you have a chance at an almost stationary target.

Puddlers that are jumped from field potholes will flush into the wind, allowing the experienced gunner to concentrate his attention in a small arc instead of a complete circle. The stalking hunter's approach should be made downwind to gain the most advantageous shooting positions.

Puddlers jumped in timbered potholes where wind is negligible will usually take the route by which they can get out of the trees the quickest. That's an advantage for a team of two hunters, since one man jumps the birds and the other gunner enjoys wide-open shooting by locating under probable flyways.

Divers will seldom tower when surprised or shot at. They'll curve away in a broad arc, depending on sheer speed for escape. Divers coming in with their wing tips just clearing the water will almost always decoy perfectly, enabling the gunner to hold fire until the first ducks are well within range. He then fires his first shot at a bird in the rear of the flock and his last shots at front birds which are still within shooting distance.

Divers crossing high and fast will usually pass by, so the gunner must be prepared to shoot at the exact instant the flock passes closest to the blind.

So, if we accept the fact that successful

This gunner may look as if he's behind his target, but he's swinging smoothly and will follow through before touching off shot. Chief basic mistake in waterfowl gunnery is failing to swing ahead and lead birds enough.

shotgunning is knowledge, what are the tricks that will help our score?

One big factor is the realization that misses derive from one of only two sources, natural causes and manmade troubles. We can forget natural causes because we can't control them. For instance, you may make a perfect swing on a gliding mallard, touch off the shot at exactly the right instant and still miss, simply because a tree intercepts your shot charge. Maybe you are diver hunting from a boat and the boat rocks just as you touch the trigger. A list of such excuses is unending. They're legitimate. They happen to all of us. But manmade troubles can be controlled, at least partially.

I feel that one of the biggest troubles confronting most gunners is lack of familiarity with their shotguns, simply lack of experience with actual shooting. Since good shotgunning results from reflex action, it follows that the more shooting you do the more automatic this reflex action becomes. And here I differ somewhat from the opinions of many gun experts.

I believe that any shooting helps, whether in the field or not. The more you shoot the more you get the feel of your gun. Clay target games are a tremendous help for this reason alone. Crow shooting is better yet, since it's so similar to waterfowling. Regardless of how or at what, get out and run shells through that gun, especially in the weeks just before hunting season.

Nobody can ever hit a flying target without lead, and I don't believe it is possible for any man to tell another exactly how to figure proper lead. In the first place, no two shots are ever the same. Secondly, my interpretation of three feet of lead may be a whale of a lot different than yours. Also, you may swing your gun faster or slower than I do, and you may employ more or less follow-through. With my method, three feet may be just right, with yours the same three feet might not be nearly sufficient. So what can you do?

Well, that old cure-all, experience, is the true answer. The only point I want to make is that you shouldn't put too much faith in what somebody else tells you in regard to lead. You have to find out for yourself. Personal experimentation is a much faster shortcut to success than random advice.

But one fact is sure: Most misses result from too little lead. A flying target moves a tremendous distance from the time your brain tells you to pull the trigger until the instant the shot reaches the bird. The time lag—between when the gun is fired and the pattern arrives at target—must be compensated for by shooting where the bird is going to be, not where he is. Compensation for crosswinds must be reckoned with, too. A 30-mph crosswind will blow a shot string three feet off target at 30 yards.

The two most important factors are distance and speed. Decoying ducks and geese place such pressure on the human nervous system that most gunners can't stand the strain, and begin their gunplay at extreme ranges. Decoying birds against an open sky look much closer than they actually are. Premature shooting is against all logic, because if a duck is already decoying within 80 yards, he is fooled enough to come within 40 assuming, of course, that decoys are properly arranged.

The problem most hunters have is appreciating the real flight speed of waterfowl. Even veteran gunners frequently find it difficult to realize how far a duck moves in the time a load of #6 shot travels 40 yards. I'd guess that 90 percent of all missed ducks are led only half enough. It is almost impossible to overlead, since shotgun pellets string out in a line. The rearward part of this so-called "shot string" would intercept a flying target even if your main charge passed slightly too far forward. If you're missing, keep shoving out additional lead until you connect. Sometimes the amount will seem ridiculous, but you'll know it's right when you start hitting.

One of the major causes of misses is flock shooting. It's an awful temptation to empty your gun into the midst of a flock of decoying ducks or geese. It seems you can't miss. The trouble is that it's ridicu-

In this situation, inexperienced hunters tend to be flustered by sheer number of targets. Temptation is strong to shoot into flock and just hope, but with all that open space between ducks you'd better stay with one target.

lously easy to miss because you're shooting at a lot more air than birds. It may not look that way but it's fact. I lick this problem with a simple trick. I try to pick the biggest bird in the flock. I concentrate on that individual. This concentration changes confusion to definite purpose. When I'm ready to shoot I have my mind zeroed on one target. This trick becomes second nature with experience, and works to perfection.

Many published opinions still promote the standard waterfowl gun as a long-barreled 12-gauge, full-choked and weighing up to eight pounds. Whenever ammunition advice pops up it's usually a plug for heavy shot backed with a maximum powder charge. Is it possible that some of us are missing limit bags by adhering strictly to the letter of these time-worn principles? Under some circumstances, yes.

Let's say we are gunning divers over an open-water rig. Incoming ducks bore straight into the decoys, then flare broadside as the guns come up. If the decoys are spread properly most of our shots will be somewhere under 35 yards. The man shouldering a full choke and touching off Magnum 4's has to aim mighty close to connect with a pattern that's just beginning to open up. But the guy shooting a modified bore with maximum-load 6's is knocking his bird dead with a just-right, more-open pattern of properly dispersed density.

How about mallard shooting over decoys in river bottoms or other thick cover? Most of these shots present another close-range situation. Say you're huddled in a brush blind or pressing against a pin oak tree and mallards are dropping in all around you. How fast are you going to swing that 12-gauge Magnum at targets crossing behind or roaring up through tree branches? Could you get to them quicker with a fast-pointing 20-gauge? A lot of today's hunters have found that they can. They also know that a Magnum charge of #6's from that 20 is just as deadly as the regular maximum #6's from the standard 12-gauge load.

The all-around duck gun is as much of a myth as the all-around decoy, duck boat, dog, or anything else. It's very likely that the "ideal" big gun with its choked-to-the-limit barrel and maximum loads of heavy shot has crippled more unrecovered ducks and geese and contributed to more clean misses than any other single factor in waterfowling.

The big-gun concept originated in the days of less effective shotshells, at a time when a good share of duck and goose hunting consisted mainly of pass-shooting. Here it was, and still is, the most efficient piece of hardware the gunner can use. Pass-shooting ranges are usually long, requiring the additional killing range of tight chokes and Magnum loads.

The weight of the big gun is no handicap in view of the fact there's plenty of time to swing with your targets. The heavy gun, in the hands of experienced gunners, produces a smoothness of swing highly beneficial in catching up with and swinging past the high fliers. The heavy gun also will absorb much more recoil than a lighter one, a factor in repeated overhead shooting.

Another important fact that many gunners refuse to accept as truth is that Magnum loads are no more powerful from a velocity standpoint than regular maximum loads. The Magnum charge simply puts more shot in a given area at extreme

ranges. In order to push the additional shot, the powder charge has to be increased proportionately.

The average initial shot velocity of a 12-gauge maximum load of #6's three feet from the end of the barrel is approximately 1331 fps. That of a three-inch Magnum load is 1315 fps. The striking force per pellet from each load is roughly the same. What dumps the duck way out there is the *number* of pellets that smack him. The standard load is well opened up, perhaps only a pellet or two hitting the bird. The increased density of the Magnum pattern may bust the duck with half a dozen hits. The Magnum kills at extreme range *only* because you hit the duck with more shot.

While we are dwelling on ballistic facts, let's toss in some more surprises. The arms and ammunition people have long since discovered that maximum shot velocities produced by modern powders are fully reached in a maximum barrel length of 24 inches. They also know that choke constuction does its full job within inches of the muzzle.

To the practical gunner these are important facts. Why burden yourself with the extra weight of a 30- or 32-inch barrel if it doesn't accomplish anything? Many shooters settle at 28 inches. All factors considered, the 28-inch barrel is probably used by more smart waterfowlers than any other length.

Early-season native ducks will be thinner-feathered and easier to kill than late-season birds from the North that are heavily feathered and laced with thick down. Modified-choked 7½'s may be just the ticket early in the season, while the same ranges may require the full-choked knockdown blast of Magnum 4's to up-end hardy late-season migrants. The tight bore and heavy shot, in this case, have nothing to do with extreme range, but give the additional push to ram shot home through the armor-plate exteriors of big, fully matured birds.

Hunting conditions may vary quickly from close-range jump-shooting in heavy cover to long-range work over open water. I do most of my waterfowling in the Mid-west where both situations are frequently enjoyed during a single day. Such variables quickly indicate the advantage of several different powder and shot combinations.

Today's waterfowler is blessed with the opportunity to choose exactly the gun and load combinations that will suit his particular needs best. And today's guns and loads are so good that if you miss you have no one to blame but yourself.

Accomplished waterfowl hunters know what to expect from their shotguns and their targets. This shooter "waited it out" as mallard swung in low over decoys, and now he has comparatively short, easy shot.

Notes on Blinds and Pass Shooting

by Grits Gresham

49

The most traditional and widespread method of hunting ducks and geese is from a blind of some kind, with the birds lured to the area by decoys. Mouth-blown calls are used in connection with the decoys in many instances, but in most of them the birds come despite the calls, not because of them.

Being accustomed to the blind's type and location can mean a great deal to the hunter's success or lack of it. I learned that the hard way on a hunt for Canada geese in the Louisiana marshes. I was hunting with a giant of a man named R. J. Stine on his land southwest of Lake Charles. We shot from a pit sunk in a natural knoll in the marsh, which had been left brush-covered while the surrounding area was drained and planted to winter wheat. R. J. gave me the left side of the box, my favorite, but perhaps his ideas were other than charitable.

When the first flock began to work, responding first to R. J.'s excellent calling and then to the decoys set in the wheat out front, my host cautioned me to keep down. Each time I tried to peek through the brush around the pit, to orient myself and the geese, he repeated the warning.

"Keep down! Keep down! I'll watch 'em . . . I'll tell you when!"

So I remained seated on the bench in the pit, head down, listening to the flock of Canadas get nearer and nearer. Finally when it seemed as if they were coming in the pit with us, R.J. said, "Let's get 'em!"

With the command, however, I felt the pressure of a ham of a hand on my shoulder. R. J.'s three hundred pounds unyieldingly rooted me to the bench while he stood there and killed two geese, shooting with one hand. When the flock was safely in the distance he lifted his hand and asked, "Why didn't you shoot?"

The Stine land is in the Gum Cove section of Louisiana, south of Vinton, and was the heart of superb Canada-goose shooting before the up-flyway refuges and shooting grounds shortstopped the birds. It was there that Elton Bordelon taught me a trick I wouldn't have believed.

Elton worked for a rice company in Orange, Texas, but hunted with R. J. and helped him guide his guests. One morning

*Texas wildfowlers, left, get fine pass
shooting over typical "white spread" of decoy
rags. Garbed in white, gunners need no
blind. Rags attract not only snows
but other geese, and ducks, too. Hunting Canadas
in Louisiana, below, shooters keep low in
their blind so birds won't flare out of range.*

he had Mary and me in tow and he called a flock of a dozen or so into our pattern. But almost within range the birds slid off to one side to light in the wheat 100 yards away.

Boom! The sound of Elton's gun going off lifted Mary and me from our seats, but he cautioned us to stay down. He had deliberately shot into the air, spooking the geese, and he immediately began calling again. This time he called that flock of spooked geese back around and over our decoys, where we killed two of them to round out our limits. "They don't know where the shot came from," Elton explained in answer to my puzzled query. "I've worked that time and again. They don't always come back, but your odds are good."

Even when hunting from a blind using decoys, you'll get many pass-shooting opportunities. Ducks or geese will fly by within range, either by chance or lured on that course by the decoys, although they have no intention of decoying.

But pass shooting by itself is a popular and effective method of hunting waterfowl in many parts of the country. One of the best examples—if "best" is the right term to use—is the firing lines which surround goose concentration areas.

Such areas as Horseshoe Lake, Swan Lake, and Horicon provide a rest area and protection for the birds, and a certain amount of food. When that food is exhausted, the birds range from the refuge each day (or night) to forage in the surrounding fields.

It is when they leave the refuge early each morning that gunners quickly are conditioned to seek altitude when they leave the refuge, placing most of them far out of gun range of the firing-line shooters.

But there are always stragglers which fly low enough, and there always seem to be gunners who try 100-yard shots. The unfortunate thing is that a tremendous amount of crippling takes place.

The firing-line fiascos aren't as numerous as they once were. Buffer zones in which shooting is prohibited have been established around some refuges, and most hunters have discovered that they are much more successful hunting from pits or blinds out in the feeding fields. Commercial hunting operations have sprung up around most of these goose refuges, and the harvest is heavy.

For several years a harvest quota has been set for the area of the Horicon Refuge in Wisconsin. When the kill reaches a certain figure, the season is closed.

Although the huge concentrations of Canada geese which have become routine at a few spots in the Mississippi Flyway have furnished good hunting in those areas, the phenomenon has several unfortunate aspects. One, perhaps the least important, is that they have eliminated gunning for these birds in the states south of these shortstopping areas.

Most pathetic, to me, is that the majestic Canada goose has changed from a wild and wary bird, king of the skies, to a ward of state and federal governmental agencies. Jammed into the concentration areas, fondly called "refuges," they have lost most of their fear of man and, consequently, most of their wariness. Each morning they figuratively line up for their handouts, their food supplements. Only the food stamps are missing.

Most serious, however, of the dangers attending the goose refuges is the potential for devastating disease. With a hundred thousand birds or more crowded into a

Some choice decoy and pass-shooting locations like this can be reached only by "mud buggy," or "marsh buggy." Material for blind is vegetation natural to the area, and it won't warn geese away despite high visibility.

tiny area for months, conditions are ripe for an epidemic which would decimate the population.

The "pass" I hunted with Bob Erickson on the Minnesota River is one he has leased for years, and is typical of many pass-shooting situations in the northern Midwest. We hunted from blinds or hides, on dry land between lakes or ponds, without decoys. The shooting was at ducks trading back and forth from lake to lake up and down the river bottom.

In the marshes of Louisiana and Texas, and elsewhere, pass shooting is sometimes more effective than hunting over decoys. This is particularly true late in the season, when blinds stick out like sore thumbs because the natural vegetation has been beaten down by weather, and when ducks

are wary and gun-shy, having survived four months of gunning from Canada southward.

Ducks tend to fly a particular route, a pattern, which may change from day to day. Watch where the flight line seems to be, and position yourself along it.

On many occasions in the marshes my gunning day has been saved by moving from a blind to a pass-shooting situation. If ducks continue to skirt my spread, I don't hesitate to move. I try to select a spot where most birds have been working, then just squat, sit, or kneel down in the marsh grass. Sometimes two or three changes of location are necessary before getting in the "right" place.

There are times, of course, when nothing works.

Crafty Calls for Ducks and Geese

by Bob Hinman

50

The first morning I was allowed to attend an opening-day breakfast, my grandfather handed me a duck call. Then, along with eggshell coffee, jowl bacon, and buckwheat cakes, came explicit instructions that I was not, under any circumstances, to blow it while in the blind.

I was young then. Since that time I've mingled with some pretty fair hoot-and-grunters such as "Dud" Faulk, Phil Olt, Chic Major, and others. They *still* give me the same advice.

You can learn to call ducks. Even if you don't have anyone to teach you, there are records available to at least let you hear what a call should sound like. Instruction records by Faulk, Olt, and others will, with practice, teach you enough to actually lure birds under favorable conditions.

Of course, you need know not only the sounds, but which calls to use and when to use them. That, my friend, is not a skill acquired by a correspondence course. You see, calling is a regional art. They don't call ducks the same in Illinois as in Arkansas, even though they may be the same

birds. A classy caller from Chesapeake Bay might easily strike out on a Dakota pothole. Even on home grounds, you don't blow the same in timber as you do on open water. And as with all good musicians, you must learn to vary tempo and tone.

Tone is odd. I've heard some calls that sound awful, but really pull 'em in. Some of those little old squeaky calls grab ducks like they were on a string. In fact, when there is a lot of calling going on around you, you'll find that a very high-pitched call will produce better results than a more normal tone.

Even with the best of calling and conditions, there are days when the birds just won't respond to any amount of pleading, and there isn't much you can do about it but wait 'em out. On the other hand, any call that makes a noise may turn the trick on those nice, sunshiny mallard-morns, or when the barometer busts its bottom on the afternoon before the big freeze.

If you are serious about learning to call, pick a few pointers from the *real* experts. Listen to the raspy quack of that old hen mallard lost in an early-morning fog, and the contented chuckle of birds at feed. Try a duck marsh on a quiet, moonlit night—it's all part of your training.

Don't overlook records made for the electronic callers. Though mostly live recordings that are illegal to use while hunting, they can be of great help in learning basic calls in your living room.

The problem today is that you seldom have enough space to properly call ducks into your decoys. You may be a caller of championship caliber, but all the cater-wauling around you will nullify your most artistic efforts. You can work on birds for 10 minutes and just when they decide to drop in, the guy in the next blind will choose that moment to ground-swat a mudhen and you can watch your birds claw for altitude.

How much calling to do is a much mooted question. One school of thought considers calling only an "advertisement" or attention getter—you make a few quacks at a passing duck to draw his attention to the decoys. Once this has been done, all calling is stopped. It's a theory usually founded on experience of those who have never truly mastered the duck call. Because of their lack of proficiency, it is probably the wisest course—for them.

The opposite is the guy who never stops blowing from the time he gets into the blind until he leaves. But in duck calling, as most of life, moderation seems to be the key. Between the two extremes is the hunter who has learned several different calls, but most importantly has learned to judge callable ducks.

Rare is the caller who can produce any results at all from large flocks of high- and fast-flying birds. Instead, the wise caller saves his breath for the bird that is loafing along with slow-flapping wings and alternate glides.

This is a working duck, head moving to-and-fro, seeking just such a safe and sheltered area as your decoys now occupy. Often he is leery, wanting to come in but still by instinct somewhat decoy-shy. He'll probably continue to circle until quite sure everything is safe. And this is where the expert caller can help him make up his mind, settling him down with soft burring sounds and an almost continuous feeding chuckle. Even then, never call when birds are directly overhead; just remain motionless and very quiet.

The greeting, or highball, is the primary call. Its purpose is to attract and interest passing birds in your decoys. It's also by far the most difficult. It is done in different ways in different areas, but retains one point in common wherever it is done successfully. No matter what the preamble, it reaches a certain note and stays there in perfect pitch without break.

There are many different calls, again depending on the locale in which you are hunting and the type of bird to be lured. Strangely enough, almost any breed of duck will respond to a good mallard call. Even big-water canvasbacks and bluebills will swing toward your blocks on a mallard call instead of their own "burrrrrrrssssss." This, of course, means the call has drawn their attention to the decoys, which are a stronger attraction than the sound of the call.

The West Coast pintail shooter is addicted to his whistle call, while the Midwestern hunter does quite well on sprig with the mallard quack, produced with a conventional wooden or hard rubber call utilizing a reed—usually a Mylar reed nowadays. Actually, the pintail calls in both ways. There are wooden and plastic whistle calls sold for pintail purposes but a regular metal dog whistle with the pea re-

Most hunters find it reasonably easy to call Canadas and specklebellies, though snows respond poorly. Goose call can be blown correctly in fairly short time, whereas proper duck calling takes anyone years to master.

Two or more callers can almost always outpull just one. If they have only fair talent they may cover each other's mistakes instead of spooking birds; of course, two expert "grunters" will do much better.

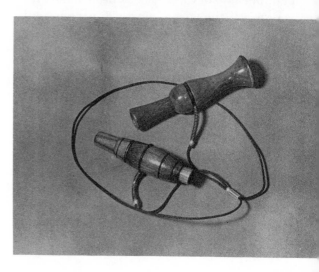

Though hard rubber calls may be the best sellers ever made, traditionalists in many regions prefer wood; walnut is most common, but materials range from rosewood and zebrawood to cherry, myrtle, apple, and even bamboo.

moved has more volume and can be held in the mouth, leaving both hands free for the gun.

To the novice, the most mystifying aspect of calling is that good and successful calling seldom sounds like a duck. This is not to say it can't, just that many styles of calling do not, even though they produce deadly results.

Fortunately, goose calling is a considerably less demanding art than duck calling, and almost anyone can become a respectable caller on the big Canadas with only a few hours of instruction and a good call. This is probably due to the fact that while a duck call is blown from the diaphragm and is actually more like grunting than blowing, the goose call is blown from the mouth, which requires much less practice.

The call should be grasped on the tone end between the web of your thumb and forefinger, the other hand then brought up to form a cup, using both hands. The opening should be straight up. By so doing, you can control the tone and volume of the call by closing or opening your fingers.

In spite of what you may have heard, the call is not made by starting on a low note and breaking into a high. The highball for Canadas is simply one note—a short, high-pitched honk most easily done by saying the word "hut" or "hoot."

You first call to passing geese by making this one "hut" and pausing five to ten seconds. Simply repeat and pause until the birds break and head toward you. Then immediately shorten and speed up the "hut" barks of the feeding call. Do not let up on this call until you are ready to shoot. And keep in mind you are trying to imitate the call on only one goose. There is no reason for you to try to sound like a flock.

Some hunters become very good at calling geese by mouth. But for even those so talented, there are drawbacks, the main one being that it's hard to call for many days straight. Another is that the range of the voice is much more limited than that of a call, and hence most hunters find that as their voice deepens with age the effectiveness of their calling suffers.

For sheer unpredictability, snow and blue geese take the cake. These silly damn birds usually sit and travel in large numbers, making too much noise themselves for a call to be heard. You might call to passing skeins for 10 years without results; then again, perhaps the first honk you let out will find a couple hundred trying to sit in your lap. Most guides I've watched calling snows simply utter an occasional "yelp" which doesn't seem to either frighten or attract the birds.

My personal opinion is that these geese respond to calling just about as poorly as my palate responds to them. I'll cast my vote instead for the whitefronted goose, or "specklebelly." He decoys readily to a good caller, and he roasts up well, too.

Ducks Are Where You Find Them

by Leonard Lee Rue, III

51

Ducks are where you find them—and you can find them by knowing enough about their feeding and general life habits. I hope you noticed that I put feeding first. Food is much more important than habitat because the ducks have to eat. While they may temporarily tolerate habitat that is not satisfactory, they cannot inhabit an area that lacks food. *Good* habitat contains both preferred food and shelter. It's true there are times when food is not the primary key to the ducks' location but I find that this condition exists only during migration.

I'm not going to discuss the usual "picture-book" methods of hunting waterfowl, the ones employing large spreads of decoys, boats, pit blinds, floating blinds, guides, etc. As a rule, that sort of big-time waterfowl hunting involves lots of time and money, chiefly lots of money. Most of the best waterfowl lands along our coasts are owned, leased, or controlled by gun clubs. Some are owned by local groups, some are the playgrounds for the wealthy. I fault none of the clubs, but the shooting done in such areas is already well known,

most often written about and seldom within reach of the average hunter. I propose to tell how you can have more success using little or no special equipment, the main expenditure being the time and effort to locate the type of conditions that I'll describe. And some, if not all, of these conditions can be found in most parts of our country.

For 17 summers I guided canoe trips into the virgin wilderness areas of the headwaters of the Ottawa River in Quebec. Ordinarily, the canoe trips were over and I was back home in New Jersey by Labor Day. The couple of times that I stayed till the last of September provided me with duck shooting that was really fantastic.

Above Lac Pikianikijuan, a huge flat area of marshland stretches up toward Lac Stramond and Lac O'Sullivan. The Ottawa River twists, turns, writhes, and ox-bows itself through this area for miles. The land is so flat that the river has very little current. Perhaps I shouldn't call this land a marsh; it is fairly well drained because the river has cut its channel deeply. The entire

*Mallard flock, surprised by author at edge of pond, leaps into air
at close range. He expected to jump ducks here or on nearby resting areas
because they'd been feeding in big cornfields close to these waters.*

area is a sea of waving grasses and sedges, looking very much like a vista of the Everglades. I don't really know what the ducks were feeding on in this area or if they were feeding there at all but they surely were using it as a resting area. American mergansers and the American or common goldeneye were the only ducks that nested in the area during the summer. But come fall, the black ducks moved in in force.

It took two men to a canoe to hunt the area because there just was not enough time for a man paddling alone to drop his paddle, grab up his gun and get off a shot before the ducks disappeared. It was jump-shooting at its finest.

With the man in the bow doing the shooting, the stern paddler would quietly ease the canoe along the river, cautiously nosing around each bend. We always watched the water for telltale ripples that would often clue us as to whether ducks were just ahead of us. Sometimes we could hear them gabbling. When the ducks saw the canoe they'd jump into the sky, their wings beating frantically as they sought to gain altitude. If all went well, at the sound of the shots, a plump black duck or two would splash back into the water. If the shots were just shots and not hits, it really didn't matter because there were hundreds of ducks still to be flushed around the many bends that lay ahead. It was shooting that rivaled all the tales of duck hunting in days gone by.

Strangely, the noise of the shots did not flush the rest of the ducks from the marsh. The explanation may have been any one of several possibilities. As most of the ducks were on their first migration south, most of

Rue came on this pair of ringneck ducks (drake in foreground, hen behind him) on fair-sized New Jersey pond, almost hidden in woods. There were also scaup, blacks, and mallards—resting here and feeding in shallower pond nearby.

Author found black ducks feeding on land rimming marshy stretch of Ottawa River. Canoe-hunting with his partner, he was able to jump some from banks and many more from water—usually in easy range.

Pintails occasionally came to same wooded New Jersey ponds where Rue discovered good hunting for scaup, mallards, ringnecks, and black ducks. Birds evidently were feeding on duckweed, pondweed, and other aquatic plants.

them had never had contact with man, nor had they ever heard a shot. Also, the deep-cut river channel probably funnelled most of the sounds straight up and as we could never see the ducks till we flushed them, they couldn't see us either. Ducks that were shot at and missed did not leave the area but settled down on the river again somewhere in the marsh. We then had a chance to jump the same bunch again as we went on upstream or sometimes we would find them on our trip back down.

Although I always checked the crop contents of the black ducks we dropped, I could not recognize any of the seeds or plant material as being from the vegetation in the area. The ducks had probably fed elsewhere and were just using the marsh area to rest.

Many hunters in my home state of New Jersey use a canoe to float the little rivers to jump-shoot ducks. Here, mallards and wood ducks outnumber the black ducks, although a fair number of the latter are also encountered. Because of the drop to the land, these little rivers, especially in my hilly northern section, run too fast to be worked upstream, so they are just floated down. And to make this work easiest requires two automobiles, one left at the site where you intend to get off the river and the other to ferry the canoe up to where you plan to start. Floating the rivers through farming sections means that you must be alert to strands of barb wire crossing the river to keep the farmers' cows from straying.

Another type of jump-shooting is done by simply walking the river banks of these little rivers, banging away at the ducks as you flush them. Although chest-high waders are uncomfortable to walk in, they're a must because most of the ducks will be dropped on the opposite side of the stream. Unless you have a retriever, you will have to cross over to pick up your ducks.

While the birds may be in almost any spot along the river, your best chance of finding them is near stands of oak. It seems incredible that a duck can swallow an object as large as an acorn, yet the acrons of the pin and white oaks are favorite duck foods in the fall, particularly for the mallards and wood ducks.

During the years that I hunted New Jersey's Pahaquarry River flats on the Coventry Hunting Club for pheasants, I shot a good number of ducks along the Millbrook. This little stream snaked its way through the valley on its way to meet the Delaware River, and a large part of the valley was wooded. Wood ducks could almost always be found on the stream, especially in the stands of oak timber.

Every so often, the stream and parts of the valley bottom would be flooded by hard rains and by the river rising. Then all we had to do was to wear hip boots and camouflage clothing and stand next to one of the large tree trunks so that we did not offer a silhouette; no blind was needed. If we threw out three or four decoys, it helped but wasn't absolutely necessary. A good duck call definitely did help to turn a flock of ducks when they flew over. A real loud quacking run and a little flutter at the end of the call was usually sufficient. This well-known sound of a feeding mallard hen lured many a duck to its last supper. And so long as these conditions lasted, perhaps for as long as a week, the hunting was of the type, though admittedly never of the quantity, of the famous flooded oak flats of Arkansas.

Early icing conditions along the larger rivers make for good pass shooting on the scaup, goldeneye, buffleheads, and mergansers. Still water freezes first, leaving the fast riffles and shallower stretches open. The aforementioned ducks will feed on small fish and eelgrass by starting at the top of the open water, floating with the current and feeding as they go. When they reach the end of the open water, they fly back up again to start over. A retriever is a must for this type of shooting, which is best done from a blind hidden along the shore. If you have to retrieve the ducks by boat, you scare off the rest of the birds for too long a period of time. Even though a duck may be frightened off by the shooting, it will not be long before more ducks drop into the area as they trade up and down the river throughout most of the morning.

In another spot I have located several good-sized ponds almost hidden in the woods. The one pond is fairly large and deep and the other is shallow with loads of duckweed, bur reed, milfoil, and other duck foods. The ducks, mainly mallards, ringnecks, some scaups and blacks, and an occasional pintail spend a lot of time flying back and forth between the two ponds. As the ponds are within half a mile of each other, the ducks fly low over the trees; they have no need to fly higher. Again, just using camouflaged clothing, especially a face mask to prevent flare, will produce good shooting. I have found that if I'm not in a good position when the first ducks go over, all I have to do is move to the crossing they are using. These little flyways change according to the time of day, wind, and weather conditions. However, the flight crossing that the first ducks use will undoubtedly be used by the rest of the ducks until something drastically alters conditions.

Ducks and geese are diurnal feeders by nature, foraging under cover of darkness only if they are forced to do so by hunting pressure. Along our coasts, most waterfowl sleep out on the safety of the bays or the open ocean during the night, coming in at the first crack of dawn to feed. Most of the time as the sun comes up, so does the wind, putting a chop on the water that the waterfowl dislike. So in any event, dawn is the most productive time for most waterfowl pass shooting. Locating your blind between the salt-water areas and the feeding areas is excellent. And so is a blind located between the salt water and a large, open, fresh-water pond. Some sea ducks can drink salt water but most of the birds will go great distances to get fresh water whenever possible.

Your intimate knowledge of your home area should pay off handsomely if ducks are common in your area. I know of one farm field that is just a little too wet to be cultivated. The spring and fall rains always put up to a foot or so of water in this spot, which then dries out again in the summer and in the winter. But the area is always moist enough to produce luxuriant vegetation, including many kinds of duck food. What makes the area particularly attractive to waterfowl is that it is in the middle of land that is usually planted in either corn or wheat and the spilled grain provides a bumper food attraction. Another advantage is that this little hollow is out of sight of the main road so it is relatively unknown. The farmer who owns the land occasionally shoots a few ducks there and is not reluctant to let his friends try their luck, too. Most farmers would have ditched this area to drain it for the small amount of land that might be gained to be put into production but my friend would rather see a few ducks on it.

Locate every little pond in your area. You can bet that the ducks have already done so. With beaver being on the increase in most areas, more little ponds are being built as the result of their activities. Most beaver ponds are usually quite shallow, and this allows the food plants to grow. And most beaver ponds are located in or near woodlands where they are seldom seen and most often their locations are not even suspected. These are really good "safe" places for ducks to rest; such places give the birds a real sense of security. A periodic check of these ponds during the hunting season can usually be counted upon to teach some of the ducks the errors of their ways.

There are probably as many preferred ways of hunting as there are hunters but I do know that the hunting methods just described produce ducks. And that's what duck hunting is all about.

Woodies are usually timid but this hen (left) and drake, feeding near shorelines of streams, seem to be posing for author's camera. Both wood ducks and mallards love acorns, and Rue was scouting area because of abundance of oaks.

Snipe and Other Oddballs

by John Wootters

52

"Dun't know why yer care 'bout shootin' them damned old snipe," the old-timer snorted. "Back in the market-huntin' days we sluiced 'em a dozen to the shot. They ain't nothin' to 'em but a long bill, a bundle of feathers, an' 'bout a table-spoonful o' meat!"

"You just don't understand," I told him. "It's not that I want a snipe pie; it's just that I don't want to go to my grave thinking I was defeated by a long bill, a bundle of feathers, and a tablespoonful of meat. Just once in my life, I want to prove that I'm man enough to hit a jacksnipe on the wing!"

At that time, I had a perfect record on Wilson's snipe, America's most maddening game bird: I'd gone something like oh-for-fifty. I'd missed snipe every way it's possible to miss a flying bird . . . and then I'd invented a few unique and exclusive ways to miss them. I was beginning to believe that snipe are immortal, at least in the face of gunfire, and I had a somewhat paranoid conviction that this insignificant "bundle of feathers" flew all the way to Texas every winter just to plague, harass, and persecute me.

Killing a snipe with a shotgun—even one lonesome snipe—had become something of an obsession; I was determined to kill a jacksnipe if it harelipped every cow in Texas!

My psychiatrist and I are pleased to report that I have now slain a few snipe in fair chase, honest and above-board, on the wing. Few accomplishments have ever given me deeper, more soul-satisfying gratification.

Jacksnipe shooting is one of the last remnants of the great days of shorebird hunting, when market gunners slaughtered snipe, plover, yellowlegs, willets, curlews, and turnstones for the jaded palates of the wealthy. They didn't leave us much. I have shot curlew and plover in old Mexico, back in the days when that was legal, but of the migratory shorebirds still on the game list in this country only Wilson's snipe, the various rails and gallinules, and the unlovely and unwanted coot are abundant.

Of these, jacksnipe are by far the sportiest challenge. They're not hard to find, wherever there is boggy ground, but they're extremely tricky targets. There's not much to them, cleaned for the table, but those few hunters who have tried them generally consider them tasty. Limits are generous (and well they might be!) and the season is lengthy in most states.

Best bet on snipe is walking them up where the soft ground they prefer has enough low cover to permit the gunner to get within range before the birds flush. Most opportunities are at singles, and a good trick is to move upwind when there's a stiff breeze blowing. Snipe tend to climb fast, and usually tower straight up in a wind and fall back over the gunner's head, going ninety to nothing but flying pretty straight, for a jacksnipe.

If there is a secret to hitting snipe with a charge of shot, it is not to fire too quickly. Upon flushing, the birds zig and zag and dipsy-doodle in a manner which would make a mourning dove hang his head in shame. But within a few seconds, they give their raspy chirp, relieve their bowels, and straighten out. The rule is, "Wait until he chirps and craps, then shoot!"

I doubt if there is a "best" gun for snipe, but I hang my pitiful hopes upon a swift 20-gauge double, bored improved and modified and loaded with skeet loads or field loads with one ounce of #9 shot.

This isn't a bad combination for railbird shooting, either, although the problem is different with these marsh hens. They tend to hug cover until absolutely forced to take wing, and then they flutter up like an arthritic butterfly, long legs dangling, and drop limply back into the reeds after a few yards. They're slow and not really hard to hit, provided you can handle a gun fast enough to get on them before they disappear.

In the coastal ricefields of Texas, we used to hitch a ride on the rice farmers' harvesting machines during rail season. As

Related to woodcock but slightly trimmer in body and more than slightly trickier in flight, this little shorebird is jacksnipe—also known as Wilson's snipe or common snipe. It's usually hunted in boggy lowlands.

the machine plowed along in the mucky fields, we could see rails darting here and there, but rarely got a shot until the giant combine began to chew up the last swathe in a field. Then the shooting would get wild and woolly as dozens of rails burst from the diminishing cover in all directions. Of course, shooting from the moving, lurching harvester added an interesting dimension to the ballistic problems.

More conventional rail-hunting techniques involve shooting from a flat-bottomed skiff or pirogue as it is poled slowly through wet marshes. The poling gets to be pretty hard work, and so the rails—king, clapper, and sora—have been subjected to very light hunting pressure along the Atlantic seaboard in recent years.

Hunter rests with limit of snipe, walked up on marsh he reached by boat. On waters like this, there's also chance of putting up railbirds or coot; hunting pressure on all these oddball species is light, seasons and limits generous.

Snipe hunting can be messy, but "bog-slogging" is often rewarding if you carry light 20-gauge double like this Winchester Model 101, feed it #9 skeet loads, and keep yourself from firing until birds level and straighten out.

The rails' larger and more colorful cousins in the marshes are the gallinules. These are long-legged, chicken-like skulkers of the lily pads and reeds. There is an open season and a bag limit on them in many areas but, except for an occasional shot at a gallinule while rail hunting, I have never discovered a way (or a reason) to hunt them. Those I have shot have been by mistake or out of curiosity and a desire to examine the birds closely. Both species—common, or Florida, gallinule and the purple gallinule—are inhabitants of freshwater swamps and marshes, whereas the rails may be found in either fresh or saltwater, depending upon species. They swim well and fly very poorly, if at all. I have never eaten a gallinule, and those who have don't exactly rave about the flavor.

This is a consideration in hunting the remaining oddball of this mixed lot of game birds, the American coot. I keep hearing rumors of chefs who have learned to make epicurean dishes with coots, but I have yet to find a recipe which can make a coot palatable. It's a shame, since the birds are plentiful, with generous bag limits and long seasons in most states. They offer poor sport at best, however, with most shots offered as they flush, running comically across the water until they labor into low flight. In 30 years of waterfowling, I have yet to have an incoming shot at a coot on the wing, and they do not decoy; the coot decoys you've seen were meant to add a confidence factor to stools for ducks.

They're found almost anywhere ducks may be hunted, however, and if anyone ever discovers a way to get some sport and a good meal out of a coot, I'd like to hear about it.

These are the "other" waterbirds which are legal game in the United States. The rest of the shorebirds—plovers, curlews, avocets, stilts, yellowlegs, willets, dunlins, even sandpipers or "peep"—will very properly never be added to the game lists again, having only barely survived (a few species didn't) the market-hunting slaughters around the turn of the century.

Of those still available to gunners, the little jacksnipe is worth all the rest.

Part VIII: Near Home or Far Afield

The Preserve Picture

by Dave Duffey

53

The hunt was just a half hour old when the shiny black Labrador proudly placed the fifth long-tailed cock pheasant in the grasp of his handler.

"Well, that makes this hunt five times better than Iowa," one of the hunters remarked. "I drove 900 miles, got one shot, and missed because of the tall corn."

"You better believe it," one of his two companions chimed in. "The guys we hunted with would go out of their minds if they could see this kind of cover. If I didn't *know* there were birds released here you could fool me. It's just like hunting native birds."

As the dog sat alertly alongside his handler the third hunter stepped over and gave him a pat. "You may not believe this, but I about gave up hunting 10 years ago because of amateur dogs. Every one of my buddies had a dog of some kind that wouldn't mind or didn't hunt and we were hollering at or chasing dogs more than we were shooting birds. I just might start hunting seriously again. It's a pleasure to hunt behind a dog that does what his master says he's going to do and does it right."

Those are near verbatim statements made by three sportsmen who were sampling shooting preserve hunting for the first time. They were all successful in their chosen professions, serious hunters, but often pressed for time. They were willing to pay for good hunting. They found it on a privately managed hunting area.

Not every "pay-for-your-birds" hunting club is top notch. A few are pretty sorry. But the successful ones provide hunting that no sportsman can fault. They offer the serious hunter a chance to hone his wing-shooting skills, and they provide relaxation and sure results for the busy man who can't afford the time away from his profession or family to take an extended out-of-state trip in search of good hunting.

Hunting preserves have much to offer, from the essentials—good grounds, and enough birds to test the skills of dogs and gunners—to complex business operations offering food and lodging, training and boarding of dogs, skeet and trap shooting, guides and dogs, bird cleaning, you name it. By shopping around, instead of driving for miles trying to find an unposted piece of land, a sportsman can locate a good preserve that matches his needs and budget.

Every state now offers long hunting seasons, licensed and regulated by natural resource agencies, on a variety of domestically reared game birds, chiefly pheasant, bobwhite quail, chukar partridge, and mallard duck, for the hunter who is willing to cough up the fee, just as he pays for his other recreational pursuits. He may find it less expensive but more rewarding than scouring the vicinity of his home base looking for a landowner who will allow him to seek game that may not be there, competing for state-stocked birds on public hunting areas, or travelling great distances to enjoy the annual "big" hunting trip to another state that has reasonably good population of the game birds he seeks.

A properly operated commercial hunting establishment is not only obligated to furnish its guests with what they want but must do so if it is to stay in business, break even, or show a profit. So the sportsman can expect good numbers of strong birds in a natural setting as a basic benefit, plus whatever additional services he desires and will pay for.

And most important, perhaps, is the fact that a preserve is a place where hunters are not only permitted but are actually welcomed, and where the atmosphere revolves around hunting, guns, dogs, birds, and shooting.

But getting the most out of a shooting preserve also involves some contribution by the hunter, beyond the payment of a membership or birds-bagged fee. Chiefly it boils down to acting like a sportsman.

Attitude plays an important role. Some men are convinced that "hunting should be free" (which it isn't anymore, no time,

no place), and that the private landowner or the state owes them their recreation. For these chaps, preserve hunting is out of the question.

If a man leans toward the view of modern "ecologists," his distaste for killing animals and his hatred of firearms may blind him to the fact that a hunting preserve can be a wildlife oasis, providing space, food, and cover for birds and animals other than the game that is stocked for shooting; a wild area that might otherwise succumb to industrial, residential, or agricultural development inimical to nature and its wildlings.

The man who thinks hunting on a commercial area marks him as a dude because it is a fish-in-a-barrel proposition is in for a surprise, too. It is true shooting of this type can be furnished upon demand. Birds are purchased or raised by the operator, eventually paid for by the customer. That customer can demand his due any way he chooses, such as shooting birds as they fly out of the crate or having necks wrung if he must display his prowess as a hunter but missed the sporting chances he had at hard-flying birds in the field. But most shooting preserve operators emphasize hunting. For just shooting, they can furnish clay targets. Hunting is many-faceted: the sight and sound of game birds, a dog's tail rattling dry corn stalks as he works a devious running pheasant; the rigid intensity of a pointing pose telling the world there's a covey of quail ready to bust out a few yards in front, a bird folding in full flight when intercepted by a well-placed shot charge flung by a properly swung shotgun; the recovery of downed game by a well-trained retriever; the camaraderie and kidding with other like-minded men.

A practical man requires no great imag-

As bobwhite hunter reloads after scoring double on preserve quail, dog handler accepts retrieved birds from brace of stylish and efficient English pointers; most preserves will furnish dogs, or you can work your own.

ination to figure out that when all of the things that make up hunting are there the only major difference between commercial hunting in a licensed, designated area and "free" hunting on a private back 40 or a public hunting ground is the guarantee that somewhere in the area being hunted there are some birds to be found and shot.

The fee he pays to enjoy this sport to the utmost covers not just the birds he bags but the opportunity to hunt freely and properly and to savor all the highlights a day in the field with gun and dog provides.

Some men express a reluctance to hunt on preserves, despite enjoying it, because of possible criticism. "My buddy, Tom, says it's a rich man's game, for the privileged few and the state ought to own all that land so everybody can hunt on it."

But any thoughtful person would be no more deterred from good sport by such carping than would a reasonable man think of spouting such foolishness.

One of the tenets of the American way of living is the right to own real and personal property and do pretty much what one chooses with it. That right also carries the responsibility of paying taxes and fees to exercise a hold over the land and decide to what use it should be put. If fees, making it feasible to maintain and operate recreational lands as such, were not forthcoming from hunting customers the land, in many cases, would be put to another use of no benefit to any sportsman.

Commercial hunting operations contribute to the economy in numerous ways beneficial to both hunters and nonhunters who do not patronize them, in addition to the

John Falk congratulates young shooter who has just brought down his first ringnecked pheasant. Preserves like this Northeastern one offer good upland terrain, long seasons, and fine training ground for new hunters.

payment of taxes to provide governmental services. And, despite large expenditures to purchase and lease "free" land for the general public, there is an increasing tendency for states to find reasons for charging a use-fee for such areas and to restrict the number of persons allowed to enter.

While it is true that the wealthy will always be able to afford more of the better things in life and the poor very little or none, the bulk of American hunting license buyers, through wise use and budgeting of the money they choose to spend on recreation, can afford at least some hunting on shooting preserves. Where and how often will depend upon how important hunting is to them and how much of their spendable income they feel is warranted as payment for personal pleasure and recreation.

Finally, the patron of fee-hunting areas can make legitimate claim to being a more conscientious and responsible sportsman than the free-hunting advocate. The preserve hunter is in fact a benefactor to those who cannot or will not expend money for the privilege of hunting on privately owned property.

When hunting domestically propagated game birds, the sportsman is exerting no pressure on native game which inhabits both private and public lands outside the boundaries of the commercial establishment. Nor is he competing with the "wild bird" hunter for hunting space or bagging birds that might provide shooting opportunities for the man unable or unwilling to spend more than a state hunting license fee to enjoy his sport.

Under most state licensing arrangements, private hunting clubs are not allowed to harvest all the birds they release, even if it were possible, which it is not, given the vagaries of birds, weather, dogs, and shooting ability. Most arrangements allow the recovery of about 75 percent of the total birds released. Many clubs do not even approach that return percentage. Many of the birds not shot within the preserve boundaries will spill out on the outside for the public's benefit. While few artificially propagated birds contribute to a natural-hatch population, stocked birds do drift considerable distances and provide shooting opportunities to hunters who haven't paid for that privilege.

If enjoyment of dog work, good shooting, and all the other things that go with hunting in a natural setting, plus a very real justification for hunting in this manner

aren't enough, the sportsman who pays for his birds can take comfort in numbers. Each year more and more hunters, by both choice and necessity, have turned to preserve hunting as the answer to their needs.

Today's experienced hunter has all the requirements for participation in the good hunting well-managed preserves offer. And for the adult just "taking up" hunting or the youngster being introduced to the game, preserves can provide the fundamental facilities and know-how.

Sportsmen who wish to get the ultimate out of hunting on a commercial game management area can attain this goal with a bit of insight, a reasonable attitude, and the recognition that, if not now, certainly in the near future high-quality hunting will be enjoyed only by those willing to pay for it.

Flushed by dog handler, center, two quail go up out of palmetto on Southern preserve as author, left, and friend swing their guns. Such preserves offer ideal place to polish up your dog's performance—as well as your own.

An Outfitter's Plea

by Les Bowman

Outfitting—like hunting—is not what it used to be. Twenty or thirty years ago, most of the big-game animals, from deer and antelope to bighorn sheep, were fairly plentiful in most good game areas. Trophy heads were abundant, and because game wasn't hunted too much by too many, the outfitter had little trouble finding a respectable trophy for his hunter.

Today, however, hunting pressure has increased the wariness of game animals while at the same time decreasing their numbers. Some states with high game populations have tried to sell every license they can and have shortened their hunting seasons to 12 or 14 days. Others have split the seasons on elk and deer in order to decrease the overall kill and sell more licenses. To make matters worse, the intrusion of industrialized man has destroyed some of the best hunting areas and has pushed game animals out of their natural habitat, further diminishing their numbers. Little wonder that the modern outfitter has a tough row to hoe.

In the 1970s there is no such thing as a guaranteed big-game hunt. No outfitter can promise that a hunter will fill his licenses or permits 100 percent. In many areas the success percentages for game animals such as elk have fallen from the 75 percent (and sometimes as high as 100 percent) averages of just a few years ago to as low as 16 percent. And as far as trophy heads go—which is not as far as they used to—the hunter can expect very few in the record or even near-record class.

But despite all this gloomy talk and all these discouraging statistics, a successful big-game hunt is still possible. It can be achieved with just three elements: a good hunter, a good outfitter, and a good deal of cooperation between the two.

In most cases, the hunter who needs or desires the services of an outfitter (or guide) is the nonresident hunter. Let's assume that you are one of these people, planning a big-game hunt in a state or province you have never visited. Here is what to remember in contacting an outfitter.

First, make your plans well in advance of the actual hunt. A good outfitter, if contacted well in advance, will give you all the help and advice you need. If he doesn't, then he's not a good outfitter and you'd better try someone else. But do call well in advance. No outfitter can be expected to answer many questions during his busiest season. Besides, if he *is* good, he'll be booked full anyway. Another reason to plan well ahead is that many states require licenses or permits to be secured through a drawing, and applications for these drawings must be received several months ahead of the actual hunt. Only in Canada and Alaska can you be reasonably sure of getting a license at the eleventh hour.

When you contact an outfitter for the first time, you should be ready to ask several questions and answer a few yourself. First, be sure to ask him for his rates. Failure of the hunter to check all the costs of a hunt, including the deposit and especially the extras that may be added at his request, can cause a real misunderstanding. For instance, in some states that have the guide rule, the hunter-to-guide ratio is whatever the guide wishes to make it. Most states limit the number of hunters a guide can take to two hunters at one time. As a rule, outfitters hire guides on the two-to-a-hunter basis. So, if you request a personal guide after your hunt starts and make no inquiries about the additional cost, you are apt to be pretty shook up when it appears on your bill at the end of the hunt. The cost of a personal guide may add from $15 to $30 a day.

Be sure to ask your outfitter what kind of hunting terrain will be encountered, and how he proposes to cross that terrain (on foot or on horseback). You should try to get an idea of the probable weather (always the toughest question for an outfitter to answer), and you should determine just how much equipment will be furnished by him

and how much by you. Different outfitters have different requirements that are determined somewhat by the areas in which they operate and the types of hunts they conduct.

Veteran guide-outfitter Les Bowman displays record-book trophy taken during Wyoming elk hunt by Bob Edgar of Cody. Success of hunting trip often hinges on planning by, and cooperation between, client and outfitter.

One question you will have to *answer* concerns your physical fitness. The condition of a hunter is of great importance to his outfitter. Most of the mountain areas in the western part of the states, and a great part of the plains hunting areas are around 4,500 feet in altitude, or higher. Nearly all the good elk hunting ranges are in the high country, some at 10,000 feet or more. Even though most elk hunting is by the pack-in, horseback type of hunting, there is usually some walking to be done, especially if a stalk must be made. If an outfitter knows how much his hunter can take, he can regulate the hunt to a certain extent, so his hunter has a better chance of success. During the early part of the elk season the real high country ranges are productive of far the best and biggest trophy heads. However, if you are not up to high-country hunting, it is still possible to have a good hunt later in the season, and at an altitude you can handle. So let your outfitter know. He wants your *continued* business and he'll do his best to see that you have a good hunt where you can enjoy it.

Proper clothing and particularly the right kind of footwear is something else you should inquire about. No one can enjoy a hunt if he is shivering and limping. Most good hunting altitudes, even in early fall, can be cold, and warm clothing is a necessity. If you are in a pack-in camp, the best-quality sleeping bag you can buy will certainly contribute to your well being and the enjoyment of your trip. Incidentally, some outfitters furnish sleeping bags. We never did, as I always felt that a good sleeping bag was a necessary part of a hunter's belongings. A good bag will last a lifetime of hunting and is well worth the investment.

Too many hunters try for too many types of game on one hunt. In some states the big-game license includes elk, deer, bear, and even fishing. A hunter gets one of these and wants his outfitter to get everything on the license for him, and all in the ten-day time he booked. But what many hunters don't understand is that each game animal requires a little different type of hunting. During elk season, although deer are in the same area, the deer stay in the heavy timber and brush. Getting a bear in

the fall is just a happening. Fishing is sometimes good in the high elk country, sometimes just so-so, and often there is none at all. Don't blame your outfitter. If you want the whole package, make arrangements ahead of time, and stay long enough to get them all.

Although preference in guns is largely a personal matter, it's a good idea to check with your outfitter to see what he suggests in the way of caliber and bullet weight. He should know what is right for the particular type of game you're after and the sort of terrain you'll be covering.

When you are satisfied that you've made the proper arrangements, well in advance, keep in contact with your outfitter once in awhile. It will benefit both of you, as there are always lots of little details that may be worked out in advance, contributing to a more enjoyable time for all.

In conclusion, I would like to give you an example of the almost perfect hunter. I haven't made him up. He did hunt with us and he is this good.

He booked his hunt well in advance, he told us of his physical capabilities, his shooting experience, and his special requests and likes. He told us he had permits for elk, sheep, deer, and antelope, and had us arrange for a trophy-size buffalo. He said that he had only 14 days to spend with us and he knew that many animals would be a problem to get but we could try. He also let us know that, while he had sprained a knee on an Alaskan hunt the week before, he would be able to get around on foot quite well, although not as fast as usual. He told us he was used to extremely high-altitude hunting so our high elk and sheep ranges would not bother him. He said that he owned and rode his own horses, but would like a saddle that fit well. He told us that he could eat most anything we furnished in the way of food, but would like his own sleeping tent. And last, he said he shot rather well (the understatement of the year), and used a 7 x 57 custom-built Winchester and Imperial 139-grain factory loads on all but the very largest type of game.

I advised him that the chances of filling all his permits in such a short time weren't very good, but that we'd give it a try. I would take him in alone with just a helper and we would try for the hardest animal to get, the bighorn sheep first. We would be in an area where we might also get an elk or big timberline buck on the same hunt.

On our first morning out of camp five rams surprised us by coming down a wide open ridge we were crossing. He was off that horse in a flash, a cartridge in the chamber, and a fast offhand try that raked some hair off the last ram's hip before they disappeared in the timber. I knew then that I had a real experienced hunter along. Three days later he took a ram that just missed the record book by three points. He took his sheep after a one-hour-and-45-minute stalk, down into a deep canyon, from the 10,000-foot level where we spotted the sheep and tied our horses, up a rough creek bed to the 11,000-foot level, then a short distance around the side hill to a point where he could take a rest. One shot at 300 feet was all it took. Two days later, from the same camp, he got an elk that went into the record book by several points.

We packed up, came into the ranch, and took off for the eastern edge of the state where he got his record buffalo. In the following two days he took two excellent typical mule deer and two trophy antelope.

I seriously doubt that anyone could duplicate this hunt today due to the lack of game now as compared to then (1962). I think one certainly couldn't find an elk in this same class and definitely not in the time we hunted. But the success of this hunt was due more than anything else to the close cooperation between hunter and outfitter. I understood how to hunt with him and what he could do and he left it entirely up to me as to what to do and how to do it.

He was one of the most pleasant hunters I have ever been out with and one of the easiest to get along with. His name is Abdorezza Pahlevi, Prince of Iran.

Guided by experienced outfitter, Adair Nunally of Atlanta took this fine six-point elk right at timberline in high country (elevation, 10,300 feet). Range was 200 yards, and she needed just one shot with her .270 bolt-action.

What Every Hunter Should Know About Canada   55

by Jerome J. Knap

Stories on hunting in Canada are as numerous in the outdoor press as cottontails on the bramble-choked "back 40" of an Iowa farm. By and large, these stories are accounts of how the writer got his big bull moose or trophy sheep.

Yet strangely enough, this is not always the type of information that an American hunter planning his first trip to Canada wants to know. In letters to the provincial fish and game departments and to the tourist departments, the most-often-asked questions deal with the nitty gritty of travelling in Canada and of crossing the international border. How much red tape is involved in crossing the border? How do I get my rifle in? How much ammunition can I bring? What documents do I need? What are the highways like? Do I need to know French? This is the type of mundane information that is seldom given in articles on hunting in Canada.

Frankly, I too would rather write about stalking a Dall sheep on a mountain meadow in the Yukon or gunning for geese on the wind-swept coast of Hudson Bay. The laws and regulations of Canada Customs don't exactly make stirring, sinewy prose. But it's about time that someone write this piece.

Crossing into Canada, in most cases, is not much more difficult than crossing boundaries from one state to another. Automobiles and baggage, even at airports, are seldom searched and the traveller generally has to answer only a few simple questions such as: Where were you born? Where do you live? Where in Canada are you going? How long will you be visiting Canada? What is the purpose of your visit? Are you bringing any gifts for anyone?

You may or may not be asked to show proof of American citizenship. However, you should have identification papers with you in case you are.

American citizens and permanent residents of the U.S. do not need passports for entry into Canada. For native-born U.S. citizens, a birth, baptismal, or voter's certificate is ample proof of citizenship. Naturalized U.S. citizens should bring along a naturalization certificate. An Alien Registration Receipt Card (U.S. form 1-151) is needed by permanent residents of the U.S. who are not American citizens.

One good piece of advice in dealing

with customs officers is to be cheerful and courteous. This applies not only to Canadian customs officers on entering Canada, but also to U.S. officers when returning to the United States. A smile goes a long way, and it's free.

Bringing guns into Canada is generally the biggest worry of the American hunter. First, forget about handguns. You cannot bring them in for hunting and you won't need them for self protection. (Target shooters have a loophole, but more about this later.) Fully automatic arms are, of course, prohibited. So are firearms shorter than 26 inches, and firearms that can be fired when folded or collapsed to a length of less than 26 inches. Otherwise, bringing rifles or shotguns into Canada is largely free of red tape for any visitor over 16 years of age. There are no caliber restrictions with regard to the importation of rifles and shotguns. There are, of course, caliber restrictions for hunting. These are set by the provincial game departments and vary from one province to another. Again, these will be discussed later.

The first step in bringing rifles or shotguns into Canada is to construct a legible list of each gun by make, model, caliber, and serial number, on a piece of paper. Then take this list, when you leave, to the U.S. Customs Office at the border or airport from which you are departing. The customs officer may or may not look at these guns, but he will issue you a certificate listing all the guns you are exporting. This is not any sort of gun registration. You will have the only copy of this form. The purpose here is for you to be able to prove that these guns were taken by you to Canada when you are returning home. The form proves that you did not purchase the guns in Canada and that you are not trying to smuggle them into the States. All of the

empty spaces on this customs certificate will be crossed out by the customs officer so that you cannot add any items to it. It's perhaps needless to say that you should keep this certificate in a safe place so you don't lose it. And don't change anything or scribble on this certificate or it will be suspect. When you cross the border, inform Canada Customs that you have firearms with you. If requested, show them the description list of the guns and, if necessary, the guns themselves. The Canada Customs official may issue a Temporary Admissions Permit to cover the guns. The issuance of such a permit is at the discretion of the officer. If he believes that you will return with the guns, he may not bother with the form. The sole purpose of this permit is to ensure that the guns are taken back into the United States and not sold in Canada. If you intend to leave a gun in Canada as a gift, you must pay import duty, excise, and sales taxes on the gun.

There is a special provision in the Canada Customs regulations for temporary importation of handguns when the visitor is travelling to a bona fide handgun marksmanship competition. The sponsoring club of such a competition generally obtains the necessary permit for the importation of a target handgun. The competitor himself can clear such a gun by applying directly to the Collector of Customs and Excise at the point of entry. The competitor must have proof that he is a participant in a bona fide handgun competition.

American hunters travelling to Alaska via the Alaska Highway may temporarily import handguns into Canada under special permit, but this is conditional to the fact that the guns are enclosed in a case or container and can be sealed by Canada Customs officers at the point of entry.

A nonresident hunter may bring as

Canada offers plenty of hunting for moose like this big bull, hurriedly leaving water at Fox Lake, Ontario. You can bring 200 rounds of ammunition into Canada duty free, but check with provincial game department for permissible calibers.

It pays to make advance inquiries regarding types of game available in any given region. On big-game trip, for instance, you might want to bring shotgun for change-of-pace outing to hunt rock ptarmigan.

much as 200 rounds of ammunition with him duty free as personal baggage. These can be either shot shells or rifle cartridges. Participants in rifle matches or in trap or skeet competitions organized by the Dominion of Canada Rifle Association, the Canadian Civilian Association of Marksmen, the Amateur Trapshooting Organization, or the National Skeet Shooting Association are allowed to import 500 rounds of ammunition duty free as personal baggage.

The American hunter or target shooter will find that sporting-goods and gun stores in Canada stock the same brands of ammunition in the more popular calibers and gauges as stores back home. Also, Canadian brands of ammunition are of high quality. This will come as a relief to hunters who intend to fly to Canada. By buying ammunition in Canada, you not only save on bulk and weight, but also on the headaches associated with the current airline regulations regarding transporting ammunition. If, of course, your pet rifle is chambered for an exotic cartridge or for a wild-

cat, you have no choice but to bring your ammunition with you.

What about other equipment that a hunter may want to bring with him on a trip? All items of a personal nature or sporting equipment may be brought in by a visitor for his own use. This includes boats, motors, snowmobiles, camping equipment, fishing rods and reels, binoculars, and cameras. Again, these should be listed in a fashion similar to the gun list, so that you can obtain a registration certificate from U.S. Customs to ensure that you have no problems in bringing the items back into the United States. Canada Customs may also want a record of these items on a Temporary Admissions Permit to ensure that you not leave them behind.

As I stated before, Customs officials rarely bother with the Temporary Admissions Permit. It is generally only used when the officer is suspicious that the items in question may be left in Canada. Incidentally, they do have the right to ask for a deposit, in cash or bond, to further ensure that the items be returned to the

United States. Such a deposit is demanded only in extreme cases. A tourist travelling to Canada need not worry that a deposit will be demanded of him on items that he is bringing in for his own use.

Bringing hunting dogs into Canada doesn't present any serious problem. A dog being brought or shipped from the United States must be accompanied by a certificate signed by a licensed veterinarian stating that the dog has been vaccinated against rabies during the preceding 12 months. The certificate must have on it a good, clear, legible description of the dog. If the dog has a registry tattoo on its ear or inner thigh, it's a good idea to quote this on the certificate as well. If you're travelling with the dog, keep this certificate with your personal identification.

A visitor to Canada may bring with him a "reasonable amount of film and flash-bulbs appropriate to the nonresident's visit." The definition of "reasonable" is rather fluid. Canada Customs officials are rather generous in their interpretation of this. A hunter with a dozen rolls of film would not encounter any problem. The visitor may also bring with him, duty free, 40 ounces of liquor or wine or 24 pints of beer, up to 50 cigars, two pounds of tobacco, and 200 cigarettes. He may also bring food for two days.

Hunters intending to drive to Canada may be happy to learn that there is no gasoline shortage north of the border. You should also keep in mind that the Canadian gallon (Imperial measure) is 20 percent larger than the American gallon. Some Canadian provinces require that the driver of a car provide proof of financial responsibility, should he be involved in an automobile accident. The easiest way to do this is for the motorist to obtain a Canadian Nonresident Interprovince Motor Ve-

hicle Liability Insurance Card. This pale-yellow card is available only in the United States through the insurance company that insures your car. Your insurance agent can obtain one for you. A driver's license from any state is recognized in Canada.

In general the highways in Canada are good. There are, however, fewer four-lane expressways. Speed limits and directions are generally well marked. Canada is conscious of the motoring tourist. The secondary and back roads are much like those in your home state.

For some reason, many Americans believe that the French language is spoken universally in Canada. Although it is one of the official languages of the country, it is universally spoken only in Quebec and in the northern portion of New Brunswick. But even in these places, people associated with the tourist trade usually speak English. Your guide on a northern Quebec moose hunt may not speak English well enough to carry on much of a campfire conversation, but he will be able to say "big bull, shoot!"

Every hunter should familiarize himself with the hunting regulations in the province where he intends to hunt. Summaries of regulations are available from the provincial game departments and are generally included with the brochure outlining open seasons. This is something that many nonresidents neglect. Hunting regulations vary from province to province. In some provinces a firearm in a car must be dismantled or encased, while in other provinces the firearm need only be unloaded and not encased. Some provinces do not allow large-caliber rifles to be carried during closed big-game seasons, and others limit the size of shot in shotguns. Some provinces place caliber restrictions on big-game rifles; others do not. Some provinces pro-

Most U.S. residents think of Canadian hunting solely in terms of big game,
neglecting exceptional opportunities for waterfowling and upland
hunting. These sharptails were collected near abandoned homestead in Alberta.

hibit the use of bullets with solid-steel jackets. Shotguns must be plugged to a maximum of three shots almost universally in Canada for both waterfowl and upland game. And just as in the U.S., no shotgun larger than a 10-gauge may be used for waterfowl hunting.

Hunting regulations in Canada are largely a matter of commonsense, but it's wise to become familiar with them. For example, legal shooting time for most provinces begins a half hour before official sunrise and ends a half hour after official sunset. This includes waterfowl, upland game, and big-game hunting, but there are exceptions.

Many of the articles in the outdoor press portray Canada as a vast wilderness with abundant game. This probably stems from the fact that writers generally go into wilderness areas. And, of course, you never read stories where the writer didn't get his trophy. Such stories are never written. Yet Canada is not all wilderness; indeed many areas are densely populated.

For example, the farming countryside on the Canadian shores of Lakes Erie and Ontario has no more game than the farmlands on the American side of these lakes. This area of Canada has a dense human population with very large cities. Agriculture is clean and intensive. Either condition is not conducive to producing abundant game.

Providing specific information on where to hunt in Canada is beyond the scope of one short chapter. About the most practical advice I can give is for you to plan your trip into an area of Canada with sparse population, into the vast tracts of wilderness. You are already investing a fair sum of money for nonresident licenses, travel costs, and the services of a guide or outfitter, so you might as well invest a bit more and go deep into the bush.

One of the first steps that an American hunter planning a Canadian hunt should take is to acquaint himself with Canadian geography. The simplest way to do this is with a map. Write to the Canadian Government Office of Tourism, 150 Kent Street, Ottawa, Canada, and ask for a copy of the "Canada Highway Map"—even if you intend to fly up. This map shows the highway network over the entire country as well as through the northern United States. From this you will see what parts of Canada are heavily settled and which parts are largely wilderness.

And even before you begin to plan the trip, you must of course decide what you want to hunt and where these species are found. This may strike you as being naive and simple, but every year the Ontario Ministry of Natural Resources gets dozens of letters inquiring as to the whereabouts of the best areas for grizzly in the province. There hasn't been a grizzly in Ontario since the last ice age.

The prospective hunter should find out what game is available and where. Some provinces require that nonresidents hire a guide or hunt with a resident hunter. Or a guide may be required by law only in certain wilderness areas or only when a hunter is after certain big-game species such as grizzly or sheep.

In some provinces it is still possible for a hunter to make a do-it-yourself hunt by flying in to remote areas. But the success rate of hunters on such hunts is lower than those who hire a guide. The average nonresident hunter is better off investing a little additional capital for a guide.

Of course the outfitter's or guide's success rate is not necessarily indicative of trophy quality. Some of the western outfitters boast of a 90-percent success rate on sheep, but frequently this means that their clients are shooting rams just beyond the legal ¾ curl. Such rams are not trophy-class specimens. They are only about five or six years old and should not really be le-

gal game. It takes at least eight or nine years to produce a trophy ram.

Canada has some excellent wing shooting to offer. Outstanding duck and goose shooting is found on the Canadian prairies, around Hudson and James Bays, and in the Gulf of St. Lawrence in Quebec. New Brunswick woodcock and ruffed grouse gunning has been well known to a small group of devotees. But grouse and woodcock are also abundant in areas of Quebec's Eastern Townships, the area south of the St. Lawrence River, the eastern corner of Ontario, the upper portion of the Bruce Peninsula between Lake Huron and Georgian Bay, and Manitoulin Island. All these locations have grouse and woodcock covers.

Manitoba and Saskatchewan offer good grouse gunning, but sharptails overshadow the ruffed grouse, particularly in Saskatchewan. Although the prairies of Saskatchewan probably offer the best sharptail gunning on the continent, the Hungarian partridge hunting may be just as good.

The sharptails and Huns continue on into Alberta which also has fine ruffed and blue grouse gunning in some of the forested areas of the foothills. To many Albertans the bonanza bird is the ringnecked pheasant. The best pheasant hunting is around Lethbridge in southwestern Alberta. In good years the hunting there compares favorably to the halcyon years of South Dakota. This fact has already been discovered by small groups of Californians.

The big-game hunting in British Columbia completely overshadows the fine blue grouse shooting on the forested slopes of this mountain province, and the good duck and goose hunting in many of the coastal bays and marshes.

There are only three other provinces I have not mentioned. These are Newfoundland, Prince Edward Island, and Nova Scotia. Newfoundland is moose and caribou country, but it also has some fine goose shooting and duck shooting. Ptarmigan are the important upland game birds here. Hunting these birds over a setter may seem somewhat unique until one learns that the legendary game bird of Scotland—the red grouse—is nothing but a Scottish race of the willow ptarmigan.

Prince Edward Island also has some fine goose and duck shooting on the coastal marshes, while the picturesque Nova Scotia has good ruffed grouse and woodcock gunning and even some pheasant and Hun shooting in the Annapolis Valley.

Barring a few exceptions, the small-game hunter planning a gunning trip to Canada is faced with a do-it-yourself proposition. New Brunswick has ruffed grouse and woodcock guides with good dogs whose services can be hired. The fabulous goose hunting along the James and Hudson Bay coasts of Manitoba, Ontario, and Quebec is likewise well organized and there are a number of outfitters with package trips in each province. There are also several outfitters who specialize in duck and goose hunting on the Gulf of St. Lawrence in Quebec. Many sportsmen's outfitters in northern Quebec, Ontario, and Manitoba will cater to grouse and duck hunters, but very few are organized to offer meaningful services. Many are not even located in good grouse or duck country.

About the only way a hunter can savor the fine wing shooting on the Canadian prairies is to travel there on his own. Although the odd farmer will act as a guide, finding such a man is largely a word-of-mouth proposition. Hunters can either camp out or stay in country hotels in small farming towns. Accommodation is generally comfortable and surprisingly inexpensive.

Any hunter planning a do-it-yourself hunt should have a fair knowledge of how to hunt and the type of cover the birds are found in. Dogs are almost indispensable, even on the game-rich Canadian prairies. For upland game birds, pointing dogs are the best bet, while a retriever will save crippled ducks in the weed-choked prairie sloughs and potholes.

There is no secret, no shortcut to a successful Canadian hunting trip. If there were such a thing, it would be planning. Over the years I have noticed that hunters who do their homework, who plan everything carefully before shelling out their money and going on a trip, generally are the ones who have a good hunt.

Tips on Hunting Trips

by Jack O'Connor

56

As a writer of hunting tales, I get many dozens of letters each year asking for assistance in planning hunting trips. Some of my correspondents want to do nothing more complicated than make a modest trip for Wyoming antelope, but others want sheep in the Yukon or a general bag of everything from leopard to elephant in Africa.

But no matter where my correspondents want to go or what they want to hunt, they almost never tell me the three things I must know if I am to answer them intelligently—how long they can stay, how much money they can spend, and what they can stand physically.

Obviously, the man with a week to hunt and $200 or $300 to spend cannot plan to make a 30-day pack trip in northern British Columbia or the Yukon at $75 or $85 a day. One must have time and money to hunt big game in distant places. The man with a lot of time (and some know-how) can sometimes get by with spending relatively little money, and the chap who is loaded can use money to save time. However, everyone needs some of both.

Many years ago I did a lot of hunting in Mexico for desert bighorn sheep, javelinas, and desert mule and whitetail deer. I had little money, but I knew the deserts, I spoke enough Spanish to get by, and I either used no guide or I picked up some local cowboy for a few pesos a day. I was able to make hunts for peanuts that cost others many hundreds of dollars.

In contrast, I have a very wealthy friend who could light his cigarettes on $100 bills the rest of his life and not be bothered. He uses money to save time. He will send a pack train into a piece of good game country, then fly in to meet it by chartered plane, land on a nearby lake, and start hunting.

Any man planning a hunt should be realistic about his own physical condition and his ability to climb and hike. The day before I began this modest article, a chap called me about a hunt. He had read, he told me, that the desert sheep was probably the most prestigious of all North American trophies. He wanted therefore to begin his sheep hunting on desert rams. He was a man of great influence (he said) and was convinced he would be able to manage the necessary permits.

It developed he was 62 years old, weighed 260 pounds, was a chain smoker, and suffered from emphysema. It was necessary, he said, that he do his sheep hunting from a Jeep. I told him that no matter how much money and influence he had he couldn't bribe the desert rams to come down out of their rugged hills and canyons so he could plink at them out of a car.

Sadly enough, many who plan trips are not very realistic about their time, their money, or their physical ability—and the hearts of most of us are full of larceny. Hunting trips have to be paid for in one way or another—in money, in time, or in physical exertion.

But all too many of us would like to get by without paying these costs. I get many letters from those who would like to have me take them to the Yukon or to Africa (all expenses paid, of course) and give them a jolly hunting trip in return for companionship and modest services such as helping me skin out heads or take pictures.

The only time I ever felt like taking anyone up on such a proposition was when a very pretty airline stewardess asked me if she couldn't come along with me on safari as a secretary. For the first time I realized that a secretary was practically a necessity on safari and that without the assistance of a cute little trick like this I had been roughing it.

I also get many letters from those who want a first-rate trip but at bargain rates. I have had many dozens of letters from those who don't want a "champagne safari." They are willing to do with just the simple necessities—a good crew, a crack white hunter, hunting car and lorry in first-class condition, comfortable and adequate tents and sleeping gear, and a guarantee of record-class trophies. Assured of these bare necessities, my correspondents are willing to scrimp along without champagne. They do, however, expect at least a 50 percent reduction.

Before making distant trip, decide what single trophy you'd rather have than any other. You might get very lucky and take moose like this in one day, or you might need almost entire trip to fill one tag, without time for other game.

Akin to the lads who are willing to pass up champagne are those sturdy fellows who want a pack trip at a greatly reduced price by working their way. They would be willing to wrangle the horses, cut the wood, pitch the tents, do the packing. They always tell me that they are tough as boots and are good hunters and woodsmen (they have shot three whitetail deer) and they really do not need guides. They forget that every man is a dude when he is out of his own backyard. The best sheep guide in the Yukon has a lot to learn if he goes after a desert ram, and the finest ivory hunter in Africa is out of his element if he tries to get himself an Adirondack whitetail.

So the man planning a distant big-game hunt should be realistic about his time, his money, and his hunting skills and physical condition. There are many interesting hunts that can be taken with little expenditure of time or money. Many eastern hunters pool resources, share expenses as they drive out West, and hunt mule deer and antelope without rupturing the family budget. Sometimes they pull a trailer. Sometimes they take tents with them, camp on public land, or get permission to pitch their tents on some rancher's place.

In the West today, roads into elk country are usually lined with cars, and country accessible by automobile is crowded with hunters. However, in many western states there are packers who will for a fee pack hunters back into good hunting country far from the road hunters. After an agreed time, the packer returns, loads the hunters' tents, equipment, and meat on their horses or mules and takes them back to the road. This way, the man of modest means who owns his own equipment and who can take care of himself in the sticks can have a wilderness hunt at a modest price. In this case he is substituting know-how and hard work for money.

Probably the best way for the man planning a hunting trip to locate good country and a good outfitter is to get the information from someone who has hunted in the particular country. Correspondence with an outfitter will tell the perceptive hunter much. Beware of the glib outfitter who promises the moon. It is much easier to talk a good hunt than to lay on one. Stories in the hunting and fishing magazines will give leads on good outfitters and good areas. One can always write to the author of a story in care of the magazine in which it appeared. Often he will pass out information he didn't care to include in his tale.

If he can afford it, the prospective hunter should always avoid mass-produced hunts. If he signs up for a "bargain" hunt, he should do so with his eyes open. Some cut-rate outfits furnish one guide for every four hunters. Two hunters to a guide can work out very well if the two hunters happen to be husband and wife. In most cases, though, such an arrangement is poison. Suppose two hunters go together with one guide. On the whole trip they see one good ram with a 44-inch head or one big bull elk. Who is to do the shooting? More than one lifelong friendship has floundered on questions such as these.

The choice of a hunting companion is perhaps even more critical than the choice of an outfitter. I know of more than one pair of companions who have come back not speaking. Hunting trips are an acid test of compatibility. People who are charming enough in everyday life may turn into selfish slobs, whiners, poor sports, and game hogs on hunting trips. I know people I get along with well enough in everyday life but with whom I wouldn't be caught dead on a hunting trip—and there are undoubtedly people who wouldn't be caught dead going on a trip with me. Not many people are cheerful when they are exhausted, cold, and wet—or when they miss an easy shot at a fine trophy after a companion brings in coveted trophies.

The man planning a distant trip should decide before he starts what one trophy he would rather have than anything else. He should make up his mind to choose his

In choosing right kind of Western trip for you, consider whether you ride well, whether you're in shape for long, arduous climbs, how much money you can afford to spend, and how long you can be away from your home and business.

country with this trophy in mind and, when he gets there, he should plan to hunt hard for it. For many years I have been a dedicated sheep hunter, and good rams have been my prime objective on most of the many hunts I have taken in the mountains. As a consequence I have usually done pretty well on rams—and generally I also have bumped into other trophies while hunting sheep.

The man who demands everything doesn't often do too well as he scatters his efforts. The man who wants to go on a 14-day hunt, shoot a 40-inch ram, a 60-inch moose, a black bear, a goat, a mule deer, knock off a few dozen blue grouse, and catch trout and grayling generally will be disappointed.

A large party should be avoided on a pack trip. The more people, the more noise; the more shooting, the quicker a piece of country is burned up and the game chased away. The larger the party, the more the members are at cross purposes. One man wants to stay and hunt

sheep, the others want to move on into moose or caribou country. Yet another becomes homesick and wants to hurry back to the little woman and his desk at Widgets, Inc.

And the prospective hunter should plan on as long a trip as possible. Miracles have been accomplished in a short time. I once knew two chaps who packed into a good piece of country in the Yukon. In one week they shot two fine rams, two good caribou, two good moose, and a grizzly. In nine days they had packed in, had hunted, and were back on the Alaska Highway.

But one should never count on exceptional luck. Instead he should make allowances for some *bad* luck. Suppose he has arranged for only two weeks. Packing in and out will take, let us say, four days. Moving camp twice will take two days more. That leaves him only eight days to hunt. Then a four-day storm comes up. That leaves him four days to hunt. A bunch of horses runs away. Another day is gone. He winds up with three days. If he has allowed himself 21 days, his chances of bad luck ruining his trip are less; if he has allowed himself 30 days, he is still better off.

The prospective hunter should always ask his outfitter for suggestions as to clothing and equipment needed and he should pay attention to them. People who have spent their lives in a country know more about conditions than those who have never been in it. The ideal is to have just enough. I like to take a sufficient variety of clothes so I will be reasonably comfortable in any kind of weather I am likely to encounter and enough clothes so that I can change if I get wet. Obviously, different clothes are needed on a hunt for giant brown bear on Admiralty Island in Alaska than on a hunt for desert mule deer in southern Arizona. On Admiralty it is almost always raining, and in southern Arizona it seldom rains. On Admiralty one hunts in hip boots. In Arizona they would be worthless. It is silly to load up with useless gadgets and unnecessary clothes, but it is equally foolish to take so few things that you are uncomfortable. It is better to have a few garments too many than too few.

Another piece of what I consider wisdom is to have an extra rifle in the party. Chances are that it will not be needed, but if it *is* needed, it is needed badly and there are no sporting-goods stores on the other side of the hill. Many outfitters don't like to take the trouble to pack the extra rifle, but don't let them talk you out of it.

Plan a trip you can handle physically and that is within your means and one that you have time for. Pick out the one trophy you want most, then go where your chances are best and hunt like hell. Pick your companions as carefully as you do your outfitter. Take enough of everything, but leave the gadgets at home.

Author Jack O-Connor's hunts have taken him around world. Here he is (right) with Louie Jacquot at Jacquot's cabin on Kluane Lake during 1945 sheep hunt. Jacquot and his brother Gene packed their outfit over Chilkoot Pass in '98.

Appendix: Best Times and Places to Hunt the Major Species

by John Madson

Making long-range predictions of the best places to hunt is a sure way to get out on a limb that can be sawed off by weather, politics, and sundry events that never show up in a crystal ball.

But in a handbook that's meant for hunters at all levels of experience, we reckon that someone has to crawl out on that limb and prognosticate. So here goes.

The material in the following tables is largely based on the annual game forecasts that Winchester's Conservation Department has been making for 18 years with the help of state and provincial conservation agencies. These forecasts always rate the hunting prospects for each game species in each state or province, ranking them "excellent," "good," "fair," or "poor." Which works out fine in an annual state-by-state forecast, but doesn't help much in a national forecast because hunting quality is always *relative*. "Good" antelope prospects in Wyoming hold more fine hunting for more hunters than "excellent" antelope prospects in Texas—and although wild-turkey prospects may be "excellent" in both states, Wyoming hardly compares to Texas as a turkey state. Such relativity has been considered here, and we have tried to skim off the cream and emphasize the best national areas for hunting each game species. There are many exceptions to these generalities, but "mainly it war so," and in noting the "best places" for hunting we will stay loose and general. We might be able to name the township that will have the best pheasant hunting in North America for the next couple of years—but we're not going to. To do so would be unfair to the reader, the landowners, and the game.

And as far as "availability of good hunting" is concerned—well, that depends mostly on the hunter himself. There is good hunting to be found almost anywhere there is good game habitat, but you can be certain that such hunting is going to cost more in terms of money, effort, or time. In which commodity are you richest? Which can you best afford to spend? (Of the three, effort and time may buy more full hunting enjoyment than will money.)

But one thing is certain: the best hunting comes to the man who spends his personal resources freely, and his returns are relative to his investments. That was true a million years ago; it will be true as long as men go hunting.

BIG GAME

SPECIES	BEST HUNTING PLACES	BEST TIMES	HOW MUCH GOOD HUNTING AVAILABLE?
White-tailed deer	East: the seaboard states of Virginia, the Carolinas, Georgia, and Florida have had high deer crops for a number of years. Of the "farm states," Missouri is one of the best. In the West, the whitetail continues to spread in western Dakotas and Montana.	December	Access to good hunting lands should be no real problem. Remember that some of the best whitetail hunting is in cultivated land where permission is necessary. However, there are extensive public lands in these states that offer good deer hunting.
Mule deer	Montana, Wyoming, Colorado. Although muley hunting is statewide, some of the best is in brushy draws in open rangeland, and in rough "breaks" beside rangeland rivers. Such country is often lightly hunted.	Special late hunts and post-season hunts.	There is much public land for mule-deer hunting, and the National Forests are favorites. But don't overlook relatively treeless public lands, such as National Grasslands and Bureau of Land Management holdings.
Elk	Wyoming and Colorado have had excellent elk herds for several years, and there is much public land on which to hunt. Washington probably has the nation's top elk herd, but tends to discourage nonresident hunters.	Early season in high country, when bulls may be called.	Most elk hunting is on public lands—and especially in remote areas accessible only by horseback or off-road vehicles. There's plenty of elk country, but the best of it is costly and/or difficult to get into.

SPECIES	BEST HUNTING PLACES	BEST TIMES	HOW MUCH GOOD HUNTING AVAILABLE?
Antelope	Wyoming—although the demand for pronghorn tickets there is very heavy. Eastern Oregon is a good bet, and so is Montana.	Late September	A great deal of our antelope hunting is on private rangeland, and arrangements *must* be made with the rancher. There are some public BLM lands in the antelope range, but these may be difficult to locate.
Black bear	In the Lake States, Michigan is hard to beat. Out West, it's Colorado.	Early October for the fall hunting, but spring hunting will produce better meat.	Plenty of good bear-hunting country. How do you want to hunt? For the classic hunt, go with someone who runs good bear dogs. In the West and Southwest there are excellent commercial guides for a good horse-and-dog bear hunt.
Grizzly bear	Alaska. (Kodiak, Alaska Peninsula, S.E. Panhandle.) Northwest Territories of Canada may be very good.	August-September	There are good numbers of grizzlies in Alaska and the Northwest Territories, and no end of country to hunt them in. But it demands guides and outfitting, and plenty of time. British Columbia has not had good grizzly prospects in recent years.
Cougar	Vancouver Island (B.C.) has many lions, but few lion guides. Colorado and Arizona have good guided cougar hunts. For scenery and top action, we choose southern and eastern Utah.	November	Good places to hunt are no problem— if you have a good guide and a good pack of lion dogs. Most of this is in rocky wilderness country and public domain.

SPECIES	BEST HUNTING PLACES	BEST TIMES	HOW MUCH GOOD HUNTING AVAILABLE?
Bighorn sheep	Stateside, there's probably good bighorn hunting anyplace you can get a permit. There are few bighorns, but even fewer permits. Alberta may be the best north of the border, although nonresident hunting restrictions will stiffen.	October	Very limited populations everywhere, and subject to intense management. All hunting is on public lands.
Dall sheep	Central and interior Alaska.	August-September	Plenty of good hunting available for the hunter who can afford it.
Mountain goat	Alaska in the S.E. Panhandle and southern coastal mountains; British Columbia in the Skeena, Atlin-Stikine, Laird, and Peace areas.	September	Again, a northern wilderness species that requires guide and outfitting for the average hunter.
Moose	Canada: western Quebec, Northwestern Ontario, Northwest Territories. Alaska: Kenai Peninsula, Alaska Peninsula, southern Alaska.	Early September-October	Plenty of good hunting available, but guides and outfitters are generally required.

SMALL GAME

SPECIES	BEST HUNTING PLACES	BEST TIMES	HOW MUCH GOOD HUNTING AVAILABLE?
Ringnecked pheasant	Iowa, especially the south-central and southwestern parts. South-central Nebraska and north-central Kansas often have some real hotspots. South Dakota is raising much more grain these days, but far fewer ringnecks.	Mid-November	Access to good pheasant hunting in Midwestern farmlands is surprisingly good by most eastern standards. But permission to hunt is essential—especially in Iowa, with its tough new trespass law.

SPECIES	BEST HUNTING PLACES	BEST TIMES	HOW MUCH GOOD HUNTING AVAILABLE?
Bobwhite quail	For sheer numbers, you can't beat the Southeast: the Carolinas, Georgia, northern Florida. But access to good quail coverts may be hard for nonresidents to find. For better access, and good numbers of birds, try Missouri, Iowa, eastern Nebraska and Kansas, Texas amd Oklahoma.	December and later in the South; November in the Midwest.	Plenty—but it takes some finding, and some good contacts and advance preparation. Traditional quail range of the Southeast is more likely to be tied up than are Midwestern quail ranges where bobs aren't taken quite as seriously.
Mourning dove	Again, the South has it. Georgia, the Carolinas, and along the Gulf Coast to Texas and beyond. Northern dove hunting can be superb, but is rather brief by comparison to the southern wintering concentrations.	Early September in the North and Midwest; October and early November in the South.	Access to good shooting is no particular problem, and is probably never as difficult as access to resident upland game birds. The best shooting in the South is often found in carefully managed fields open to fee gunning.
White-winged dove	Arizona in Maricopa, Pima, Pinal, and Yuma counties. In Texas, the four southernmost counties.	September	Generally good. Free hunting is not difficult to find, and there is probably an upswing in fee hunting in both Texas and Arizona.
Ruffed grouse	All in all, we like the Lake States—especially northeastern Minnesota, northern Wisconsin, and Michigan. Elsewhere, southeastern Ohio, western North Carolina, and western Virginia.	October	Excellent. Even in farm woodlots there is usually good access, and there are many public forestlands in the best grouse country.
Hungarian partridge	Southwestern North Dakota, southeastern Washington, southeastern Idaho.	September-early October	Generally good. Hunting is in grainfields and farmlands, but in regions without great upland hunting pressure—and access is no big problem.

SPECIES	BEST HUNTING PLACES	BEST TIMES	HOW MUCH GOOD HUNTING AVAILABLE?
Chukar partridge	Southeastern Washington and northeastern Oregon along the main valley and tributaries of the Snake River.	October	Excellent. Chukar hunting is usually in rough, steep wastelands that are rarely closed to hunting.
Sharptail grouse	Western North Dakota, especially in the Little Missouri drainage. Eastern Montana in brushy coulees in rangeland.	September–early October	Excellent. Big country and plenty of it.
Wild turkey	In the East, Pennsylvania, Maryland, and West Virginia are among the best. Farther west, the nod goes to Missouri and Arkansas.	Spring	Generally very good, since much of this hunting is in public forest lands.

WATERFOWL

Canada geese	Tidewater country of Maryland; southern Illinois; the Dakotas and Nebraska.	November	There are usually commercial shooting grounds along the main flyways and concentration areas of honkers. Such areas also have controlled public shooting; in either case, plan to hunt during the middle of the week. Do-it-yourself goose hunting is harder to find and requires much equipment but is possible—such as on the sandbars of rivers like the Platte and Missouri.

SPECIES	BEST HUNTING PLACES	BEST TIMES	HOW MUCH GOOD HUNTING AVAILABLE?
Black duck	Maryland	November	Good black-duck shooting is available to almost anyone willing to spend the time and/or money required to have it. It isn't easy to come by—and there's no reason why it should be. Anyone unwilling to spend time and effort (and some money) can't expect to have good black-duck shooting.
Mallard	Arkansas, the Dakotas	November–early December	See general note below.

General Note: Everything considered, the Central Flyway is probably the best in the nation for waterfowl hunting. There are flyways with more birds, but from the standpoint of readily available gunning this flyway—with its vast regions of prairies and plains—has waterfowling that is virtually untouched. There are countless ranch ponds, little sloughs, rivers, and creeks that are scarcely hunted at all. For example, in early November, 1973, on a cold Wednesday when the mallards and pintails were moving, there were exactly four of us hunting a 4,000-acre public marsh in southern Colorado.

Index